Everyday Denazification ii

In the wake of World War II, the victorious Allied armies implemented a radical program to purge Nazism from Germany and preserve peace in Europe. Between 1945 and 1949, 20 million political questionnaires, or Fragebögen, were distributed by American, British, French, and Soviet armies to anxious Germans who had to prove their non-Nazi status to gain employment. Drafted by university professors and social scientists, these surveys defined much of the denazification experience and were immensely consequential to the material and emotional recovery of Germans.

In *Everyday Denazification in Postwar Germany*, Mikkel Dack draws the curtain to reveal what denazification looked like on the ground and in practice and how the highly criticized vetting program impacted the lives of individual Germans and their families as they recovered from the war. Accessing recently declassified documents, this book challenges traditional interpretations by illustrating the positive elements of the denazification campaign and recounting a more comprehensive history, one of mid-level Allied planners, civil affairs soldiers, and regular German citizens. The Fragebogen functions as a window into this everyday history.

Mikkel Dack is Assistant Professor of History at Rowan University and Director of Research at the Rowan Center for the Study of the Holocaust, Genocide, and Human Rights.

Everyday Denazification in Postwar Germany

The Fragebogen and Political Screening during the Allied Occupation

Mikkel Dack
Rowan University

CAMBRIDGE
UNIVERSITY PRESS

Shaftesbury Road, Cambridge CB2 8EA, United Kingdom

One Liberty Plaza, 20th Floor, New York, NY 10006, USA

477 Williamstown Road, Port Melbourne, VIC 3207, Australia

314–321, 3rd Floor, Plot 3, Splendor Forum, Jasola District Centre, New Delhi – 110025, India

103 Penang Road, #05–06/07, Visioncrest Commercial, Singapore 238467

Cambridge University Press is part of Cambridge University Press & Assessment, a department of the University of Cambridge.

We share the University's mission to contribute to society through the pursuit of education, learning and research at the highest international levels of excellence.

www.cambridge.org
Information on this title: www.cambridge.org/9781009216357

DOI: 10.1017/9781009216326

© Mikkel Dack 2023

This publication is in copyright. Subject to statutory exception and to the provisions of relevant collective licensing agreements, no reproduction of any part may take place without the written permission of Cambridge University Press & Assessment.

First published 2023
First paperback edition 2024

A catalogue record for this publication is available from the British Library

Library of Congress Cataloging-in-Publication data
Names: Dack, Mikkel, 1982- author.
Title: Everyday denazification in postwar Germany : the Fragebogen and political screening during the Allied Occupation / Mikkel Dack.
Description: Cambridge, United Kingdom ; New York : Cambridge University Press, 2023. | Includes bibliographical references and index.
Identifiers: LCCN 2022036171 (print) | LCCN 2022036172 (ebook) | ISBN 9781009216333 (hardback) | ISBN 9781009216357 (paperback) | ISBN 9781009216326 (epub)
Subjects: LCSH: Denazification–Germany. | Germany–Politics and government–1945-1990. | Government questionnaires–Germany–History–20th century. | Employee screening–Germany–History–20th century. | National socialism–Social aspects–Germany. | Germans–Attitudes.
Classification: LCC DD257.2 .D24 2023 (print) | LCC DD257.2 (ebook) | DDC 943.087–dc23/eng/20220802
LC record available at https://lccn.loc.gov/2022036171
LC ebook record available at https://lccn.loc.gov/2022036172

ISBN 978-1-009-21633-3 Hardback
ISBN 978-1-009-21635-7 Paperback

Cambridge University Press & Assessment has no responsibility for the persistence or accuracy of URLs for external or third-party internet websites referred to in this publication and does not guarantee that any content on such websites is, or will remain, accurate or appropriate.

Contents

List of Illustrations	*page* vii
List of Tables	viii
Acknowledgments	ix
List of Abbreviations	xii

Introduction	1
Denazification and the Fragebogen	5
Interpreting Denazification	10
Methodology, Sources, and Scope	16
Outline of the Book	19

1 **An Army of Academics: Planning the Denazification of Germany** — 21
   - The Problem of Denazification — 22
   - Civilianizing the Military, 1943–1944 — 31
   - The Neo-Marxist War on Nazism — 43
   - Inter-Allied Planning for Denazification — 55
   - Conclusion — 63

2 **"A Miserable Paper Substitute for a Spontaneous Revolution": Drafting the Questionnaire** — 65
   - Italian Origins: Defascistization and the *Scheda Personale* — 66
   - Drafting the Fragebogen — 74
   - The Handbook Controversy — 88
   - French and Soviet Questionnaires — 99
   - Conclusion — 108

3 **"Land of the Fragebogen": Screening the German Population** — 111
   - Allied Invasion and Early Distribution of the Questionnaires, 1944–1945 — 113
   - The Questionnaires under Military Government Administration, 1945–1946 — 125
   - The Questionnaires under German Administration, 1946–1949 — 144
   - Conclusion — 158

4 The "Little Man's Nuremberg": Germans
  and Denazification   162
  The Everyday Experience of Denazification   164
  Passing or Failing: The Consequences of Political Screening   180
  Case Study: Kreis Hersfeld (Hesse), 1945–1949   191
  Conclusion   206

5 Writing Away Culpability: The Unintended Outcomes
  of Denazification   209
  Resorting to "Gestapo Methods": Denunciation and Denazification   211
  Tailoring Truth: Memory Construction and Whitewashing the Nazi Past 226
  Conclusion   251

  Conclusion: Everyday Denazification   253

  Appendix: The Fragebogen Questions   264
  Bibliography   273
  Index   295

Illustrations

FIGURES

1.1 Cover of the satirical magazine *Das Wespennest*,
    October 7, 1948 — page 29
1.2 US officers attending a lecture at the School
    of Military Government at the University of Virginia
    (Charlottesville), April 1943 — 41
2.1 First page of the SHAEF Fragebogen — 82
2.2 First page of the US Fragebogen — 95
3.1 Two civil affairs officers sort through captured Nazi
    records at the Berlin Document Center, 1946 — 128
3.2 First page of the Meldebogen — 155
4.1 Submitting a denazification questionnaire in Berlin's Steglitz
    district, 1946 — 170
4.2 A crowd of German citizens filling out questionnaires
    in Frankfurt am Main — 171
5.1 "The Bridge to Freedom," by former Nazi caricaturist
    Walter Hofmann ("Waldl"), 1946 — 239

MAP

1 Germany under Allied Occupation, 1945–49 — xv

Tables

TABLES

3.1 US Special Branch review of Fragebögen in Bavaria, Württemberg-Baden, and Hesse (prior to May 31, 1946)   134
3.2 Questionnaire activities by US Special Branch in Bavaria (August 13–19, 1946)   148
3.3 Questionnaires processed in each zone/sector (1945–49)   160
4.1 Removal and exclusion from public office and private business in each zone/sector   186
4.2 Hersfeld Military Government and Spruchkammer rulings, sample group   204
5.1 Denazification case files, sample group   231

Acknowledgments

This book bears the imprint of many people whose advice, support, and friendship sustained me at different times and in different places. The project had a long gestation period, and while research and writing are solitary endeavors, I regularly relied on the knowledge and input of others.

In 2006, as a bright-eyed Canadian exchange student, I had the privilege of meeting several prominent scholars at the Frei Universität Berlin, notably Uta Gerhardt and Gisela Bock, who, unbeknownst to me then, set me on a new research path. They encouraged me to seek out a more inclusive history of the Allied occupation, one about people not policies, and also to reconsider the legacies of the political purge. Some years later, a chance discovery of thousands of mislabeled denazification case files at the US National Archives led to the writing of this book.

My doctoral supervisor and mentor, Annette Timm, guided the project through the dissertation stage. She allowed me room to explore and discover, while also pushing me to broaden my historical purview and question conventional interpretations. Annette continues to be a source of support and inspiration and I owe her a deep debt of gratitude. The dissertation was further advised on by Holger Herwig, Devin Pendas, Frank Biess, Petra Dolata, Florentine Strzelczyk, and Frank Stahnisch – each of them provided critical perspectives and valuable commentaries.

Decisive academic support in embarking on and sustaining this research project was provided by a number of organizations. Foremost among them was the German Historical Institute (GHI) in Washington DC, which was a pillar of support during the early stages of research, as well as the German Academic Exchange Service (DAAD) and the Social Sciences and Humanities Research Council (SSHRC) of Canada. Grants and fellowships from these agencies allowed for extended stays in Washington, London, Berlin, and Koblenz.

The twelve-year project involved research at no less than twenty archives in four countries and the exploration of hundreds of record collections, a labyrinth of sources that I could have never navigated on my own. Among the many archivists and librarians who guided me, I must mention the generosity of Amy Schmidt and Eric van Slander at the US National Archives in College Park, Maryland; Lars Amelung and Martin Luchterhandt at the Bundesarchiv in Berlin and Koblenz; and Bernd von Kostka and Florian Weiß at the AlliiertenMuseum in Berlin. I am also indebted to several historians in Hesse, especially Sebastian Hild, Treasurer of the Hersfeld Historical Association, who went above and beyond to educate me on the history of the town and district of Hersfeld. Thank you to the Stiftung Haus der Geschichte der Bundesrepublik Deutschland, the AlliiertenMuseum, and the Staatsarchiv Ludwigsburg for donating images for the book.

I would also like to express my appreciation to the men and women who shared private stories with me about growing up in postwar occupied Germany. They opened up their homes and hearts to me and recounted very difficult family histories.

Rowan University is an extraordinary place to be a historian. Since arriving in the fall of 2018, my department and college have given me uninterrupted support for the writing of this book. My colleagues workshopped chapters, offered constructive criticism, and even taught some of my classes to free up time for revisions. It is a privilege to be a member of this community of scholars, one that is as much revered as it is collegial. I am also thankful to my students and advisees, whose unique viewpoints and creative thinking convinced me, more than once, to amend the manuscript.

My editor, Liz Friend-Smith, shepherded me through the publication process. Already familiar with the history of post-WWII Germany, she has always been a strong advocate of the project and its intellectual aims. In the latter stages, Laheba Alam, Elliot Beck, and Vinithan Sedumadhavan provided critical assistance, revealing to me the many hidden parts of the publication machine. I am also grateful to the anonymous reviewers for their careful commentary, which improved the book in many ways. Kate Blackmer created a beautiful map and Tanya Izzard a comprehensive and highly accessible index.

Working in different countries and at the intersection of several subfields, I have had the pleasure of making friends and finding mentorship in many corners. At every stage of the project, fellow scholars have inspired and advised me. Some of them are Jason Crouthamel, Kate Horning, Gary Bruce, Matthew Berg, Richard Wetzell, Marie-Bénédicte Vincent, Benjamin Nienass, Jonathan Bach, Hanne Leßau, William Brustein, Helen Roche, Bill Niven, Ryan Dahn, Katya Motyl, Melissa Kravetz, Michael Jonas, Detlef Österreich, Eva Schultze, Brandon Bloch, Robert Terrell, Paul Steege, and Jay Lockenour. Sharing my research at the GHI Transatlantic Doctoral Seminar, the

Heidelberg Center for American Studies Spring Academy, and the Philadelphia Area Modern Germany Workshop led to the project being reborn multiple times, always for the better. I also received vital experience while studying at Helmut Schmidt Universität in Hamburg. It was there that Bernd Wegner and Michael Jonas preserved a rigorous intellectual environment for me to develop my research topic. Meanwhile, my fourteen Bundeswehr officer housemates warmly welcomed me, a civilian foreigner, into their *Kameradschaft*. These experiences exposed me to some unique perspectives and advanced my understanding of German military history and cultural memory.

And then there are those friends who contributed in so many intangible ways, which are hard to measure but impossible to disregard. To include all of their names would fill its own book, yet special mention must be made of Shannon Murphy, Victoria Bucholtz, Will Pratt, Stuart Barnard, Beau Cleland, Andrew McEwen, Celeste Sharpe, Erna Kurbegović, John Woitkowitz, Jess Knights, René Smolinsky, Rodrigo Sermeño, Tessa Murphy, Junko Takeda, Norman Kutcher, and Jordan Smith. On both sides of the Atlantic, I have met so many incredible people who have sustained me emotionally.

My deepest gratitude is to my family – Kate, Jordan, Skye, Jason, and Scarlet – for supporting my stubborn passion for history and providing me with a continuous outpouring of love and encouragement. But nobody has contributed more to this book than my father, Philip Dack, who is my hero. He is a storyteller and a mover of mountains, and it is his creative instinct, intellectual prowess, and playful demeanor that made this project possible and also enjoyable. This is why, as a small token of appreciation, this book is dedicated to him.

A final and special note of gratitude goes to my wife and closest friend, Evangeline. She has lived with this book for as long as she has known me. It is a stepchild that she lovingly adopted. She is such a positive force, and over the last few years, I have too often relied on her patience and generosity. Furthermore, she continues to be unwavering in her support of my vocation, regardless of where it has taken me, and us.

Abbreviations

ACC (G)	Allied Control Council (Germany)
ACC (I)	Allied Control Commission (Italy)
ACDP	Archiv für Christlich-Demokratische Politik (Archive for Christian Democratic Policy)
ADMAE	Archives diplomatiques, Ministère des Affaires Étrangères (Diplomatic Archives, Ministry for Foreign Affairs)
AdsD	Archiv der sozialen Demokratie (Archive of Social Democracy)
ADW	Archiv des Diakonischen Werkes (Archive for Diaconal Work of the Evangelical Church in Germany)
AFHQ	Allied Forces Headquarters
AM	AlliiertenMuseum (Allied Museum)
AMFA	Administration militaire française en Allemagne (French Military Administration in Germany)
AMG	Allied Military Government
AMGOT	Allied Military Government for Occupied Territories
APW	Armistice and Post-War Committee
ASTP	Area Specialized Training Program
BAB	Bundesarchiv, Berlin (German Federal Archives)
BAF	Bundesarchiv-Militärarchiv, Freiburg (German Federal Archives/Military Archives)
BAK	Bundesarchiv, Koblenz (German Federal Archives)
BDC	Berlin Document Center
BDM	Bund Deutscher Mädel (League of German Girls)
BHStA	Bayerisches Hauptstaatsarchiv (Bavarian State Main Archives)
CAC	Civil Affairs Center
CAD	Civil Affairs Division
CAO	Civil Affairs Officers
CASC	Civil Affairs Staff Centre
CATS	Civil Affairs Training School

List of Abbreviations

CC	Control Council
CCAC	Combined Civil Affairs Committee
CCG(BE)	Control Commission for Germany (British Element)
CCS	Combined Chiefs of Staff
CDU	Christlich Demokratische Union (Christian Democratic Union)
CES	Central European Section
CIC	Counter Intelligence Corps
COSSAC	Chief of Staff to Supreme Allied Commander
DAF	Deutsche Arbeitsfront (German Labor Front)
DCCAO	Deputy Chief of Civil Affairs Officer
DP	displaced person
DRA	Deutsche Rundfunkarchiv (German Broadcasting Archive)
DVP	Deutsche Volkspartei (German People's Party)
EAC	European Advisory Council
EAD	Europe–Africa Division
EKD	Evangelische Kirche in Deutschland (Evangelical Church in Germany)
ETOUSA	European Theater of Operations, United States Army
EZA	Evangelisches Zentralarchiv (Evangelical Central Archives)
FBI	Federal Bureau of Investigation
FDP	Freie Demokratische Partei (Free Democratic Party)
FEA	Foreign Economic Administration
FORD	Foreign Office Research Department
FRG	Federal Republic of Germany
FSF	Field Security Force
G-5	Civil Affairs Division (SHAEF)
GCU	German Country Unit
GDR	German Democratic Republic
Gestapo	Geheime Staatspolizei (Secret State Police)
HJ	Hitler Jugend (Hitler Youth)
IfZ	Institut für Zeitgeschichte (Institute for Contemporary History)
ITC	Intelligence Training Centre
JCS	Joint Chiefs of Staff
KfD	Kraft durch Freude (Strength through Joy)
KPD	Kommunistische Partei Deutschland (Communist Party of Germany)
LAB	Landesarchiv Berlin (Berlin State Archives)
LDP	Liberal Demokratische Partei (Liberal Democratic Party)

List of Abbreviations

MG	Military Government
MOII	War Office Section of Military Operations
MVD	Soviet Ministry of Internal Affairs
NARA	National Archives and Records Administration
NKVD	People's Commissariat for Internal Affairs
NSDAP	Nationalsozialistische Deutsche Arbeiterpartei (National Socialist German Workers' Party)
NSV	Nationalsozialistische Volkswohlfahrt (National Socialist People's Welfare)
OMGUS	Office of Military Government, United States
OSS	Office of Strategic Services
PMG	Office of Provost Marshal General/War Office
PNF	Partito Nazionale Fascista (National Fascist Party)
POLAD	Political Affairs Division
POW	prisoner of war
PWD	Psychological Warfare Division
R&A	Research and Analysis Branch
RM	Reichsmark
SA	Sturmabteilung (Storm Detachment)
SCAO	Supreme Civil Affairs Officer
SD	Sicherheitsdienst (Security Service)
SED	Sozialistische Einheitspartei Deutschland (Socialist Unity Party of Germany)
SHAEF	Supreme Headquarters, Allied Expeditionary Force
SIS	Secret Intelligence Service
SMA	Soviet Military Administration
SOE	Special Operations Executive
SPD	Sozialdemokratische Partei Deutschlands (Social Democratic Party of Germany)
SS	Schutzstaffel (Protection Squadron)
Stasi	Ministerium für Staatssicherheit (Ministry for State Security)
TNA	The National Archives
UNRRA	United Nations Relief and Rehabilitation Administration
USFET	United States Forces, European Theater
USGCC	United States Group Control Council
USSR	Union of Soviet Socialist Republics
ZFO	Zone française d'occupation (French Zone of Occupation)

Map 1 Germany under Allied Occupation, 1945–49

Introduction

> Unlike the priest with the poor sinner remote from the world in the secrecy of the quiet confessional, A.M.G. [American Military Government] sends its questionnaire into my home and, like an examining judge with a criminal, barks its one hundred and thirty-one questions at me: it demands, coldly and flatly, nothing less than the truth; it even threatens twice – once at the beginning and once at the end – to punish me, and the nature and scope of the punishment envisaged I can only too vividly imagine.[1]
>
> —Ernst von Salomon, 1951

The bestselling book in West Germany during the 1950s was an 800-page memoir written by a fanatical right-wing nationalist and convicted criminal.[2] Ernst von Salomon's 1951 *Der Fragebogen* (The Questionnaire) sold a quarter of a million copies in its first year alone.[3] The densely written autobiographical novel is a literary assault on the American military occupation, which had begun in 1945, and a scathing critique of the Allied nations' messianic campaign to

---

[1] Ernst von Salomon, *Der Fragebogen* (Reinbeck: Rowohlt, 1951), 9.
[2] In 1922, von Salomon was convicted as an accessory to the murder of Foreign Minister Walther Rathenau, for which he received a five-year prison sentence. Despite his ultranationalism, von Salomon never joined the NSDAP, as he considered its ideology too "western" and "capitalist" but also as a "more advanced" form of bolshevism. Ernst von Salomon, *Fragebogen (The Questionnaire)*, trans. Constantine Fitzgibbon (New York: Doubleday, 1955), 238; Jost Hermand, *Ernst von Salomon. Wandlungen eines Nationalrevolutionärs* (Leipzig: Hirzel, 2002), 14.
[3] Axel Schildt, *Medien-Intellektuelle in der Bundesrepublik* (Göttingen: Wallstein, 2020), 372. The book was translated into English in 1954 under the title, *The Answers of Ernst Von Salomon*, trans. Constantine Fitzgibbon (London: Putnam, 1954), and then for an American readership as, *Fragebogen (The Questionnaire)*, trans. Constantine Fitzgibbon (New York: Doubleday, 1955). Italian and French editions were also produced. The book was sold in East Germany, although not in the same numbers. The Soviets originally banned all von Salomon's titles, but the anti-American sentiment of *Der Fragebogen* must have changed minds in Berlin. A 1965 literary studies review counted the book among the "anti-fascist autobiographies." See Hans-Georg Werner, *Deutsche Literatur im Überblick* (Leipzig: Reclam, 1965), 295. In 2011, Rowohlt published its nineteenth edition of *Der Fragebogen*.

"ideologically cleanse" the defeated population of National Socialism. The "Fragebogen" itself was well known to von Salomon's readers; this was the widely distributed and much despised political screening instrument used by the occupying armies to identify, categorize, and punish Nazi Party members and sympathizers. The questionnaire asked for information on family, education, military service, and most importantly, membership in Nazi-affiliated groups. As a prerequisite for employment in jobs deemed influential, including most civil servant positions, millions of German civilians and returning soldiers completed the form. With a hyperbolic tone, von Salomon uses the questionnaire as a synecdoche for the entire denazification project and employs it for the narrative framework of the book – he recounts his life story by "responding" to the survey's 131 questions, while intermittently denouncing the force-fed politics of defeat. He describes the form as an absurd bureaucratic blunder and a self-righteous "examination of conscience" (*Gewissenserforschung*).[4]

The stunning success of *Der Fragebogen*, and the flurry of letters, lecture tours, and discussion panels that followed its publication, demonstrates that von Salomon's emotional diatribe resonated with Germans, who were, by the early 1950s, collectively opposed to any remnant of denazification. Many viewed themselves as victims of both the war and the subsequent occupation; they were, according to a popular entertainer of the time, "*fragebogenkrank*" (questionnaire sick).[5] However, the novel should not be interpreted as sensationalist literature, subject only to a brief burst of popularity. Literary critics of the time professed that von Salomon's words were paradigmatic for an entire generation of Germans.[6] Commenting on the general reception of *Der Fragebogen*, one British reviewer wrote:

---

[4] As quoted in Werner Sollors, "'Everybody Gets Fragebogend Sooner or Later': The Denazification Questionnaire as Cultural Text," *German Life and Letters* 71, no. 2 (April 2018): 149.

[5] Just Scheu, "Der Fragebogen," in *Kleinkunststücke*, vol. IV, *Wir sind so frei: Kabarett in Restdeutschland 1945–1970*, ed. Volker Kühn (Weinheim: Quadriga, 1993), 61–62. Anna M. Parkinson interprets the cultural and emotional implications of von Salomon's book in *An Emotional State: The Politics of Emotion in Postwar West German Culture* (Ann Arbor: University of Michigan Press, 2015), here 67–111.

[6] W. H. Rey, review of *Der Fragebogen*, by Ernst von Salomon, *Books Abroad* 27, no. 1 (1953): 48. See also Teresa Seruya, "Gedanken und Fragen beim Übersetzen von Ernst von Salomons 'Der Fragebogen'," in *Konflikt-Grenze-Dialog: Kulturkontrastive und Interdisziplinäre Textzugänge*, eds. Jürgen Lehmann et al. (Frankfurt am Main: Peter Lang, 1997), 227–37, here 229. Not all reviews were positive. Some media outlets criticized *Der Fragebogen* for being an overtly antidemocratic publication, calling it an "embarrassing stink bomb" written by an "immature youth" and "incompetent advocate for fascism." For negative press, see Schildt, *Medien-Intellektuelle in der Bundesrepublik*,

Introduction

When I visited Germany in 1951 Ernst von Salomon's 'Der Fragebogen' blossomed in all book-store windows and agitated all reviewing columns. On a second visit in 1953 many other works had strutted into and vanished from the literary Lebensraum [living space], but the cover of 'Der Fragebogen' still shone from the display racks, the public still bought it by the thousands, and the reviewers, hostile or friendly, had made it into a critical standard of reference.[7]

Made notorious by von Salomon's novel, but also because of its centrality in the denazification experience, the Fragebogen has become eternalized. Since the 1950s, the survey is remembered by Germans and non-Germans alike as the physical embodiment of a failed purge. To many, it represents everything wrong with the political screening program: the redundant legislation, tireless bureaucracy, and indiscriminate punishments.

During the Allied occupation, which existed in various forms between 1945 and 1955, Germans colloquially referred to the Fragebogen as the "tapeworm" (*Bandwurm*), due to its long length and their general repulsion to it.[8] Novelist Wolfgang Borchert complained that it rendered individual freedom meaningless, while election posters called for an "End to the Fragebogen Regime!"[9] In fact, a similar disdain was held by members of the Allied military governments, who considered the questionnaire too detailed and complicated.[10] To the Germans, the form was uncompromising and ignorant to the nuances of living under dictatorship, and to the Americans, British, French, and Soviets it was too ambitious a program and economically burdensome.

Despite its popular portrayal as being central to the miscarriage of denazification, the Fragebogen has never been seriously studied. The origins and impact of this survey, one of the largest in history, are virtually unknown. Apart from a superficial examination of the general

---

here 372–75, and Angela Borgstedt, "Der Fragebogen. Zur Wahrnehmung eines Symbols politischer Säuberung nach 1945," *Der Bürger im Staat* 56 (2006): 166–71, here 166–67. Written correspondence between von Salomon and his editor, Ernst Rowohlt, reveals much on the book's initial reception. These letters are included in the von Salomon Nachlass at the Deutsches Literaturarchiv in Marbach.

[7] Frederic Morton, "One Prussian's Story," review of *Fragebogen (The Questionnaire)*, by Ernst von Salomon, *The Saturday Review*, January 1, 1955, p. 54.

[8] Bianka J. Adams, *From Crusade to Hazard: The Denazification of Bremen Germany* (Lanham, MD: Scarecrow Press, 2009), 66.

[9] Sollors, "'Everybody Gets Fragebogend Sooner or Later'," 147–48; Poster, "Im Namen de Wahrheit der Freiheit und der Rechts," 1950, Archiv der sozialen Demokratie (hereafter, AdsD), B6/FLBL003050.

[10] Letter, CC for Germany (British Element) to SHAEF, G-5, December 22, 1944, US National Archives and Records Administration (hereafter, NARA), RG 331, SHAEF, G-5, Secretariat, Box 32, Doc. 21/1108.

purpose and scope of the program, historians have made little attempt to understand this principal weapon of the ideological war against fascism or the consequences that it held for Germans.

This book is the first in-depth study of the Fragebogen. In many ways, the story of this survey instrument, and the screening system it embodied, is a history of everyday denazification; that is, the campaign at its most rudimentary level and the routine experiences of common people – civilians, soldiers, and administrators. Of course, individual denazification experiences have been investigated before, but these studies rarely examine all four occupation zones, nor do they account for the perspective of both the occupiers and the occupied. They certainly do not engage with the political questionnaire in a meaningful way. There were many denazification experiences – interrogation, internment, tribunal hearings, institutional dismantling – all of which are addressed in this book, but it was the Fragebogen that governed nearly all activities, affected by far the most citizens, and accounted for as much as 90 percent of denazification budgets.

A more nuanced assessment of denazification is needed, not least because of the campaign's ambivalent results and its misunderstood scope and impact. In this study, emphasis is placed on the individual, be they an Allied wartime researcher, occupation soldier, or German citizen. These postwar actors were not passive bystanders to a large statistic-driven screening campaign; they did not know about the coming Cold War. Based largely on recently declassified materials, this book draws the curtain to reveal what denazification looked like on the ground and in practice, and how the highly criticized vetting program impacted the lives and livelihood of individual Germans and their families as they recovered from dictatorship and war. It revisits the ideological purge and seeks clarity about its origins, implementation, reception, effectiveness, and legacy. Therefore, what follows is a more comprehensive history of denazification than has previously been written.

I do not claim to account for every activity but instead to communicate a denazification story that is more inclusive and commonplace. This book is a study of both soldiers and civilians, tracing mostly American, British, and German experiences, but also those of the Soviets and French. Some readers may be surprised at, and even uncomfortable with, the ease with which I move between occupation zones. This approach is deliberate, for although there were important differences in the undertakings of the four military governments, especially between the Soviets and their Western counterparts, the mechanics of the purge, and the German experience of denazification, were remarkably similar across zones. By recognizing the questionnaire as an international project and rare common denominator of the Allied denazification campaigns, this study contributes to a growing body of scholarship that applies a holistic approach to studying the immediate postwar years.[11]

Ultimately, I conclude that the Fragebogen was an inadequate mechanism for the complex task of judging Germans. The form possessed inherent flaws in its structure and content, and it was too contradictory an investigatory device. The project was overly ambitious and cumbersome, and the Allies underestimated the resources it required. However, despite such shortcomings, the questionnaire achieved much of what it intended and offers meaningful lessons, or at least serious considerations, for future political screening and reorientation campaigns. It permanently disrupted the careers and hence influence of many former Nazis and introduced the notion of individual accountability. The program brought denazification into the homes of millions of German citizens, far from the courts at Nuremberg, and made average people account for the personal decisions they made during the Third Reich. It also encouraged respondents to build and rehearse non-Nazi narratives.

This is the conflicting legacy of the Fragebogen, the bureaucratic catastrophe that helped discredit Nazism. The ideological transformation was messy and perhaps superficial, but the inclusivity and grassroots nature of the political screening system ensured that a permanent non-Nazi imprint was left on German society. As such, this study is revisionist, at least in part, as I argue against the existing scholarship that has largely emphasized that the Fragebogen program not only failed in its own right but destabilized the entire denazification campaign. As you will learn, the questionnaire was by far the most pervasive and powerful tool of the political purge.

Denazification and the Fragebogen

The term "de-nazification" was first used by military planners in the Pentagon in 1943 to refer to proposed postwar reforms of the German

---

[11] There are only a handful of published studies that examine denazification activities in all four zones. Among them are Andrew H. Beattie, *Allied Internment Camps in Occupied Germany: Extrajudicial Detention in the Name of Denazification, 1945–1950* (Cambridge: Cambridge University Press, 2020); Perry Biddiscombe, *The Denazification of Germany: A History, 1945–1950* (Stroud, Gloucestershire: Tempus Publishing, 2007); Constantine Fitzgibbon, *Denazification* (London: Joseph, 1969); and Justus Fürstenau, *Entnazifizierung: Ein Kapitel deutscher Nachkriegspolitik* (Neuwied am Rhein: Luchterhand, 1969).

legal system, and perhaps as an analogy to the already familiar act of demilitarization.[12] By the spring of 1944, the implication of the word had been expanded by policymakers and adopted by the other Allied nations to refer to any concerted effort to rid German and Austrian society, culture, politics, economy, and judiciary of National Socialism and militarism. This included liquidating the Nazi Party (*Nationalsozialistische Deutsche Arbeiterpartei*, NSDAP) and its affiliated and subsidiary organizations, repealing legislation, destroying symbols and monuments, and arresting Nazi leaders and influential supporters. However, the much larger and more substantial action was the investigation of regular Germans, mainly civil servants and professionals, and removing or barring those identified as Nazis or Nazi sympathizers from positions of responsibility and influence. The purge of public offices and private businesses dominated all serious discussion of denazification.[13] To most wartime planners, the campaign was not meant to be a forum for moral discussion or a teaching institution of the nation, or even an investigation of legal guilt. It was, instead, about political responsibility and the physical exclusion of individuals who had been in close proximity to the Nazi regime from the building of a new democratic Germany.

Recognizing they were venturing well outside their wheelhouse, all four major Allied-nation armies recruited experts from civilian life to formulate strategies to eradicate Nazism. These specialists introduced social scientific approaches into the denazification curriculum, including innovative theoretical, statistical, and applied research methods, as well as modern perceptions of political, ideological, and sociological transformation. Inspired by procedures used to identify Fascists in occupied Italy (1943–45) and the progressive ideas of a handful of American-based scholars, many of them German-Jewish intellectuals, a simple yet unorthodox strategy was chosen. Denazification would be achieved primarily by screening Germans for employment using standardized questionnaires. Every adult who wished to work, or continue to, in a public or semi-public position of responsibility or in a leading private enterprise would be required to complete a survey. They would not be arrested or

---

[12] Political scientist Elmer Plischke, who headed the denazification desk for the US Office of the Political Advisor to General Eisenhower, claimed to have coined the word in April 1944, but there are several instances of it being used earlier. Elmer Plischke, "Denazification in Germany: A Policy Analysis," in *Americans as Proconsuls: United States Military Government in Germany and Japan, 1944–52*, ed. Robert Wolfe (Carbondale: Southern Illinois University Press, 1984), 207; Biddiscombe, *Denazification of Germany*, 9.

[13] Elmer Plischke, "Denazifying the Reich," *The Review of Politics* 9, no. 2 (April 1947): 156; Directive, "Annex XXXIII (Denazification)," April 24, 1945, NARA, RG 331, SHAEF, SS, SD, Box 77, pp. 4–5.

made to face a military tribunal, but rather asked to fill out some paperwork, notifying the military government if they had ever been a member of a Nazi organization.

American and British civilians, working together under the Western command's Supreme Headquarters, Allied Expeditionary Force (SHAEF), wrote the first denazification questionnaire in the spring of 1944, referring to the form by the German name: "Fragebogen" (or the plural Fragebögen).[14] It did not take long for the French and Russians to adopt similar surveys and for analogous forms to be drafted for distribution in occupied Austria (1945–55) and Japan (1945–52). This seemed to be the only way to gather political intelligence on such large populations. Enrolling the defeated enemy in its own vetting process was an unconventional strategy, but so too was the task of transforming their worldview. Never before had a military victor attempted to screen the personal beliefs of civilians to ensure a lasting peace.

Despite popular representations, judicial actions taken against war criminals, including the Nuremberg Trials, as well as the reeducation of citizens, were not part of formal denazification proceedings; these activities had separate protocols. Instead, the purging of Nazism from public life was realized almost exclusively by the investigation of regular Germans, most of them middle-class educated men – teachers, doctors, civil servants, and managers. While the Nazi leadership faced the International Military Tribunal, the general population was subjected to a political examination directed by the Fragebogen.

The original form contained seventy-eight questions, most of which related to professional biography and positions held in the institutional structure of the National Socialist regime. In the longest section, the applicant was instructed to provide details on membership in the NSDAP, SS, SA, and twenty-nine other organizations. They were also required to include information on their education, military service, and financial history. Over the course of the occupation, all four Allied armies drafted their own version of the questionnaire, each slightly different from the one prior. One of the most widely circulated forms was the American Fragebogen, printed in May 1945, which contained 131 questions

---

[14] Staff Study, "Measures for Identifying and Determining Disposition of Nazi Public Officials in Germany," May 28, 1944, NARA, RG 331, SHAEF, GS, G-5, IB, HS, Box 104, p. 7, Doc. 9959/181. SHAEF had sixteen Allied nation members: Australia, Belgium, Canada, Czechoslovakia, (Free) France, Greece, India, Luxembourg, Netherlands, New Zealand, Norway, Poland, South Africa, Yugoslavia, United Kingdom, and United States.

printed on six pages; this was the form that Ernst von Salomon (supposedly) completed, along with millions of other Germans.[15]

A caveat was printed at the top of all versions of the Fragebogen, warning respondents that if they did not answer every question or if they submitted false information, they would be subject to judgment by a military tribunal. To ensure veracity, completed forms were crossed-checked against seized and salvaged Nazi Party and government records, collected locally and in zonal and national document repositories. After being inspected for any responses that necessitated mandatory removal or arrest, the remaining forms were divided into predetermined categories of Nazi affiliation. This, in turn, could result in the immediate termination of the respondent's job or a prohibition from entering influential employment.

However, the Fragebogen was not a typical questionnaire composed of just checkboxes and columnar lists. The survey allowed for the inclusion of supplementary materials, such as a *Lebenslauf* (resumé), within which applicants could add comments to their answers and provide any other information that, they believed, would improve their chances of being cleared for employment. These allowances seemingly granted the former Nazi a fair trial, which some wartime planners and politicians were opposed to. Nevertheless, these additional records run into the millions of pages submitted by citizens trying to keep their jobs by convincing the occupiers that they were innocent of the excesses of the Nazi regime.

The first Fragebögen were distributed in early 1945 by the civil affairs officers who followed American, British, and French armies into German territory. Soon after, the Red Army began using the form. Referred by some Allied administrators as the "political litmus test," the questionnaire quickly came to govern most denazification efforts, dwarfing all other activities in scale, scope, and expense. Nearly every facet of the larger campaign, and many other undertakings such as food ration allocation and management of refugees, relied on these or similar forms. The Fragebogen system changed regularly over the course of the occupation and there existed significant differences between and even within each zone. The character of the program was affected by local circumstances

---

[15] A complete list of the questions in the US Fragebogen can be found in the book's Appendix. As suggested by Werner Sollors, von Salomon may have never completed the long-form questionnaire that his book was structured around. In a 1948 letter, von Salomon explained that the idea for the book came from his editor, Ernst Rowohlt, who had informed him that the British authorities required all authors to complete a political questionnaire. See Sollors, "'Everybody Gets Fragebogend Sooner or Later'," 151–52, and Schildt, *Medien-Intellektuelle in der Bundesrepublik*, 366.

and the discretion of individual officers just as much as international affairs, including the developing events of the Cold War. The most significant change, however, came in 1946, when the Allied Control Council announced the transfer of denazification responsibilities to German authorities. Gradually, all four occupiers approved the establishment of a network of German-staffed denazification commissions (or tribunals) within their respective zones and the introduction of a standardized system for categorizing Nazi affiliation.

All German ministries adopted the Fragebogen of their respective military government overseers and the information the surveys provided continued to form the basis for investigative screening. In the spring of 1946, the Office of Military Government, United States (OMGUS) oversaw the drafting of a shorter questionnaire, which acted as a political census; its completion was required by all citizens over the age of eighteen. At times, distributed alongside the Fragebogen, this *Meldebogen* (registration form) was completed by more than thirteen million people.[16]

Due to a growing discontent with denazification by Germans, the impracticality of processing millions of questionnaires, and rising tensions between the Soviet Union and the West, political screening was gradually phased out, the Fragebögen along with it. Beginning in late 1946, the purge devolved into a watered-down and routine system of civilian-staffed commissions that coincided with the issuing of exoneration certificates, the enactment of far-reaching political amnesties, and a popular public sentiment of "forgive and forget."[17] By 1948, questionnaires were still being used in all four zones but to a much lesser degree. The early impetus of denazification had given way to a program of amnesty and reintegration. In early 1948, the Soviets declared that their war against fascism had been won. Soon after, in the West, Konrad Adenauer's Christian Democratic Party (*Christlich-Demokratische Union*, CDU) formally denounced all remaining denazification activities. The American, British, and French armies acknowledged their campaign's failures. After the founding of East and West Germany in 1949, the questionnaires gradually disappeared from circulation and stacks of completed forms were moved from offices to archives.

---

[16] Jeffery Herf, *Divided Memory: The Nazi Past in the Two Germanys* (Cambridge, MA: Harvard University Press, 1997), 204.

[17] Lutz Niethammer, *Entnazifizierung in Bayern: Säuberung und Rehabilitierung unter Amerikanischer Besatzung* (Frankfurt am Main: S. Fischer, 1972), 613; Ernst Klee, *Persilscheine und falsche Pässe: wie die Kirchen den Nazis Halfen* (Frankfurt am Main: Fischer, 1991).

The US Military Governor of Germany, Lucius D. Clay, wondered if "perhaps never before in world history has such a mass undertaking to purge society been undertaken."[18] More than twenty million German civilians and returning soldiers completed at least one of the forms, making it, likely, the largest survey in history to that point.[19] It is difficult to comprehend the magnitude of resources required to manage such a project. The fact that the Allies allowed extensive written supplements, which had to be translated, authenticated, and evaluated, makes the challenges presented by the program almost unfathomable.

Although the lifespan of the Fragebogen was limited, it had a substantial and lasting impact on the millions of Germans who completed it, nearly a third of the population. The questionnaire affected income, professional status, and community reputation. It directly influenced, and in many cases determined, physical lifestyle and mental well-being in the postwar years and it generated heightened feelings of anxiety and distrust. "Failing" the Fragebogen usually resulted in the loss of employment and career. Most importantly, the surveys shaped how the Nazi regime was remembered because, for many, it was the first time they had to seriously address their recent past under the Third Reich. This peculiar instrument provided Germans an opportunity, and an imperative, to recreate themselves in the aftermath of the war and to rewrite their personal histories, which would then be "approved" by the occupiers, in essence granting exoneration. The Fragebogen was therefore not only a fundamental instrument of the Allied occupation but a mindful record of the German past and a site of memory distortion and recreation.

Interpreting Denazification

For decades, denazification has been characterized as a wholesale failure. In rare unanimity, scholars across disciplines and generations mostly agree that the Allies' ideological war against fascism was ill-conceived and that it failed to achieve its basic objectives.

Loud criticism began immediately upon arrival of the occupiers, in the early months of 1945. Soldiers, politicians, legalists, humanitarians, and journalists accused denazification of being ineffective, illegal, and immoral. As censorship loosened, German critics, including new and revived political parties, as well as the Protestant and Catholic churches, joined in the chorus. Adenauer's coalition government rejected denazification outright, passing amnesty laws in 1949 and 1954 that reintegrated

---

[18] Lucius D. Clay, *Decision in Germany* (Garden City, NY: Doubleday, 1950), 259.
[19] A calculation of questionnaires processed in the four zones can be found in Chapter 3.

hundreds of thousands of former Nazis into the workforce. At the same time, the German Democratic Republic (*Deutsche Demokratische Republik*, GDR) carried out an effective propaganda campaign against the West, claiming that the "fascist successor state" had failed to denazify, having reemployed hundreds of former high-ranking Nazis in prominent political and commercial positions. Combined with a memory of defeat and hard-fought postwar survival, it is not surprising that the verdict against denazification became cemented in the minds of early scholars.

Negative assessment was based on a variety of factors and critics are right to recognize fundamental deficiencies in the denazification project. Still, such overwhelming consensus is peculiar considering the absence of clearly defined aims against which to judge success and failure. How does one evaluate the eradication of Nazism and militarism from society? What timeline should be used for the measurement of success? Does Germany's current role as a world leader in democracy feature in this assessment? The concept of denazification has always been vague, and its lofty objectives, complex activities, and uncertain legacies make any evaluation difficult, especially when resorting only to short-term quantitative data related to job dismissals and amnesties. It is equally curious that the crowded field of scholarship has ignored perhaps the most crucial piece of evidence, the Fragebogen. The political screening instrument consumed much of the resources dedicated to ideological disarmament and it defined the denazification experience for most Germans. The enormous success of Ernst von Salomon's book elevated the questionnaire to an arena of popular conversation, but this also had the effect of permanently condemning the screening program and discouraging scholarly investigation. The Fragebogen has almost always been presented as a statistical annotation, relegated to footnotes and appendices, and referenced only in passing and with superficial analysis to illustrate the overly ambitious, bureaucratic, and flawed character of denazification. After seventy years, the full story of the Fragebogen and its legacies is beginning to be told. A small number of studies have recently emerged that examine different components of the questionnaire program, as well as its public and private reception.[20]

---

[20] Among them is Hanne Leßau's published dissertation, which is an investigation of how denazification documents, including the Fragebogen, allowed Germans an opportunity to confront and negotiate their own Nazi pasts. Leßau examines a sample of eight hundred case files from North Rhine-Westphalia in the British occupation zone. Hanne Leßau, *Entnazifizierungsgeschichten. Die Auseinandersetzung mit der eigenen NS-Vergangenheit in der frühen Nachkriegszeit* (Göttingen: Wallstein, 2020). My own interpretation of these mental processes can be found in Chapter 5. The remaining

Researchers struggled for decades to gain access to political screening records. In fact, before 1975, no archive in any country had declassified its denazification holdings. It was not until 2015 that most Fragebögen were available in German, American, British, and French collections. The majority of Soviet records are still unavailable, however; reportedly hundreds of thousands of questionnaires remain under lock and key at the State Archive in Moscow.[21] The slow release of records is unsurprising. Case files contain personal information, much of it incriminating, and they are protected by information privacy laws.[22] It does not help that the questionnaires that are available to researchers are scattered across dozens of archives in no fewer than five countries. Due to these obstacles, the course of scholarship has progressed unevenly. The Fragebogen program, and therefore individual experiences of denazification, has been largely ignored, while studies continue to be siloed into individual zones and nation groups. The focus remains overwhelmingly on the western zones and the perspective of the Allied occupiers, and historians continue to conduct mostly policy-based critiques, using a top-down analytical approach and, until recently, adhering to the well-worn thesis that denazification was a monumental failure.

The first period of what can be considered independent scholarship occurred between the 1950s and 1970s and was dominated by American historians and political scientists who surveyed denazification activities in the US zone. This exploratory stage of research drew mainly from the firsthand experiences of the authors and the limited archival records available, mostly government research reports. No serious debate on any topic emerged, only a joint venture to discover the reasons *why* denazification failed. Former chief of the US denazification program in Bavaria, William Griffith, claimed in his unpublished but influential

---

studies are, Sollors, "'Everybody Gets Fragebogend Sooner or Later'," 139–53; Mikkel Dack, "Retreating into Trauma: The Fragebogen, Denazification, and Victimhood in Postwar Germany," in *Traumatic Memories of the Second World War and After*, eds. Peter Leese and Jason Crouthamel (London: Palgrave Macmillan, 2016), 143–70; Mikkel Dack, "Tailoring Truth: Political Amnesia, Memory Construction, and Whitewashing the Nazi Past from Below," *German Politics and Society* 39, no. 1 (Spring 2021): 15–36; Mikkel Dack, "A Comparative Study of French Denazification: Instruments and Procedures in Allied Occupied Germany," in *La France et la dénazification de l'Allemagne après 1945*, eds. Sébastien Chauffour et al. (Brussels: Peter Lang, 2019), 109–27; and Borgstedt, "Der Fragebogen. Zur Wahrnehmung eines Symbols politischer Säuberung nach 1945," 166–71.

[21] The denazification records of the East German KPD and SED were released in 1990, along with some relevant SMA collections, but most files housed in Russian archives remain inaccessible to researchers.

[22] Unless stated otherwise, all German civilians referenced in this book have been assigned a pseudonym. Their true initials are included in the relevant citation.

1950 dissertation that the Americans abandoned denazification too early and that they should have put more trust in German antifascists.[23] Similarly, John D. Montgomery accused American urgency to contain communism of undermining the war against Nazism.[24]

In the 1970s, the study of denazification changed considerably, as a new school of revisionist historians challenged traditional arguments and theoretical constructs about the postwar era. Sustained by the release of tens of thousands of *Spruchkammer* (special denazification tribunal) files in West German state archives, this resource-rich period was populated by a younger generation of researchers who were not as concerned with high-policy studies as they were with *Alltagsgeschichte* (history of the everyday). The new wave of scholarship was championed by social historian Lutz Niethammer with his landmark book, *Entnazifizierung in Bayern* (1972).[25] Consulting archival materials on both sides of the Atlantic, Niethammer concluded that denazification had indeed been a failure, but that the war on fascism could have very well succeeded if the Americans had not allowed fundamental political reform and economic goals to overshadow the need for social and ideological change. The argument that he forwarded did little to upset traditional interpretations, but his research did admit the German-administered screening commissions to historical review. No longer was the story of denazification being told only by Americans and investigation confined to the actions of the occupiers.

Niethammer's seminal work initiated the publication of a series of microstudies in which mostly German historians examined denazification measures in individual *Länder* (states) and *Kreise* (districts).[26] But these *Alltagsgeschichten* of the 1970s and 1980s were not concerned with grassroots denazification experiences. Like earlier works, they evaluated the screening campaign from the perspective of authoritative institutions. Instead of military governments, they investigated the activities of German-run screening commissions, pooling data on rulings and amnesties in hopes of answering the same question of why denazification failed. Niethammer and his followers continued to measure "success"

---

[23] William Griffith, "The Denazification Program in the United States Zone in Germany" (PhD diss., Harvard University, 1950).
[24] John D. Montgomery, *Forced to Be Free: The Artificial Revolution in Germany and Japan* (Chicago: University of Chicago Press, 1957), 1–9.
[25] Niethammer, *Entnazifizierung in Bayern*.
[26] Among them are Irmgard Lange, *Entnazifizierung in Nordrhein-Westfalen: Richtlinien, Anweisungen, Organisation* (Siegburg: Respublica Verlag, 1976); Boyd L. Dastrup, *Crusade in Nuremberg: Military Occupation 1945–1949* (Westport: Greenwood Press, 1985); and Elmar Ettle, *Die Entnazifizierung in Eichstätt: Probleme der politischen Säuberung nach 1945* (Frankfurt am Main: Lang, 1985).

according to the number of former Nazis permanently removed from positions of influence. The Fragebogen featured prominently in these histories, but only as statistical evidence of the overly ambitious bureaucratic screening program.

The concurrent release of many British and French occupation records, in 1975 and 1986, respectively, saw researchers scrambling to catch up with the existing scholarship on the US zone. The origins, scope, and scale of the "other" Western campaigns were studied at length, mainly for the purpose of comparison. With the American model firmly typecast as the epitome of administrative failure – and the "American Fragebogen" as its showpiece – the unique and perhaps more positive characteristics of the British and French programs were highlighted. British historians emphasized the features of a more moderate screening campaign, and scholars of the French occupation unanimously concluded that denazification in the smallest zone was more personalized, consistent, and forward thinking.[27] These authors did not go as far as to celebrate the British and French campaigns, but only to attest that they had not been as redundant as the American project. Furthermore, they continued to operate in the same historical timeframe, evaluate denazification based on employment data, and mostly ignore the experiences of individual Germans.

Unsurprisingly, the most significant shift in scholarship occurred in the 1990s and early 2000s, following the collapse of communism in Eastern Europe. The gradual release of occupation-era documents in the former GDR and in Russia resulted in a landslide of literature on varying aspects of the Soviet occupation, including violence, censorship, education, and political reform. Post-reunification debate on Soviet denazification intersected with a reevaluation of East German politics and culture, including "de-Stasification" and a wider comparison of Germany's two

---

[27] Notable studies include Barbara Marshall, "German Attitudes to British Military Government, 1945–1947," *Journal of Contemporary History* 15, no. 4 (October 1980): 655–84; Jill Jones, "Eradicating Nazism from the British Zone of Germany: Early Policy and Practice," *German History* 8, no. 2 (June 1990): 145–62; Klaus-Dietmar Henke, *Politische Säuberung unter französischer Besatzung: Die Entnazifizierung in Württemberg-Hohenzollern* (Stuttgart: Deutsche Verlags-Anstalt, 1981); Rainer Möhler, *Entnazifizierung in Rheinland-Pfalz und im Saarland unter französischer Besatzung von 1945 bis 1952* (Mainz: V. Hase & Koehler, 1992); Reinhard Grohnert, *Die Entnazifizierung in Baden 1945–1949* (Stuttgart: Kohlhammer, 1991). Prior to the 1980s, most discussion of denazification in the British zone was absorbed by studies on the larger occupation, such as Michael Balfour and John Mair, *Four Power Control in Germany and Austria, 1945–1946* (London: Oxford University Press, 1956). At this time, the only serious study of the French occupation was Roy Willis, *The French in Germany, 1945–1949* (Stanford: Stanford University Press, 1962).

dictatorships.[28] These studies either drew critical attention to the inconsistencies in the application of denazification policy within the Soviet zone or emphasized the differences between the Russian and Western campaigns.[29] Such a comparison is made, for example, in Timothy Vogt's indispensable work, *Denazification in Soviet-Occupied Germany* (2001), which is the first monograph to explore the Soviet Fragebogen program in any detail. Vogt argues that much like in the West, denazification in the Soviet zone was a failure, but that this was never admitted publicly.[30]

In more recent years, the study of the *Nachkriegzeit* has splintered into different avenues of historical inquiry, accounting for multiple perspectives and methodologies. Research on soldier–civilian encounters, individual and collective memories, trauma, victimhood, gender, and justice has produced a more sophisticated interpretation of the postwar.[31] These works move beyond the short-sighted and single-framed evaluation of the military occupation, to consider the impact of war and dictatorship on German society, including the emotional state of the citizen and the political and cultural effects of foreign subjugation.

Unfortunately, these rich and mostly German-oriented studies have only engaged tangentially with the topic of denazification. What this cultural history has done, however, is chip away at the foundation of traditional interpretation and encourage a new cohort of scholars who are more reflective in their analysis of denazification and willing to challenge long-held historiographical assumptions. Equipped with better access to relevant archival records, researchers no longer shy away from conducting multi-zone studies and even highlighting similarities between

---

[28] On de-Stasification, see John O. Koehler, "East Germany: The Stasi and de-Stasification," in *Dismantling Tyranny: Transitioning between Totalitarian Regimes*, eds. Ilan Berman and J. Michael Waller (Lanham, MD: Rowman & Littlefield, 2015), 43–74; and Christiane Wilke, "The Shield, the Sword, and the Party: Vetting the East German Public Sector," in *Justice As Prevention: Vetting Public Employees in Transitional Societies*, eds. Alexander Mayer-Rieckh and Pablo de Greiff (New York: Social Science Research Council, 2007).

[29] Such as Damian van Melis, *Entnazifizierung in Mecklenburg-Vorpommern: Herrschaft und Verwaltung 1945–1948* (Munich: Oldenbourg, 1999).

[30] Timothy Vogt, *Denazification in Soviet-Occupied Germany: Brandenburg, 1945–1948* (Cambridge, MA: Harvard University Press, 2000), 232–34.

[31] Some notable works include Norbert Frei, *Vergangenheitspolitik: die Anfänge der Bundesrepublik und die NS-Vergangenheit* (Munich: Beck, 1996); Herf, *Divided Memory*; Atina Grossman, *Jews, Germans, and Allies: Close Encounters in Occupied Germany* (Princeton, NJ: Princeton University Press, 2007); Frank Biess, *Homecomings: Returning POWs and the Legacies of Defeat in Postwar Germany* (Princeton, NJ: Princeton University Press, 2006); Mary Fulbrook, *German National Identity after the Holocaust* (Cambridge: Polity Press, 2002).

Western and Soviet approaches to screening and internment.[32] More noteworthy is an inclination to acknowledge the positive legacies of denazification. Revisionist scholars tend to adopt a longer timeframe to measure effectiveness and point to the democratic success story of the Federal Republic.[33] However, this emerging scholarship has not yet fully embraced a bottom-up history of denazification. Conducting multi-zone comparative studies and reevaluating ideological effectiveness are essential tasks, but so too is an examination of everyday shared experiences. Furthermore, few studies have successfully combined the history of Allied denazification efforts with the subsequent experiences of the German population.

Methodology, Sources, and Scope

This book is a history of mass political screening in occupied Germany – what I refer to as *everyday denazification*. The research reminds us that the occupying authorities were involved in the day-to-day lives of the people they governed and that they influenced how Germans rebuilt their lives after the war. It deconstructs what is currently a compartmentalized history of the military occupation to garner an appreciation that soldiers and civilians populated the same physical space and interacted closely with each other, especially during the denazification process.

From the Allied perspective, an investigation of the Fragebogen program allows for a more comprehensive understanding of the ideological war against fascism. The number of people arrested, discharged, and rehired are weak quantitative proxy measures of program success, as they fail to reflect how Germans actually felt about Nazism. By studying the mechanics of the machine and its operation in the field a more precise interpretation of the American, British, French, and Soviet campaigns is achieved. An inclusive study of the first nonviolent de-radicalization project in modern times also speaks to contemporary issues, as seen in the pervasive public concern for the rising wave of political extremism and right-wing populist movements.

---

[32] Biddiscombe, *Denazification of Germany*; Beattie, *Allied Internment Camps in Occupied Germany*.

[33] Among them are Konrad Jarausch, *After Hitler: Recivilizing Germans, 1945–1995* (Oxford: Oxford University Press, 2006); Frederick Taylor, *Exorcising Hitler: The Occupation and Denazification of Germany* (New York: Bloomsbury, 2011); Uta Gerhardt and Gösta Gantner, "Ritualprozeß Entnazifizierung: eine These zur gesellschaftlichen Transformation der Nachkriegszeit," *Forum Ritualdynamik* 7 (July 2004): 1–80; and Harald Jähner, *Aftermath: Life in the Fallout of the Third Reich, 1945–1955*, trans. Shaun Whiteside (New York: Knopf, 2022).

From the German perspective, the book explores how average citizens living under military occupation experienced denazification and how it affected their lives – family welfare, employment, financial status, community reputation, mental health, etc. It individualizes political screening, shifting the analytical gaze away from high-level administrators to the common German citizen and their immediate community. At its core, the Allied crusade to eradicate Nazism was about changing the views and beliefs of Germans; this study refines the investigation of whether this in fact happened. Moreover, it extends the already rich literature on postwar German cultural history by asking overdue questions about how denazification impacted community relations and memory.

In this book, "denazification" is interpreted as both the sociological imperative to eradicate National Socialism from public life and permanently discredit the ideology in the minds of German citizens, as well as the actual approved multifaceted administrative program designed to achieve such goals. This is aligned with the often-proposed dual definition, which accounts for both "expansive" and "narrow" interpretations.[34] The former includes any actions taken to discourage Nazism and serve transitional justice, such as mass dismissals, criminal prosecutions, internment, and reeducation initiatives. The "narrow" definition, which was subscribed to by the occupying armies, is confined mainly to vetting (or purging) processes and the removal of personnel.[35] In defining success and failure, I do not take the "narrow" view or adopt an uncompromising system of measurement; destroying National Socialism did not hinge on a long-standing exclusion of every Nazi from postwar public service. Instead, effective denazification meant a prevailing community rejection of the regime and its ideology, rendering them culturally taboo and thereby ensuring that Nazism would not reemerge in any meaningful form. Unlike scholars who evaluate denazification based on pooled statistics, I measure the campaign's success by interpreting the firsthand accounts of people who in fact underwent political screening. That being said, it is not the main intention of this book to evaluate the

---

[34] See Beattie, *Allied Internment Camps in Occupied Germany*, 10; Rebecca Boehling, "Transitional Justice? Denazification in the US Zone of Occupied Germany," in *Transforming Occupation in the Western Zones of Germany: Politics, Everyday Life and Social Interactions, 1945–55*, eds. Camilo Erlichman and Christopher Knowles (London: Bloomsbury, 2018), 65.

[35] In the relevant literature, "purging" is generally used to refer to the targeting of individuals for their affiliation in a certain group, while "vetting" is a systematic evaluation of personnel based on specific criteria. In this study, the terms are used interchangeably.

effectiveness of denazification. While a critique is unavoidable, especially when introducing a crucial piece of evidence to the investigation, it is my opinion that the habitual fixation of producing a definitive verdict has distracted from the interpretation of many significant experiences and influences.

To account for more perspectives, a multitude of sources have been reviewed for this study. They include government and military files, soldier and civilian diaries, commission documents, church and party records, and newspapers drawn from German, American, British, and French archives and libraries. A small number of interviews were conducted with Germans who experienced the denazification process firsthand. Unsurprisingly, the predominant source is the questionnaire itself. Thousands of Fragebögen, completed by citizens of varying backgrounds, living in different occupation zones, between 1945 and 1951, were examined. They contain more than a million short answers, but I was more interested in the descriptive and ofttimes evocative responses found in the appended documents – personal biographies, sworn statements, and letters. For the purpose of this study, "Fragebogen" refers not only to the standardized form, but the sheets of written commentary attached to them, submitted by respondents during their screening. The study of a mass-distributed questionnaire, one that produces an exhausting amount of quantifiable data, makes the traditional stochastic method of analysis appealing. However, to generate a history of everyday denazification, this study avoids a statistical approach.

American and British zone activities are featured more prominently in the book, which is intentional. The questionnaire program originated as an Anglo-American project. The French and Soviet programs were distinct, as were those instituted under the various *Land* governments, but the questionnaires used by every authority were based on the American and British model. Furthermore, the American zone witnessed by far the widest distribution of Fragebögen. Of the more than 20 million questionnaires submitted for review, 16 million were processed by OMGUS or by German offices operating under American supervision.[36] Moreover, the US National Archives and Records Administration maintains the largest accessible collection of records related to the Fragebogen program. Therefore, while activities in all four zones are examined, the Soviet zone perspective, and to a lesser degree the French viewpoint, are more circumstantial.

---

[36] Tony Judt, *Postwar: A History of Europe since 1945* (New York: Penguin Press, 2005), 56.

Outline of the Book

The book's temporal frame extends from the Allied invasion of Europe, in July 1943, to the formation of the two German states, in late 1949. Some consideration is given to residual denazification activities in the early 1950s, under the watchful eye of the Allied high commissioners. The work adopts a mix of chronological and thematic organization. Overlaps in timeline reflect the difficulty of neatly periodizing late 1940s Germany and the uneven transition from war to peace to stable government. The book is divided into five chapters and accommodates three undefined sections, each with its own vantage point and timeframe.

The first section traces the ideological and practical origins of the inter-Allied denazification campaign and the unorthodox questionnaire program that it proposed. Chapter 1 surveys the wartime planning landscape in 1943 and 1944 and introduces the individuals and institutions that created the Fragebogen. Hundreds of civilian experts, including college professors, police officers, lawyers, and Jewish refugees, were employed to build denazification policy and to overhaul military civil affairs programs. In Chapter 2, the Fragebogen is introduced – it sits the reader down at the drafting table and explains what the civilian specialists envisioned for Germany after the collapse of the Nazi dictatorship. The structure and content of the original survey is scrutinized, and conclusions made as to why so much confidence was placed in such an experimental project. Although the French and Soviet questionnaires are not the principal focus of this book, they are an essential part of the denazification story. Neither of these lesser-known political screening programs has been subject to thorough scholarly review; both are examined here in detail.

Chapters 3 and 4 act as the centerpiece of the book and together comprise a study of everyday denazification. Here, the lived experiences of both the civilian occupied and the military occupiers are explored, describing to the reader what political screening looked like on the ground and in action. Chapter 3 lifts the incomplete and unevaluated Fragebogen off the desks of planners in England and delivers it to American, British, French, and Soviet soldiers operating in Germany. It analyzes the implementation and gradual institutionalization of the *Fragebogenaktion* (questionnaire campaign) beginning in 1945; how the form was distributed, collected, and evaluated, and what role it played in the larger military occupation. In Chapter 4, the second vantage point of the book is introduced, that of the German citizen. It describes what denazification was like for most men and women; how they reacted to the Allies' war on Nazism and how it impacted their daily lives. This chapter concludes with a detailed case study of denazification experiences in Hersfeld (Hesse), a moderately sized district (*Kreis*) in the US occupation zone.

In the final section of the book, the reader is introduced to a conversation about the psychological and social consequences of denazification, particularly community relations, emotional well-being, memory and identity, and the national process of coming to terms with the Nazi past. Despite being heralded at the time as a campaign to change the hearts and minds of Germans, no comprehensive investigation of the ideological effects of denazification has been conducted. Chapter 5 includes a more nuanced interpretation of denazification, beginning with an investigation into how the Fragebogen encouraged the already widespread practice of political denunciation, likely delaying the healing of the dysfunctional society left after the war. It then turns its focus on how Germans remembered and recorded memories of the Nazi regime. Consideration here is given to narrative psychology and the power that written language has on memory. The Fragebogen is presented as an autobiographical ego-document with performative features. Emphasis is placed on the German appropriation of denazification and the transformative role that the questionnaire played in the emotional lives of a morally culpable people.

A comprehensive assessment of the Fragebogen is presented in the book's conclusion, including speculation about the enduring effects of denazification on the two German successor states. The unexpected achievements of the zonal screening programs are measured against their many weaknesses and negative results. Consideration is also given to more recent political screening projects in different parts of the world, and the historical lessons ascribed to denazification.

1 An Army of Academics
Planning the Denazification of Germany

> Perhaps there has rarely been a reasonably high-level organization where low-ranking university professors were more appreciated and sought than in the German Country Unit.[1]
> —Professor Harold Zink, Staff Officer, German Country Unit

In a March 1920 report to the Chief of Staff of the American Forces in Germany, Colonel Irwin L. Hunt, Officer in Charge of Civil Affairs, testified that the United States' Army of Occupation in the Rhineland "lacked both training and organization to guide the destinies of the nearly 1,000,000 civilians whom the fortunes of war had placed under its temporary sovereignty."[2] Hunt reminded his superiors that in the aftermath of the Great War, no attempt had been made to study the civil responsibilities involved in an occupation of enemy territory. He recommended that, in the future, soldiers be equipped with "scholastic knowledge" and a thorough comprehension of the "psychological, economic and political factors" relevant to the country they occupied.[3] Although Hunt's report was initially shelved by the War Department, it was reevaluated some twenty-three years later, when Western Allied armies began mobilizing for their invasion of Germany; it forever changed American civil affairs doctrine.[4]

---

[1] Harold Zink, *The United States in Germany, 1944–1955* (New York: Van Nostrand, 1957), 21.
[2] Colonel Irwin L. Hunt, "American Military Government of Occupied Germany, 1918–1920," March 4, 1920 (Washington DC: US Government Printing Office, 1943), 65. After the 1918 armistice, a large portion of the Rhine region (mostly the left bank) was subject to military occupation by American, British, French, and Belgian troops. The occupation lasted until June 1930, but American troops left in January 1924, handing over their administrative district to the French.
[3] Ibid., 63–64. For the original Hunt Report, see Report, "American Military Government of Occupied Germany, 1918–1920," n.d., NARA, RG 260, OMGUS, EO, Box 303.
[4] A summary of "lessons learned" from the occupation of the Rhine region was distributed to SHAEF army formations in November 1944. See Report, "Experiences in Occupied Rhineland, 1919–1925," November 8, 1944, NARA, RG 331, SHAEF, GS, G-5, IS, HS, Box 196.

This first chapter traces the wartime development of American and British army civil affairs programs and the complex bureaucracies that built the denazification campaigns. At all levels of planning, there was a unanimous commitment to the eradication of Nazism, but mid-level military and government offices struggled to translate high-policy goals into workable procedures. The Fragebogen was a product of this challenging and ultimately dysfunctional policy-planning environment.

The two offices accredited for devising and drafting the political screening questionnaire for Germany were the Central European Section, a small research group within the US Office of Strategic Services (OSS), and the German Country Unit, which operated under the Western inter-Allied command of SHAEF. The primary function of civilian specialists in the formulation of denazification strategy is most apparent in these working groups. Both OSS and SHAEF, and dozens of other wartime agencies and planning units, went to great lengths to recruit civilian experts to draft and implement occupation policy. Still, the enlistment of historians, political scientists, criminologists, legalists, and engineers, from various institutional settings and political persuasions, to write denazification procedures was an unprecedented and experimental undertaking. This "army" of academics brought with them innovative social scientific approaches and instruments, such as theoretical and applied research methods, as well as new perspectives and concepts regarding ideological, sociological, and political transformation. To appropriately understand the Fragebogen program, we must begin by surveying the political, military, and intellectual landscape in which denazification developed.

The Problem of Denazification

On the evening of November 29, 1943, sitting around a large oak table at the Soviet Embassy in Tehran, Joseph Stalin, Winston Churchill, and Franklin Roosevelt deliberated on what to do with Germany after the war. The Russian dictator demanded that 50,000 officers of the German Commanding Staff be "physically liquidated," perhaps even 100,000, and that the eastern territories be permanently dismembered.[5] Fearing an economically crippled Europe and consequent communist encroachment, Prime Minister Churchill advocated for a softer peace and temporary division of the defeated Reich. President Roosevelt, who was

---

[5] Foreign Relations of the United States: Diplomatic Papers, the Conferences at Cairo and Tehran, 1943, Tripartite Dinner Meeting, 8:30 p.m. (document 368), Bohlen Collection, p. 554.

careful not to make any long-term commitments to Europe, remained mostly silent on the issue.

At this first wartime conclave of the Big Three powers, the only point of agreement was that conventional terms of defeat, such as those ratified in the Treaty of Versailles twenty-four years earlier, would not suffice. Taking away weapons, territory, and industrial capacity was not enough to permanently solve the "German problem" and ensure a lasting peace. The Tehran Conference was merely a diplomatic forum for the exchange of opinions, but the Allied leaders left with an understanding that an unconventional strategy was needed. A fatal blow had to be struck against what was perceived to be a culture of political authoritarianism and entrenched militarism. Interpreted by a Swedish journalist attending the conference, Germany was portrayed as a "patient ... Europe's 'sick man', in desperate need of injections of anti-Nazi serum."[6] An American commitment to a postwar curative campaign was confirmed by Roosevelt in a radio broadcast one month later: "we intend to rid them [Germans] once and for all of Nazism and Prussian militarism and the fantastic and disastrous notion that they constitute the 'Master Race.'"[7] It was in the wake of the Tehran Conference that the major Allied powers began developing a strategy for the denazification of Germany.

From the beginning, the eradication of Nazism was a problematic endeavor; it was never a clear-sighted campaign. The most fundamental problem was that no one – not military intelligence officers, civilian specialists, or even captured Germans – could define Nazism, at least in so much that it could be effectively targeted for elimination. A card-carrying Nazi Party member was easy enough to identify, but "fascists" and "militarists" were not. What exactly was a Nazi sympathizer? How could individuals be screened for ideology? While a number of markers were ultimately identified, such rudimentary questions were never sufficiently answered by any authority. As reported retrospectively by one discerning British intelligence officer, "there was widespread agreement that 'Nazis had to be rooted out'. ... Fewer still stopped to define what they meant by Nazism or to consider the implications of too sweeping a definition."[8]

---

[6] Stig Dagerman, *German Autumn*, reprint, trans. Robin Fulton (London: Quartet, 1988), 59.
[7] Franklin D. Roosevelt, "December 24, 1943: Fireside Chat 27: On the Tehran and Cairo Conferences," available from http://millercenter.org/the-presidency/presidential-speeches/december-24-1943-fireside-chat-27-tehran-and-cairo-conferences (accessed December 15, 2021).
[8] Balfour and Mair, *Four-Power Control in Germany and Austria*, 170–77.

The United States, Great Britain, France, and the Soviet Union already had experience in occupying foreign territories and peoples but post-hostility transition governance had always been restricted to the employment of military personnel, who acted largely in a supervisory capacity. Previous occupations were carried out for the purpose of suppressing military renewal and ensuring the transfer of monetary and territorial compensations. Never had a modern power developed and implemented a coordinated campaign to ideologically disarm the enemy in order to ensure a lasting peace. Unsurprisingly, the underlying question of how best to eliminate Nazism did not initially concern Allied nation decision makers. Until the final victory was in sight, conversation about denazification occurred only between a small number of specialists, scattered across mid-level offices in mostly national agencies. Instead, all meaningful wartime discussion about the postwar peace was concerned with military governance and how best to punish Germany.

On the surface, inter-Allied planning was relatively uncomplicated and based on consensus. At the Moscow Tripartite Conference of Foreign Ministers, which began in October 1943, the Soviet Union, United States, and Great Britain established a European Advisory Council (EAC) to oversee multilateral planning for the post-hostilities period.[9] A year and a half later, at the much anticipated Yalta Conference, the Big Three leaders decided that after its unconditional surrender, Germany would be divided into zones of occupation.[10] The Soviet Union would administer the five most eastern *Länder* (states), those of Brandenburg, Mecklenburg, Saxony, Saxony-Anhalt, and Thuringia, while Great Britain would control the northern territories of Schleswig-Holstein and Lower Saxony, including Hamburg, as well as densely populated Westphalia and the northern portion of the Rhine province. The United States was allocated Bavaria, Hesse, and the northern half of what is today Baden-Württemberg, as well as the Bremen Enclave. The French, who were not formally represented at Yalta, received the smallest portion of territory in the southwest of the country, which included Rhineland-Palatinate, the Saarland, and the southern half of

---

[9] Beate Ruhm von Oppen, *Documents on Germany under Occupation 1945–1954* (London: Oxford University Press, 1955), 2–4.

[10] United States Department of State, *Foreign Relations of the United States: Conferences at Malta and Yalta, 1945* (Washington, DC: US Government Printing Office, 1945), 970–71. The first official inter-Allied agreement regarding the future occupation of Germany was the Atlantic Charter (signed August 14, 1941), within which the United States and Great Britain established preliminary goals for the postwar world and promised the "final destruction of Nazi tyranny." This was merely a statement of ethical objections to the Nazi regime and an affirmation of common principles for postwar international peace.

Württemberg-Baden.[11] The Reich's capital of Berlin would be granted special four-power status, with each occupying authority governing an individual "sector" of the city. To ensure policy uniformity, an Allied Control Council (ACC) would be formed, although each member nation would administer their respective territory independently. Further agreement came in policy objectives. The occupation would be governed by the so-called "Five D's": Germany would undergo demilitarization, deindustrialization, decartelization, denazification, and democratization. These mandates were reaffirmed at the Potsdam Conference in July 1945, including a joint commitment to "destroy the last vestiges of Nazism and Fascism."[12]

Beyond the agreement that the enemy state should be divided, punished, and reoriented, Allied leadership struggled to reach a consensus on the character of the occupation, including its duration. According to Roosevelt, the United States was not prepared to undertake any detailed planning for the occupation of a country "which had not yet been defeated."[13] The emerging superpower was reluctant to make any long-term commitments to postwar Germany, or to Europe for that matter, at least not until its surveyors had assessed the war damage and measured political conditions firsthand. Roosevelt was also not willing to test his interventionist policy on the eve of the 1944 presidential election; he worried that after the war's conclusion, the American public would prefer to revert back to familiar isolationism and leave the management of Europe to the newly established United Nations.[14] Furthermore, he was continuously being pressured by his advisors not to dwell on such matters but instead focus on forcing a quick defeat of Germany, so that American troops and material resources could be relocated to the Pacific Theater. What resulted was a general unwillingness on the president's behalf to approve the drafting of a formal plan for the occupation.

Unofficial American policymaking ended abruptly in August 1944, when Secretary of the Treasury Henry Morgenthau intervened. His hard brow vision for Germany included the permanent division of the country

---

[11] The *Land* Rhineland-Palatinate was created by the French in 1946, from the southern portion of the Rhine province (Prussia) and parts of Hesse and Bavaria. Bremen and Bremerhaven (together, the "Bremen Enclave") originally came under the jurisdiction of the British but was later incorporated into the US zone after the Americans demanded access to a seaport. Tony Sharp, *The Wartime Alliance and the Zonal Division of Germany* (Oxford: Oxford University Press, 1975), 90–101.

[12] James K. Pollock and James H. Meisel, eds., *Germany under Occupation: Illustrative Materials and Documents* (Ann Arbor: George Wahr, 1949), 14–20.

[13] Barbara Marshall, *The Origins of Post-War German Politics* (London: Croom Helm, 1988), 1.

[14] Adams, *From Crusade to Hazard*, 1.

into separate states, including an "international zone," from which reparations would be extracted. Although the "Morgenthau Plan" was endorsed by many influential figures, including the Supreme Allied Commander, Dwight D. Eisenhower, the proposal was eventually thrown out, or at least watered down.[15] It was replaced by a more moderate policy, one that abided by the traditional US Army doctrine of "welfare of the governed," calling for a just and humane administration.[16] But even though Morgenthau's draconian program was discarded, the general tone of a "tough peace" continued to infiltrate occupation planning, tightening up regulations in nearly all areas of military government administration, including denazification. What resulted was a strategy rife with ambiguous goals and conflicting instructions for civil affairs officers operating in the field. Some programs were clearly oriented on dismantlement and punishment while others favored reconstruction and rehabilitation.

Much like their American counterpart, the British were determined not to become entangled in the politics of occupation, at least not until Japan had been defeated. Still, planning for postwar government began earlier in Churchill's administration. The principal concern was national security and preventing Germany from ever again being in a position to wage an aggressive war in Europe. For British planners, this meant stripping the Reich of its military capabilities and industrial strength, as well as eradicating Nazism from popular society. However, the Foreign Office, as well as a number of Churchill's key advisors, believed that in order to revive the British economy and restore the United Kingdom to its prewar world-power status, a more temperate policy was required. Britain's recovery was tied to the restoration of European trade and the opening of market agreements, conditions that relied on the stability of the German economy. Furthermore, Britain feared the spread of communism on the continent; it worried that the Soviets would move into the political vacuum left by the defeat of Germany and expand their empire west.[17] This dilemma, how to balance territorial security and economic and political stability, made the job of British planners difficult.

---

[15] A January 1944 poll conducted by *Fortune Magazine* postulated that 30 percent of Americans favored the dismemberment of Germany into smaller states. Taylor, *Exorcising Hitler*, 111.

[16] Championed by US Secretary of War, Henry Stimson, the occupation policy that emerged in the final months of the European war favored the recovery of German industry and the reintegration of the German economy into the larger European market.

[17] Marshall, *The Origins of Post-War German Politics*, 1.

France was the only major Allied nation that had been fully occupied by the Germans, and due to the fragile state of its government-in-exile and sole focus on national liberation, occupation planning was carried out much later and with an even greater degree of uncertainty. Complicating matters was the existence of political and social divisions within France, some of which predated the war, and the fact that many French citizens had collaborated with the Nazis under the Vichy regime.[18] Despite the accomplishments of Charles de Gaulle's Free French movement, the role that France would play in the postwar occupation of Germany was dictated largely by the Big Three powers, especially Great Britain and the United States.[19] France's main purpose in occupying Germany was to maintain the integrity of its own borders. The desire to implement a program of territorial and economic revenge was popular within the provisional government, but de Gaulle's senior administration viewed the occupation as a constructive undertaking and as a possible long-term remedy for the maintenance of peace. Perhaps the occupation could also act as a physical statement that signified the restoration of France as an independent political agent in Europe and a revived great power.

Detailed planning in the Soviet camp also came relatively late, but the reason for remaining in Germany after the war was clear. The Red Army was charged with permanently crippling the German war machine and ensuring that Nazism was forever purged from the country's economic and political systems.[20] Apart from these most basic goals, the Russians were determined to extract war reparations in the form of industrial output and broaden its sphere of influence into central Europe while preventing the spread of capitalism. Some members of Stalin's inner circle advocated for a "hard peace," but more hopeful planners projected a homegrown social transformation in Germany, one led by a loyal vanguard of local antifascists who would ensure the eventual liberation of the working class. This latter strategy was eventually adopted, at least partially, and the leaders of the *Kommunistische Partei Deutschland* (Communist Party of Germany, KPD), such as Walter Ulbricht, Anton Ackermann, and Gustav Sobottka, were appointed as pro-Soviet revolutionaries.[21] Nevertheless, the administrative character of the Soviet occupation government and its German auxiliaries was not clearly outlined prior to the invasion.

---

[18] Willis, *The French in Germany*, 77.   [19] Ibid., 7, 15–19.
[20] Vogt, *Denazification in Soviet-Occupied Germany*, 19.
[21] Norman Naimark, *The Russians in Germany: A History of the Soviet Zone of Occupation, 1945–1949* (Cambridge, MA: Belknap Press, 1995), 10.

If wartime planning for the political administration of Germany was lacking, the denazification campaign was nothing more than an afterthought. Still, the inter-Allied commitment to a prolonged war against Nazism was established early on, as this was viewed as an essential prerequisite to sustaining peace in Europe. Alluded to in the Atlantic Charter (1941) and confirmed at the Moscow and Tehran conferences (1943), as well as in subsequent statements by all four major Allied nations, the eradication of Nazism was an essential component of the occupation.[22] However, no serious joint-Allied planning occurred until the eve of the invasion, again because of the preoccupation with winning the war but also due to disagreement on how to interpret National Socialism.

Popular was the belief that the phenomenon of Nazism had been conceived and propagated by a criminal organization of fascist "gangsters" – that it was a sort of "sickness" that had infected the German people and now required treatment (see Figure 1.1).[23] Another common explanation was that aggressive nationalism and militarism were inherent to the German character and that Nazism had merely brought natural tendencies to the surface.[24] This cultural interpretation evoked notions of collective guilt and encouraged the treatment of Germany as a nation of criminals.[25] But it would be a vast simplification to suggest that there existed only these two schools of interpretation, one that believed in the existence of an "outlaw party," the other an "outlaw race," even though staunch supporters of each existed within all four Allied-nation governments. Instead, it is more appropriate to depict these theories as being in constant conversation, and often competition, with each other throughout the occupation including the initial phase of denazification planning.

For the Americans, at the highest administrative level, basic policy for denazification was determined by the president's Cabinet Committee on Germany. Due to disagreements within the committee, especially regarding the dismemberment and deindustrialization of Germany, but also perhaps because of the cyclical resurgence of Roosevelt's Germanophobia, an agreed-upon policy for denazification was never achieved prior to the invasion.[26] In their attempt to accommodate all

---

[22] Ruhn von Oppen, *Documents on Germany under Occupation*, 1–2; Taylor, *Exorcising Hitler*, 4. Tripartite plans for the punishment of Nazi war criminals were first outlined at the Moscow Conference (October 18 to November 11, 1943), then refined at Tehran (November 28 to December 1, 1943), Yalta (February 4–11, 1945), and Potsdam (July 17 to August 2, 1945).
[23] Jarausch, *After Hitler*, 46–47.   [24] Biddiscombe, *Denazification of Germany*, 27–28.
[25] Jarausch, *After Hitler*, 47.
[26] According to General Lucius Clay, Roosevelt's distaste for German "arrogance and provincialism" originated in his youth, when he and his family vacationed in Germany. Clay, *Decision in Germany*, 5.

Figure 1.1 Cover of the satirical magazine *Das Wespennest*, October 7, 1948. Cartoon by Stury.
Source: Haus der Geschichte, Bonn

in-house interpretations of Nazism and appease the American public, occupation planners ultimately advocated a highly ambitious and diversified campaign. There remained a desire to conduct a wholesale purge of the German political and economic spheres, but also strong interest in implementing an extensive reeducation program and to "convince" Germans to aspire to democratic principles.

Although anti-German sentiments ran throughout its wartime administration, the British were less inclined to adhere to a policy drawn from any notion of collective guilt or to implement a far-reaching purge. Instead, policymakers concentrated their efforts on the rehabilitative goals stated in the Yalta communique. Draconian policies were advocated by key political figures, who warned of a deep-seeded flaw in the German national character, but overwhelming opinion within the British government was that political and moral blame should be directed at the Nazi regime's leadership.[27] Popular was the belief that with the appropriate amount of guidance, historical practices could be undone and Germans converted into committed democrats.

The French were, at first, not as pragmatic and remained unconvinced by the theory that a "sickness" of Nazism had infected the general populace. A long history of conflict and four years of military occupation had resulted in a deep animosity toward Germany and confirmation of the country's *Erbfeind* (archenemy) status. While certainly influenced by this popular sentiment, French leaders were surprisingly realistic in their mission, recognizing that the maintenance of national security could not be achieved through an *esprit de revanche*. Instead, the French were determined to judge each case on its own individual merits rather than deferring to categories of guilt, as some American offices were recommending. They hoped to wean the German people from Nazism through mandatory reeducation projects and to replace the ideological void with an imported brand of French political culture.[28]

Soviet denazification policy was unique in that it was guided by Marxist theory on class consciousness and the historical development of economic systems. Planners in Moscow viewed the war against Nazism as an opportunity to not only cleanse German society of fascist elements but also construct and nurture a workers' state. However, some advocated a radical overhauling of political and economic institutions, coupled with mass arrests and dismissals, while others believed that the "German problem" could be solved through a large-scale mandatory reeducation program.[29] Some planners thought it best to align their disciplinary measures with American policy, while others preferred to

---

[27] Ian D. Turner, "Introduction: The British Occupation and Its Impact on Germany," in *Reconstruction in Post-War Germany: British Occupation Policy and the Western Zones, 1945–55*, ed. Ian D. Turner (Oxford: Berg Publishers, 1989), 4–5.

[28] Willis, *The French in Germany*, 149–50.

[29] Vogt, *Denazification in Soviet-Occupied Germany*, 8–9. For a detailed analysis of the Soviet debate on the nature of German Nazism/fascism, see Christian Kanig,

target only the Nazi leadership and industrial elites.[30] According to historian Timothy Vogt, this fundamental disagreement led to an "ideological quandary and the crippling of the formulation of a clear-cut denazification program."[31]

While most tasks seemed relatively straightforward, the removal of former Nazis from positions of responsibility was not, as it produced difficult questions upon which the success of the purge rested: What exactly is a Nazi? Should Nazi status rest entirely on party membership? If so, what should be done with those Germans who joined the party out of opportunism or force of circumstance? Should all 8.5 million Nazi Party members (10 percent of the population) be barred from the civil service? How does one measure Nazi sympathy? More fundamental still, is denazification primarily an action against a political party or an ideology, or an entire population? The negative prefix suggested that "nazification" could in fact be reversed, but what exactly was it that would be reversed? Furthermore, will the necessary intelligence for screening Germans for employment be available to occupying armies? The general lack of inter-Allied coordination did not help answer these questions, nor did the vastly different interpretations of Nazism or an occupation strategy that clumsily mixed programs of retribution and rehabilitation; denazification was supposed to fall somewhere in between.

Civilianizing the Military, 1943–1944

The political objectives that arrived from wartime conferences were not accompanied by executive oversight or even a clear allocation of responsibility for policymaking. Commitments had been made to occupy, punish, and reorient Germans, but no strategy was delivered. This had two outcomes, both of which impacted the final character of denazification. First, British and American mid-level planning groups flourished. With complicated bureaucracies and competing chains of command, a myriad of agencies working under orders from different domestic offices developed. These groups were mostly uncoordinated and much of their work repetitive. The creation of inter-Allied planning groups only further upset the decision-making hierarchies and produced more bureaucratic confusion.

"Reeducation through Soviet Culture: Soviet Cultural Policy in Occupied Germany, 1945–1949" (PhD diss., Indiana University, 2011), 28–116.

[30] Richard Bessel, *Germany 1945: From War to Peace* (New York: HarperCollins, 2009), 199; Vogt, *Denazification in Soviet-Occupied Germany*, 9.

[31] Vogt, *Denazification in Soviet-Occupied Germany*, 9.

The second consequence was a rise in creative thinking and a greater willingness to experiment with unconventional strategies. With the absence of traditional military overseers, considerable room was given to a new generation of policymakers. American and British officers, who dominated Allied wartime planning, recognized there was an inherent problem in traditional civil affairs operations and advocated for a major program overhaul. Despite some moderate infighting, it was generally recognized that the Treaty of Versailles represented a policy failure and that the function of military government needed greater attention. The same criticisms voiced by Col. Irwin Hunt in his 1920 report are found in the recorded meeting minutes of these early planning groups.[32]

Civil affairs was quickly redefined to include a multitude of civic responsibilities for liberated and occupied territories, such as government administration, public safety, finance, health, and infrastructure.[33] It was determined that the most suitable candidates for implementing and managing these expanded mandates were experts from private companies and universities – including civil engineers, physicians, legalists, political scientists, historians, and healthcare workers. In addition to supplying civilian aid relief, coordinating displaced peoples, restructuring Germany's political and economic systems, and installing military government, civil affairs officers were assigned the task of planning and executing denazification. Nazism was viewed as an unprecedented phenomenon and therefore unprecedented strategies were required. As early as 1940, the military began recruiting specialists and collaborating with universities, research institutions, and intelligence agencies.[34]

---

[32] See, for example, "Planning Directive No. 9," June 19, 1944, The National Archives, UK (hereafter, TNA), WO 171/72, Doc. 5640/58.

[33] Earl F. Ziemke, *The U.S. Army in the Occupation of Germany, 1944–1946* (Washington, DC: Center of Military History, US Army, 1975), 3–22; Zink, *The United States in Germany*, 5–42; Eric James Bohman, "Rehearsals for Victory: The War Department and the Planning and Direction of Civil Affairs, 1940–1943" (PhD diss., Yale University, 1984). The terms "civil affairs" and "military government" were often used interchangeably, even though military government was simply the primary component of civil affairs. To some American planners, a "civil affairs office" administered a liberated territory, while a "military government" controlled a defeated nation.

[34] It should be noted that the enrollment of civilians in military apparatuses was by no means restricted to civil affairs. The American and British governments hired thousands of academics, businesspersons, and other professionals to assist in the war effort, undertaking tasks such as intelligence gathering, psychological warfare, economic planning, and the screening of military personnel. Much has been written on this subject; see, for example, David H. Price, *Anthropological Intelligence: The Deployment and Neglect of American Anthropology in the Second World War* (Durham, NC: Duke University Press, 2008); Mark Guglielmo, "The Contribution of Economists to Military Intelligence during World War II," *Journal of Economic History* 68, no. 1

The propensity to employ civilian experts also reflects the changing nature of higher education in the Western world and the rising popularity of the applied social sciences. Since the 1880s, the social sciences in the United States and Great Britain had developed rapidly in response to both real and perceived social problems and the anxieties that accompanied them.[35] Mass industrialization and urbanization, changing class structures, declining religious assurance, and a general rise in liberalism spurred bourgeois society and its governments to turn to the examination and application of social science knowledge. WWI exacerbated this search for meaning and order, as did fears of feminization, communism, unemployment, and the rise of the welfare state. In response to these widespread concerns, governments, private businesses, and universities looked to new methodologies to diagnose national character and the political health of the state, a process that led to what has been described as a "scientization of the social."[36] The professionalization of the social sciences occurred simultaneously, helping to channel the political and social anxieties of the post–WWI world into an arena suited for scientific investigation.

By the late 1930s, social science methods of observation and analysis had been thoroughly integrated into industry, government, higher education, and popular culture.[37] Therefore, during World War II, when military planners began to reevaluate their traditional civil affairs programs and draft plans to screen, punish, and reeducate defeated enemies, they did not have to look far for innovative strategies. New methodologies were readily available, including the standardized questionnaire, an instrument already being widely used by public institutions and private businesses on both sides of the Atlantic. While skepticism of the utility of

---

(2008): 109–50; Trevor J. Barnes, "Geographical Intelligence: American Geographers and Research and Analysis in the Office of Strategic Services, 1941–1945," *Journal of Historical Geography* 32, no. 1 (2006): 149–68; and James H. Capshew, *Psychologists on the March: Science, Practice, and Professional Identity in American, 1929–1969* (Cambridge: Cambridge University Press, 1999).

[35] Lutz Raphael, "Embedding the Human and Social Sciences in Western Societies, 1880–1980: Reflections on Trends and Methods of Current Research," in *Engineering Society: The Role of the Human and Social Sciences in Modern Societies, 1880–1980*, eds. Kerstin Brückweh et al. (New York: Palgrave Macmillan, 2012), 44, 50.

[36] Kerstin Brückweh et al., "Introduction: The Scientization of the Social in Comparative Perspective," in *Engineering Society: The Role of the Human and Social Sciences in Modern Societies, 1880–1980*, eds. Kerstin Brückweh et al. (New York: Palgrave Macmillan, 2012), 21.

[37] For further reading on the development of the applied social sciences in the United States and western Europe, see Roger E. Backhouse and Philippe Fontaine, eds., *The History of the Modern Social Sciences* (Cambridge: Cambridge University Press, 2010), and Dorothy Ross and Theodore M. Porter, *The Modern Social Sciences* (Cambridge: Cambridge University Press, 2003).

the social sciences was prevalent within the armed forces, enough members of the Allied armies were receptive to these new practices and to the enrollment of civilians, even though they possessed different capabilities for application.

France may have had a longer legacy of post-conflict occupations, but it was less prepared for the installation of military government in Germany and therefore adopted many American strategies and structures. Some preparations were made, however, in the winter of 1944/45, when a French school for military government was established in liberated Paris under the direction of General Louis-Marie Koeltz.[38] Civil affairs recruits were enrolled in a four-week program at the Sorbonne and School of Political Sciences, attending lectures by the country's foremost experts in German history, law, and culture, such as André Siegfried and Edmond Vermeil.[39] Almost all of the school's 1,500 students were recruited from civilian life, including specialists from public ministries within the French government and employees of private industry.[40] The *Administration militaire française en Allemagne* would eventually be comprised almost entirely of civilians in uniform.[41]

During the violent and disorderly closing months of the war, the Soviets also found little time to organize military government and recruit and train civilians. In fact, they did not establish a formal civil affairs division within their military apparatus until November 1944.[42] As a result, the original directories of the Soviet Military Administration (SMA) were modeled on ACC structures and early denazification programs were strikingly similar to those of the Western Allies. In early 1945, while the Russians scrambled to build up the staff organization of its military government, Red Army commanders occupied towns and villages in eastern Germany and set up local headquarters, or kommandatura, from which they exercised administrative authority over the surrounding region. These offices did not receive detailed instructions for civil administration and carried out denazification independently with little oversight. Instead of consulting SMA headquarters in Berlin for policy guidance, early commandants depended largely on German

---

[38] Grohnert, *Die Entnazifizierung in Baden*, 12–13.

[39] Corey J. Campion, "Negotiating Difference: French and American Cultural Occupation Policies and German Expectations, 1945–1949" (PhD diss., Georgetown University, 2010), 87–88.

[40] Some private firms believed that sending its employees to Germany on government-sponsored missions would prove profitable in the long run, as this might give them a direct hand in the extraction of reparations and play a greater role in the subsequent economic rehabilitation of Europe. Campion, "Negotiating Difference," 87–88; Willis, *The French in Germany*, 71–72, 88.

[41] Willis, *The French in Germany*, 66.   [42] Naimark, *The Russians in Germany*, 21–22.

antifascists and reeducated Prisoners-of-War (POW). By September 1945, SMA employed some 5,000 people in its administration, most of them civilians, of which only 500 were Russian.[43] Many more specialists were later recruited in the Soviet Union, but relatively few participated in the wartime planning for the occupation.

The Anglo-American story of army civil affairs is much more important, at least in relation to the development of a shared denazification policy. It was American and British civil affairs officers who drafted the original Fragebogen that the other Allied armies adopted. They also built the military governance apparatus that was assumed, at least initially, by the French. The American–British planning partnership began in January 1942, when Washington and London agreed to collaborate in the execution of all major military operations. One year later, after the Casablanca Conference, inter-Allied planning for the postwar was organized under the Civil Affairs Division of the newly formed Chief of Staff to Supreme Allied Commander (COSSAC).[44] This large organization, which was renamed SHAEF in late 1943, dominated occupation planning during the final two years of the war.

Because of its long imperialistic tradition of relying on the army to govern foreign territory, the British were reluctant to trust civilian agencies. However, the experimental campaign of denazification forced the military to look beyond its ranks. In early 1942, while the United States continued to rely solely on military intelligence, London mobilized hundreds of academics and professionals from private institutions to provide analytical support, experimenting with "new men and new methods."[45] Economists, statisticians, historians, and political scientists assessed the economic impact of the Allied bombing campaign,

---

[43] Ibid., 23. In the final months of the war, Moscow instigated the formation of KPD teams, or "initiative groups," which were placed under antifascist German leadership and charged with reorganizing local political bureaucracies. See Biddiscombe, *Denazification of Germany*, 123; and Naimark, *The Russians in Germany*, 16–20.

[44] These included the Civil Affairs Directorate in the War Office, the German Advisory Section in the Foreign Office, and the Armistice and Post-War Committee (APW), which was formed in April 1944 to coordinate occupation policy and chaired by the Deputy Prime Minister and Labour Party leader, Clemens Attlee. The most important group, however, was the Official Committee on Armistice Terms and Civil Administration, which was composed of a small panel of civil servant advisors who more or less dictated occupation policy because they determined which Foreign and War Office papers were forwarded to the APW for review. See F. Donnison, *Civil Affairs and Military Government North-West Europe, 1944–1946* (London: His Majesty's Stationery Office, 1966), 9–10.

[45] Nelson MacPherson, "Reductio Ad Absurdum: The R&A Branch of OSS/London," *International Journal of Intelligence and Counter Intelligence* 15, no. 3 (November 2002): 391.

processed topographical intelligence, and wrote reports on German politics and culture. This unconventional recruitment drive, one that was carried out by nearly all military offices, resulted in what one British diplomat of the time referred to as "an adventure playground for conscripted social scientists."[46] Not everyone embraced this influx of civilians. In fact, Field Marshal Bernard Montgomery envisioned an occupation force composed entirely of combat veterans. Disagreements between civil affairs officers and regular army recruits persisted after the German surrender, so much so that lecture tours were carried out in the field under the unadorned title of "Selling Civil Affairs to the Army."[47]

One of the most influential civilian-staffed organizations formed by the British government for the purpose of postwar planning was the Foreign Office Research Department (FORD), which was established in April 1943 under the renowned historian and professor, Arnold Toynbee.[48] Much of FORD's workforce was drawn from academia and many members were previously employed by the independent Royal Institute of International Affairs (or Chatham House), who wrote research guides intended for denazification agents operating in the field.[49] Among FORD's staff was Thomas H. Marshall, professor of sociology at the London School of Economics, who headed the German Section and advocated a denazification system that exercised individual discretion and targeted only senior Nazi civil servants. The renowned Oxford University classics professor, E. R. Dodds, was another academic who had far-reaching influence on the British denazification campaign. Dodds also called for a modest purge, one that targeted high-ranking Nazis and managerial-level civil servants.[50] He wrote in a 1944 FORD-commissioned report that:

The purge of personnel should be based on the principle not of revenge but of security: fanatical Nazis could not be safely left in office, but the very numerous trimmers whose conversion to Nazism dated from 1933 might be given the

---

[46] Christopher Andrew, "F. H. Hinsley and the Cambridge Moles: Two Patterns of Intelligence Recruitment," in *Diplomacy and Intelligence: Essays in Honour of F. H. Hinsley*, ed. Richard Langhorne (Cambridge: Cambridge University Press, 1985), 32–33.
[47] Adams, *From Crusade to Hazard*, 8.
[48] Christopher Thorne, "Chatham House, Whitehall, and Far Eastern Issues: 1941–1945," *International Affairs* 54, no. 1 (January 1978): 7; Robert A. Longmire and Kenneth C. Walker, "Herald of a Noisy World – Interpreting the News of All Nations, the Research and Analysis Department of the Foreign and Commonwealth Office: A History," Foreign Policy Document Series No. 263 (London: Foreign and Commonwealth Office, 1995).
[49] Jones, "Eradicating Nazism," 149–51.
[50] David Phillips, "War-time Planning for the 'Re-education' of Germany: Professor E.R. Dodds and the German Universities," *Oxford Review of Education* 12, no. 2 (1986): 195.

opportunity of a second conversion where suitable qualified successors were not available.[51]

Dodd's three-tiered conceptualization of Nazi allegiance within German society influenced the drafting of the widely circulated "black" (Nazis), "grey" (Nazi followers), and "white" (anti-Nazis) lists and contributed to the pragmatic tone of the British denazification program. "Black lists" were used to cross-reference Fragebogen responses, especially in the early months of the occupation, when the Nazi Party membership records had not yet been located.[52] In October 1944, the War Office released its handbook for *Germany and Austria in the Post-Surrender Period: Policy Directives for Allied Commanders in Chief*. Although vague in its instructions, this manual was the only policy guidance on denazification provided by the British government prior to the invasion of Germany; its content reflected the principles and strategies advocated by academics like Marshall and Dodds.[53]

The Americans were not far behind the British in "civilianizing" military government. As avowed in the 1920 Hunt Report, the relatively short hundred-year history of US civil affairs could not be relied upon when planning the future occupation of liberated and defeated territories. The United States Army was already familiar with post-conflict government, but previous occupations were carried out by regular soldiers, untrained in civil affairs matters, and often uneducated in the language and culture of the occupied territory.[54] Furthermore, they had been stationed in regions with small populations and where the political and economic infrastructures were largely intact. In December 1941, soon after the declaration of war on Japan, key offices within the War Department began drafting plans for a different kind of occupation.

---

[51] Ibid., 197–98.
[52] For an example of how these lists were used in the field, see Report, "Black, White, and Grey List for Information Control Purposes," October 10, 1945, NARA, RG 498, ETOUSA, Historical Division, Box 4115.
[53] Jones, "Eradicating Nazism," 149–50; Biddiscombe, *Denazification of Germany*, 91. For a list of early British denazification proclamations and ordinances (from January 1944 to January 1945), see "Proclamations and Ordinances – Denazification," Jan. 45, TNA, WO 219/3588, Doc. 1599/818.
[54] Susan L. Carruthers, *The Good Occupation: American Soldiers and the Hazards of Peace* (Cambridge, MA: Harvard University Press, 2016), 4; Carl J. Friedrich, ed. *American Experiences in Military Government in World War II* (New York: Rinehart, 1948), 25. Prior to World War II, the US military governed, either directly or through local leaders, the following territories: Mexico (1846–48), New Mexico (1846–51), Cuba (1898–1903, 1906–09), Puerto Rico (1898–1900), the Philippine Islands (1899–1901), Guam (1899–1950), American Samoa (1899–1951), Nicaragua (1909–10, 1912–25, 1926–33), Haiti (1915–34), Dominican Republic (1916–24), Honduras (1924–25), Panama Canal Zone (1903–2000), and German Rhine region (1918–23).

They envisioned a much larger and more capable civil affairs bureaucracy, one that could differentiate between liberated and defeated peoples and confront ideological institutions, such as Nazism.

As the war progressed and the reality of military governance loomed ever greater, American planning for the postwar expanded and diversified. The president's Cabinet Committee on Germany debated policy, including the objectives of denazification, while the organization of military government was informally delegated to several offices overseen by the War Department's General Staff.[55] The most important was the Civil Affairs Division (CAD), created in March 1943 under the direction of Major General John H. Hilldring. Reporting directly to the Secretary of War, the two-star general was tasked with coordinating "all matters within the purview of the War Department, other than those of a strictly military nature."[56] While other planning groups interpreted the role of military government along more traditional lines – that of maintaining military supervision and security – the CAD had a greater understanding of the complex job that lay ahead. According to one of its members, Dr. Harold Zink, the CAD had a "broader outlook, a different psychology, and more imagination."[57]

Farming out of intelligence-gathering activities to academics and other civilian experts occurred in conjunction with major changes to the British and American civil affairs training programs. As early as 1941, the British War Office began educating civilian recruits in postwar occupation activities at its Intelligence Training Centre (ITC) at St. John's College, Cambridge. Here, students enrolled in an eight-week program, attending lectures in history, geography, economics, and politics, which were intended to provide general background knowledge of Germany and other enemy territories.[58] Two US officers were registered in the third ITC course, which began in October 1941. The university-run program was refurbished in February 1943 as the Civil Affairs Staff Centre (CASC) and relocated to Wimbledon Common in London. At the new school, students participated in a thirteen-week program (later reduced to five), receiving military and technical training, but also attending

---

[55] Knowing all too well the radical policy swings of the Cabinet Committee on Germany and the "wild card" Morgenthau, the War Department was reluctant to integrate high-level occupation planning into its civil affairs program. Hajo Holborn, *American Military Government: Its Organization and Policies* (Washington, DC: Infantry Journal Press, 1947), 8.
[56] Ibid.   [57] Zink, *The United States in Germany*, 7.
[58] "History of the Civil Affairs Centre Wimbledon," n.d., NARA, RG 331, SHAEF, GS, G-5, IB, HS, Box 211, pp. 1–2, and Ziemke, *The U.S. Army in the Occupation of Germany*, 4–5.

history and economics classes taught by prominent British scholars. A denazification training component was added to the curriculum in August 1944.[59] The program graduated 150 students in its first year, including 19 Americans and 14 Canadians.[60]

The American officers who attended the ITC program at Cambridge endorsed its academic framework, which influenced the decision to establish a similar training center at the University of Virginia in Charlottesville. The school was founded in April 1942, with Brigadier General Cornelius W. Wickersham, a lawyer by trade, as its first commandant and director.[61] In accordance with the US Army's Field Manual 27-5, a document heavily influenced by the Hunt Report, recruits were to possess the appropriate technical skills required for civil affairs service, as well as sufficient knowledge of the history, culture, and language of the population that was to fall under their administration. Prior to its opening, the Office of Provost Marshal General outlined the kind of students and faculty it planned to enroll: "A group of officers possessing some special or promising talent and their instruction in ... the historical, political, social and economic backgrounds of the occupied regions in which they may be called upon to function."[62]

However, only a small number of enlisted soldiers met these high standards of specialization, and an even smaller number were approved by their field units for reassignment. As a result, most students who attended the school were recruited directly from civilian life, mainly engineers, businesspersons, economists, civil servants, and police officers. It is estimated that the Army screened more than 75,000 civilian candidates for potential enrollment in the program.[63] The teaching staff was also predominantly nonmilitary, and included prominent scholars such as historians Arnold Walters and Henry Powell, and political scientist Joseph P. Harris.[64] During the four-month program, students underwent training in public administration, healthcare and sanitation, and

---

[59] "History of the Civil Affairs Centre Wimbledon," n.d., NARA, RG 331, SHAEF, GS, G-5, IB, HS, Box 211, p. 7.
[60] Ibid., 2–3. [61] Carruthers, *The Good Occupation*, 23.
[62] As quoted in Rebecca L. Boehling, "Socio-political Democratization and Economic Recovery: The Development of German Self-Government under U.S. Military Occupation: Frankfurt, Munich, and Stuttgart, 1945–1949" (PhD diss., University of Wisconsin-Madison, 1990), 55.
[63] Joseph P. Harris, "Selection and Training of Civil Affairs Officers," *American Political Science Review* 38, no. 2 (April 1944): 703. The Office of Provost Marshal General was responsible for the selection and training of military government recruits, while the actual administration of civil affairs was carried out by the CAD.
[64] Ziemke, *The U.S. Army in the Occupation of Germany*, 7; Harris, "Selection and Training of Civil Affairs Officers," 694.

communications, as well as scenario-based civil affairs problem-solving exercises and academic courses covering the history, culture, politics, and economies of Germany, Italy, and Japan (see Figure 1.2).[65] In its four-year existence, the School of Military Government graduated 9,905 students.[66]

The school at Charlottesville had considerable problems, however, as its curriculum was largely focused on broad-area orientation, not the specific people, institutions, and geography that officers would encounter. Furthermore, the time allotted for foreign-language lessons was inadequate and missing entirely from the first few classes.[67] One instructor estimated that only 5 percent of students acquired the German language skills necessary to interact with the occupied population, even at the most basic level of communication.[68] Training for political screening was also insufficient and often neglected altogether. As late as spring 1943, the CAD was still planning to leave the Nazi government administration structure intact after the invasion and limit the removal of government employees.[69] With no confirmed plan to carry out mass dismissals, denazification training was not considered a priority.

Only six months after its opening, criticism about the school's curriculum and quality of students reached the ear of the president.[70] A high-level controversy ensued regarding the "civilianization" of civil affairs, leading to a major reevaluation of the Army's future role in military government. As a result, but also because of a general need for more civil affairs officers, a new schooling system was established in July 1943 that was directly overseen by the War Department and ran parallel to the school at Charlottesville. This network of Civil Affairs Training Schools (CATS) operated at ten different universities across the country, including Yale, Harvard, and Stanford.[71] These schools

---

[65] John Brown Mason, "Lessons of Wartime Military Government Training," *Annals of the American Academy of Political and Social Science* 267 (January 1950): 184–85.
[66] Ibid., 184.   [67] Zink, *The United States in Germany*, 13.   [68] Ibid.
[69] Biddiscombe, *Denazification of Germany*, 20.
[70] To make matters worse, the media had branded Charlottesville a "school for Gauleiters," due to a belief that officers were being trained to wield absolute authority over the German people and the unfounded rumor that the school's faculty had been infiltrated by fascists. Earl Ziemke, "Improvising Stability and Change in Post-War Germany," in *Americans as Proconsuls: United States Military Government in Germany and Japan, 1944–1952*, ed. Robert Wolfe (Carbondale: Southern Illinois University Press, 1984), 54.
[71] For information on the training at Fort Custer, see Klaus Dietmar-Henke, *Die amerikanische Besetzung Deutschlands* (Munich: R. Oldenbourg, 1995), 223.

Figure 1.2 US officers attending a lecture at the School of Military Government at the University of Virginia (Charlottesville), April 1943.
Source: US Library of Congress

drew nearly all of their students from civilian life; 70–80 percent were college graduates.[72]

Charlottesville continued to train students in civil affairs, but by the summer of 1943, most recruits were attending the CATS program, which emphasized knowledge-based "area learning." Curriculum was focused more on the day-to-day operations of running an occupied town or district. Approximately half of the course program consisted of

---

[72] Mason, "Lessons of Wartime Military Government Training," 185–86. The forerunner to the CATS was the Area Specialized Training Program, another civil affairs curriculum setup on various university campuses throughout the country.

foreign-language study, either German, Italian, French, or Japanese, while the remainder was composed of lectures on the history, culture, politics, and economy of the occupied area to which each student had been assigned.[73] Much attention was given to the study of "national psychology," with hopes that students would acquire a greater understanding of "local points of view" and, for example, why so many Germans came under the influence of Nazism.[74] The instructional staff were hand-picked professors, including political scientists John B. Mason and James K. Pollock and the German-born political theorist Carl J. Friedrich.[75]

This specialized education surely affected the way in which civil affairs officers interpreted denazification in the field. When the CATS program came to an end, in January 1944, many of its students were dispatched to England, where they played a pivotal role in civil affairs planning, this time at the inter-Allied level. Most of these young men did not have a direct hand in writing denazification procedures but they did participate in distributing, collecting, and evaluating questionnaires. Therefore, the professional and educational background of these recruits is important to trace, as is the civil affairs environment in which they were immersed. This can be said of graduates from all of the civil affairs schools; whether trained in Wimbledon, Charlottesville, or one of the CATS, almost every British and American recruit was selected and valued as specialists in civil administration. This allowed for the introduction of new methods and perspectives into the realm of traditionally military-minded civil affairs.

It is also important to note that these men (and few women) were not experts in punitive and debilitating measures, something that much of denazification policy called for, but instead trained in technical and academic fields that revolved around models of growth and education. Whether engineers, teachers, or economists, they were familiar only with constructive strategies and solutions. They were also trained largely by academics who promoted a deeper understanding of German culture, which likely further discouraged their receptivity of the punitive measures of denazification. This civilian contingent, although initially small in size and dispersed across many different schools and offices, grew quickly,

---

[73] Harris, "Selection and Training of Civil Affairs Officers," 700.
[74] Mason, "Lessons of Wartime Military Government Training," 185.
[75] For a complete list of political scientists teaching at CAT schools, see Charles S. Hyneman, "The Army's Civil Affairs Training Program," *The American Political Science Review* 38, no. 2 (April 1944): 352–53. Some of these professors would go on to publish books on military governance. For example, Friedrich, ed., *American Experiences in Military Government*.

and became increasingly influential when high-level attention finally turned to the impending occupation.

The Neo-Marxist War on Nazism

Perhaps the most pronounced example of the growing civilianization of military civil affairs was the activities of the Office of Strategic Services (OSS). The predecessor of today's Central Intelligence Agency was founded in July 1941, and in addition to espionage, produced research-based intelligence for the federal government and armed forces, and their allies that supported the war effort. The OSS embraced the social sciences with open arms by enlisting a small army of civilian experts to help defeat Nazism. This represented the advent of a new kind of intelligence. Underscored by historian Richard Harris Smith, the OSS made "the first concerted effort on the part of any world power to apply the talents of its academic community to official analysis of foreign affairs."[76] It was also the first government agency of any Allied nation to systematically grapple with the task of denazification.

Born out of the political culture of New Deal liberalism and nurtured by wartime necessity, the OSS was the United States' first foray into the world of international secret intelligence.[77] It had been decided by the highest levels of government that the new organization would be entirely civilian in its makeup and responsible only to the White House. For the first year of its existence, these fundamentals held true, as the agency remained independent of the War and State departments and from all special wartime executive committees. To lead the new agency, Roosevelt appointed William "Wild Bill" Donovan, a former Wall Street lawyer and staunch republican interventionist, who believed that the most valuable political intelligence was obtained through hard-driven scholarly research.[78]

The largest and most valued branch within Donovan's intelligence-gathering agency was Research and Analysis (R&A), which was charged with accessing government materials and firsthand and secondary sources to write factual reports on topics that had direct implications

---

[76] Richard Harris Smith, *OSS: The Secret History of America's First Central Intelligence Agency* (New York: Lyons Press, 2005), 11.

[77] Further reading of the OSS should begin with Smith, *OSS*, and George C. Chalou, ed., *The Secrets War: The Office of Strategic Services in World War II* (Washington, DC: National Archives and Records Administration, 1992).

[78] Lawrence H. McDonald, "The OSS and Its Records," in *The Secrets War: The Office of Strategic Services in World War II*, ed. George C. Chalou (Washington, DC: National Archives and Records Administration, 1992), 80.

for American foreign policy. It was especially interested in addressing political, economic, legal, and administrative problems that might befall liberation and occupation forces. Justification for the establishment of an academic-natured research branch was summarized in a 1942 OSS memorandum that echoes the words of Col. Irwin Hunt:

> It is obvious that the United States Government urgently requires studies leading to the understandings of conditions and developments abroad. The United States has suffered in the past because of the lack of competent and objective estimates of economic and military capabilities and political tensions of other nations ... the particular ability of the OSS to make these studies stems from two facts ... it is staffed by political, economic and topographical experts ... its agents and officers can operate in foreign countries in a manner impossible for the accredited representatives of the United States Government.[79]

After Pearl Harbor, the OSS's budget was increased from 1.15 to 13 million dollars, and thereafter R&A grew quickly, eventually employing more than 900 researchers and clerks attached to offices in more than a dozen countries.[80] Like other branches, R&A struggled to build its reputation as a reliable source of political intelligence, effectively collaborating with outside government departments only after William L. Langer, an endowed professor of history at Harvard University, was made branch chief in September 1942.[81] External relationships were improved further in 1943, when the agency relinquished its purely civilian image and began to recruit army and navy personnel.[82] This nominal militarization helped R&A, with its still mostly civilian staff, to extend influence into the War and State departments and thereby contribute more to planning for the occupation of Germany.

Detailed reports on every topic imaginable were drafted, from "The Role of Communism in the Balkans," to "Concentration Camps in Germany," to "Radio Broadcasting in Japan."[83] These analytical reports were delivered to more than a dozen domestic and foreign offices for

---

[79] Report, "Justification for Problem," n.d., NARA, RG 226, OSS, Box 1, p. 1.
[80] Bradley Smith, *The Shadow Warriors: O.S.S. and the Origins of the C.I.A.* (New York: Basic Books, 1983), 69.
[81] Ibid., 122. R&A's previous chief was James P. Baxter, president of Williams College, who lost control of the Branch after falling ill in 1942.
[82] Relations with the War Department improved in July 1942, when the OSS came under the management of the Joint Chiefs of Staff and was thereafter assigned security classifications for its research studies. Smith, *The Shadow Warriors*, 76, 175, 203.
[83] Paul Kesaris, ed., *A Guide to O.S.S./State Department Intelligence and Research Reports – Germany and Its Occupied Territories During World War II* (Washington, DC: University Publications of America, 1977), 3–4, 17.

assistance in postwar policymaking.[84] Relevant reports were also incorporated into the curriculums of the civil affairs schools at Charlottesville and Wimbledon, and among the CATS, as well as delivered to SHAEF offices, where they influenced planning for the purge of German personnel.[85]

In the summer of 1943, an OSS representative at the Pentagon, Hajo Holborn, convinced General Hilldring to assign all intelligence gathering for US civil affairs operations in Europe to R&A's Europe-Africa Division (EAD).[86] This did not stop other government agencies and research groups from collecting their own intelligence, but it did narrow the planning bureaucracy. For the remainder of the war, the EAD spent countless hours producing nearly one hundred handbooks that addressed topics relevant to military governance. Further down the organizational ladder, the EAD's Central European Section (CES) wrote guidebooks specifically for civil affairs operations in Germany and Austria.[87] Between 1942 and 1945, R&A produced around 2,000 research studies, which were circulated widely in the United States and Europe.[88] The reach of this intelligence was extended when the OSS began placing liaison officers in inter-Allied, British, French, and Canadian agencies, and setting up European field offices.[89] Some R&A agents were given new and sometimes dangerous assignments, such as disseminating propaganda, capturing enemy records, conducting

---

[84] Within a sample of fifty completed reports, twenty-seven were written at the request of the War Department's Civil Affairs Division and eleven by the State Department. For a breakdown of which offices commissioned studies from the CES, see "Central European Section, Europe Africa Division," January 27, 1944, NARA, RG 226, OSS, Container 1, pp. 1–4.

[85] After the war, R&A was involved in the Nuremberg Trials, assisting the Chief US Prosecutor in gathering and interpreting information about the Nazi political system. For more on the role of the OSS in war crimes trials, see Bradley F. Smith, *Reaching Judgement at Nuremberg* (New York: Basic Books, 1977), 270–71 and Barry Katz, *Foreign Intelligence: Research and Analysis in the Office of Strategic Services, 1942–1945* (Cambridge, MA: Harvard University Press, 1989), 49–57.

[86] Katz, *Foreign Intelligence*, 70.

[87] Ibid., 73–75. In total, the CES completed thirty of its proposed forty *Civil Affairs Guides for Germany*. See Franz Neumann, Herbert Marcuse, and Otto Kirchheimer, *Secret Reports on Nazi Germany: The Frankfurt School Contribution to the War Effort*, ed. Raffaele Laudani (New Haven: Princeton University Press, 2013), 12.

[88] Barry M. Katz, "The OSS and the Development of the Research and Analysis Branch," in *The Secrets War: The Office of Strategic Services in World War II*, ed. George C. Chalou (Washington, DC: National Archives and Records Administration, 1992), 46; Katz, *Foreign Intelligence*, 18.

[89] Katz, *Foreign Intelligence*, 23, 78–90. At this time, OSS offices were also located in Great Britain, France, Germany, Holland, Belgium, Spain, Portugal, Norway, Sweden, Austria, Italy, Greece, and Hungary.

psychological warfare, and collaborating with resistance fighters.[90] As the war developed, the need for up-to-date research-based intelligence increased. By the summer of 1944, the OSS had approximately 6,000 personnel operating overseas and another four thousand in the United States.[91]

Many sections within R&A were comprised entirely of academics, the majority recruited directly from the universities at which they taught or studied. In a 1959 speech, Allen Dulles, then director of the CIA, remembered that "Donovan assembled the best academic and analytical brains that he could beg, borrow, or steal from the universities, laboratories, and museums."[92] Scholars from nearly every discipline in the social sciences and humanities were represented, but historians, political scientists, geographers, psychologists, economists, and anthropologists were favored. These recruits were anything but amateur. Among R&A's roster were historians Sherman Kent, Gordon Craig, Walter L. Dorn, Carl E. Schorske, H. Stuart Hughes, classicist Norman O. Brown, and economists Charles Kindleberger and Carl Kaysen.[93] An estimated 900 university professors and researchers served in R&A, forty of whom were historians, including seven future presidents of the American Historical Association.[94] Although as much as 25 percent of the R&A staff were women, most worked in low-status positions, carrying out secretarial work and gaining little recognition.[95] These veterans of academe were happy to temporarily leave their tenured posts and relocate to Washington for the duration of the war, not only because of a dramatic drop in university enrollment and therefore lack of courses to teach, but because of the general appeal of supporting the war effort while working alongside esteemed colleagues.

---

[90] On the nature of R&A operations in occupied Germany, see Letter, William L. Langer to Harold C. Deutsch, "OSS Mission for Germany, European Theater of Operations," June 28, 1945, NARA, RG 226, OSS, Box 1.
[91] Smith, *The Shadow Warriors*, 203.
[92] Speech by Allen Dulles, "William J. Donovan and the National Security," to the Erie County Bar Association, Buffalo, New York, May 4, 1959. For further reading on the role of academics in the OSS, see Robin Winks, *Cloak and Gown: Scholars in the Secret War, 1939–1961* (New York: William Morrow, 1987).
[93] Katz, *Foreign Intelligence*, 10.
[94] Ibid., xii. The personnel files of R&A employees are declassified and available for viewing at NARA (RG 226).
[95] Scholars such as Vera Sandomirsky Dunham, the renowned Russian literary critic, and Harvard anthropologist Cora DuBois, who headed the R&A Indonesia Section, should not be overlooked. For additional reading on women employed by the OSS, see Elizabeth P. McIntosh, *Sisterhood of Spies: The Women of the OSS* (Annapolis, MD: Naval Institute Press, 1988).

Through an informal network of personal and professional contacts, R&A also sought out young, bright-minded graduate students who were versed in the history and politics of particular geographical regions. For example, EAD researcher Rudolph Winnacker contacted a former colleague at the University of Michigan, writing that the OSS was "looking for good boys who will ruin their health for about $2,000 per annum, who have a reading knowledge of French or German ... who have been trained by the European historians of your noble faculty in methods of research."[96] Instead of waiting for these students to be drafted, Winnacker continued, "let us have the pick of the crop."[97] Through a similar channel of recruitment, Harold C. Deutsch, historian and assistant chief of the EAD, went to great lengths to enlist Franklin L. Ford, a PhD student from the University of Minnesota. Fearful that the twenty-two-year old would soon be attached to an active army unit and sent overseas, Deutsch appealed to the War Department, explaining that Ford is "exceptionally fitted for an assignment to the R&A Branch of the OSS ... he has an outstanding record at the Universities of Minnesota and Cornell."[98] Such efforts to recruit students were instigated from above by both Donovan and Langer, both of whom believed that young idealists could embody the liberal mandate that the OSS had been built around and institute fundamental change within wartime planning groups.

Even more unusual, and more important to the story of denazification, was the sizable contingent of German "refugee intellectuals" employed by R&A's Central European Section. These recruits were predominantly German-Jewish scholars who had fled Germany after the Nazi ascendency in 1933; many were self-proclaimed Marxists. Langer was adamant that the leftist ideologies of these academic mandarins should be overlooked by the US government, as their political, regional, and linguistic expertise were unparalleled.[99]

At the core of this group were leading members of the exiled *Institut für Sozialforschung* (Institute for Social Research), or Frankfurt School, affiliated with Columbia University since 1935. After obtaining Federal Bureau of Investigation (FBI) clearance that confirmed his loyalty to the United States, the first to be called to Washington was Franz L. Neumann, who was appointed research director of the CES in early

---

[96] Letter, Rudolph Winnacker to Mr. A. E. R. Boak, September 19, 1942, NARA, RG 226, OSS, General Correspondence, 1941–45, Container 2.
[97] Ibid.
[98] Letter, Harold C. Deutsch to Colonel E. F. Connelly, October 6, 1943, NARA, RG 226, OSS, Box 243.
[99] Katz, *Foreign Intelligence*, 32.

1943. The former Berlin labor lawyer turned political theorist had recently published his book, *Behemoth: The Structure and Practice of National Socialism, 1933–1944*, which secured his reputation as an expert on the political nature of Nazism in German society.[100] Upon his own recommendation, Neumann was soon joined by his former colleague Herbert Marcuse, already a well-known philosopher and political scientist, and a few months later, Otto Kirchheimer. Throughout the summer and fall of 1943, other Frankfurt School exiles trickled into the CES, including Friedrich Pollack and Arkadij Gurland, again at the recommendation of Neumann. In fact, Neumann had nominated a long list of cultural luminaries of the defunct Weimar Republic, including fellow political theorist Theodor Adorno, playwright Bertolt Brecht, Bauhaus director Walter Gropius, and even Heinrich Brüning, the former German chancellor.[101] Through this network of personal contacts and because of a desire by the OSS leadership to acquire firsthand intelligence on Germany, the Frankfurt School eventually formed a sizable assembly within R&A.

Not all German-born recruits came from the political left. In the spring of 1943, while Neumann and his fellow neo-Marxists were reuniting, a more conventional cast of German academics were enlisted. Prominent among them were historians Hajo Holborn and Felix Gilbert, art historian Richard Krautheimer, jurist Henry Kellerman, and international relations expert John H. Herz.[102] These émigré scholars, some of whom were also German-Jewish refugees, adhered to the well-established tradition of German historiographical thought. They were the students of Leopold von Ranke and Friedrich Meinecke and upheld the values of objective, source-based research and scientific scholarship; standards that R&A was striving to achieve in its written reports.[103] Although their

---

[100] Franz Neumann, *Behemoth: The Structure and Practice of National Socialism, 1933–1934* (New York: Octagon Books, 1964). Neumann was first recruited by the US government to act as chief consultant for the Board of Economic Welfare, but in August 1942, was appointed chief economist in the Intelligence Division of the Office of the US Chief of Staff. It was not until early 1943 that he assumed the position of deputy chief (later chief) of the R&A Central European Section.

[101] Regina Ursula Gramer, "The Socialist Revolutionary Dilemma in Emigration: Franz L. Neumann's Passage Toward and Through the Office of Strategic Services" (MA thesis, Arizona State University, 1989), 62. The FBI was generally suspicious of the Germans employed by R&A and even called for the dismissal of some staff members, including Horst W. Bärensprung, who had been identified as a KGB asset. In fact, there is evidence that Neumann himself was an informant. See Smith, *OSS*, 217, and Letter, Lt. Raymond Deston to Sherman Kent, September 21, 1944, NARA, RG 226, OSS, Container 5; Neumann et al., *Secret Reports on Nazi Germany*, 7.

[102] Biddiscombe, *Denazification of Germany*, 22.

[103] For further reading on the German academic émigrés and their role in wartime US politics, see Franz Neumann, ed., *The Cultural Migration: The European Scholar in America* (New York: Arno Press, 1977); Daniel Snowman, *The Hitler Émigrés Revisited*

colleagues in the "Neumann group" were also trained in the European classical-humanist tradition, they were of a more conservative school of historical thought, one that valued critical research over social and economic theory.

The third and final group of CES researchers was formed by members of the American academy, mostly grizzled Ivy League professors. They came from affluent backgrounds and held conservative values but were put to work alongside an enthusiastic and liberal-minded group of doctoral students, many of whom had humbler origins and spoke passionately about progressive change and social reform; they also trumpeted the use of applied social science research techniques.

By the end of the war, the R&A Branch was, according to historian Barry Katz, "something like a huge social science research institute."[104] It employed a diverse group of empirical researchers with varying methodological and interpretive approaches. Despite their country of origin and political ideology, all of the researchers recruited by the OSS were forced to adapt their academic training and intellectual knowledge for the demands of war.

In late 1943, the War Department ordered the OSS to outline a program for the denazification and democratic reconstruction of Germany. The project quickly came to dominate CES work, despite the knowledge that other domestic, as well as inter-Allied agencies, were drafting similar reports. Neumann directed the assignment, and he and his colleagues agreed that the eradication of Nazism could not be treated as a singular task assigned to a specific military government divisional office. Instead, it had to be widely disseminated throughout the entire occupation apparatus and incorporated into all postwar directives and procedures. Whether it concerned programs aimed at economic revival, democratization of government infrastructure, or integration of displaced persons, denazification had to be considered. Nearly all of the fifty CES studies completed or initiated before January 1944, either independently or in collaboration with other agencies, referenced denazification procedures and their consequences.[105]

The two most important CES reports, completed in the spring and summer of 1944 respectively, were "The Abrogation of Nazi Laws in the Early Period of MG [Military Government]" and the "Dissolution and

---

(London: Research Centre for German and Austrian Exile Studies, 2013); and Felix Rösch, *Émigré Scholars and the Genesis of International Relations: A European Discipline in America?* (Basingstoke, Hampshire: Palgrave Macmillan, 2014).

[104] Katz, *Foreign Intelligence*, 84.
[105] Report, "Central European Section, Europe Africa Division," January 27, 1944, NARA, RG 226, OSS, Container 1, pp. 1–4.

the Nazi Party and its Affiliated Organizations."[106] In the latter study, Marcuse recommended a comprehensive purge of the German civil service at all administrative levels and the immediate arrest of 222,000 active Nazi officials.[107] Another influential report was Kirchheimer's "General Principles of Administration and Civil Service in Germany," which provided a detailed breakdown of the German government's central agencies and the extent to which Nazism had penetrated the civil service. It made repeated warnings about the many active Nazis who could potentially evade the administrative purge due to their low-level bureaucratic standing or nonparty status.[108] Kirchheimer estimated that between 7,000 and 8,000 higher officials would need to be dismissed during the initial occupation.[109]

The majority of these denazification studies were written for the Civil Affairs Division, but copies were circulated to other agencies and committees, as well as some foreign governments. For example, the *Civil Affairs Handbook on Germany*, with sections on screening and dismissing civil servants, was drafted for the CAD but also distributed to the War College, Navy Department, FBI, MI-6, and both the British and Canadian military headquarters.[110] If security clearance had been granted, denazification reports were even shared with the Soviets through the European Advisory Council.[111] In fact, in preparation for the invasion, all four Allied armies consulted OSS-compiled lists of prominent Nazi officials and trusted Germans. The British Foreign Office Research Department had compiled its own capacious "black-grey-white" lists, but R&A's reports were more extensive, including thousands (not hundreds) of names.

At the heart of the CES's plan for eliminating fascism lay the methodology of Critical Theory. First defined by the Frankfurt Institute's director Max Horkheimer in 1937, Critical Theory postulates that an

---

[106] Memo, "Office of Strategic Services, Research and Analysis Branch, Interoffice Memo," January 18, 1944, NARA, RG 226, OSS, Container 1.
[107] Neumann et al., *Secret Reports on Nazi Germany*, 257. [108] Ibid., 302–17.
[109] Ibid., 307.
[110] Memo, "Interoffice Memo from Projects Committee to Division Europe-Africa," November 23, 1943, NARA, RG 226, OSS, Correspondence, 1943–45, Container 1. It should be mentioned that the wartime relationship that existed between the OSS and British secret service agencies, namely, the Secret Intelligence Service and the Special Operations Executive, was not always one of mutual trust and cooperation. However, both national security networks, at different times during the war, relied on one another for intelligence, training, and technical equipment. Smith, *OSS*, 24–25; Smith, *The Shadow Warriors*, 374.
[111] Memorandum Draft, Editorial Committee to General Hilldring, "The Purpose, Objectives, and Functions of a Military Government Program for Germany," n.d., NARA, RG 226, OSS, Container 1.

entrenched ideology, such as Nazism, acts as the principal obstacle in achieving human liberation.[112] It maintains that in order for individuals to acquire a clear understanding of the politico-social relationships that exist within society, they must undertake a self-conscious social critique of their political, economic, and cultural surroundings. According to the Frankfurt School theorists working in R&A, the Nazi regime, which represented bourgeois society and state capitalism, created an attractive ideological narrative of the world in order to legitimize its rule and had been successful in enslaving the German people and preventing their social and spiritual enlightenment.[113] Neumann himself maintained that National Socialism was not in fact a true political philosophy but a deceptive criminal partnership between four centers of power: the Nazi Party, the army, the bureaucracy, and the industrial elites.[114] According to his theory, this "lawless" non-state power system dominated all elements of society by providing Germans with a false consciousness by means of an ideology, thereby suppressing the development of working-class identity and the achievement of social justice.[115] The CES analysts did not believe that the Nazi state was the result of a historical accident (i.e., the ascendancy of a particularly charismatic leader), nor part of a larger German *Sonderweg* (special path) toward political modernity, or an expression of the German national character. Instead, Nazism was understood as a deceptive and criminal belief system formulated by groups of the industrial bourgeoisie. Neumann, Marcuse, and Kirchheimer believed that Critical Theory could be used as a practical tool to eliminate Nazism from German society.[116]

Research for denazification was not restricted to the work of neo-Marxist intellectuals, and there was sometimes unyielding resistance from other CES researchers, but the Neumann group did write the majority of the relevant reports.[117] Although it is difficult to trace the

---

[112] Max Horkheimer, "Traditional and Critical Theory," in *Critical Theory: Selected Essays*, ed. Max Horkheimer, trans. Matthew J. O'Connell (New York: Continuum, 1972), 188–243.

[113] Ibid., 244. For a thorough explanation of the differing opinions within the Frankfurt School on the nature of Nazism, particularly between Neumann and Pollack, see Neumann et al., *Secret Reports on Nazi Germany*, 3–6.

[114] Neumann, *Behemoth*, 3.   [115] Ibid., vii.

[116] There exists some skepticism about whether Marcuse fully agreed with Neumann about the applicability of Critical Theory for the postwar political revival of Germany. See Tim B. Müller, *Krieger und Gelehrte: Herbert Marcuse und die Denksysteme im Kalten Krieg* (Hamburg: Hamburger Edition, 2012).

[117] For example, Felix Gilbert and Richard Krauthammer, both German émigré scholars unaffiliated with the Frankfurt School, worked extensively on formulating recommendations for the denazification of teachers and professors and the reconstruction of the German education system. Katz, *Foreign Intelligence*, 75–77.

influence of any idea, by deconstructing R&A studies and remaining mindful of how their authors conceptualized the Nazi state, the impact that the neo-Marxists had on shaping American and Allied strategy for denazification, and on the formulation of the questionnaire program specially, is apparent. All core components that constituted the Neumann group's early vision for denazification can be linked to the subsequent decision to use a mass-distributed standardized political questionnaire.[118]

First, the CES recommended that denazification reach every corner of the country and impact all of German society, not only because the political "illusion" of National Socialism had infiltrated every facet of public and private life, but only a renewed consciousness of the German people as a whole could produce the desired social revolution.[119] While punitive actions would be selective, targeting individuals who had held important political and economic positions and high military rank, the entire country must come under review; hence, a comprehensive system of political and ideological screening had to be implemented.

Second, although denazification had to be enforced aggressively by the occupation authorities, the CES believed that a genuine critique of Nazism and subsequent change of consciousness could only occur voluntarily by the individual German. Not to be mistaken for lenient treatment – which many future critics believed it to be – the occupiers had to collaborate with the German people in order to achieve longer-term objectives. As stated in an R&A summary of its intelligence reports, democratic government "can only be accomplished by the German people themselves."[120] Moreover, the CES researchers believed that once the placeholders within the Nazi regime had been removed from positions of power, the people could emancipate themselves politically and economically. A self-administered questionnaire would be a practical instrument to survey millions of citizens and also accomplish the CES goal of enrolling individual Germans in their own political liberation and granting them some measure of autonomy.

---

[118] For an excellent interpretation of how the political views of members of the Neumann group impacted CES research, see Petra Marquardt-Bigman, *Amerikanische Geheimdienstanalysen über Deutschland 1942–1949* (Berlin: De Gruyter Oldenbourg, 2015), 67–118.

[119] Neumann et al., *Secret Reports on Nazi Germany*, 254. After the war, Karl Jaspers had similar views on moral regeneration and national rehabilitation. He believed that for a genuine societal transformation to occur, all Germans had to undergo self-reflection and ultimately accept some responsibility for the Nazi regime and its crimes. See Karl Jaspers, *Die Schuldfrage* (Heidelberg: Lambert Schneider, 1946).

[120] "Directions for the Preparation of Civil Affairs Guides and other Planning Documents," n.d., NARA, RG 226, OSS, Container 1, pp. 3, 15.

Third, it was generally agreed that denazification should extend beyond the political and military realms by undermining Nazism's economic program. Marcuse in particular called for a dismantling of financial power structures, which he viewed as having stimulated the growth of the NSDAP and sustained the strength of the regime. In his report on the dissolution of Nazi organizations, Marcuse targeted not only official party members but financial benefactors and opportunists. The CES also published a list of nongovernment and nonparty organizations that it believed had been "essential for the rise and maintenance of Nazism," to which was appended the names of 1,800 businesspersons and economic leaders who Neumann and Marcuse believed should be treated as active Nazis.[121] The desire to extend denazification to the private sector and target business elites, many of whom were not party members, was initially dismissed by the US Military Government. However, this changed in the fall of 1945, when a new law required the removal of all former party members from managerial positions in private businesses.[122] Moreover, every version of the Fragebögen included an entire section pertaining to the professional standing and income of the respondent, questions that were intended to identify potential Nazi-era "profiteers." With some trace of irony, the questionnaire born in part out of Marxist ideologies, was remarkably elitist; it targeted influential employees, especially business managers and other officers of authority.

Finally, instead of judging each individual case based on its own specific circumstances, the émigré theorists recommended that Germans be classified into criteria-based categories of Nazi affiliation – for example, "active Nazi," "nominal Nazi," and "anti-Nazi."[123] It was suggested that each category have a corresponding punishment, often denoting whether an individual was subject to "mandatory" or "discretionary" dismissal from his or her position of employment. This system of categorization, endorsed by Neumann's office, was incorporated into nearly every Allied-nation denazification directive, and provided the general

---

[121] Guide, "Draft of Civil Affairs Guide, 'Principles for the De-Nazification of Non-Government and Non-Party Institutions,'" August 8, 1944, NARA, RG 226, OSS, Container 3, pp. 1, 12; Guide, "Dissolution of the Nazi Party and Its Affiliated Organizations. Supplement: Denazification of Important Business Concerns in Germany," November 27, 1944, NARA, RG 226, OSS, Box 1. It has been argued that in their prolonged exile from Germany, members of the Neumann group no longer understood the complexity of Nazi hierarchies and loyalties. See Pamela M. Potter, *Art of Suppression: Confronting the Nazi Past in Histories of the Visual and Performing Arts* (Berkeley: University of California Press, 2016), 91.

[122] Pollock and Meisel, *Germany under Occupation*, 179.

[123] This system of delineating political guilt was first applied in R&A "black-grey-white" lists, later evolving into a strict set of categories of Nazi affiliation.

framework for all screening activities. The entire Fragebogen program was predicated on a similar uncompromising system of categorization.

The CES research reports provided the first and most widely circulated strategy to combat National Socialism. The eradication of Nazism was not so much the embodiment of American culture, as it has almost always been portrayed, but the brainchild of mostly leftist German intellectuals. Likewise, the denazification questionnaire, which the CES planners inspired, was not necessarily the product of American and British minds. As explained by Werner Sollors, "The Americanness of the 'Fragebogen' may thus be just another myth surrounding a text that has given rise to more than its fair share of post-war myths."[124]

Some scholars of American wartime intelligence are firm in their belief that the OSS had little discernable influence in shaping foreign policy; that the war ended before R&A could begin developing full-scale procedures and that its intelligence-gathering techniques and the civilian and foreign makeup of its staff made it difficult to acquire rewarding partnerships in and outside of the United States.[125] This argument does hold true in some regard, as CES reports were regularly criticized, altered, and ignored by policymakers. It is well known that R&A faced considerable challenges working with other agencies, especially in Great Britain.[126] But while it is difficult to accurately trace the influence of ideas more generally, a close examination of the research carried out by the CES challenges this position. The very specific ingredients of the denazification campaigns can be traced to the offices of R&A and suggests that OSS-sourced intelligence was influential on the joint-Allied planning groups in Europe, those that built much of the denazification framework adopted by all invasion armies.

By 1944, R&A was the world's largest research institution and it acted as the Allies' most productive source of political intelligence on Germany. Coupled with the partnerships that R&A had with nearly every American

[124] Sollors, "'Everybody Gets Fragebogend Sooner or Later'," 153.
[125] Skeptical of the OSS's influence on US foreign policy is Nelson MacPherson, *American Intelligence in Wartime London: The Story of the OSS* (Portland, OR: Frank Cass, 2003), 260–69; Smith, *The Shadow Warriors*, 390–419; Boehling, "Socio-political Democratization and Economic Recovery," 46; and Michael Desch, *Cult of the Irrelevant: The Waning Influence of Social Science on National Security* (Princeton, NJ: Princeton University Press, 2019), 42–64.
[126] An example of such criticism can be found in the State Department's review of the first draft of one of R&A's civil affairs guides: "[T]he plan for the de-nazification of 13,000 judges and prosecutors in two months by 20 MG [Military Government] officials dealing with seven cases a day does not appear particularly practical." Howard Trivers, "Report on the Civil Affairs Guide Draft Entitled 'The Abrogation of Nazi Laws in the Early Period of AMG'," April 28, 1944, NARA, RG 226, OSS, Container 1, pp. 1–7.

and Allied political and military body on five continents, it is difficult to render its influence on postwar planning as inconsequential. This extraordinary group of academics formulated the first comprehensive approach to denazification. It devised the laws that formally abolished the Nazi Party, and many of its memorandums on Germany were retained as reference works by Allied planning groups, as well as various departments within the US government and armed forces.[127] Some CES reports may have ended up in office wastebaskets, but they were first read and deliberated over by the most important policymakers within the Western alliance; all OSS reports were distributed to the White House, State Department, War Department, FBI, and numerous SHAEF offices.[128] Amid an environment of high-policy indecision, civil-military distrust, and the drafting of overlapping and contradictory directives, these early OSS studies acted as an important common source of reference for multiple agencies and offices.

Moreover, beginning in late 1943, R&A agents advised American and British civil affairs officers on how to effectively screen for Fascists in occupied Italy. At least a dozen reports related to the nature of Italian Fascism and the removal of former Fascists from civil servant positions were distributed to military government offices. Soon after, an R&A outpost was established in London, staffed by civilian experts who worked closely with SHAEF in its development of an Anglo-American denazification program. SHAEF's German Country Unit (GCU), the office that built the military government apparatus for all three Western Allied armies, essentially farmed out intelligence gathering for denazification purposes to R&A.

Inter-Allied Planning for Denazification

As the war began to turn and the Western Allies prepared for their invasion of Europe, more domestic and inter-government offices requested OSS research reports. Opening a second front would inevitably result in millions of liberated and defeated peoples coming under the control of foreign armies and therefore civil affairs guidelines were needed. COSSAC's Civil Affairs Division was charged with planning and coordinating many noncombat operations, including denazification in Germany.[129] The OSS researchers in Washington were well aware

---

[127] Katz, *Foreign Intelligence*, 35; Smith, *The Shadow Warriors*, 289–90.
[128] A chart depicting the flow of R&A intelligence is printed in Gramer, "The Socialist Revolutionary Dilemma in Emigration," appendix.
[129] There were earlier attempts to establish civil affairs planning units, namely, the European Theater of Operations, US Army (June 1942) and the British Administration of Territories (Europe) Committee (July 1942), but at this stage of

that while they churned out empirical studies related to the political vetting of public and private offices, formal strategy for denazification would be decided in London; they were, after all, intelligence officers not policymakers. Hence, while the theoretical inspiration for the Fragebogen project and political intelligence used to formulate its questions came from the OSS and other overseas offices, the task of actually drafting the questionnaire and building the larger denazification campaign belonged to inter-Allied planning groups.

In February 1944, the Supreme Headquarters Allied Expeditionary Force (SHAEF) replaced COSSAC as the Allied command structure for the invasion of north-west Europe. Civil affairs was likewise reorganized under the new banner and expanded to include all operational planning for the occupation of Germany; it was given the divisional title "G-5."[130] SHAEF's G-5 Division was mainly composed of civilian specialists who worked in public administration, healthcare, and law enforcement, recruited equally from American and British sources.[131] Despite its largely civilian makeup, the unit existed under the direct authority of the joint-Allied military command. Speaking to a large group of G-5 personnel in May 1944, SHAEF Supreme Commander, General Dwight D. Eisenhower, reminded his recruits that "you are not politicians or anything else but soldiers."[132]

Even before the establishment of SHAEF, a steady stream of American officers had begun arriving at the new Civil Affairs Center (CAC), located in the village of Shrivenham, eighty miles west of London. The CAC acted as an administrative hub for all US civil affairs operations in Europe. Here, students attended classes on military governance and enrolled in intensive language courses.[133] Nearly 40 percent of recruits were commissioned from civilian life, the remainder having already served in armed service branches or the National Guard, but they too

---

the war, military government planning was largely ignored by Roosevelt and Churchill. Ziemke, *The U.S. Army in the Occupation of Germany*, 24. The first joint-civil affairs operations occurred in November 1942, when Allied troops landed in French North Africa. See Harry L. Coles and Albert K. Weinberg, *Civil Affairs: Soldiers Become Governors* (Center of Military History, US Army, 1964), 30–62.

[130] SHAEF had six divisions: Personnel (G-1), Intelligence (G-2), Operations (G-3), Supply (G-4), Civil Affairs (G-5), and Publicity and State Department (G-6). For a detailed breakdown of organizational structure, personnel, and leadership, see Forrest C. Pogue, *The Supreme Command* (Washington, DC: Office of the Chief of Military History Department of the Army, 1954), 67, 529–35.

[131] Donnison, *Civil Affairs and Military Government North-West Europe*, 26.

[132] "Notes on a talk given by General Dwight D. Eisenhower to Civil Affairs personnel at Shrivenham, 9 May 1944 at 1530 hours," n.d., NARA, RG 331, SHAEF, GS G-5, IB, HS, Box 133, Doc. 5611/223.

[133] Ziemke, *The U.S. Army in the Occupation of Germany*, 64–65.

Inter-Allied Planning for Denazification 57

were selected because of their prewar civilian education and expertise.[134] Much like at Charlottesville and the CATS, this overseas American school employed mostly university professors and other scholars. The British established its own civil affairs training center at Eastbourne, south of London on the channel coast. Recruits who passed through this facility were usually graduates of the Wimbledon school and their instruction was comparable to the American program.[135] At both Eastbourne and Shrivenham, students were organized by "detachment" and trained according to the specific region where they would eventually be deployed. After their training, graduates were assigned to either the British 21st, US 6th, or US 12th army groups.[136]

Most civil affairs officers were moved into active service directly from one of these two training schools, but a select few were put to work in the "country houses" set up within the G-5 Division. In early 1944, there existed six independent "houses" – France, Norway, Netherlands, Belgium, Denmark, and Germany/Austria – each of which undertook detailed planning for civil affairs missions in their respective country. It was their job to write procedural manuals, train new recruits at Shrivenham, Wimbledon, and Eastbourne, and build the administrative offices that would eventually be moved to the continent to form "SHAEF Missions" in liberated nations or, as in the case of Germany and Austria, "Military Governments."[137]

The German Country Unit met for the first time on February 16, 1944 at Prince's Gardens in central London.[138] This planning group, which was relocated to Shrivenham some weeks later, employed 269 American and British staff members and was under the direction of the former chairman of the Charlottesville school, US Col. Edgar Lewis.[139] According to an early executive report, the GCU had three tasks: (1) to build the machinery for military government in Germany and Austria; (2) to produce a comprehensive handbook detailing the administration of military government; and (3) to train other civil affairs

---

[134] Ibid., 64. According to Harold Zink, the language and regional education at Shrivenham was far from adequate; that it "probably did more harm than good." Zink, *The United States in Germany*, 15.
[135] Donnison, *Civil Affairs and Military Government North-West Europe*, 32–33.
[136] A handful of American recruits were trained at Eastbourne and British officers at Shrivenham, as it was assumed at this early stage that SHAEF army units would be integrated.
[137] Directive, DCCAO/Special Staff, February 19, 1944, NARA, RG 331, SHAEF, GS, G-5, IB, HS, Box 103, pp. 294–95.
[138] "Historical Statement of the German Country Unit," Aug. 44, NARA, RG 331, SHAEF, GS, G-5, IB, HS, Box 133, Doc. 5611/36.
[139] Ziemke, *The U.S. Army in the Occupation of Germany*, 80–81.

58   Planning the Denazification of Germany

personnel who were to be stationed in Germany or Austria.[140] However, the British War Office refused to extend its full support to the GCU, as the unit presumably took its cues from the Combined Chiefs of Staff (CCS), which was based in Washington. For similar reasons, the group's function as the primary director for military government was challenged by members of the European Advisory Council (EAC), a larger inter-Allied planning group that included the Soviets. The GCU, therefore, maintained a precarious existence. Even after the Normandy landings, in June 1944, the role that it would play in the future governance of Germany was uncertain.[141] According to one of its early members, Earl Ziemke, "no one really expected SHAEF's German Country Unit to last out the summer."[142]

Much like domestic research groups, the majority of GCU staff members had no military background and were recruited directly from civilian life. They were employed for their technical abilities, civil knowledge, and worldly experience. Spread across nineteen separate offices, the average age of a GCU employee was close to forty, but as remembered by one administrator, "maturity was considered to be an asset in a civil affairs officer."[143] On account of a shortage of British officers, the GCU was disproportionally staffed by Americans.[144] This lopsided composition had an effect on the formulation of denazification procedures, mainly because of the considerable amount of influence given to OSS advisors working in London. Remembered by one GCU officer, it was the OSS that provided the "basic data" and "essential research" for building "appropriate" arrest and removal categories.[145]

---

[140] "Historical Statement of the German Country Unit," Aug. 44, NARA, RG 331, SHAEF, GS, G-5, IB, HS, Box 133, Doc. 8/957.

[141] One day after the Normandy landings, the GCU office in London was partially destroyed by a German V-1 rocket. Luckily, the attack occurred early in the morning when the building was empty.

[142] Ziemke, *The U.S. Army in the Occupation of Germany*, 82.

[143] Ibid., 64. The nineteen GCU offices were: Financial, Transportation, Economics, Planning, Food, Labour, Historical, Personnel, Interior, P.T.T., Political Intelligence, Displaced Persons, Legal, Supply, Property Control, Education and Religious Affairs, Administration, Org. and Per. Planning, Austrian. The recruits who staffed them had initially been exempted from military conscription due to their age, student status, or necessity to some specific domestic industry, or because they had simply been "called up" relatively late in the war at a time when their specific skill sets were needed.

[144] In a letter to the DCCAO on April 21, 1944, GCU Head Edgar Lewis explained that due to "the difficulty in obtaining British personnel, it is expected that the German Section will be composed of not more than 25% British personnel." Letter, Edgar Lewis to DCCAO (SS) CA, SHAEF, April 21, 1944, TNA, WO 219/3851, Doc. 9301/14.

[145] Zink, *American Military Government in Germany* (New York: Macmillan, 1947), 131.

Receiving a customary military rank, GCU recruits came from all walks of life.[146] Lawyers were overrepresented, the majority of whom had experience practicing civil law, as were engineers, mainly with mechanical, industrial, civil, and resource-based specialties. Col. Lewis himself, head of the GCU, was a lawyer.[147] Also represented were economists, industrialists, bankers, doctors, teachers, editors, social workers, and police administrators, recruited from government agencies and private companies. Among them was J. C. Cation, a retired banker born in London but living in Los Angeles, who was enlisted by the Financial Section, and Paul R. Heitmeyer, a broadcasting station manager and newspaper editor from Washington, DC, employed in the Administration Section.[148] Special mention should be made of the three Scotland Yard detectives, the Anglican pastor, and the former vice-presidents of General Motors and Bank of America.[149] Nearly two dozen women worked for the GCU, but they all performed secretarial work, received no military rank, and are not listed as "official personnel" in the G-5 records.

Social sciences and humanities doctorates were not uncommon. Fifteen university professors worked in the GCU, some of whom also taught courses at civil affairs schools. Historians, political scientists, economists, and sociologists from Harvard, Yale, Berkeley, Cambridge, Oxford, and other universities filled out the multidisciplinary staff. They included Milton E. G. Muelder, professor of history and political science at Michigan State College, and Arnold L. Zemple, an economist and statistician at Washington University in St. Louis.[150] Some of these academics were born in Germany, or had studied there, and were recruited for their linguistic abilities and firsthand knowledge.[151]

Despite the overwhelming predominance of middle-aged civilian experts and academics, the GCU also employed regular soldiers and career officers. Some of these men had been transferred from active duty because of their prewar profession, while others were veterans of the Great War. Such was the case of the GCU's most decorated officer,

---

[146] It was common for civilian recruits to be assigned a military rank because they required access to top secret or sensitive information that held rank classification.
[147] "Biographical Data for Personnel of German and Austrian Units," June 15, 1944, NARA, RG 331, SHAEF, GS, G-5, IB, HS, Box 133, Doc. 5611/163.
[148] Ibid., Docs. 5611/152, /159.
[149] Ibid., Docs. 5611/162, /166, /170, /172; Carolyn W. Eisenberg, *Drawing the Line: The American Decision to Divide Germany, 1944–1949* (Cambridge: Cambridge University Press, 1996), 30.
[150] Biographical Data for Personnel of German and Austrian Units," June 15, 1944, NARA, RG 331, SHAEF, GS, G-5, IB, HS, Box 133, Docs. 5611/165, /174.
[151] Ibid., Docs. 5611/150, /163, /165, /172.

Lt. Col. Sir Vincent W. Troubridge, a graduate of the Royal Military College who had served in Belgium, France, Italy, and Greece.[152] Some GCU officials had participated in the occupation of the Rhineland, between 1919 and 1930, while many more had performed civil affairs operations more recently in North Africa and Italy.[153] Still, military men were a minority in the German Country Unit. For every career officer, there were twenty civilian specialists, most of whom held multiple degrees and had extensive experience in a particular trade or profession. It was their job to collect, review, and revise the wide-ranging and disparate intelligence that trickled in from the OSS, CAD, War Office, FORD, and Allied Military Government in Italy.

Developing procedures for denazification existed within a larger assignment to write a comprehensive handbook. Based loosely on a similarly purposed guide for Italy, the *Handbook for Military Government in Germany* aspired to the traditional US civil affairs mantra of "welfare of the governed," suggesting a "firm, just, and humane" administration.[154] The *Handbook* was intended to be the "only essential document carried by a civil affairs officer in the field."[155] Denazification was addressed at length, but more detailed instructions were provided in a supplemental publication called the *Public Safety Manual of Procedures*, first printed in September 1944.[156] The GCU began drafting both guides, along with other technical manuals, in early March 1944. They were joined by a handful of OSS researchers, who sat on joint-committees and attended weekly staff meetings. Felix Gilbert, a German-born historian, was transferred to the London OSS/R&A outpost in February 1944, and acted as a sort of intermediate between his radical-minded Washington colleagues and the more practical SHAEF planners.[157]

The GCU's vision for the eradication of Nazism was, at first, soft in scope, calling for a "minor and calculated" purge of the German political

---

[152] Ibid., Doc. 5611/171.   [153] See, for example, ibid., Docs. 5611/154, /164, /165.
[154] As stated in an August 14, 1944 US CAD post-surrender directive.
[155] "Historical Statement of the German Country Unit," Aug. 44, NARA, RG 331, SHAEF, GS, G-5, IB, HS, Box 133, Doc. 5611/56.
[156] For the first edition of the *Public Safety Manual of Procedures*, see "Public Safety Manual of Procedures, Military Government of Germany," Sept. 44, NARA, RG 331, SHAEF, SS, AG, ES, Box 9.
[157] Biddiscombe, *Denazification of Germany*, 26. The OSS/R&A outpost in London was staffed mainly by academics who had more conservative inclinations than their CES colleagues in Washington. Katz, *Foreign Intelligence*, 80. On the troublesome relationship between OSS/London and SHAEF, see MacPherson, *American Intelligence in Wartime London*.

Inter-Allied Planning for Denazification 61

system. The original version of the *Handbook* stipulated that the NSDAP would be abolished, and senior party members expelled from office, but it also allowed for many of the existing government structures to be preserved and officials employed as a means to avoid administrative collapse.[158] Instead of specifying who exactly to dismiss, the GCU granted much discretion to local military government officials. The name "Special Branch" was adopted to refer specifically to denazification units operating at the national (*Staat*), district (*Kreis*), and municipal (*Stadtkreis*) levels of military government, while regular Public Safety officers would administer denazification in smaller towns and in rural regions (*Landkreis*).[159]

The *Handbook* was subject to an exceptional amount of controversy, and as a result, it underwent three major revisions in less than a year, a topic discussed in Chapter 2. It was viewed by some policymakers as far too lenient a document. Morgenthau believed that it gave "the impression that Germany was to be restored just as much as the Netherlands or Belgium."[160] Perhaps the most important revision concerned the employment of "active Nazis" and "ardent sympathizers." While the GCU had originally recommended that military government utilize the technical skills of some former Nazis, the final draft prohibited such practices: "Under no circumstances shall active Nazis or ardent sympathizers be retained in office for purposes of administrative convenience or expediency."[161] However, it also stated that the "administrative machinery of certain dissolved organizations may be used when necessary to provide essential functions." At no point were the terms "active" and "nominal" Nazi, "Nazi sympathizer," or "militarist" defined, despite being referenced throughout the *Handbook*.[162] Such ambiguities, coupled with the unopposed GCU decision to delegate discretion to local commanders, would eventually lead to administrative problems in the field.

The *Public Safety Manual of Procedures*, of which there were two versions, published in September 1944 and February 1945, respectively,

---

[158] This decision was also made to circumvent international occupation law, which prohibited foreign occupiers from altering the legal or social structures of a conquered state. Legal considerations were held in the utmost regard by the GCU staff, especially by the *Handbook's* principal architect, Keith Wilson, who was a jurist.
[159] Griffith, "The Denazification Program in the United States Zone in Germany," 11.
[160] Biddiscombe, *Denazification of Germany*, 30.
[161] SHAEF, *Handbook for Military Government in Germany: Prior to Defeat or Surrender* (SHAEF, December 1944), Part I, Chapter I, Introduction.
[162] Ibid.; SHAEF, *Public Safety Manual of Procedures, Military Government of Germany*, 1st ed. (September 1944), 41.

addressed denazification in greater detail. It was, after all, the Public Safety Branch that was assigned the task of purging government offices and private business. The *Manual* called for the "removal of leading active Nazis from the civil administration" and provided instructions for examining Fragebögen.[163] A blank copy of the questionnaire was included in the appendices. Although the *Manual* stipulated that only "objective criteria and standard procedures must be used to determine the 'degree of Nazism' of German officials rather than heresy, denunciations or rule of thumb measures," it relied on the same ambiguous language and undefined terms as its parent handbook. Terms such as "active" and "nominal" Nazi were frequently mentioned but never defined.[164] Furthermore, denazification agents were permitted to retain former Nazis for essential functions of civil administration.[165]

Both of these GCU-drafted procedures contained a fundamental dilemma. On the one hand, they outlined an inflexible system of identification and punishment and promoted a reliance on rigid categories of Nazi affiliation, but they also granted considerable discretion to officers operating in the field and made allowances for local conditions. These contradictory instructions were inherited, in part, by OSS researchers and had the effect of disrupting SHAEF's screening program in the early months of the occupation. Throughout its entire albeit short existence, the GCU operated independently and with little to no guidance from executive government offices or high-level Allied organizations. It had been assigned the nearly impossible task of translating the lofty goals for denazification laid out by the Allied leadership, while being pulled in many different directions by various American and British agencies, including the OSS. As remembered by one of its members, William E. Griffith, a professor of history and later Chief of the US Denazification Branch in Bavaria, "The almost complete lack of policy direction from governmental levels was shown by the fact that as late as May 1944 the German Country Unit had received no directive concerning the basic policy to be adopted in respect to removal and exclusion from public office in Germany."[166]

---

[163] Ibid., 40–51.
[164] It was not until the spring of 1945, months after the invasion, that SHAEF directives began providing definitions, but even then, criteria for removal were unclear and regularly contested within denazification branch offices. Directive, "Removal from Office of Nazis and German Militarists," March 21, 1945, NARA, RG 331, SHAEF, SS, AGO, ES, Box 134.
[165] SHAEF, *Public Safety Manual of Procedures*, 41.
[166] Griffith, "The Denazification Program in the United States Zone in Germany," 7.

The GCU planners were also aware that no matter how much work they accomplished, their reports and manuals remained provisional and subject to change. They were writing denazification procedures in an office that was consistently under threat of dissolution and within a larger organization that was scheduled to be disbanded immediately after Germany had been defeated.[167] Considering the little attention paid, or direction given, to the GCU, the criticism that befell its members and their work in the final months of the war seems unwarranted. Nevertheless, it was this small planning group that built the denazification program that was eventually adopted by all occupying armies. Equipped with political intelligence from the OSS in Washington, the GCU formulated the only practical denazification strategy offered by any wartime office.

Conclusion

By late 1943, Col. Irwin L. Hunt's muffled warnings had finally been heard. The young forward-thinking officer had insisted on the recruitment of civilian specialists and the establishment of schools "devoted to the higher training of officers."[168] At the time, in 1920, no one had listened, but in grappling with the global dimension and mechanized nature of the new conflict, the Allied leadership recognized the need for a new postwar transition strategy. Summarized by one of the principal architects of American military government, Hajo Holborn, "total war had changed the old pattern of peacemaking."[169]

This chapter has acted as an introduction to high-level policymaking and mid-level planning for the occupation and denazification of Germany. It has traversed the complex and often changing bureaucracy landscape and surveyed the intellectual climate. During the war, the American and British armed forces, and to a lesser degree the French and Soviets, recognized and attempted to correct the inherent weaknesses in traditional post-hostilities doctrine. Key political and military figures were willing to experiment with new concepts and strategies in order to achieve their unorthodox objectives, such as the ideological reorientation of the enemy. What resulted was a mobilization of nonmilitary intellectual resources. Civilian-administered offices were established, training schools with academic curricula founded, and channels of political and research-based intelligence pursued. Even more

---

[167] Zink, *American Military Government in Germany*, 131.
[168] Hunt, "American Military Government of Occupied Germany," 64.
[169] Holborn, *American Military Government*, x.

profound was the recruitment of thousands of civilian specialists who were put to work in planning the occupation of Germany. This was the civilian-engaged environment that permitted the adoption of an experimental self-administered political questionnaire.

The OSS researchers' idealistic vision for denazification was translated and negotiated to meet the GCU's practical requirements for civil affairs administration. One office generated a grand idea, supporting it with research intelligence, while the other employed that idea within the bureaucracies of inter-Allied military government. Both groups were largely populated by academics, who promoted unconventional approaches to the political cleansing of German society. However, they were also subject to the same dysfunctional decisionmaking processes that existed at the executive level. Unsupervised mid-level bureaucracies are common during times of war but planning for denazification was especially crowded and confused. The unamiable relationship that existed between political and military institutions at the national level and between members of inter-Allied groups exacerbated this state of affairs.

The academics working for the CES and GCU were continuously challenged by an inherent contradiction in all strands of occupation policy: the pursuit of both punitive and restorative goals. While short-term objectives, such as the punishment of Nazi war criminals, extraction of economic reparations, and demilitarization, dominated all levels of occupation planning, longer-term considerations, including economic partnerships and continental political dynamics, could not be ignored. The determination of the Allied leaders to pay lip service to both the punishment and rehabilitation of Germans made the assignment of mid-level planners to produce a cohesive program extremely difficult. The result was that a practical strategy for the occupation was never produced. Denazification procedures were drafted, but a shared consensus on postwar political screening activities was not achieved.

It is easy to criticize the wartime planning apparatus, but it was this confusion and dysfunction that allowed civilian planners to cut a path into unknown territory and produce creative outcomes. Perhaps, if Germany had been subject to a traditional form of military governance a much less effective approach would have emerged. The civilian-crafted screening program was highly experimental and can be considered an ideological and administrative compromise. The "army" of academics forced through many social scientific approaches, but their most enduring contribution was an unassuming four-page political questionnaire. At the time, they did not realize the breadth and consequence that the form possessed, nor that it would come to underpin most denazification activities and alter the lives of millions of Germans.

2 "A Miserable Paper Substitute for a Spontaneous Revolution"
Drafting the Questionnaire

> The objection may be quite naturally raised that we are depending on the "Fragebogen" and that any German would be foolish to give answers against his own best interests ... we know of no other way of tackling this almost impossible task of eliminating the Nazi.[1]
> —Lt. Col. William T. Babcock, Public Safety Branch, USGCC

Chapter 1 charted the history of denazification planning at the national and Allied levels, with emphasis placed on small research groups operating in the United States and Great Britain. What follows here is an examination of the questionnaire itself, specifically its origins and the early implementation of the political screening system in Germany. It moves the analytical focus away from the policymaking architecture and the interchange of ideas between civilian-staffed offices to the rudimentary construction of a functioning vetting program. As such, this chapter bridges the historiographical gap that has long existed between the interpretation of high-policy goals and the mass application of the denazification campaign.

First, the practical origins of the Fragebogen are traced to 1943 Allied-Occupied Italy, where military agencies first used screening instruments on a defeated enemy population. Then we revisit the German Country Unit and investigate the reasons why its members adopted the Italian form. This section pays close attention to the motivations and behaviors of the SHAEF officers who developed the denazification questionnaire. We then scrutinize the structure and content of the original Fragebogen, published in May 1944. Finally, this chapter observes how the questionnaire came under immense criticism from high-level officials during the final months of the war and follows the subsequent fragmentation of the screening program into national camps. It analyzes and compares the independent Fragebogen projects that emerged under American, British,

---

[1] In early 1945, Babcock was Head of Public Safety. "Public Safety and the Removal of the Nazi," January 29, 1945, NARA, RG 331, SHAEF, AGD, Box 69; Jones, "Eradicating Nazism," 154.

French, and Soviet administrations and corrects previous interpretations about the scope and character of denazification.

The decision to adopt a self-administered questionnaire as the key screening instrument was bold and experimental. The GCU planners were delegated the challenging task of translating the contradictory goals of occupation policy into a workable program for implementation. But while their ultimate accomplishments are remarkable, the Fragebogen itself was an inadequate mechanism for the complex task of judging Germans. The form was hastily written and contained both punitive and redemptive features and, by today's standards, included undemocratic and arguably immoral questions. While trumpeted as a device for objective screening, the program allowed for subjective responses and discretionary evaluation. The development of the project did not show clarity and confidence, but stumbled forward out of necessity and indecision, and because of the absence of any alternative strategy. The OSS and SHAEF planners had an idealistic, even revolutionary, vision of what denazification could be, but their hopes never materialized in the way they expected. Candidly explained by a British civil affairs officer involved in drafting the questionnaire, "Denazification was ... a miserable paper substitute for a spontaneous revolution that would have freed the soul of Germany. But since the revolution did not happen, there was nothing for it but the fragebogen."[2]

Italian Origins: Defascistization and the *Scheda Personale*

From the moment American and British civil affairs officers stepped foot on the beaches of Sicily, in early July 1943, they encountered serious problems. Simply put, they were not equipped for the tasks that they had been assigned. Organized under the jointly administered Allied Military Government of Occupied Territories (AMGOT), later the Allied Military Government (AMG), these mostly civilian recruits were ordered to relieve combat forces by providing the "liberated" population with the necessary means of subsistence and to establish local administration, public health services, and law and order.[3] However, at this early stage

---

[2] Donnison, *Civil Affairs and Military Government North-West Europe*, 378.
[3] "AFHQ Plans Proposes an Equal Partnership and a Nonzonal System," March 24, 1943, in *Civil Affairs: Soldiers Become Governors*, United States Army in WWII Series, eds. Harry Lewis Coles and Albert Katz Weinberg (Washington, DC: United States Army Center of Military History, 1964), 162; Kimber Marie Quinney, "The United States, Great Britain, and Dismantling Italian Fascism, 1943–1948" (PhD diss., University of California, Santa Barbara, 2002), 43–44.

of the invasion of Europe, the civil affairs schools at Charlottesville and Wimbledon had not yet finished developing their curricula, and training for such operations was rushed and conducted in the field over a mere matter of days.[4] Aside from a handful of civilian agents who had been deployed to North Africa in late 1942 and early 1943, most officers had absolutely no experience in local governance or in rehabilitating a country devastated by war. After arriving in Italy, one soldier recalled his shock to find that the region where he was stationed had no civil transport, intercommunication, or administration to speak of, confessing that "officers could work hard and well for 2 to 3 months without doing any more than 'learn.'"[5]

The shared Allied objective to purge Italian government and industry of fascist influences seemed hopeless.[6] No discernible definition of "fascism" had been produced by any group – party membership was not considered a sufficient standard – and the Americans and British did not see eye to eye on the matter of political screening. Planners in Washington desired a more direct form of governance and the removal of all former fascists from positions of influence, while London sought a system of indirect rule and planned to dismiss only senior party members. Then again, these differing opinions mattered little in the summer of 1943, because no inclusive policy for what was then being referred to as "epuration" or "defascistization" had been confirmed.[7] AMGOT memorandums reiterated the shared commitment to eradicate fascism but contained little instruction on how to carry out a political purge of personnel. Defascistization was not viewed as a priority of military government, at least not in the early months of the occupation,

---

[4] The first US/British civil affairs training center for officers assigned to Sicily was established in Algeria in May 1943. C. R. S. Harris, *Allied Military Administration of Italy, 1943–1945* (London: Her Majesty's Stationary Office, 1957), 25; Joseph Albert Hearst Jr., "The Evolution of Allied Military Government Policy in Italy" (PhD diss., Columbia University, 1960), 16.

[5] "Report on Experience with A.M.G. in Italy," March 1944, NARA, RG 331, SHAEF, GG, G-5, IB, HS, Box 196, File 27.02, Doc. 76 1024/10 929.

[6] Scholarship on the Allied Occupation of Italy is plentiful, but there are few books that deal specifically with defascistization. The best studies are Roy Palmer Domenico, *Italian Fascists on Trial, 1943–1948* (Chapel Hill: University of North Carolina Press, 1991); Hans Woller, *Die Abrechnung mit dem Faschismus in Italien 1943 bis 1948* (Munich: Oldenbourg, 1996); Romano Canosa, *Storia dell'epurazione in Italia* (Milan: Baldini e Castoldi, 1999); and Michele Battini, *Peccati di memoria. La mancata Norimberga italiana* (Rome: Laterza, 2003).

[7] The term "epuration," which roughly translates to "purification," was borrowed from the French usage (*épuration*) in North Africa. Valeria Galimi, "Circulation of Models of Épuration after the Second World War: From France to Italy," in *Dealing with Wars and Dictatorships: Legal Concepts and Categories in Action*, eds. Liora Israël and Guillaume Mouralis (The Hague: TMC Asser, 2014), 197–208.

while the fighting continued. In an AMGOT report circulated on August 2, 1943, civil affairs officers operating in Sicily were reminded that the "first aim [of military government] is not defascistization but avoidance of administrative breakdown."[8] In fact, defascistization would never achieve the priority status that denazification would later hold for the Allied armies in Germany, and it was not pursued with the same vigor.

Distinct from the popular notion of the collective guilt of Germans, American and British political intelligence reports tended to portray Fascism as an ideological system imposed on the Italian population by Benito Mussolini's inner clique of *Squadristi* thugs, rather than an intrinsically Italian phenomenon.[9] However, AMGOT planners also recognized that, unlike Nazism's short tenure, Fascism had governed Italian society for twenty-two years and, therefore, had likely penetrated all social strata and professional institutions. Consequently, party membership could not be relied upon as a cause for dismissal. Mandatory membership in the Partito Nazionale Fascista (National Fascist Party, or PNF) was common in Mussolini's Italy. In many cases, to gain employment, enroll in university, obtain a marriage license, collect veteran benefits, or garner a pension, applicants were required to join the PNF.[10] Another problem was that the distinction between a "defeated" and "liberated" person had been complicated when, in July 1943, Mussolini was ousted from power by his own Grand Council and arrested by order of King Victor Emmanuel III. The new government installed under General Pietro Badoglio signed an armistice with the Allied powers on September 3, 1943, which was followed by a formal Italian declaration of war against Germany. Soldiers loyal to Mussolini, or those simply exhausted by the war, abandoned their posts, and partisan warfare broke out on both sides of an ever-changing frontline. To advancing Allied soldiers, it was unclear who was an ally and who an enemy.

A standardized criterion for screening did not exist, and even if it had, civil affairs officers did not possess the political intelligence needed to identify fascists. AMGOT relied on OSS "black lists," incomplete government records, local newspapers, and voluntary denunciations from

---

[8] Ibid., 195.
[9] Andrew Buchanan argues that US defascistization policy for Italy was always more redemptive than punitive because policymakers viewed Italian Fascism as something that had been "imposed upon a malleable people" and therefore it required the military government to restore the Italians to the "dignity of human beings." Andrew Buchanan, "'Good Morning Pupil': American Representations of Italianness and the Occupation of Italy, 1943–1945," *Journal of Contemporary History* 43, no. 2 (2008): 218–20.
[10] Quinney, "The United States, Great Britain, and Dismantling Italian Fascism," 56.

Italian citizens.[11] Furthermore, the Sicilian campaign, and much of the fighting on the Italian mainland, was fast-paced, and officers often found themselves stationed far behind the frontline with no administrative guidance on policy or intelligence support.[12] Referring to the task of defascistization, a Public Safety officer wrote in a May 1944 staff study that "there was no precise guiding policy, no plan or procedure and no clear cut delegation of authority ... there were no objective criteria for separating the 'sheep from the goats.'"[13] This resulted in a drastically inconsistent program, one that was forced to function locally on a case-by-case basis and without the necessary resources.

The most sustained voice of criticism of the existing defascistization program belonged to Lt. Col. Charles Poletti, the first Supreme Civil Affairs Officer (SCAO) for Sicily. Poletti was an outspoken Italian-American lawyer and politician who had briefly served as governor of New York.[14] He had overseen the drafting of the original occupation guidelines and, with the support of Lt. Col. Charles M. Spofford, a fellow lawyer and chief of the Military Government Section, he sought to standardize defascistization procedures for all Italian territories.[15] Poletti was an idealistic and innovative manager who was receptive to the use of social sciences research for the purpose of welfare state intervention and education.[16]

---

[11] The OSS also provided AMGOT/AMG with firsthand intelligence gathered from interviews with "foreign experts" living in the United States and from several Italian-American organizations, including the Sons of Italy and Fier di Marsala. For these intelligence reports, see "Survey of Foreign Experts, Progress Report #7," NARA, RG 226, OSS, Container 5.

[12] The Military Government also turned to the United States Army's Counter Intelligence Corps and British Field Security Force to assist in identifying Fascists, but these security officers were attached to active military units and only in a particular region for a day or two. Gary A. Trogdon, "A Decade of Catching Spies: The United States Army's Counter Intelligence Corps, 1943–1953" (PhD diss., University of Nebraska, 2001), 37.

[13] Staff Study, "Measures for Identifying and Determining Disposition of Nazi Public Officials in Germany," May 28, 1944, NARA, RG 331, SHAEF, GS, G-5, IB, HS, Box 104, Doc. 9959/175.

[14] Martin Kyre and Joan Kyre consider Poletti "probably the most controversial American occupation official in the theater" because of his outspoken criticism of AMGOT bureaucracy and the military chain of command, as well as rumors of his affiliation with the Italian mafia. Martin Kyre and Joan Kyre, *Military Occupation and National Security* (Washington, DC: Public Affairs Press, 1968), 102; Salvatore Lupo, *History of the Mafia*, trans. Antony Shugaar (New York: Columbia University Press, 2009), xiii.

[15] In March 1943, Spofford wrote the "Appreciation and Outline Plan," which was adopted as the "basis of the development in detail of military government in Sicily." As quoted in Isobel Williams, *Allies and Italians under Occupation: Sicily and Southern Italy, 1943–45* (London: Palgrave Macmillan, 2013), 25. For a full draft of the "Appreciation and Outline Plan" (commonly referred to as the "Spofford Report"), see "Draft Report by Charles M. Spofford," March 1944, TNA, WO 204/3159.

[16] Domenico, *Italian Fascists on Trial*, 32–33.

In formulating solutions to civil affairs problems, the former governor was also an advocate of calculated bureaucracy and the use of experimental and cost-effective administrative techniques. Historian Roy Domenico argues that civil affairs officers like Poletti "viewed Italy as their own laboratory where goodly doses of American-style democracy could be applied."[17]

When defascistization was extended to the Italian mainland in September 1943, administrative problems reached a state of crisis, which spurred Poletti into action. He created a Political Intelligence Section to formulate criteria for the retention and removal of former Fascists, thus institutionalizing defascistization.[18] This small unit was headed by Maj. Aldo Raffa, a political science instructor at Georgetown University.[19] Influenced by Poletti's bureaucratic thinking and openness to using social science methods, as well as incoming OSS reports on the political and cultural life in the Fascist state, Raffa and his staff drafted a defascistization questionnaire, or *scheda personale* (personal questionnaire/form). This precursor of the Fragebogen was printed in late September 1943, five months before the creation of the German County Unit.

The three-page, seventy-five-question survey, which "every individual in Italy who held a prominent position during the Fascist regime" was required to complete, was meant to solve two defascistization problems: the lack of political intelligence, and the mounting criticism from the Italian people, who viewed job dismissals as arbitrary and unjust.[20] Raffa understood that defascistization officers would still be required to access Italian archives, private employment records, and newspapers in order to cross-reference *scheda personali*, but he also believed that the self-completed form would save civil affairs officers countless hours of administrative work. It is important to recognize that at its heart, the questionnaire program, as envisioned by Raffa, was intended not only to classify Fascists and expunge right-wing ideology from Italian society but

---

[17] Ibid., 32.
[18] Hearst, "The Evolution of Allied Military Government Policy in Italy," 154; Staff Study, "Measures for Identifying and Determining Disposition of Nazi Public Officials in Germany," May 28, 1944, NARA, RG 331, SHAEF, GS, G-5, IB, HS, Box 104, Doc. 9959/177.
[19] Aldo L. Raffa, NARA, RG 331, SHAEF, GS, G-5, IB, HS, Box 119, Doc. 5601/620; Personnel File, "Raffa, Aldo L.," NARA, RG 226, OSS, Box 630.
[20] Letter, AMGOT HQ (Col. Charles Spofford) to all SCAOs, "Questionnaires for Civil Official and Employees," October 6, 1943, NARA, RG 331, ACC-Italy Subject File, HQ, PSB, Box 1412; Memo from Maj. Aldo Raffa, "A Questionnaire Is Developed to Standardize Epuration Investigations," November 1, 1943, in Coles and Weinberg, *Civil Affairs*, 383–84.

also to identify "good Italians" who could be trusted by the Allied authorities in civil service positions.

Most questions in the *scheda* required a simple "yes" or "no" answer, and unlike the subsequent German form, no allowances were made for personal remarks or commentaries.[21] The questionnaire asked for information on political party and militia membership, as well as employment in Fascist corporative and syndical organizations, sources of income, and military service. For example:

> Question 5b: Did you at any time belong to the Squadristi?
> Question 10b: Were you at any time a functionary in a syndical union?
> Question 13e: Were you a "volunteer" in the Spanish Civil War?

Members of certain Fascist organizations (e.g., Mussolini's bodyguard unit, the *Moschettieri del Duce*) and holders of particular positions of authority (e.g., manager of a PNF-administered farming cooperative, or *consorzio agrario*) were to be immediately dismissed from employment. All questions were answered "under oath," and respondents were warned at the top of the form that "severe penalties, both penal and monetary, are provided for whoever makes false statements in the present questionnaire."[22]

First circulated in Sicily in late September 1943, it did not take long for the *scheda personale* to reach other Italian provinces. As the Allied Forces pushed the enemy further north, Poletti was reassigned to new military government offices, first in Calabria then Lucania, Latium, Umbria, and finally Lombardy. Wherever stationed, he promoted the use of the political questionnaire.[23] Defascistization proved easier on the Italian mainland because the Badoglio government had already removed many leading Fascists from influential positions. In an October 6, 1943 memorandum circulated to SCAOs stationed in all provinces, Spofford formally announced the commencement of the program. He stated that "all persons who are being considered by SCAOs as candidates for public offices must complete the questionnaire before action is taken" and that "Raffa or his associates will soon visit all SCAOs for assistance/

---

[21] For a copy of the English translation, see Letter, AMGOT HQ (Col. Charles Spofford) to all SCAOs, "Questionnaires for Civil Officials and Employees," October 6, 1943, NARA, RG 331, ACC-Italy Subject File, HQ, PSB, Box 1412.

[22] Original Italian: "Penalità severissima, di prigione e di ammenda sono previste per chiunque facesse delle dichiarazioni false nella presente scheda."

[23] Domenico, *Italian Fascists on Trial*, 26.

training."[24] This dispatch was followed by a memo from Raffa himself, in which he explained that the project was a logical alternative to the ad hoc judgments that had previously characterized political screening.

Despite the early circulation of these proclamations, the *scheda* did not become commonplace until the spring of 1944, nearly one year after the invasion of Sicily. In a March 17, 1944 directive titled "Screening Italian Officials in AMG Areas," commanders of all Occupied areas were ordered to circulate questionnaires, and a guide on "What to look for in a completed Scheda" was published along with descriptions of the various categories of guilt.[25] Problems with screening procedures continued, however, mainly due to the lack of staff available to process the massive influx of completed forms. Despite these shortcomings, the questionnaire program was maintained, and when defascistization was handed over to the Bonomi government in the spring of 1945, the *scheda* continued to act as the cornerstone of the campaign to rid the political administration of Fascist influences.[26]

In some respect, the Italian questionnaire was the model for the Fragebogen, and in this regard, some characteristics of the program should be highlighted. Firstly, the *scheda personale* project was not manageable given the limited resources assigned to it. Distributing and processing questionnaires required a small army of civil affairs officers and a steady stream of reliable political intelligence, neither of which existed. The strain that the program had on military government is evidenced by dozens of letters sent to AMG headquarters from local offices that anxiously asked for more staff.[27] More than 11,000 *scheda personali* were distributed in Sicily in the first seven months of the Occupation, but only 3,671 were processed, resulting in the removal of a mere 111 employees from public office.[28]

Secondly, terms such as "active Fascist," "Fascist sympathizer," and "minor" and "major" officials were never defined, although mentioned

---

[24] Letter, AMGOT HQ (Col. Charles Spofford) to all SCAOs, "Questionnaires for Civil Officials and Employees," October 6, 1943, NARA, RG 331, ACC-Italy Subject File, HQ, PSB, Box 1412, pp. 1–2.

[25] ACC Memorandum, "Screening Italian Officials in AMG Areas," March 17, 1944, NARA, RG 331, ACC-Italy, HQ, PSB, Box 1412, Docs. 5460–65.

[26] Stipulated in the Italian armistice, the Badoglio government (July 1943–June 1944) was required to continue defascistization after the military occupation. In spring 1945, the ACC turned over its collection of completed *scheda* to the Italian authorities. Quinney, "The United States, Great Britain, and Dismantling Italian Fascism," 93.

[27] For example, see Letter, ACC HQ – Region III, Public Safety Branch Office, to Public Safety Sub-Commission, ACC, "scheda personale," March 23, 1944, NARA, RG 331, ACC-Italy, HQ, PSB, Box 1412, Docs. 5458–59.

[28] ACC Report, "De-fascistization," June 8, 1944, NARA, RG 331, ACC-Italy, HQ, PSB, Box 1412, Doc. 5494.

regularly during epuration activities and printed in the questionnaires themselves. In February 1944, the ACC published a "Glossary of Terms for the Scheda Personale," but it only listed political, economic, and military organizations and not any of the terms used as qualifiers to employ, dismiss, and arrest former party members.[29] The German Country Unit would struggle with similarly vague definitions.

Thirdly, the *scheda personale* program did not achieve administrative consistency. As late as June 1945, ACC reports spoke of "uncontrolled epuration" in regions throughout the country due to the late onset of the questionnaire program and because different versions of the *scheda* were being circulated at different times, in different provinces, and in different capacities.[30] Samuel Reber, the most senior US political officer in Italy, confessed that he had no instruction or any ideas on how to implement defascistization, even though its procedures had apparently been standardized.[31] The same problem would be encountered in Germany.

Fourthly, the questionnaires allowed the military government to incriminate and punish Italians based on categorical determination. By using a screening instrument to determine an individual's affiliation with the Fascist regime, a strategy first endorsed by the OSS but nurtured by Poletti's and Raffa's own backgrounds, defascistization was immediately reduced to a bureaucratic system, one reliant on arrest and dismissal categories. Such rigid classification vastly simplified the Fascist political and social experience and ignored the specificities of each individual case.

Finally, the AMG made no effort to measure public opinion or even evaluate the questionnaire as an effective instrument. If it had, it would have quickly learned that the Italian people did not take the *scheda personale* program seriously. A standardized survey used to measure political sentiment and affiliation was an unusual concept to Italians, and after witnessing the initial leniencies given by the occupying armies, many decided not to complete a form or submitted false information.[32] The Italian jurist Mario Bracci would later note that "Colonel Poletti's scheda ... will remain in the museums of Italy as a single document of historical incomprehension ... and of total ignorance of things Italian."[33]

Nevertheless, the Italian screening program, which functioned in various forms and capacities between 1943 and 1945, was exported for use

---

[29] Letter, ACC HQ, Interior Sub-Commission, to Vice President, Administrative Section Operations Security and Intelligence Public Safety, "scheda personale," February 6, 1944, NARA, RG 331, ACC-Italy Subject File, HQ, PSB, Box 1412, Docs. 5440–46.

[30] Memo, "Uncontrolled Epuration in Private Business Will Be Stopped," June 1945, in Coles and Weinberg, *Civil Affairs*, 567.

[31] Domenico, *Italian Fascists on Trial*, 26. [32] Ibid., 33. [33] Ibid.

by the German denazification planners in SHAEF. In March 1944, Aldo Raffa and his Political Intelligence Section arrived in England with the sole purpose of drafting a German questionnaire. They knew that the *scheda personale* campaign had proven unmanageable, that it had never been implemented with any level of consistency, and that it relied on ill-defined terms of identification and strict categories of political affiliation.[34] Even more surprising is that when the GCU drafted its Fragebogen, in May 1944, the *scheda personale* was still being reconsidered and revised.

Drafting the Fragebogen

When the defascistization specialists arrived in Shrivenham in March 1944, they encountered a planning group not so different from the one they had formed in Italy. The GCU, populated by lawyers, economists, police officers, and political scientists, was much larger but equally ill-equipped to organize a massive purge of the enemy's political and economic systems.[35] Much like AMGOT's Political Intelligence Section, the GCU had a handful of vague policy directives to work with, including the Yalta Agreement and the later published CCS 551, which was a Combined Chiefs of Staff pre-surrender directive.[36] These decrees simply ordered the occupation government to "destroy Nazism-Fascism and the Nazi Hierarchy" and "remove all Nazi and militarist influences from public offices and from cultural and economic life."[37] Their job was made more difficult because the GCU's planning section charged with formulating a denazification program had no permanent administrative head for the first two months of its existence, when the Fragebogen was in fact written.[38] Furthermore, staff recruits were still trickling in from Charlottesville, Wimbledon, Washington, London, and Italy, and the administrative makeup of the office remained uncertain.

---

[34] Milton Bracker, "Reich Gives AMG Biggest Problems," *New York Times*, April 2, 1945, p. 8.

[35] For consistency, I defer to using the office's original name, the German Country Unit, but at different times and by different sources, the group was also referred to as the German Country Section.

[36] The "Combined Directive for Military Government in Germany prior to Defeat or Surrender" (April 24, 1945), or CCS 551, restated the Yalta objectives, but, in a twist, granted considerable discretion to military commanders operating in the field in formulating a necessary balance between the dismantlement and preservation of existing German political and economic structures.

[37] Holborn, *American Military Government*, 137; Pollock and Meisel, *Germany under Occupation*, 2.

[38] "Notes of Meeting of the German Country Unit, Special Staff, C.A. SHAEF," March 8, 1943, TNA, WO 219/3851, Doc. 9301/32.

Drafting the Fragebogen

However, it was exactly because of these uncertainties, and due to its status as a temporary planning group, that the GCU exercised so much autonomy in developing a rubric for joint-Allied denazification.[39] This did not mean, however, that the unit possessed the time or expertise to carry out new research on the Nazi system.[40] Instead, its planners relied heavily on intelligence from external partners, most notably the OSS, but also MI6 and the Royal Institute of International Affairs, as well as operational guidance from civil affairs officers who had served in Italy.

As learned in Chapter 1, the principal mandate of the GCU was to plan for and later constitute the military government for Germany and to produce a comprehensive manual for its functioning. Outlined in a February 22, 1944 memo, the group was charged with producing a document "similar to the so-called 'AMGOT Bible' for Sicily, which will be both a plan and detailed application of the various functional directives now in course of issue to the conditions likely to obtain in Germany."[41]

Major Aldo Raffa, the principal architect of the Italian *scheda personale*, was recruited by SHAEF for a specific task, to produce a standardized system for political screening.[42] It was well known within the GCU that other offices and agencies were building programs for the eradication of Nazism, but Raffa was told that his curriculum would ultimately be adopted by all Allied armies operating in Germany, at least during the pre-surrender phase. The Italian-born, Harvard-educated political science instructor had originally been recruited by the OSS and assigned to R&A's North Africa Section, before being deployed to the Mediterranean Theater to help build the defascistization campaign.[43] When he traveled to England, Raffa was accompanied by Capt. M. Keith Wilson, another veteran of Italy and collaborator on the *scheda personale* project. Wilson was a lawyer who had undergone civil affairs training at Fort Custer and Yale University (CATS program), before

---

[39] The GCU was not technically part of SHAEF but a "special staff subsidiary" of G-5.
[40] The GCU conducted its own staff studies on Germany, but these reports contained mostly amalgamated information gathered from external intelligence agencies.
[41] Report, "Formation of the German Unit," February 22, 1944, TNA, WO 219/3472.
[42] Niethammer, *Entnazifizierung in Bayern*, 58; Griffith, "The Denazification Program in the United States Zone in Germany," 12.
[43] After the war, Raffa taught political science courses at American University in Washington, DC. In 1953, he joined the Central Intelligence Agency, but not before returning to Sicily to enroll in a doctorate program at the University of Palermo. "Biographical Data for Personnel of German and Austrian Units," June 15, 1944, NARA, RG 331, SHAEF, GS, G-5, IB, HS, Box 133, p. 27, Doc. 5611/166; Author unknown, "Appointments and Staff Changes," *The American Political Science Review* 46, no. 3 (September 1953): 941.

being assigned to Sicily and later Sardinia as a Public Safety officer.[44] After the German surrender, he was appointed Chief of the Denazification Section for the US Military Government, but prior to that served in the GCU alongside Raffa. Although the writing of the first *Fragebogen* can be attributed to Raffa, Wilson was intimately involved.[45] The other GCU members who had an immediate hand in devising the project were Lt. Col. Orlando W. Wilson, a criminology professor from the University of California, Berkeley, and Sinclair Armstrong, a professor of history at Brown University and OSS liaison, who relayed information between the GCU and his colleagues back in Washington, particularly Neumann and Marcuse.[46] All of these men were American academics, and apart from Armstrong, had firsthand experience with defascistization in Italy.

The absence of military executive interest meant that the decision to create a denazification questionnaire was made by this small group of civilian specialists. Raffa, M. K. Wilson, O. W. Wilson, Armstrong, and eight other planners comprised the Public Safety Branch (PSB), an office created in early 1944 within the Interior Section of the GCU. It was assigned to drafting two chapters in the comprehensive *Handbook for Military Government in Germany* and producing its own *Public Safety Manual of Procedures*, within which the Fragebogen system would be detailed. Raffa and his colleagues were aware of the potential pitfalls of a mass screening campaign, including the "hit-and-miss methods" of identifying fascists that had prevailed in Sicily.[47] Still, they agreed that a similar strategy should be pursued for Germany.

This decision was made for two reasons. First, the GCU believed that the general framework of the Italian defascistization campaign was sufficient; it was late implementation that caused its problems. They concluded that if a standardized screening system was confirmed prior to the

---

[44] "Biographical Data for Personnel of German and Austrian Units," June 15, 1944, NARA, RG 331, SHAEF, GS, G-5, IB, HS, Box 133, p. 27, Doc. 5611/173.

[45] Antony Mann, *Comeback: Germany 1945–1952* (London: Macmillan, 1980), 69.

[46] "Biographical Data for Personnel of German and Austrian Units," June 15, 1944, NARA, RG 331, SHAEF, GS, G-5, IB, HS, Box 133, pp. 2, 27, Docs. 5611/149, / 173. After the occupation, M. K. Wilson, previously a circuit judge, became the personal aid to O.W. Wilson, who was appointed police superintendent of Chicago in 1960. "Minor Wilson Would Run in 43rd Ward," *Chicago Tribune*, February 20, 1967, p. 3. For a detailed biography of Orlando Wilson and his contribution to the professionalization of law enforcement, see William J. Bopp, "In Quest of a Police Profession: A Biography of Orlando W. Wilson" (PhD diss., Florida Atlantic University, 1975).

[47] Staff Study, "Measures for Identifying and Determining Disposition of Nazi Public Officials in Germany," May 28, 1944, NARA, RG 331, SHAEF, GS, G-5, IB, HS, Box 104, Doc. 9959/177.

invasion and clearly communicated in the relevant manuals circulated to civil affairs officers, then denazification could achieve the consistency that defascistization had not. Second, and perhaps more importantly, Raffa and his team could not come up with a better strategy to screen millions of people. Other approaches were forwarded – such as mass internment and the conducting of individual in-person interviews – but none were practical.[48] The breadth of denazification, as intended by the Allied governments, was enormous, and no one could formulate a better plan than the one currently being haphazardly applied in Italy.

The decision to adopt a political questionnaire was also influenced by the recent institutionalization of the applied social sciences and rising popularity of mass public polling in the United States and Great Britain. The GCU's academic staff was already accustomed to collecting and interpreting research data and using problem-oriented and knowledge-based research methods. While the sample survey was introduced in Europe around the turn of the nineteenth century, the basic method of opinion polling was popularized in the United States during the 1930s. Introduced by George Gallup, Elmo Roper, and Archibald Crosslet, these new technologies of mass feedback syndicated surveying on a broad range of topics, including political elections, labor unions, wartime mobilization, and venereal disease.[49] In the years leading up to the outbreak of World War II, dozens of private polling institutions were established in the United States, the largest being Gallup's American Institute for Public Opinion, and Roosevelt's public opinion survey of its Works Progress Administration.[50] The popularization of scientific surveying unfolded differently in Britain, but the use of questionnaires had also became commonplace. In 1937, the British Institute of Public Opinion was established, and the ambitious research project of Mass Observation launched, the latter being a privately funding nationwide initiative to record and catalogue the "everyday lives of ordinary people in Britain."[51] This

---

[48] Ibid.
[49] Sarah E. Igo, *The Averaged American: Surveys, Citizens, and the Making of a Mass Public* (Cambridge, MA: Harvard University Press, 2008). For a history of the social scientific survey, see Martin Blumer, Kevin Bales, and Kathryn Kish Sklar, eds., *The Social Survey in Historical Perspective, 1880–1940* (Cambridge: Cambridge University Press, 1991); Andrew Whitby, *The Sum of the People: How the Census Has Shaped Nations, from the Ancient World to the Modern Age* (New York: Basic Books, 2020); or Céline Bessière et al., "L'enquête par questionnaire," *Genèses* 29 (December 1997): 99–122.
[50] George Gallup and Claude Robinson, "American Institute for Public Opinion Surveys, 1935–1938," *Public Opinion Quarterly* 2, no. 3 (July 1938): 373–98; Nick Taylor, *American Made: The Enduring Legacy of the WPA: When FDR Put the Nation to Work* (New York: Bantam Book, 2008).
[51] Gary S. Cross, *Worktowners at Blackpool: Mass-Observation and Popular Leisure in the 1930s* (London: Routledge, 1990), 1–11.

controversial program saw the surveillance of unsuspecting British residents and the distribution of hundreds of open-ended questionnaires.

By 1939, universities, private businesses, and regional and federal governments were using questionnaires for every purpose imaginable. Corporations hired industrial psychologists to monitor the mental state of their workers, government agricultural offices surveyed farmers to inform their rural policymaking, national sentiment was being measured, and militaries were appraising soldier morale.[52] As explained by historian Kerstin Brückweh, questionnaires were often presented by marketers during this period as a "democratic instrument that was indispensable to modern societies."[53] Furthermore, by December 1943, SHAEF was using quantitative and qualitative surveys for many purposes, such as identifying problems of mass military mobilization and interrogating German POWs about war crimes and rocket technology.[54]

Standardized surveys had also long been deployed by American and British police departments to compile crime data and collect intelligence on dangerous or suspicious individuals.[55] During the war, law enforcement agencies in both countries used self-administered questionnaires to screen immigrants from enemy countries for potential security threats. Because the PSB employed several police officers, this method of systematic screening was well received. In a December 1945 meeting, Col. Gerald Halland, the British inspector general of the PSB, explained to the UK Control Council that the Fragebogen was "an old police technique similar to that used in 1940 in this country."[56] Police influence is also apparent in the GCU's decision to name denazification units

---

[52] Sarah E. Igo, "Hearing the Masses: The Modern Science of Opinion in the United States," in *Engineering Society: The Role of the Human and Social Sciences in Modern Societies, 1880–1980*, eds. Kerstin Brückweh et al. (New York: Palgrave Macmillan, 2012), 216–17.

[53] Brückweh et al., "Introduction," 29. For further reading on the history of mass surveying, see Martin Bulmer, Kevin Bales, and Kathryn Kish Sklar, eds., *The Social Survey in Historical Perspective, 1880–1940* (Cambridge: Cambridge University Press, 2011) and Jean M. Converse, *Survey Research in the United States: Roots and Emergence, 1890–1960* (Berkeley: University of California Press, 1987).

[54] For example, "Personal Register," November 44, NARA, RG 331, SHAEF, GS, G-5, IB, HS, Box 110, Doc. 5604/164; Report, "Summary of Findings of Civilian Investigations," June 25, 1944, NARA, RG 331, SHAEF, GS, G-5, IB, HS, Box 111, Doc. 5605/99.

[55] Griffith, "The Denazification Program in the United States Zone in Germany," 17. See also David Smith, "'Trusted Servants of the Population': The Public Safety Branch and the German Police in the British Zone of Germany," in *Policing and War in Europe*, ed. Louis A. Knafla (Santa Barbara: Greenwood Press, 2002), 145–69.

[56] Ian D. Turner, "Denazification in the British Zone," in *Reconstruction in Post-War Germany: British Occupation Policy and the Western Zones, 1945–1955*, ed. Ian D. Turner (Oxford: Berg Publishers, 1989), 245.

"Special Branch," nomenclature borrowed from Scotland Yard. Some GCU planners wanted to adopt other, more cutting-edge, police techniques for denazification purposes, such as the then experimental science of fingerprinting. In fact, O. W. Wilson insisted, with little avail, that every German citizen over the age of fourteen be fingerprinted and 4,000 FBI agents deployed as denazification investigators.[57]

The utilization of questionnaires was also compatible with the OSS's vision for denazification. Its researchers imagined a massive administrative campaign that extended to all corners of Germany and impacted every citizen; this could only be implemented through a standardized system to identify Nazis. In agreement with Critical Theory, Neumann's team required that the campaign be personalized by involving each individual German in their own denazification. It needed to allow a self-reflective process, one that would ultimately result in a personal emancipation from Nazi political-economic culture.[58] The OSS also recommended that the vetting of civil servants and professionals be based upon a uniform system of categorization that evaluated Nazi "activeness" according to political membership and military rank and placed each individual into a defined and fixed class of Nazi affiliation.

In March 1944, Sinclair Armstrong and Felix Gilbert delivered the uncompromising agenda of their OSS colleagues. Several members of the GCU refused to extend the purge to all members of Nazi organizations or political screening to the entire economic sphere, but they did agree on nearly all other points.[59] Raffa was particularly receptive, as he had once been a R&A researcher himself. Despite some reluctance on the part of its British officers, the GCU agreed to adopt a system of classification and sanctions. All Germans who came under review would be investigated and placed into a specific category of Nazi affiliation. Armstrong referred to the OSS "black-grey-white" lists that the GCU was already using and the failure of flexible arrest and removal categories in Italy. It was agreed that applicants would be classified into four employment groups:

---

[57] "Fingerprints of Persons in Germany," June 14, 1945, NARA, RG 331, GS, G-5, Secretariat, Box 30, Docs. 21/159–21/165; Letter, Ambassador Murphy to Mr. Beam, April 23, 1945, Bundesarchiv-Koblenz (hereafter, BAK), POLAD 731/18; "Americans Tackle a Big Task: Will Fingerprint Three Million Germans," *Press and Journal*, July 17, 1945, p. 3.
[58] "Directions for the Preparation of Civil Affairs Guides and Other Planning Documents," n.d., NARA, RG 226, OSS, Container 1, pp. 3, 15.
[59] Sinclair agreed with the GCU planners that Neumann's and Marcuse's proposed purge was too extensive and impractical. Biddiscombe, *Denazification of Germany*, 26.

1. Mandatory removal (e.g., SS, SA, NSDAP members prior to 1933)
2. Discretionary removal (mild to moderate Nazi activity, i.e., nominal Nazis)
3. No objection (no evidence of Nazi activity)
4. Employment recommended (evidence of anti-Nazi activity)[60]

Much to the pleasure of Neumann, it was also agreed that all Germans in the SHAEF-administered territories would be directly involved in their own denazification. When some of the Public Safety officers voiced concern about the inevitability of Germans falsifying their questionnaires, Armstrong reassured them that this would cease after a few hundred offenders had been publicly punished.[61]

All of these influences persuaded the GCU that a self-administered screening instrument was appropriate to underwrite denazification or at least was a feasible approach when the simple truth was that no other practical strategy existed. In a staff study circulated on May 28, 1944, the GCU explained that "specific criteria was needed to distinguish between leading or active Nazis and those who are only nominal Nazis" and that "the best method for applying the criteria is to incorporate it into a MG [military government] questionnaire to be filled out by all public officials."[62] Their proposal for denazification, as communicated to SHAEF G-5 Main Office, recommended that "the 'Fragebogen' attached as Appendix 'B' be adopted, with necessary corrections or additions, as the official CA [civil affairs] questionnaire for all Germans in civil administration and for such other German personnel whose 'degree-of-Nazism' needs to be determined."[63] While this decision was being made in the spring of 1944, the *scheda personale* program, which the Fragebogen was in part modeled on, had not yet been uniformly organized in Italy nor had its effectiveness been formally evaluated or limitations addressed.

After agreeing to use a questionnaire for denazification screening, the GCU began formulating procedures for its implementation. In an internal study, it was concluded that there were four basic options for denazification officers who entered a German town or district: (1) They could allow all persons in public office to remain in their posts pending screening; (2) remove all persons from public office pending screening;

---

[60] Niethammer, *Entnazifizierung in Bayern*, 58–59; Griffith, "The Denazification Program in the United States Zone in Germany," 13.
[61] Biddiscombe, *Denazification of Germany*, 24.
[62] Staff Study, "Measures for Identifying and Determining Disposition of Nazi Public Officials in Germany," May 28, 1944, NARA, RG 331, SHAEF, GS, G-5, IB, HS, Box 104, p. 7, Doc. 9959/181.
[63] Ibid., p. 8, Doc. 9959/182.

Drafting the Fragebogen   81

(3) suspend all members of the NSDAP pending screening, or; (4) remove and exclude high-ranking Nazi officials and allow all others to retain employment in public office, subject to later review by military government.[64] The report explained that if the goal was to avoid the kind of leniency that had prevailed in Italy, while also preventing administrative breakdown, the final option was the most practical.[65] It concluded that "on the basis of the Italian experience, the most effective method of utilizing the 'yardstick' in practice is to incorporate the criteria into a Personnel Questionnaire (*Fragebogen*)."[66] The twelve-page report did not explain how denazification agents would in fact acquire the necessary intelligence to evaluate questionnaires.

The Fragebogen was written in May 1944. GCU records indicate that only two thirty-minute meetings were held to discuss the form's content, the extent of its dissemination, and its administrative requirements.[67] The final version had several spelling mistakes. Circulated first within the Interior Section and then sent to General Julius C. Holmes, head of SHAEF G-5, for approval, the questionnaire was exhibited as the primary mechanical device of administrative denazification. Processing these forms was to comprise the main task of American, British, and French Special Branch officers operating within SHAEF-administered territories. It was also suggested that the Soviets might eventually adopt the form. In late August 1944, the Fragebogen went to press and by year's end, three months prior to the full-scale invasion of western Germany, more than 500,000 forms had been printed.[68]

The original SHAEF survey (see Figure 2.1) contained seventy-two questions, divided into ten sections, across four pages. It began with a stern warning, printed in German and English: "Omissions or false or incomplete statements will result in prosecution as violations of military ordinances." The first section asked routine questions about the applicant's identity, such as date of birth, citizenship, permanent address, and occupation. It also inquired about the position that the applicant hoped to fill or retain. The longer second section asked if the respondent had ever been a member of the Nazi Party or held a key political position in the National Socialist government. Those in any high-level political position were to be immediately dismissed, or denied employment, and

---

[64] Ibid., p. 5, Doc. 9959/179.   [65] Ibid., p. 6, Doc. 9959/180.
[66] Ibid., p. 7, Doc. 9959/181.
[67] German Country Unit War Diaries, TNA, WO 171–72, p. 219.
[68] "Public Safety Forms for Military Government," August 19, 1944, NARA, RG 331, SHAEF, AG, War Diaries 1943–1945, Box 46.

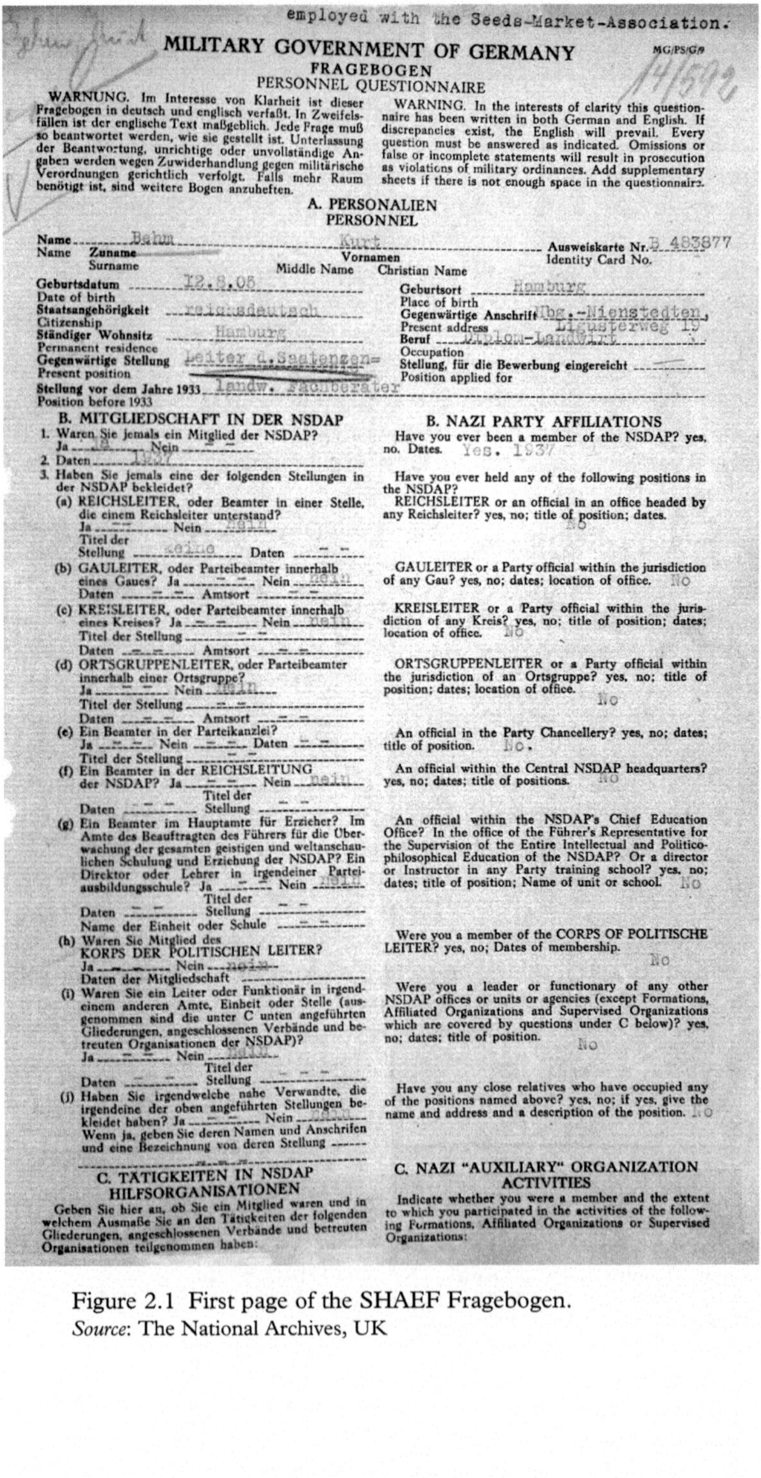
employed with the Seeds-Market-Association.

MILITARY GOVERNMENT OF GERMANY

MG/PS/G/9

FRAGEBOGEN

PERSONNEL QUESTIONNAIRE

14/592

WARNUNG. Im Interesse von Klarheit ist dieser Fragebogen in deutsch und englisch verfaßt. In Zweifelsfällen ist der englische Text maßgeblich. Jede Frage muß so beantwortet werden, wie sie gestellt ist. Unterlassung der Beantwortung, unrichtige oder unvollständige Angaben werden wegen Zuwiderhandlung gegen militärische Verordnungen gerichtlich verfolgt. Falls mehr Raum benötigt ist, sind weitere Bogen anzuheften.

WARNING. In the interests of clarity this questionnaire has been written in both German and English. If discrepancies exist, the English will prevail. Every question must be answered as indicated. Omissions or false or incomplete statements will result in prosecution as violations of military ordinances. Add supplementary sheets if there is not enough space in the questionnaire.

A. PERSONALIEN
PERSONNEL

Name / Name — Zuname / Surname: Bahm — Vornamen / Middle Name / Christian Name: Kurt — Ausweiskarte Nr. / Identity Card No.: B 483877

Geburtsdatum / Date of birth: 12.8.05 — Geburtsort / Place of birth: Hamburg

Staatsangehörigkeit / Citizenship: reichsdeutsch — Gegenwärtige Anschrift / Present address: Hbg.-Nienstedten, Ligusterweg 19

Ständiger Wohnsitz / Permanent residence: Hamburg — Beruf / Occupation: Diplom-Landwirt

Gegenwärtige Stellung / Present position: Leiter d. Saatengen= — Stellung, für die Bewerbung eingereicht / Position applied for: —

Stellung vor dem Jahre 1933 / Position before 1933: landw. Fachberater

B. MITGLIEDSCHAFT IN DER NSDAP — B. NAZI PARTY AFFILIATIONS

1. Waren Sie jemals ein Mitglied der NSDAP? Ja ja Nein — — Have you ever been a member of the NSDAP? yes, no. Dates. Yes. 1937
2. Daten 1937
3. Haben Sie jemals eine der folgenden Stellungen in der NSDAP bekleidet? — Have you ever held any of the following positions in the NSDAP?
(a) REICHSLEITER, oder Beamter in einer Stelle, die einem Reichsleiter unterstand? Ja — Nein nein. Titel der Stellung keine Daten — — REICHSLEITER or an official in an office headed by any Reichsleiter? yes, no; title of position; dates. No
(b) GAULEITER, oder Parteibeamter innerhalb eines Gaues? Ja — Nein nein. Daten — Amtsort — — GAULEITER or a Party official within the jurisdiction of any Gau? yes, no; dates; location of office. No
(c) KREISLEITER, oder Parteibeamter innerhalb eines Kreises? Ja — Nein nein. Titel der Stellung — Daten — Amtsort — — KREISLEITER or a Party official within the jurisdiction of any Kreis? yes, no; title of position; dates; location of office. No
(d) ORTSGRUPPENLEITER, oder Parteibeamter innerhalb einer Ortsgruppe? Ja — Nein nein. Titel der Stellung — Daten — Amtsort — — ORTSGRUPPENLEITER or a Party official within the jurisdiction of an Ortsgruppe? yes, no; title of position; dates; location of office. No
(e) Ein Beamter in der Parteikanzlei? Ja — Nein — Daten — Titel der Stellung — — An official in the Party Chancellery? yes, no; dates; title of position. No.
(f) Ein Beamter in der REICHSLEITUNG der NSDAP? Ja — Nein nein. Daten — Titel der Stellung — — An official within the Central NSDAP headquarters? yes, no; dates; title of positions. No
(g) Ein Beamter im Hauptamte für Erzieher? Im Amte des Beauftragten des Führers für die Überwachung der gesamten geistigen und weltanschaulichen Schulung und Erziehung der NSDAP? Ein Direktor oder Lehrer in irgendeiner Parteiausbildungsschule? Ja — Nein nein. Daten — Titel der Stellung — Name der Einheit oder Schule — — An official within the NSDAP's Chief Education Office? In the office of the Führer's Representative for the Supervision of the Entire Intellectual and Politico-philosophical Education of the NSDAP? Or a director or Instructor in any Party training school? yes, no; dates; title of position; Name of unit or school. No
(h) Waren Sie Mitglied des KORPS DER POLITISCHEN LEITER? Ja — Nein nein. Daten der Mitgliedschaft — Were you a member of the CORPS OF POLITISCHE LEITER? yes, no; Dates of membership. No
(i) Waren Sie ein Leiter oder Funktionär in irgendeinem anderen Amte, Einheit oder Stelle (ausgenommen sind die unter C unten angeführten Gliederungen, angeschlossenen Verbände und betreuten Organisationen der NSDAP)? Ja — Nein nein. Daten — Titel der Stellung — — Were you a leader or functionary of any other NSDAP offices or units or agencies (except Formations, Affiliated Organizations and Supervised Organizations which are covered by questions under C below)? yes, no; dates; title of position. No
(j) Haben Sie irgendwelche nahe Verwandte, die irgendeine der oben angeführten Stellungen bekleidet haben? Ja — Nein nein. Wenn ja, geben Sie deren Namen und Anschrifen und eine Bezeichnung von deren Stellung — Have you any close relatives who have occupied any of the positions named above? yes, no; if yes, give the name and address and a description of the position. No

C. TÄTIGKEITEN IN NSDAP HILFSORGANISATIONEN — C. NAZI "AUXILIARY" ORGANIZATION ACTIVITIES

Geben Sie hier an, ob Sie ein Mitglied waren und in welchem Ausmaße Sie an den Tätigkeiten der folgenden Gliederungen, angeschlossenen Verbände und betreuten Organisationen teilgenommen haben:

Indicate whether you were a member and the extent to which you participated in the activities of the following Formations, Affiliated Organizations or Supervised Organizations:

Figure 2.1 First page of the SHAEF Fragebogen.
Source: The National Archives, UK

referred to the relevant counterintelligence unit for additional screening, which could result in arrest.

The longest and most consequential section of the Fragebogen followed. Under "Nazi 'Auxiliary' Organization Activities," respondents were required to indicate whether they had been a member of any Nazi-affiliated groups, and if so, to record the duration of their membership and any offices held. The listed organizations, thirty-two in total, spanned the full spectrum of political and social life, from paramilitary formations, such as the *Schutzstaffel* (SS) and *Sturmabteilung* (SA), to professional organizations, like the *NS-Ärztebund* (NS-Physicians' League) and *NS-Lehrerbund* (NS-Teachers' League). Also included were labor and welfare agencies, including the *Deutsche Arbeitsfront* (German Labor Front) and the *Deutsche Frauenwerk* (German Women's Welfare Organization), and youth and student groups, such as the *Hitlerjugend* (Hitler Youth, HJ) and *Deutsche Studentenschaft* (German Students' Union).

Using OSS studies to determine which groups had voluntary membership and how closely aligned they were with National Socialist ideology, the GCU wrote up detailed instructions for the evaluation of this section of the Fragebogen. While any form of membership in some organizations, including the SS, called for immediate dismissal, the majority of mandatory removal affiliations were contingent on the specific rank or office held. For example, all persons who had been officers in the SA prior to April 1, 1933, at least down to and including the rank of *Scharführer* (squad leader), were to be removed or excluded from certain offices, while lesser ranks and members who had joined after this date fell into a "discretionary removal" category.[69]

The following three sections of the questionnaire required the respondent to list all writings and speeches that they had published or delivered since 1923, to detail a history of employment since 1930, including the position and duties, and to catalogue all sources of income since January 1, 1933. These questions were designed to identify fascist sympathizers and detect "financial favor at the hands of the Nazis."[70] Next, respondents were asked about membership in military and paramilitary groups since 1919 and if they had served as part of a military government in any occupied territory, including Austria and the Sudetenland. To identify individuals who had been sent to other countries as fifth columnists, or who had been members of a foreign civil

---

[69] OMGB-Special Branch, *German Denazification Law and Implementations with American Directives Included*, June 15, 1946, 168.
[70] Ibid., 172.

administration in a territory annexed to or occupied by the Reich, respondents were asked in the following section about travel outside of Germany since 1933.

The final section of the questionnaire is perhaps the most interesting, as applicants were asked about their political affiliations prior to 1933 and if they had ever participated in an "anti-Nazi underground party or group" or been dismissed from their job or otherwise discriminated against on account of their nonsupport of the government. If the respondent answered "yes" to any of these questions, they were required to provide the names and addresses of two persons who could validate the claim. The end of the questionnaire contained a limited space for "Remarks" (*Anmerkungen*), where the respondent had the opportunity to clarify any of their previous answers before signing the document to certify its truthfulness.

A subtle yet important instruction listed at the beginning of the questionnaire read: "Add supplementary sheets if there is not enough space on the questionnaire." The Fragebogen was therefore not a questionnaire in the traditional sense, as it allowed the respondent to answer at length and to include personal commentary. This simple allowance, one which was not provided to Italians, turned the form into a potential canvas for subjective narrative, an avenue explored in detail in Chapter 5.

Several questions in the Fragebogen were particularly provocative and in fact, they were later contested by military government officers in the field. Among them was a question that required respondents to denounce family members. "Have you any close relatives who have occupied any of the positions named above [executive Nazi government and party positions]? If yes, give the name and address and a description of the position."

Raffa, O. W. Wilson, and the other Public Safety planners within the GCU intended for a large yet logistically simple system of implementation. Questionnaires would be printed at occupational headquarters and distributed by civil affairs officers, preferably Special Branch, to all current or prospective German government officials and employees in the SHAEF administered territories. Fragebögen would be filled out, signed, and returned to the nearest military government office within three days. Upon receiving a completed questionnaire, a denazification officer would review the answers, along with any supplemental sheets, and place the applicant in the appropriate employment category. During this process, civil service, police, and Nazi Party records, as well as information gathered by the Counter Intelligence Corps (CIC) and from voluntary denunciations, were to be consulted. Ultimately, the largest and most valuable cache of political records was stored at the Berlin

Document Center, an American-run repository that housed, among other collections, the membership files of the Nazi Party.[71] This archive was the crown jewel in the Allies' postwar intelligence apparatus but was not fully functional as a source for verifying questionnaires until early 1946. Operating in the spring of 1944, the GCU planners simply assumed that the NSDAP central repository was intact and would be available to them as soon as the fighting ceased. There did not seem to be much worry that the massive bombing campaign against German cities had destroyed crucial intelligence, namely, party and government records. The program also assumed that there would be enough translators and other staff to review submitted questionnaires, as well as enough paper to print the required millions of forms. These assumptions were not discussed at any Public Safety meeting or listed in any GCU progress report.

In late 1944, the GCU also wrote a Fragebogen for use in occupied Austria. Drafted several months after its German precursor, the Austrian form had a similar structure and most of the same questions; the list of Nazi auxiliary organizations was nearly identical.[72] Unique to the form, however, were sections on property ownership, political party donations, and prior criminal convictions. Seeking to root out "hidden Nazis," one question asked, "Have you ever applied for membership in the NSDAP?" Some of the new questions clearly accounted for Austria's distinct history and political status within the expanded Reich, but others were likely included to remedy shortfalls in the German form. In the short time since the German Fragebogen had been printed, the GCU had learned more about the intricacies of the NSDAP, including its common practice of closing its membership rolls to maintain the party's elite status.[73] Asking new questions about financial donations was meant to identify Nazi supporters and sympathizers who did not hold party membership. All four occupying armies in Austria distributed this questionnaire, or a similar version. In total, between 1945 and 1955, it is estimated that more than 540,000 Austrians completed a Fragebogen, around 8 percent of the population.[74] Unlike in Germany, only former members of the NSDAP were required to fill out the form.

---

[71] Henry Friedlander and Sybil Milton, eds., *Archives of the Holocaust, Vol. 11: Berlin Document Center, Part I* (New York: Garland Publishing, 1992), ix–xv.

[72] In addition to the auxiliary groups listed in the German form was the *Arbeitsgemeinschaft NS-Studententinnen*.

[73] For a blank copy of the *Fragebogen* for Austria, see NARA, RG 260, USF-Austria, USCA-Austria Section, IA/DP Division, DB, Box 10.

[74] There is currently no study on the Austrian Fragebogen program, but it is discussed briefly in Dieter Stiefel, *Entnazifizierung in Österreich* (Vienna: Europaverlag, 1981). Further reading on denazification in Austria should include, Maria Mesner and Matthew Paul Berg, *Entnazifizierung zwischen politischem Anspruch, Parteienkonkurrenz*

The work of the GCU also impacted planning for the administrative purge in postwar Japan. Over a two-and-a-half-year period, beginning in February 1946, US occupying forces and trusted Japanese officials distributed political questionnaires to hundreds of thousands of political, financial, media, and education elites. The five-page, twenty-four question form was modeled on the German Fragebogen, containing a similar structure and many of the same questions.[75] When the purge ended in May 1948, some 210,000 individuals had been removed or barred from public office.[76]

By the fall of 1945, military governments in Italy, Germany, Austria, and Japan were all using questionnaires to carryout political screening. The denazification Fragebogen should therefore not be understood as a stand-alone experiment, but part of a larger global effort by the Allied victors, especially the United States, to screen for and remove fascist and militarist elements and influences from the defeated Axis nations.

As soon as the approved German Fragebogen was sent to the printers in August 1944, the program was integrated into every occupation directive and guidebook, effectively changing administrative procedures for all military government offices within SHAEF and every British, American, and French army detachment.[77] The two most important publications, the *Handbook for Military Government in Germany* and the *Public Safety Manual of Procedures*, explained the program's core objectives and provided instructions on how civil affairs officers and regular soldiers were to collect intelligence using the questionnaire. In Section 287 of the *Handbook*, the basic procedures for the program were outlined:

Each official and candidate for appointment will be required to record on a questionnaire (*Fragebogen*) detailed and specific information concerning his background and participation in Nazi activities and organizations. The information disclosed by the questionnaire will be checked against other

---

und Kaltem Krieg: das Beispiel der SPÖ (Vienna: R. Oldenbourg, 2005); Éric Dussault, *La dénazification de l'Autriche par la France: la politique culturelle de la France dans sa zone d'occupation, 1945–1955* (Sainte-Foy: Presses de l'Université Laval, 2005); and Robert Knight, *Denazification and Integration in the Austrian Province of Carinthia* (Chicago: University of Chicago Press, 2007).

[75] For a copy of the US questionnaire for Japan, see Memorandum, "Removal and Exclusion of Government Personnel from Public Office," November 45, NARA, RG 331, SCAP, GS, AD, Purge Misc. File, 1945–51, Box 2053.

[76] Hiroshi Masuda, *MacArthur in Asia: The General and His Staff in the Philippines, Japan, and Korea* (Ithaca, NY: Cornell University Press, 2012), 211.

[77] These orders also affected the denazification operations of all SHAEF partners, including Australia, Canada, and Poland.

Drafting the Fragebogen 87

sources of information, such as counter-intelligence, Nazi Party and police records, civil service certificates, publications and informants.[78]

More detailed instructions were provided in the *Public Safety Manual*, which ordered denazification officers to distribute Fragebögen to all civil servants immediately upon arrival in an occupied territory. It warned that "all German officials and employees will be required to fill out the Fragebogen truthfully and completely under pain of penalty for violation of the Military Ordinances."[79] A copy of the questionnaire was provided in the *Manual*'s appendices, along with a list of the key Nazi government positions and party ranks that mandated summary dismissal.[80] The GCU estimated that only one Special Branch officer and eight support staff (file clerks, stenographers, interpreters) for every 200,000 German residents were needed to process Fragebögen.[81] This would later prove to be a gross underestimation.

As early as spring of 1944, the GCU offered special training to civil affairs recruits on the various functions of military government.[82] This instruction took place at the US School Center at Shrivenham and at Prince's Garden in London, and included classes on administration and local government, legal principles, fiscal management, and displaced persons, as well as German language courses.[83] Recruits underwent an intensive two-week training program, which included twenty-seven hours of instruction on the Nazi Party, its history, structure, and the scale of its domestic authority, and thirty-seven hours on Special Branch activities. Seven hours were allotted to distributing, verifying, and classifying Fragebögen. More time was spent educating trainees on the questionnaire program than any other Special Branch task. The two GCU officers assigned as the principal instructors for this class were the authors of the questionnaire itself, Maj. Aldo Raffa and Capt. M. Keith Wilson.[84]

The influence of the GCU continued after SHAEF was disbanded in July 1945, when many of its members were transferred to American and British military government offices in Germany. Although relatively

---

[78] SHAEF, *Handbook for Military Government in Germany: Prior to Defeat or Surrender* (SHAEF, December 1944), Part III, Section IV, Paragraph 287.
[79] Ibid., 42. [80] Ibid., Appendices V, W, and X.
[81] Ibid., Section VI, Paragraph 226, p. 49, and Appendix K.
[82] It was one of the original tasks of the GCU to train and assign civil affairs personnel. Report, "Formation of the German Unit," February 22, 1944, NARA, RG 331, SHAEF, GS, G-5, IB, HS, Box 104, Doc. 957.
[83] "Historical Statement of the German Country Unit," August 44, NARA, RG 331, SHAEF, GS, G-5, IB, HS, Box 133, Docs. 5611/59–63.
[84] "Special Branch Personnel and Training – Appendix D: Instructors for Training Program," August 17, 1944, NARA, RG 331, SHAEF, GS, G-5, Secretariat, Box 32.

small in number, these GCU veterans were the most experienced in denazification procedures and therefore appointed to authoritative positions. For example, O. W. Wilson was made Chief of Public Safety for OMGUS and M. K. Wilson Chief of its Denazification Section, possibly the two most important positions for denazification in the US zone.[85]

The Fragebogen project evolved quickly because of various influences on and within the German Country Unit. The Allied leadership for the program provided the governing objectives, the Italian defascistization campaign the methodology, and the OSS the intelligence and scope, all while being nurtured and pushed forward by an internal academic and police culture. But despite what seems to be a unified strategy, one must not lose sight of a much simpler and less idealistic truth: the Fragebogen was the only practical program option offered by the GCU and its advisors. It is important to recognize that this linchpin of denazification was a product not of mutual agreement but of the absence of strong opposition, which transpired due to a lack of any alternative strategy and the existence of a precedent; the Italian questionnaire gave bureaucratic creditability to the Fragebogen program.

The Handbook Controversy

The SHAEF leadership agreed to use the GCU-drafted questionnaire, but such consensus did not last long. In August 1944, the Anglo-American denazification project was suddenly upset when US Secretary of the Treasury, Henry Morgenthau, visited SHAEF headquarters in London.[86] He returned to Washington with a mimeograph of the *Handbook for Military Government in Germany*, which he used to attack the Western Allies' entire occupation strategy. He argued that the proposed political purge allowed for too much discretion on the part of local military government officers and that only the NSDAP leadership was being targeted, not the middle- and lower-rank Nazis who he believed also posed a threat to the future of democracy. Reciting key passages from the *Handbook* that he found particularly offensive, Morgenthau petitioned President Roosevelt to toughen up denazification measures. He struck out at the Fragebogen directly, claiming that the form was too accommodating to Germans, as it allowed for supplemental materials. The GCU's recommendation that an appellate courts system

---

[85] Griffith, "The Denazification Program in the United States Zone in Germany," 10.
[86] Ziemke, *The U.S. Army in the Occupation of Germany*, 86; Zink, *American Military Government in Germany*, 131–32.

be established infuriated him most; such a democratic mechanism seemed inappropriate for former Nazis.

Roosevelt was immediately convinced and pledged to expand the scope of denazification. In an August 26 memorandum to his Secretary of War, Henry L. Stimson, the president wrote:

This so-called Handbook is pretty bad. I should like to know how it came to be written and who approved it down the line. If it has not been sent out as approved, all copies should be withdrawn and held until you get a chance to go over it. ... It gives the impression that Germany is to be restored as much as the Netherlands or Belgium, and the people of Germany brought back as quickly to their prewar state.[87]

To rally public support behind an enlarged campaign, the president incited the amenable wartime press. Remembered by one GCU official, Roosevelt "became so aroused that he called in the press to castigate the offenders publicly."[88] No less than a dozen daily newspapers disseminated stories of the shortcomings of joint-Allied denazification policy and praised the uncompromising American reforms. The *New York Times*, for example, reported on Stimson's promise that the "[Military] Government will be both 'tough' in its administration and 'ruthless' in carrying out a projected 'de-nazification program'."[89] Key figures in the British War Office agreed with the American hardliners, at least in principle, and this was enough to commission a joint revision of the SHAEF *Handbook*. The amended December 1944 volume took a much stricter stance regarding which Germans would be allowed to retain office, expanding the number of categories that required automatic arrest and mandatory removal. As a subsidiary guide, the *Public Safety Manual* was also republished.[90] Its February 1945 second edition lengthened the list of titles and ranks that constituted "active" Nazi status.

Some GCU planners agreed with Morgenthau about the need to intensify denazification, including the head of the Financial Section, Col. Bernard Bernstein, but the majority did not.[91] Instead, they feared that too comprehensive a purge would result in the collapse of what was left of Germany's economic infrastructure and arouse anti-Western sentiment that would impede military government's long-term goal to instill

---

[87] Quoted in Ziemke, *The U.S. Army in the Occupation of Germany*, 86.
[88] Zink, *American Military Government in Germany*, 132.
[89] Sidney Shalett, "'Tough' U.S. Rule Set up for Reich," *New York Times*, May 12, 1945, p. 1
[90] SHAEF, *Handbook for Military Government in Germany: Prior to Defeat or Surrender* (December 1944); SHAEF, *Public Safety Manual of Procedures, Military Government of Germany*, 2nd ed. (February 1945).
[91] Ziemke, *The U.S. Army in the Occupation of Germany*, 86.

a democratic political culture. Furthermore, an expanded campaign would likely clog denazification's bureaucratic machinery.[92]

Inter-Allied policy concerns mattered little, however, when, in the wake of Morgenthau's well-orchestrated policy attack, the decision was made at the February 1945 Yalta Conference that after the surrender, military government, and therefore denazification, would be organized at the zonal level. In the following months, the GCU was dissolved, and its staff reassigned to independent American and British planning groups. The war was still being fought, of course, and therefore SHAEF continued to exist, but the job of revising the *Handbook* and organizing denazification activities for the pre-surrender period was reassigned to a small SHAEF office that employed no specialists in German government or civil service.

After more than a year of waiting for a definite set of instructions from executive authorities, much of the work of the GCU was thrown out. Remembered by one denazification officer:

The net result [of the 'handbook controversy'] was that not only was the effort of many months of hard labor of several hundred persons under the most trying circumstances because of the lack of basic policy decisions more or less wasted but more important the military government personnel earmarked for Germany had no plans of any character at a time when it was extremely important that they became acquainted with their mission.[93]

The US and British denazification campaigns quickly drifted apart. While the *Handbook* and *Manual* were being revised by the few civilian planners still working within SHAEF, the newly formed United States, Group Control Council (USGCC) began designing its own occupation strategy with a revised curriculum for political screening. Former GCU members now working for USGCC were under significant pressure from Washington to take more severe actions against former Nazis. This was fueled by the home press, which continued to propagate in sensationalist articles that prominent Nazis and war criminals were already evading justice. In late September 1944, when the first few border towns were being occupied, Raymond Daniell reported in the *New York Times* about the "lackadaisical attitude" toward the enforcement of denazification and that "Nazis still hold some of the best jobs in commerce and industry."[94]

---

[92] Letter, O.W. Wilson to Lt. Col. W.T. Babcock, March 8, 1945, NARA, RG 331, SHAEF, GS, G-5, Secretariat, Box 30, Doc. 21/211.
[93] Zink, *American Military Government in Germany*, 132.
[94] Raymond Daniel, "Nazis Hit By U.S. Officers," *New York Times*, September 21, 1944, p. 10; Raymond Daniel, "Nazis Still Hold Key Jobs in Reich," *New York Times*, September 20, 1945, p. 11.

Matters were made worse in October, when a right-wing, antidemocratic German politician was "accidentally" installed as mayor of Aachen, the first large city occupied by US soldiers. The press gave generous print space to the story, which in turn generated a flurry of criticism about military government and its campaign to eradicate Nazism.[95]

Responding quickly to the scandal, a new American-drafted, SHAEF-endorsed called FACS 93 was issued, which extended the scope of the purge by targeting nearly all former Nazis for dismissal, regardless of their rank and function within the Party. FACS 93 attempted to nullify the element of discretion in the removal of former Nazis from office, stating that "in no circumstances should active Nazis be retained on grounds of administrative expediency."[96] Five months later, a new directive, "Removal from Office of Nazis and German Militarists," was delivered to all units of the US Sixth, Twelfth, and Twenty-First Army Groups, which doubled the list of offices and ranks that mandated mandatory removal and deprived local commanders of any residual powers of discretion.[97] This American-led intensification of denazification was implemented under the SHAEF banner but never fully endorsed by Churchill or de Gaulle.

The USGCC understood that the Fragebogen had to account for the broadened removal categories, which meant listing more political offices, military ranks, and Nazi-affiliated organizations. Furthermore, the new directives called for a determined effort to purge economic systems of Nazi influences and therefore the survey had to ask more questions about the respondent's business dealings. In March 1945, the USGCC's Public Safety office began discussing ways to improve the Fragebogen. All the while, American, British, and French troops were occupying towns in western Germany and distributing thousands of copies of the SHAEF questionnaire.

The Americans hoped that their modified form would eventually be adopted by all Western armies and maybe even the Russians, but first, renewed criticism within their own ranks had to be addressed. Robert D. Murphy, Chief US Political Adviser to Germany (POLAD), argued that the revised Fragebogen was far too long and also that it did not provide adequate space for the applicant to respond to some of the more

---

[95] For more information on the "Aachen incident," see Taylor, *Exorcising Hitler*, 13–17.

[96] Letter, British Embassy (Washington, DC) to Charles Peake (Foreign Office, London), September 8, 1944, TNA, WO 219/3853, Doc. 5639/400.

[97] Directive, "Retention in Office of Nazis and German Militarists," February 23, 1945, NARA, RG 260, USGCC, AG, General Correspondence, 1944–45, Box 5; Directive, "Removal from Office of Nazis and German Militarists," March 24, 1945, NARA, RG 260, USGCC, AG, General Correspondence, 1944–45, Box 3.

indefinite questions.[98] He expressed concern that it placed too much emphasis on "anti-Nazi activities," but also wished to see more questions added that could help "discover persons likely to be of service under Military Government."[99] Simply put, Murphy wanted a shorter document, but one that did not sacrifice any the questionnaire's content or capability as an analytical instrument. Such an uncompromising wish list was familiar to the former GCU planners, who had struggled to create a screening device that was both comprehensive and functional. Raffa and Wilson defended their redesign and tried adamantly to repel any additional late-stage revisions. Demonstrated in a March 8, 1945 letter to Lt. Col. William T. Babcock, head of USGCC Public Safety, Wilson wrote that "the Fragebogen ... should not be designed with the primary view to conserve paper or for the convenience of the German filling it out, but to provide all pertinent data in a form most convenient for Military Government to evaluate."[100]

The British were critical of nearly every proposal to revise the questionnaire and equally cautious of changing the parameters of its denazification campaign. As a member of SHAEF, it had, at least in theory, endorsed FACS 93 and the "Removal from Office of Nazi and German Militarists" directive, but the War Office generally disagreed with the creeping intensification of American denazification strategy.[101] Reluctance to accept the new categories of automatic arrest and dismissal was conveyed in a September 27, 1944 letter from Col. Frank Hollins of the British Control Commission for Germany to his American counterpart: "The attached note is not, of course, intended to question the policy of turning out Nazis from the German administration as quickly as possible. It does suggest, however, that in order to secure this result, it is not necessary or desirable to turn out large blocks of existing civil servants automatically."[102]

British refusal to adopt the revised Fragebogen only confirmed the policy divide, as did the subsequent rejection of the US interim document, JCS 1067, which laid out the tough new principles of American occupation policy. However, there had also been British criticism of the original questionnaire. At a December 16, 1944 meeting hosted by what was left of SHAEF's Public Safety office, the commander of the

---

[98] Letter, Political Division (Robert Murphy) to Public Safety, IA&C, April 21, 1945, BAK, POLAD 731/15, Doc. 765011.
[99] Ibid.
[100] Letter, O.W. Wilson to Lt. Col. William T. Babcock, March 8, 1945, NARA, RG 331, SHAEF, GS, G-5, Secretariat, Box 30, Doc. 21/208.
[101] Turner, "Denazification in the British Zone," 246.
[102] Letter, Hollins, CCG(BE) to Field, February 27, 1944, WO 219/3853, Doc. 5639/407.

Twenty-First Army Group voiced concern that the Fragebogen was "too detailed and complicated" a document and that there were not enough Special Branch officers to administer the forms.[103] He recommended that a new questionnaire be drafted, one of a "much simplified character." British leadership within G-5 was quick to reject this:

> It is not agreed that any attempt should be made at this stage to alter the fragebogen ... the fragebogen has been prepared after considerable discussion and examination, and whilst admitting that it is a detailed and complicated document, it is felt that no change should be made until investigating officers have gained sufficient experience to enable them to carry out their task with a shorter document.[104]

Most British policymakers subscribed to this line of reasoning. Brigadier C. D. Heyman, Chief of SHAEF's Internal Affairs Branch, announced that "the experience gained in Germany hitherto is insufficient to justify a revision of the Fragebogen of which there are over 500,000 still in stock, at this juncture."[105] A similar pragmatism was communicated by the British War Cabinet. At an April 16, 1945 War Room meeting, it was agreed that while the questionnaire indeed required revision, it was not practical to print new forms until the existing supply had been used up.[106] Some committee heads wanted to include new questions related to "civilian employment" in Nazi offices. Others recommended that the applicant be required to list at least three personal references, people who would "be in a position to vouch for the statements which he [the respondent] makes."[107] Still other officials were adamant that no new questions be added at all, as the existing Fragebogen was already too long.[108] Nevertheless, the decision was made to continue to use the original survey, at least until the current supply was depleted. This demonstrates neither complete satisfaction with the SHAEF form nor a rejection of the proposed American revision; instead, the decision was made out of ambivalence and convenience.

---

[103] Letter, CCG(BE) to SHAEF/G-5, December 22, 1944, NARA, RG 331, SHAEF, G-5, Secretariat, Box 32, Doc. 21/1108.

[104] Letter, Lt. Gen. A.E. Grasett (SHAEF, G-5) to Deputy Commissioner (Military) and CCG(BE), December 29, 1944, NARA, RG 331, SHAEF, G-5, Secretariat, Box 32, Doc. 21/1105.

[105] Letter, G.D. Heyman to SHAEF Mission to France, "Elimination of Nazi Personnel – Fragebogen," March 23, 1945, NARA, RG 331, SHAEF, G-5, Secretariat, Box 30, Doc. 21/427.

[106] Letter, SAINT (Paris) to War Room (London), "Military Government Information," April 20, 1945, TNA, KV 4/268.

[107] Letter, E.B. Stamp to W.R.C., April 12, 1945, TNA, KV 4/268.

[108] Letter, Blum (SHAEF, Counter Intelligence War Room, London) to Lt. John Martin (OSS/X-2), April 26, 1945, TNA, KV 4/268.

94   Drafting the Questionnaire

When SHAEF was dissolved in the fall of 1945, British authorities once again considered revising the Fragebogen. Their stock of printed questionnaires was beginning to run out and therefore it seemed an appropriate time to replace the original form, which the Americans had rejected six months earlier. In part because of public pressure to enact a more rigorous campaign, but also a desire to standardize screening activities across the three western zones, the newly established British military government, or Control Commission for Germany (British Element), (CCG[BE]), redrafted the questionnaire. Comprised of 133 questions, the new British Fragebogen, which came into effect on January 1, 1946, placed more emphasis on secondary and higher education and required applicants to list the names of two references, which was meant to discourage falsifications. In the words of one of the drafters, "The Fragebogen itself left plenty of loopholes for deceit; it was the attempt to close these which lengthened the list of questions until it totaled 133."[109] Still, the British form was modeled on and was essentially a duplicate of the American survey.

The revised US questionnaire (Figure 2.2; also, see Appendix), drafted in May 1945, was notably different from its SHAEF predecessor.[110] It contained more questions than the original form, 131 in total, and spanned six pages. Much like its mother document, the new Fragebogen asked questions about membership in Nazi-affiliated organizations, past employment, income, military service, writings and speeches, foreign travel, and anti-Nazi activities. New sections were added, however, including one on "Secondary and Higher Education," in which respondents listed every school they had attended since they were children, as well as membership in student organizations. It was believed that enrollment in a "politicized school" (e.g., *Adolf-Hitler-Schule*), or admission to a university after March 1939, indicated National Socialist beliefs.[111] Respondents were also asked if they had been admitted into a profession or trade since 1935, which, according to Public Safety, suggested they were viewed by the regime as politically reliable.[112] Questions pertaining to employment in specific NSDAP offices were reduced, as the senior positions listed were seen to be too scarce to be included in such a widely distributed survey.

---

[109] Balfour and Mair, *Four-Power Control in Germany and Austria*, 174–76.
[110] For all of Wilson's suggested alterations, see Statement by Col. O.W. Wilson (Public Safety Branch, GCU), May 7, 1945, NARA, RG 260, USGCC, AG, General Correspondence, 1944–45, Box 5.
[111] OMGB-Special Branch, *German Denazification Law and Implementations with American Directives Included*, 166.
[112] Ibid.

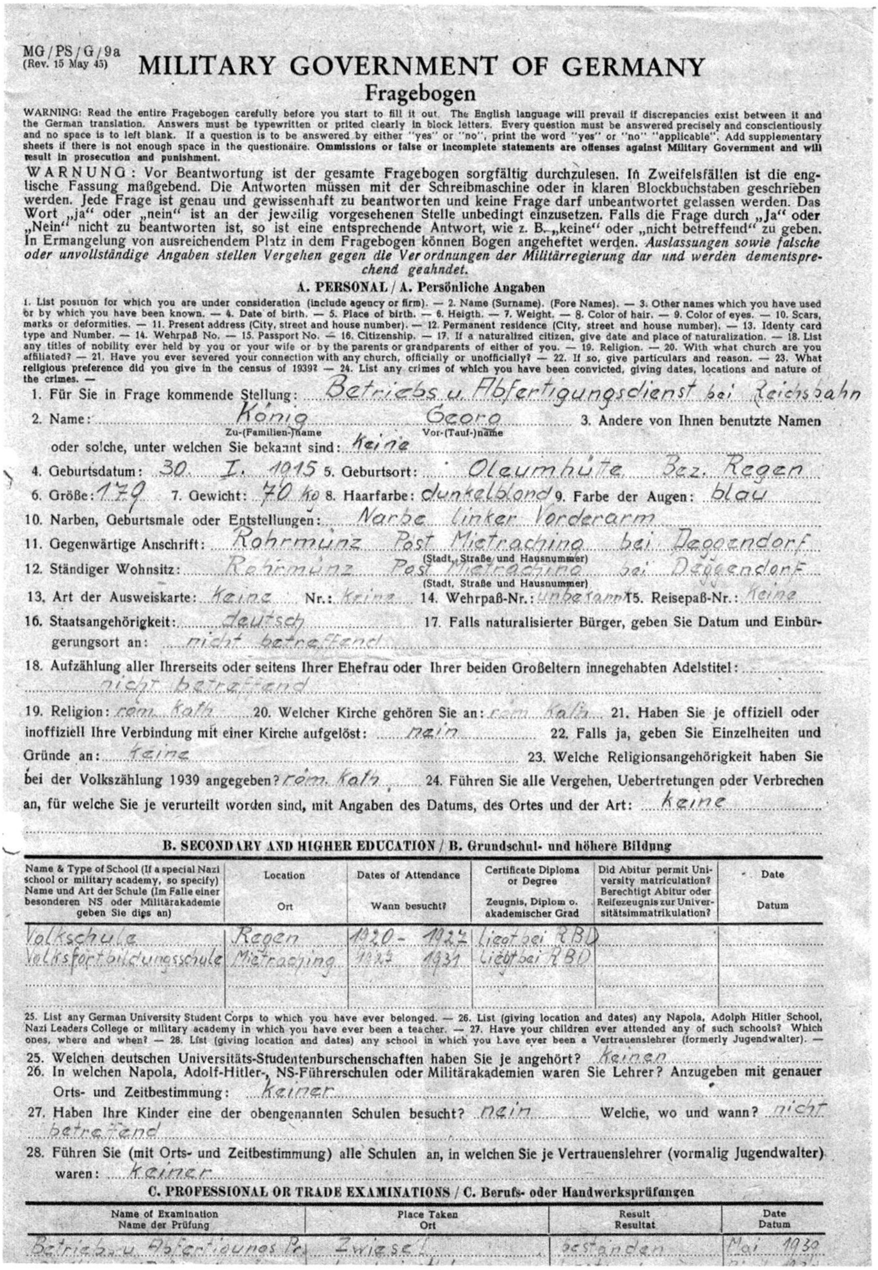

The Handbook Controversy

Figure 2.2 First page of the US Fragebogen.
Source: US National Archives

Twenty-three Nazi groups were added to the original list of thirty-one, bringing the total number to fifty-four. These additions were mostly cultural groups (e.g., *Reichskulturkammer*, *Reichspressekammer*, *Reichsmusikkammer*) and international organizations (e.g., *Amerika-Institut*, *Kameradschaft USA*, *Osteuropäisches Institut*).[113] The following section included new questions pertaining mainly to part-time and unpaid service within specialized government offices, as well as services rendered in military, paramilitary, law enforcement, intelligence, and civil defense organizations. The instructions for answering these questions reflected the recently improved American knowledge of Nazi political and social systems. The form concluded with a series of questions related to the candidate's private business dealings with the Nazi government, as well as land ownership: large landholdings were believed to reveal "Junker class status," a Fragebogen synonym for militarist.[114] A common German retort of the time ran, "in the old days it was a Jewish grandmother that caused problems, now it is having a noble one."[115]

Viewed in its entirety, the American Fragebogen contained more questions relating to education, employment and income, military service, and membership in Nazi organizations. The instructions were more detailed and questions more explicit. For example, while the original form simply asked, "Have you rendered military service since 1919?" the American redraft required the applicant to also list the name of his military unit, rank, duties and responsibilities, and the name of his commanding officer. Again, Germans in the US zone would joke about these added questions, that the Fragebogen may as well ask, "did you play with toy soldiers as a child? If so, what regiment?"[116]

The American form also included questions relating to the persecution of Jews, likely accounting for knowledge gained in early 1945 about Nazi crimes in Poland and the decision to prosecute the Nazi leadership for war crimes. Questions 87 and 93 asked respondents if they had ever been

---

[113] *Reichskulturkammer* (Reich Chamber of Culture), *Reichspressekammer* (Reich Media Chamber), *Reichsmusikkammer* (Reich Chamber of Music), *Amerika-Institut* (American Institute), *Kameradschaft USA* (USA Camaraderie), *Osteuropäisches Institut* (East European Institute).

[114] "Junker families" were invariably associated with Prussian militarism. Even if a respondent had not been an NSDAP member, if identified as a "Junker," they were immediately placed in a discretionary removal category. OMGB-Special Branch, *German Denazification Law and Implementations with American Directives Included*, 172.

[115] As quoted in Giles MacDonogh, *After the Reich: The Brutal History of the Allied Occupation* (New York: Basic Books, 2007), 346.

[116] As quoted in, Victor Gollancz, *In Darkest Germany* (London: Victor Gollancz, 1947), 102.

a member of the *Institut zur Erforschung der Judenfrage* (Institute for the Study of the Jewish Question) or the *Staatsakademie für Rassen- und Gesundheitspflege* (State Academy for Race and Health Services), while Question 121 inquired, "Have you or any immediate members of your family ever acquired property which has been seized from others for political, religious, or raciag [*sic*] reasons...?" Question 123 asked, "Have you ever acted as an administrator or trustee of Jewish property in furtherance of Aryanization decrees or ordinances?" These questions were not intended to identify war criminals for arrest, but simply to establish the respondent's affiliation and affinity to National Socialism. Still, their inclusion is significant, as the original SHAEF questionnaire made no mention of Nazi racial ideology or persecution.[117]

The new questionnaire further encouraged respondents to denounce family members for political and ideological transgressions. While the SHAEF form asked if any relatives had worked in a high-level party office, the American survey extended this question to all fifty-four of the listed Nazi-affiliated organizations. Under threat of imprisonment, the respondent was required to provide the names and addresses of all relatives who "held office, rank, or post of authority" in any Nazi affiliated group. Another question asked, "For what political party did you vote in the election of November 1932?" which one former GCU member believed inappropriate because it necessitated personal information of a political nature from a democratic secret ballot election.[118]

The revised Fragebogen was drafted and printed far too late. While the new form was being debated in Washington, American GIs were occupying dozens of German villages and towns and purging local administrations and businesses. Furthermore, when the new questionnaire was approved for circulation by United States Forces European Theater (USFET) in May 1945, it did not immediately reach officers attached to tactical units. During an interim period of administrative confusion, US Public Safety officers either continued to use the original SHAEF Fragebogen or simply relied on local informants to weed out active Nazis. The modified *Handbook* and *Manual*, which remained the principal guides for early denazification operations, provided instructions on how to process only the SHAEF Fragebogen. To make matters worse, because it was well known that an amended form would soon arrive,

---

[117] Questions pertaining to crimes against Jews did appear in revised Fragebögen distributed in some districts in the British zone. See Leßau, *Entnazifizierungsgeschichten*, 77.
[118] "Denazification – Deletion of Questions 108 and 109 from Standard Fragebogen," July 8, 1947, TNA, FO 1006/301.

political screening at the local level was often carried out indiscriminately and at the discretion of regional military government offices. Therefore, denazification did not achieve consistency during the pre-surrender period, even though all invasion armies were under the coordinated direction of SHAEF.

In the months following the German surrender, questionnaires became imbedded in the American denazification bureaucracy, despite much internal criticism. When SHAEF was dissolved in July 1945, and American forces withdrew to their designated zone, USFET/USGCC began standardizing procedures and distributing the revised questionnaire to military government offices in Bavaria, Hesse, Württemberg-Baden, and the Bremen Enclave. The "Public Safety Plan for Occupation for Allied Control and Occupation of Germany" (or Annex XXIII) integrated all denazification policies into a unitary program and identified the Fragebogen as its cornerstone.[119] By the time OMGUS was formed, in October 1945, the questionnaire alone determined the employment eligibility of applicants.

The American "handbook controversy" of August 1944 was activated by Morgenthau and exacerbated by the popular press, but it can also be interpreted as a product of a long-standing neglect of military government planning. Understandably busy fighting the war, by the time high-level attention shifted to denazification, the campaign could not be easily overhauled. What resulted was a series of impulsive decisions made by the American political and military leadership. Denazification became an even more bureaucratic endeavor, whose contradictory principals, late arrival, and lack of resources left civil affairs officers scrambling in the field. In the words of one official, the formalization of the new American tough peace model, led to a "virtual paralysis" of denazification.[120] The approach of the other Allied nation armies was eventually distorted by these fundamental problems of the American campaign, either because they were unprepared for denazification themselves or their own initiatives were consumed by their larger and more powerful benefactor. Despite resounding criticism of the early American denazification project, by the summer of 1945, the British, French, and Soviets were all circulating second generation questionnaires modeled largely on the revised American form.

---

[119] Directive, "ANNEX XXIII (Public Safety)," March 15, 1945, NARA, RG 260, USGCC, Box 32.
[120] Zink, *American Military Government in Germany*, 135.

French and Soviet Questionnaires

With little independent thought or direction, questionnaires were adopted by French and Soviet administrators. For a number of reasons, paramount among them the priority task of expelling the Wehrmacht from their respective nations, the two outsider Allied nations were underprepared for the complex task of denazification. Nevertheless, their investment in such a campaign was much greater because the French and Russians had to live with the results of denazification on their real (or proxy) borders.

For decades, scholarship on denazification has depicted the Fragebogen as a uniquely American project, one that was reluctantly adopted by the British, who used it only sparingly. There has been little scholarly investigation of French or Soviet wartime denazification planning or of the mechanics of their screening programs. In fact, only a few studies have acknowledged that the French and Soviets used questionnaires to screen their occupied populations.[121] This lack of knowledge is due in large part to the availability of sources. Many records remain classified or otherwise inaccessible in Russian archives and therefore researchers are forced to make do with the limited files that exist in German collections. Nevertheless, thousands of Soviet denazification records, including questionnaires, are available, and by piecing them together, a clearer picture of the Russian Fragebogen program emerges. A much better situation exists in France. A 2015 national decree released archival collections related to World War II, including hundreds of thousands of denazification records.[122] Because of this act, a more dedicated study of screening activities in the *zone française d'occupation* (ZFO) is now possible, one that can eliminate the somewhat speculative conclusions of the past. What follows in this section, and dispersed within subsequent chapters, is an investigation of the French and Soviet Fragebogen programs.

---

[121] Among them, Vogt, *Denazification in Soviet-Occupied Germany*, and Sébastien Chauffour et al., eds., *La France et la dénazification de l'Allemagne après 1945* (Brussels: Peter Lang, 2019). Two large research projects are currently (2023) underway in Europe that involve the mass digitization of French denazification records, including Fragebögen. One involves a partnership between the *Archives diplomatiques* and *Landesarchiv Baden-Württemberg*, while the other is an independent research endeavor by a group of scholars from universities in France, Germany, and the United States. Both projects have the potential to expand our understanding of denazification in the French occupation zone.

[122] "Arrêté du 24 décembre 2015 portant ouverture d'archives relatives à la Seconde Guerre mondiale," *Journal officiel de la République française* no. 0300 (December 27, 2015).

The newly amalgamated French First Army was a member of the Supreme Allied Command and therefore bound to the occupation measures outlined in the *Handbook* and *Manual*. The government-in-exile played no part in writing these guidelines. In fact, not a single French official appears on the GCU's summer 1944 personnel list of some 175 employees.[123] This relationship was complicated, however, and perhaps set right, by the fact that unlike regular soldiers, French civil affairs officers were not subordinate to SHAEF but to the *Cinquième Bureau* of their own *Administration militaire française en Allemagne* (AMFA). This was not the case for equivalent American and British officers. Due to this conflicting hierarchy, French postwar planners, and later military government officials, had no reservations in implementing their own occupation strategy, while merely paying lip service to the policies of their US and British sponsors.

To be sure, many influential figures within Charles de Gaulle's administration agreed with the Americans in that the purge should be rigorous and far-reaching, but ultimately a more moderate program was adopted. The chosen approach was surprisingly pragmatic considering the deep animosity felt toward Germany by the French people. As early as April 1944, the *Gouvernement de la République française* expressed a great deal of concern about the proposed SHAEF campaign of mass arrests and dismissals. It believed that such a strategy would only be effective in the short term, as it did not sufficiently root out what was understood as a German cultural disposition to aggressive nationalism and militarism. France was also the only major Allied nation that shared a border with Germany, and de Gaulle was keenly aware that any blanket campaign of revenge would only discourage long-term reconciliation. Added to this was the difficult consideration for France's own domestic purge of Nazi collaborators, which was already underway.[124] For these reasons, wartime planners advocated a denazification strategy based on mass reeducation, not mass punishment, and an evaluation of the merits of each individual case.[125]

---

[123] "Biographical Data for Personnel of German and Austrian Units," June 15, 1944, NARA, RG 331, SHAEF, GS, G-5, IB, HS, Box 133, Doc. 5611/148–78.

[124] On how the domestic Vichyite purge affected the French denazification campaign in Germany, see Grohnert, *Die Entnazifizierung in Baden*, here 54–56. A reading of the postwar *épuration légale* in France should begin with Jean-Paul Cointet, *Expier Vichy: l'épuration en France, 1943–1958* (Paris: Perrin, 2008); Peter Novick, Helene Ternois, and Jean Pierre Rioux, *L'epuration francaise, 1944–1949* (Paris: Balland, 1985); and Peter Novick, *The Resistance versus Vichy: The Purge of Collaborators in Liberated France* (New York: Columbia University Press, 1968).

[125] Willis, *The French in Germany*, 149–50.

Early French criticism of the proposed joint-Allied denazification program targeted the Fragebogen specifically. General Louis-Marie Koeltz, head of the *Mission Militaire pour les Affaires Allemandes* (Military Mission for Germany), wrote to SHAEF headquarters in March 1945, suggesting that changes be made to the form. He asked for the addition of five new questions related to military service and administrative duties in occupied countries during the war, explaining that they would "facilitate the investigation of the activities of certain Germans during the occupation of our country [France]."[126] The response from London was quick and decisive and it echoed what other critics had heard some months earlier:

> There are still over half a million Fragebogen for issue to Army Groups which should last for another 2 ½ to 3 months. For this reason, and because of the experience gained in the use of the Fragebogen is still very limited, it is not considered advisable to make any additions to or deletion from the form MG/PS/G/9 [the SHAEF questionnaire].[127]

The *Cinquième Bureau* was in no way able to sway SHAEF opinion on the matter, nor did it possess the necessary intelligence or other resources to draft its own form. Soon after Koeltz received this letter, in the spring of 1945, more than a hundred French civil affairs officers were enrolled in the "Fragebogen training session" in London. Even earlier, in the winter of 1944/45, civilian recruits had attended classes at the French School of Military Government in liberated Paris.[128] This four-week training program at the Sorbonne and School of Political Science trained students on how to process the Fragebogen.[129]

Cabinet-level planning committees for denazification were functioning in Washington and London as early as November 1943, but an equivalent office in Paris was only formed in July 1945.[130] Its administration was therefore not as prepared for political screening, and due to its late arrival to the Allied conclave, France always maintained a secondary role among its postwar partners. All early attempts to formulate a uniquely French denazification curriculum, or even to negotiate the prevailing

---

[126] Letter, L. Koeltz to Chief of the SHAEF Mission to France, March 23, 1945, NARA, RG 331, SHAEF, G-5, GS, Secretariat, Box 30, Doc. 21/428–2350.
[127] Letter, R. M. J. Martin (SHAEF, PS Section) to SHAEF Mission to France, "Elimination of Nazi Personnel – Fragebogen," March 23, 1945, NARA, RG 331, SHAEF, G-5, GS, Secretariat, Box 30, Doc. 21/429.
[128] Biddiscombe, *Denazification of Germany* 155.
[129] These courses were delivered by France's foremost experts in German history, law, and culture, including André Siegfried and Edmond Vermeil. Campion, "Negotiating Difference," 87–88.
[130] This office was referred to as the *Comité interministériel des affaires Allemandes et Autrichiennes*. See Jessica Reinisch, *The Perils of Peace: The Public Health Crisis in Occupied Germany* (Oxford: Oxford University Press, 2013), 260.

SHAEF strategy, failed. For the first six months of the occupation, civil affairs officials were forced to accept the program adopted by their much more influential military allies.[131] However, even though their hands were tied in influencing Allied policy, the French could dictate how denazification was implemented in the territories their soldiers occupied.

Instructions for the French denazification campaign were eventually written, arriving from Paris in August 1945 as the *Directives pour notre action en Allemagne*. By this time, nearly six months since the initial invasion, thousands of SHAEF Fragebögen had already been processed. The screening instrument that was grudgingly adopted could not be thrown out, but it could be revised. In September 1945, the AMFA wrote its own version of the questionnaire, intended for use in all three Länder, as well as in the Saar Protectorate and French sector of Berlin.[132]

At first glance, the French survey is noticeably different from the earlier forms; it contains only ninety-four questions organized into eight sections and printed on six pages, which was later reduced to three. Upon closer examination, however, it is revealed that the content is practically the same as the US Fragebogen. According to one official, the AMFA chose to adopt the American form because its questions and procedures were "more articulate, verbalized, and legalistic than were those of the other two Allies."[133] The same host of categories and questions about education and employment history, income, travel, and affiliation with Nazi groups are included. In the SHAEF and American questionnaires, Nazi organizations are listed in a long table, spanning an entire page or more, while the French Fragebogen groups similar organizations into a single question. For example, question fifty-four asked: "Have you ever been a member, volunteer, or professional in any of the following organizations: RdB, DAF, NSBO, KdF..." Therefore, the French questionnaire, although shorter in length, essentially listed the same questions. There is no indication if these structural changes were made because French planners genuinely believed that the document could be read or reviewed more easily, or if this was simply a superficial attempt to distinguish the questionnaire from the American

---

[131] "Traduction officielle du Manuel de gouvernement militaire en Allemagne (Mars 1945)," Archives diplomatiques, Ministère des affaires étrangères (hereafter, ADMAE), HC 0072; Report, "Progress Report – German Section," May 11, 1944, WO 219/3472, Doc. 8/1059; "Progress Report – German Country Section," May 18, 1944, WO 219/3472, Doc. 8/1063.

[132] Fragebogen of H.G., January 19, 1946, ADMAE, ZFO, WH 1298; BAK, Bundesbank Schriftgut der Filialen, B 332/110.

[133] Willis, *The French in Germany*, 154.

and British varieties. When, in early 1946, OMGUS introduced the shorter Meldebogen (examined in Chapter 3), the French again followed suit, distributing the new form, at least on an ad hoc basis.[134]

While the French used the American survey as a template to write its own form, and most of the questions were identical, there are some important differences. For example, much like the British form, the French required respondents to list the names and addresses of references, who, if called upon, could corroborate their answers.[135] The instructions asked for "one [reference] of whom is familiar with your business experiences, one with your political opinions, and one with your personal life."[136] There were also new questions about the respondent's religious affiliation, an unsurprising addition considering the French tendency to tether Catholicism to anti-Nazi sentiments. The survey also asked for additional details about past military service, which again is understandable because of the AMFA's heightened objective to eradicate militarism (*déprussianniser*) and concern with German military activities in occupied France.

More importantly, the instructions for evaluating the French form recognized a January 1, 1933 membership date to differentiate between "active" (removal mandatory) and "nominal" (removal discretionary) Nazis. The Americans, on the other hand, had attached an "active" Nazi status to all party members who had joined prior to May 1, 1937.[137] It seems that French planners were sympathetic to those Germans who might have joined the NSDAP for opportunistic reasons or unconvinced that party membership was a sufficient sign of guilt. Perhaps this is why French officials preferred the term "*épuration*" (purification) to the harsher sounding "*dénazification.*"

In the fall of 1945, in regions where civil affairs officers had not yet received the French Fragebogen, a two-page sheet of supplementary questions was simply stapled to SHAEF and American questionnaires. This seemed a practical temporary solution because tens of thousands of the older forms had already been printed. The amended questions asked respondents about their children's education, again, not at all surprising considering the emphasis that late-arriving French strategy placed on education. More interesting, however, is the new question, "Were you

---

[134] For example, Meldebogen of O.G., May 15, 1947, ADMAE, ZFO, BADE 1303.
[135] Fragebogen of J.S., December 12, 1945, ADMAE, AP0141/1a, Affaires Politiques, Service Information, Journalistes allemandes (1), 1945–49.
[136] Campion, "Negotiating Difference," 132.
[137] OMGUS, CAD, *Denazification, Cumulative Review. Report, 1 April 1947–1930 April 1948*, 1.

ever married to a Jew or Mischling?"[138] This is the only version of the Fragebogen, distributed in any zone, which asked about the racial makeup of one's family. No explanation as to why the question was included in the appended sheet has been found or why it was not incorporated into the revised form.

Soviet denazification planning was also crippled by wartime disorder. The failure to define the basic goals and parameters of its punishment and reorientation program frustrated Western leaders but also allowed them an opportunity to advance their own methods on Moscow. With the hope of building a four-power denazification rubric, SHAEF manuals were translated into Russian and circulated within the European Advisory Commission.[139] With no other practical strategy available to them, Soviet planners adopted the Anglo-American model for denazification, subscribing to a campaign defined largely by political screening and job dismissals.

However, the Russians fundamentally disagreed with US officials about the inherent nature of Nazism and how the term "nominal Nazi" should be defined. The popular Bolshevik attitude held that many rank-and-file party members, colloquially referred to as *Müssnazi*, or "Nazi by necessity," had been manipulated by the fascist dictatorship and therefore their permanent exclusion from postwar social democracy was unnecessary.[140] While a "hard peace" undercurrent was always present, the Russians ultimately favored a strategy that focused not so much on individual punishment, but the encouragement of antifascist German liberalism; the hope was this would set the enemy on a path to socialism. The professional opportunities awarded to citizens who willingly subscribed to the ruling party ideology were familiar to the Soviet authorities and perhaps contributed to more tolerant screening standards. Therefore, mass arrests would be avoided, and more attention given to reeducation programs, land reforms, and the breaking up of industrial cartels. This more tolerant program is in contradiction to the sheer brutality that defined the Red Army invasion and early occupation, including widespread murder, torture, internment, and rape.[141] In fact, as the occupation took form, in the early months of 1945, and the true

---

[138] Fragebogen of G.K., August 29, 1945, ADMAE, ZFO, WH 1298. "Mischling" (or mix-ling) was a Nazi legal term for persons deemed to have both "Aryan" and non-"Aryan" ancestry.
[139] Letter, Brig. Gen. C.W. Wickersham (USGCC) to Mr. N.V. Ivanov (USSR Embassy, London), April 6, 1945, NARA, RG 260, USGCC, AG, General Correspondence, 1944–45, Box 3.
[140] Fitzgibbon, *Denazification*, 41; Biddiscombe, *Denazification of Germany*, 124–26.
[141] Naimark, *The Russians in Germany*, 69–140.

nature of the new communist regime was exposed, attempts to implement a gradualist and more empathetic denazification campaign became extremely difficult.

During the first six months of the occupation, Red Army commanders and Soviet Military Administration (SMA) officials, as well as German antifascists, distributed SHAEF and US questionnaires. Some copies had been translated into Russian-German, but most of the forms remained in their original English-German. The Fragebögen were distributed on an ad hoc basis and orders delivered verbally or in regional ordinances. For example, on July 23, 1945, Dr. Rudolf Paul, the newly appointed *Landespräsident* (Minister-President) of Thuringia, delivered these instructions to his administration:

> The boards of authority require all suitable persons to fill out the questionnaire introduced by the American Military Government. Along with the questionnaire, personal records and a report that clearly outlines the important points of the case, accompanied by a formal proposal dealing with the case, should be submitted, if so requested, to the office of the state of Thüringen.[142]

While some Soviet branch offices circulated Western surveys, others simply wrote their own, including questions specific to the population or industry under investigation. For example, a special *Personalfragebogen* was written for refugees and displaced persons who had fled Poland and other liberated territories.[143] This form asked detailed questions about the applicant's military service and membership in Nazi organizations and required the inclusion of a short *Lebenslauf*. Similarly, a twenty-one-item questionnaire was drafted specifically for employees of the Reichsbahn.[144] In another case, after the US Army withdrew from the municipal district of Halle, the local SMA office drafted a short-version Fragebogen for all the city's civil servants that asked about membership in eleven Nazi organizations.[145] However, due to the disorganized state of early military government, the Fragebogen system was not broadly implemented in Soviet-occupied territories. Many Red Army commanders, likely the majority, chose not to use questionnaires at all. Instead, they relied on who they viewed as trusted Germans, mainly local KPD

---

[142] "Duchführungs- und Ausführungsbestimmungen zum Gesetz über die Reinigung," July 23, 1945, Bundesarchiv-Berlin (hereafter, BAB), Ministerium für Gesundheitswesen, 1945–50, DQ 1/1336, Doc. 240.

[143] "Personalfragebogen," August 18, 1946, Suchdienst für vermisste Deutsche in der sowjetischen Besatzungszone Deutschlands / im Gebiet der Deutschen Demokratischen Republik, BAB, DO 105/19028.

[144] "Fragebogen," BAB, Ministerium für Verkehrswesen, DM 1/3509.

[145] Letter, Verwaltung Halle to Horst Petermann, July 10, 1945, BAB, IG Farbenindustrie, AG Stickstoffabteilung, R 8128/5191.

members and recently liberated concentration camp inmates, to denounce former Nazis.

It was not until June 1945, after SMA had organized its headquarters in Berlin, that the Soviets began formulating their own unique Fragebogen program. The document they drafted, which was not published until August, was quite different from the questionnaires being distributed by the three other Allied armies. It contained 34 questions, a considerable cutback from the SHAEF 78 and American 131-question forms. However, the Soviet Fragebogen did share some features with its Western equivalents. The survey began with the same stern warning about the consequences of omitting or falsifying information and asked similar questions about education, employment, military service, and travel. SMA was highly receptive to the recruitment of trustworthy Germans for employment in military government, so questions about the applicant's knowledge of foreign languages and pre-1933 political activities also remained. As in the SHAEF, American, British, and French forms, respondents were encouraged to denounce family members. Question sixteen asked: "Do you have relatives remaining in fascist organizations? Indicate their names, place of work, and location of work at the present time."

However, this is where the similarities end. The Soviet Fragebogen did not contain a long list of Nazi-affiliated groups; instead, applicants were only asked if they had been a member of the NSDAP, SA, SS, Waffen SS, SD, and Gestapo. Soviet planners in Berlin believed that questions about membership in auxiliary groups were irrelevant and only meant to target nominal party members, who they believed had been manipulated by the Nazi leadership and its large conspiring group of business magnates.[146] The Russians explicitly stated that they cared little if a man had or had not been a Nazi Party member – a basic distinction that the Western Allies obsessed over – but only if he had been ideologically committed.[147] As such, the Soviet Fragebogen included new questions about pre-1933 political party status and trade union affiliation. Another departure from the Western forms, it asked about current political party membership. Circulated months after the Red Army invasion, denazification agents presumably wanted to know how active the applicant had become in postwar political institutions and whether they had embraced the socialist system that was being built.

The Soviet Fragebogen had some surprising omissions, however. There were no questions related to religion, income, or anti-Nazi

---

[146] Biddiscombe, *Denazification of Germany*, 126.   [147] Fitzgibbon, *Denazification*, 100.

activities, information that would seem to be of great interest to SMA. It is possible that any answer to these questions could not be confirmed and therefore they were not included. The Russian form also did not contain a section for "Remarks," and respondents were not encouraged to add supplementary sheets, although they often did. What we do know from the available archival records is that the Soviet questionnaire was meant to act as a simpler document, one that targeted only active Nazis and high-ranking officials. Its general tone was not as punitive and its content was more heavily weighted to economic and military matters, characteristics that fit well with the more collaborative program that was being pursued.

The Soviets were the last of the occupying armies to write a questionnaire, but they were proud of their late creation, heralding it as an instrument that had been improved upon after witnessing the failures of the Western armies. At a September 17, 1945 meeting of the ACC's Nazi Arrest and Denazification Subcommittee, where discussion was had about the feasibility of drafting a common four-power denazification form, a Russian delegate advocated the use of his government's survey:

I request members to consider the Russian Questionnaire I present to you. ... In compiling this Fragebogen, we took into consideration that it should not be very large and cumbersome, but should give a full characterisation of the persons who fill it in. Therefore the proposed Questionnaire consists of 34 items instead of the 131 questions in the American version. We consider it appropriate to eliminate the remaining questions from the American Fragebogen ... i.e. all questions that do not give the personality of the person, and his activity during the Fascist Regime. I am very grateful to the American and British Delegations, which have put in so much work and have made the work easier for us in compiling this Fragebogen.[148]

An important alteration to the Soviet program came in January 1946, when SMA enacted ACC Directive 24, the four-power order to create a uniform denazification campaign (discussed in subsequent chapters).[149] Moving closer to the American strategy, which relied on broad categories of arrest and dismissal, the new system called for the removal of all former Nazi Party members and leading officials in "other Nazi organizations" from civil service positions and as managers in big businesses.

---

[148] Meeting minutes, "Nazi Arrest & Denazification Subcommittee – Comments by the Russian Member on American Procedure and Fragebogen," September 17, 1945, BAK, OMGUS, 15/122-1/7.
[149] In an effort to establish an identical policy to govern the removal and exclusion of Nazis from employment, the ACC issued Directive 24 in January 1946, which targeted active party members. While Russian delegates in the ACC agreed to the parameters of the new directive, SMA did not implement them until the end of 1946.

There was reluctance to adopt the ACC guidelines, but four-power control of Berlin, and the relatively free movement of citizens between sectors, required that Directive 24 be implemented immediately to ensure procedural consistency across the city.[150] This change in policy led to a renewed vetting campaign, one that subjected the zone's entire adult population to reinvestigation. In December 1946, dozens of German-administered *Säuberungsausschüsse* (cleansing committees) and *Entnazifizierungskommissionen* (denazification commissions) were created across Brandenburg, Mecklenburg, Saxony, Saxony-Anhalt, Thuringia, and in Berlin, and a new Fragebogen drafted for all former Nazis holding public or private posts.[151] By the end of 1947, the enlarged purge was underway, modeled on the much-reviled American campaign.

The second Soviet Fragebogen bore the apt name "Questionnaire for the Application of Directive 24" (*Fragebogen und Antrag zur Direktive 24*) and had a much stronger resemblance to the US form. It listed ninety Nazi-affiliated organizations and professional positions and asked respondents to indicate the years in which they were members, as well as their function, rank, and office.[152] However, because the new survey was meant to act as a supplementary document, one circulated only to Germans who had already completed the original Fragebogen, questions related to employment, military service, and education were left out. In some *Kreise*, additional questions were included. For example, some versions allowed respondents to list any "antifascist activity" undertaken against the Nazi government or "antifascist organizations" to which they currently belonged.[153]

Directive 24 was a clear setback for those in SMA who desired an independent Soviet campaign. After only five short months, the uniquely Russian Fragebogen had gone the same way as the British and French forms before it, succumbing to the much more pervasive American political screening system.

Conclusion

In an April 1945 interview with the *New York Times*, Maj. Aldo Raffa introduced the Fragebogen to the American public and the unconventional strategy being taken to "ideologically cleanse" the German

---

[150] Vogt, *Denazification in Soviet-Occupied Germany*, 80.
[151] Andrew I. Port, *Conflict and Stability in the German Democratic Republic* (Cambridge: Cambridge University Press, 2007), 26. These denazification commissions were overseen by SMA but staffed by German antifascists.
[152] "Fragebogen und Antrag zur Direktive 24," July 10, 1945, BAB, IG Farbenindustrie, AG Stickstoffabteilung, R 8128/5191.
[153] Vogt, *Denazification in Soviet-Occupied Germany*, 123.

Conclusion

nation.[154] The political science instructor assured readers that the "experience and mistakes in the Mediterranean" had been carefully considered by his office and that the new screening questionnaire was a more efficient instrument of investigation, one that would ensure that jobholders in the new democratic Germany would "certainty not be 'active Nazis or ardent sympathizers.'"

Despite Raffa's display of confidence, the denazification campaign that emerged in the months surrounding the German surrender, whether implemented under a joint-Allied banner or by independent nations, was not balanced or consistent and it possessed many of the same problematic features of its Italian predecessor. Members of the GCU were optimistic that lessons learned from the Sicily experience had resulted in the drafting of a more effective screening instrument. However, the Fragebogen was hastily written in the spring of 1944 and its content and instructions represented a collision of ideas and methods, many of which were simply not compatible.

Still, the questionnaire was approved for mass printing and its procedures integrated into the bureaucratic workings of many facets of occupation policy. This was largely because the GCU staff members who wrote the form were veterans of the defascistization campaign, as well as police officers, legalists, and social scientists who supported the use of statistical methodologies. Moreover, the historians and political theorists in the OSS's Central Europe Section had recommended the use of specific categories of Nazi affiliation and a program of self-involved denazification, features that could be accommodated by a standardized questionnaire. Most important is that there was no practical alternative to carrying out a large administrative purge. With very little executive oversight, not from the SHAEF leadership, the EAC, or any national government office, the GCU was given free rein in designing the denazification campaign. When high-level offices finally shifted their attention, the opportunity to overhaul the screening program had already passed, as the invasion of Germany was underway. At this late stage, the questions in the survey could be altered, but the program itself could not be replaced.

This chapter has introduced the Fragebogen to analytical review and delivered the first history of the project's origins, including a detailed inspection of the form in its many variants. Three principal insights have been gained. First, the questionnaire was a creative and unorthodox solution to the problem of denazification. Inspired by a similar survey used to screen for Italian fascists and endorsed by academics, it was an experimental instrument adopted by traditional military apparatuses.

---

[154] Bracker, "Reich Gives AMG Biggest Problems," 8.

110   Drafting the Questionnaire

The US and British armies went to great lengths to enroll social scientists and civilian specialists in the war effort and the questionnaire program was a direct result of these efforts.

Second, the questionnaire in all its formats was an inherently flawed document. The survey was originally envisioned as a blunt, bureaucratic tool, meant to standardize screening activities through a simple classification protocol. What was in fact published was a subjective form that granted considerable discretion to individual denazification officers and allowed for respondents to append personal commentaries. As a result of these conflicting characteristics, the Fragebogen evolved and fractured quickly. The original questionnaire, drafted by the Americans and British, was an experimental working document based on an unproven model. It represented a forced compromise of the ideas and goals of academics, police officers, neo-Marxists, politicians, diplomats, and military strategists. Most planners were unhappy with the finished product. One soldier described it as a "bureaucratic solution to a political problem."[155] The subsequent US form was reactionary, drafted in the face of external criticism and political scandal, and it gave little consideration to the potential administrative or political consequences. Meanwhile, the British decision to temporarily continue to use the original questionnaire was a product of indecision, uncertainty, and convenience. The first French Fragebogen was a duplicate of the US form, adopted because of a lack of French influence within SHAEF and the general disorganized state of the *Cinquième Bureau*. The Soviets also fell back on the American and British model. By the time SMA drafted its own Fragebogen, denazification had already developed unique characteristics at the local level, making it extremely difficult for Berlin to institute a uniform program throughout the zone. The haphazard evolution of the Fragebogen system and its unaddressed shortcomings would prove to have severe consequences for the successful functioning of denazification.

Finally, this chapter has shown that the questionnaire was adopted and revised by all four Allied armies. This is a simple yet important observation considering that most of the relevant scholarship depicts the Fragebogen as a solely American endeavor. The assumption is understandable since the United States was the driving force behind drafting the original form and its revised questionnaire was later used as a template by the other three occupying powers. In the end, the Fragebogen served as a common denominator among the American, British, French, and Soviet denazification campaigns.

[155] Tom Bower, *The Pledge Betrayed: America and Britain and the Denazification of Postwar Germany* (Garden City, NY: Doubleday, 1982), 146.

3 "Land of the Fragebogen"
Screening the German Population

> No matter how long I live, I'll never get the word Fragebogen out of my head. Everything in Germany revolves around it.[1]
> —Gordon Gaskill, *American Magazine* (1947)

Sgt. Frank Eyck did not experience any direct combat during the war. The nineteen-year-old German-Jewish refugee, whose family had fled the Nazi dictatorship, joined the regular British Army in 1940, but was quickly reassigned to the Information Control Unit for "special employment."[2] This was on account of a unique skill set: Eyck spoke the enemy's language and understood its social culture. Attached to the 21st Army Group, his unit entered northwestern Germany in late April 1945, moving through several border towns. While the fighting continued to the east, Eyck was assigned to a press office in Hamburg, where he oversaw the publication of a newssheet periodical for German citizens. However, the young officer quickly grew frustrated in this new role because of the many restrictions imposed by denazification directives. He could not hire the printing staff he desired; most had "failed" their Fragebogen. Also, the mass printing of questionnaires limited the supply of paper, which forced his newsletter to suspend publication on several occasions.[3] Eyck's impression of denazification was typical of invading and occupying soldiers. The civilian work assignments of thousands of American, British, French, and Soviet officials were impacted by political screening activities, often unexpectedly, and the Fragebogen was viewed as a burdensome and ineffective device, one that obstructed more meaningful rehabilitative activities.

In their efforts to discredit Nazism, the occupiers undertook many tasks, including the removal of swastikas and other fascist paraphernalia

---

[1] Gordon Gaskill, "Leaves from the Diary of a Military Governor," *American Magazine* (March 1947): 33–36.
[2] Frank Eyck, *A Historians Pilgrimage: Memoirs and Reflections* (Calgary: Detselig, 2009), 237.
[3] Ibid., 288–89.

and marching German citizens through liberated concentration camps. Those with the prerequisite skills rewrote legal codes and revised school textbooks. Most denazification officers, however, were charged with distributing and processing questionnaires. They translated written responses and cross-checked them against salvaged Nazi records, interviewed citizens of interest, shared intelligence with other detachment offices, and delivered investigation findings to anxious job applicants and employers. Among these Fragebogen agents was an aspiring young writer named Staff Sgt. J. D. Salinger and a twenty-two-year-old Sgt. Heinz (Henry) Kissinger.[4] You did not need special training to participate in the screening program. The massive paper campaign demanded support from every kind of soldier operating in Germany, including intelligence officers, public administrators, military police, and regular security forces. Civil servants had to be vetted, POWs interrogated, newspapers censored, political parties supervised, and food rationing coordinated. All these actions required some sort of screening. In its many guises, denazification likely employed more than a 100,000 Allied army soldiers and German civilians.[5]

This chapter examines the occupier's experience of denazification by accessing army field reports, military government records, newspapers, and published and unpublished firsthand accounts. By doing so, a more intimate history of denazification administration is imparted, one that moves beyond a simplistic data-driven interpretation and the assessment of high-level policy. It expands the scope of traditional analysis to include routine screening activities in all four occupation zones.

For Allied army soldiers, denazification was by and large a paper process, characterized by the evaluation of forms, letters, and sworn statements. In most towns and regions, and in all zones, the Fragebogen lay at the center of these procedures, during the presurrender (February–June 1945), military government (July 1945–46), and civilian commission (1946–48) phases. Such inter-Allied uniformity in political screening, and the centrality of the questionnaire in the

---

[4] During the early days of the American invasion, German-born Kissinger assisted in the military administration of the city of Krefeld. He was later reassigned to the CIC and given command of a denazification team, first in Hanover then the Bergstraße district in Hesse. Salinger was also assigned to a CIC unit, but stationed in the town Weisenburg, near Nuremberg. Niall Ferguson, *Kissinger, Vol. 1, 1923–1968: The Idealist* (New York: Penguin, 2015); Margaret Salinger, *Dream Catcher: A Memoir* (New York: Washington Square Press, 2000); Eberhard Alsen, *J.D. Salinger and the Nazis* (Madison: University of Wisconsin Press, 2018).

[5] This estimate includes the roughly 50,000 Germans who staffed denazification commissions and ministries. Clay, *Decision in Germany*, 259.

wider denazification campaigns, has not been recognized in the current scholarship.

Allied Invasion and Early Distribution of the Questionnaires, 1944–1945

Invasion soldiers were shocked by the material and human devastation they encountered when entering Germany in the early weeks of 1945. The British and American bombing campaigns had reduced many cities to rubble, destroying an estimated 3.6 million homes and leaving 20 million people homeless.[6] In the east, the Soviet invasion had driven 5.8 million refugees into Germany to scratch out a living among the wreckage.[7] Essential utilities and nearly all transportation and health infrastructure had collapsed. Allied soldiers observed "endless rows of empty, burnt-out structural shells" and described the local inhabitants as "dregs and debris of war" living in "cellars and caves."[8] Reporting in Berlin for the *New York Herald Tribune*, William L. Shirer wrote that "this is more like the face of the moon than any city I ever imagined."[9]

A handful of border towns were occupied by Soviet and American armies in the closing months of 1944, including Aachen in October, but most of these incursions were short-lived due to Wehrmacht counterattacks.[10] The formal invasion of Germany, characterized by rapid military advancement, began in February 1945, and continued right up until the unconditional surrender on May 7. On all fronts, soldiers encountered "docile, obedient, and somewhat fearful" people, but in western towns, American, British, French, Canadian, and Polish troops were

---

[6] Keith Lowe, *Savage Continent: Europe in the Aftermath of World War II* (New York: Picador, 2013), 7–8.
[7] Mark Mazower, *Dark Continent: Europe's Twentieth Century* (London: Allen Lane, 1998), 217. Historians estimate that as many as 14 million German nationals and ethnic Germans fled or were expelled from central and eastern Europe between 1944 and 1950. Hundreds of thousands of people, mostly women and young children, died of malnutrition, disease, and physical violence.
[8] Dietrich Orlow, *A History of Modern Germany: 1871 to Present*, 7th ed. (Boston: Pearson, 2011), 232; Leon C. Standifer, *Binding up the Wounds: An American Soldier in Occupied Germany, 1945–1946* (Baton Rouge: Louisiana State University Press, 1997), 21; SHAEF Field Report, March 14, 1945, NARA, RG 331, SHAEF, CSS, Geographic Correspondence, 1943–45, Box 112.
[9] Quoted in Russell Hill, *Struggle for Germany* (New York: Harper, 1947), 30.
[10] The first German town occupied by US soldiers was Roetgen (North Rhine-Westphalia) on September 11, 1944, but one month earlier, the Soviets had crossed the prewar German border to temporarily occupy the East Prussian town of Stallupönen. Taylor, *Exorcising Hitler*, 3–6.

often welcomed with celebration.[11] Remembered by one American GI: "[O]ver the entire area the people were friendly and glad the war was over."[12] This was bewildering to soldiers. In the months leading up to the invasion, they had been told of the innate evils of the German character and warned of the guerilla "Werewolf" resistance that awaited them. Now that the fighting had stopped, the enemy seemed submissive and even friendly; they could not, at moments, help but feel like liberators. What emerged during these early weeks were complex relationships. As described by Norman Naimark, soldier–civilian relations, even in the Soviet-occupied territories, "ranged from brutal and exploitive to friendly and even intimate."[13]

Civil affairs officers who accompanied, or followed, combat troops into Germany were equally shocked by the level of destruction and the depressed state of the people. Much was expected of these early agents of military government. While active army units pushed deeper into the Reich, these men (and some women) were ordered to occupy, govern, and rehabilitate the war-torn country. They immediately established branch offices to transition towns from being conquered to occupied. During this pre-surrender phase, all operations were governed by a single objective, to provide an orderly environment to facilitate tactical troops in achieving military success.[14] Soldiers could not stay in any location long, so civil affairs was under tremendous pressure to quickly rebuild basic services, which meant finding local German administrators and technicians with proven ability and influence. Few denazification specialists were attached to military government offices in the early weeks of the occupation, sometimes only one or two were assigned to a city of 50,000 or more.[15] There were even fewer in the Soviet-administered territories. This resulted in regular soldiers, most of whom had no training in civil administration and little if any German language skills, carrying out political screening activities. The situation soon changed, however, as recruits began trickling in from foreign training centers, beginning in late February.

Denazification began immediately. Leading Nazis and known war criminals were arrested, the NSDAP and all its organizations were disbanded, street signs and swastikas were removed, and townspeople were made to tour concentration camps and bury bodies. Rigid curfews were

---

[11] CA Weekly Report, No. 25, 21st Army Group, May 8, 1945, NARA, RG 331, SHAEF, GS, G-5, Secretariat, Box 27.
[12] Standifer, *Binding up the Wounds*, 28.   [13] Naimark, *The Russians in Germany*, 33.
[14] SHAEF, *Public Safety Manual of Procedures* (September 1944), Section I, Paragraph 2.
[15] CA Weekly Report, No. 38, March 3, 1945, NARA, RG 331, SHAEF, GS, G-5, IB, HS, Box 218.

imposed, and the movement of people restricted. In the west, SHAEF Proclamation No. 1 was posted outside public buildings, declaring the Allied Forces intent to "... obliterate Nazi-ism and German Militarism."[16] Denazification officers operating under SHAEF's Public Safety Division dedicated most of their resources to determining who was fit to hold public office and other positions of influence. New civic governments had to be formed, managers of businesses and heads of industry appointed, and what was left of the German civil service screened for Nazi sympathizers.

Major problems were soon encountered, largely because of the incompatibility of the restorative and punitive goals of occupation policy addressed in previous chapters. Civil affairs officers were told to establish social order and revive local economies but also carry out an extensive purge of public administrations and private businesses. It did not help that SHAEF's *Handbook for Military Government* was rife with ambiguities. The terms "active" and "nominal" Nazi, as well as "militarist" and "sympathizer," had not been sufficiently defined and it remained unclear precisely which local offices were to be vetted. The Yalta communique, issued in February 1945, did little to clear up matters and a Combined Chiefs of Staff (CCS) directive on the "Removal of Nazis and Militarists" complicated procedures further by allowing for a delay in dismissals ruled to be "unduly difficult."[17] In a March 21 letter to the CCS, a leading G-5 agent wrote that "Supreme Headquarters has up to the present made no adequate attempt to define the terms 'administrative convenience or expediency', 'active Nazis' or 'ardent sympathizers'."[18]

The flurry of confused correspondence between local civil affairs detachments and American (USGCC) and British (CCG[BE]) headquarters confirms that occupation policy had not been turned into pragmatic guidelines. To make matters more challenging, the French First Army lacked a centralized command structure and felt indifferent to carrying out SHAEF polices. Meanwhile, the Soviets, operating within a heavier combat region and plagued by far greater administrative disorder, showed no serious desire to coordinate their screening program.[19] Still, Allied army ordinances were optimistic about the timeline for the vetting of Nazis. The Americans expected denazification to last only six

---

[16] "Proclamation No. 1," NARA, RG 331, SHAEF, AGD, War Diaries, 1943–45, Box 48.
[17] CCS Report, "Removal of Nazis and Militarists," June 29, 1945, NARA, RG 331, SHAEF, CSS, Geographic Correspondence, 1943–45, Box 111.
[18] Letter, G-5/Assistant Chief of Staff to Chief of Staff, March 21, 1945, NARA, RG 331, SHAEF, SS, AGD, ES, Box 134.
[19] Damian van Melis, "Denazification in Mecklenburg-Vorpommern," *German History* 13, no. 3 (1995): 359.

months, while the Soviets were confident that their campaign would be over even earlier.[20]

Denazification almost always began in a newly occupied town or region with the informal interrogation of community leaders, carried out at the discretion of the ranking officer. If the local government had fled, and many had, the entire civic administration was rebuilt from the ground up. To carry out this task quickly, former mayors were consulted, who had emerged in the wake of defeat, as well as church leaders, prominent businesspersons, and known anti-Nazis.[21] Local clergy were often allowed great authority, as it was assumed, often wrongly, that they had been formidable resisters of the regime.[22] Red Army units sometimes relied on the counsel of the "antifascist committees" that had sprung up during the early weeks of the occupation.[23] In the border town of Roetgen, an American civil affairs officer asked the town's mayor to give "hints about who was who and what in town."[24] After a full day of interviews, a trusted businessman was appointed mayor of British-occupied Hamburg and allowed to hire his own staff.[25] In Mainz, soldiers reached out to the city's Bishop for advice on municipal appointments, while in Marburg, a small group calling itself the *Ordnungs-Ausschuss* (coordinating committee) assisted the Russians in identifying former Nazis.[26] Meanwhile, the KPD leadership in Brandenburg issued guidelines to antifascist committees on how to assist the Soviet authorities in registering citizens.[27]

---

[20] "Public Safety Manual of Procedures," September 1944, NARA, RG 331, SHAEF, G-5, AG, ES, Box 9; Vogt, *Denazification in Soviet-Occupied Germany*, 46.

[21] American and British administrators were reluctant to delegate much authority to antifascists, who were mostly members of the revived KPD, but also careful not to suppress these groups out of fear they would go underground and "work counter to the interests of Military Government." Report, "Weekly Field Situation Report," June 8, 1945, NARA, RG 331, SHAEF, GS, G-5, Secretariat, Box 28.

[22] A notorious case of an occupying army wrongfully trusting a church leader occurred in Aachen, where, on the advice of the city's Catholic Bishop, the US Twelfth Army appointed several conservative antidemocrats to important municipal positions. Clemens Vollnhals, "Das Reichskonkordat von 1933 als Konfliktfall im Alliierten Kontrollrat," *Vierteljahrshefte für Zeitgeschichte* 35, no. 4 (October 1987): 681.

[23] Vogt, *Denazification in Soviet-Occupied Germany*, 31.

[24] Saul K. Padover, *Experiment in Germany: The Story of an American Intelligence Office* (New York: Duell, Sloan and Pearce, 1946), 79.

[25] Frances Rosenfeld, "The Anglo-German Encounter in Occupied Hamburg, 1945–1950" (PhD diss., Columbia University, 2006), 66–67.

[26] Biddiscombe, *Denazification of Germany*, 51; John Gimbel, *A German Community under American Occupation, 1945–1952* (Stanford: Stanford University Press, 1961), 88–90.

[27] Horst Laschitza, *Kämpferische Demokratie gegen Faschismus* (Berlin: Berlin Deutscher Militärverlag, 1969), 250–51; Welsh, *Revolutionärer Wandel auf Befehl?*, 25–31.

Priority was given to identifying Germans who fell into SHAEF's "automatic arrest categories." Investigators consulted "black lists," which named known Nazi leaders and war criminals, as well as Germans who had held a prominent membership, rank, or position in the government.[28] The OSS had recommended that 150,000 people be arrested immediately, a scale of internment agreed upon by all four invading armies, including the Soviets, who possessed even broader automatic arrest categories.[29] If available, Public Safety worked alongside CIC and other intelligence groups.[30] This led to an early wave of civilian internment. It is estimated that more than 400,000 Germans were detained: 170,000 by the Americans, 130,000 by the Soviets, 91,000 by the British, and 21,500 by the French.[31] Despite important differences in the duration and conditions of internment, detention across the four zones shared some basic characteristics, such as its function as both a punitive and preventative institution.[32] In addition to punishing former Nazis, internment was meant to uproot fascist ideology, and therefore should be considered part of the larger denazification campaign.[33]

Meanwhile, military governments were overwhelmed in fulfilling relief tasks, such as feeding local populations and restoring water supplies and electricity. These urgent responsibilities detracted from the abstract mission of eradicating National Socialism. Civilian recruitment was necessary to rebuild roads, bridges, and railways, and therefore, while most major Nazis were immediately arrested, nominal party members were allowed to remain in positions of authority, at least for the time being. Such actions varied between and within occupied regions. In some eastern districts, Red Army commanders acted swiftly, dismissing entire departments of municipal employees, while in others, former Nazis were not targeted at all and permitted to remain in office.[34] Interpreted by a British intelligence advisor, early Soviet denazification

---

[28] Some of these lists can be found here: "Black, White, and Grey Lists for Information Control Purposes," October 10, 1945, NARA, RG 498, HD, Program Files (OMGUS), IC, Container 4115.
[29] Beattie, *Allied Internment Camps in Occupied Germany*, 27, 37; *Handbook for Military Government in Germany: Prior to Defeat or Surrender* (SHAEF, December 1944).
[30] Padover, *Experiment in Germany*, 87; Trogdon, "A Decade of Catching Spies," 136.
[31] Beattie, *Allied Internment Camps in Occupied Germany*, 1.
[32] Ibid., 23–24. It should be noted, however, that it was only the Soviets who deported arrestees for the purpose of civilian labor.
[33] Ibid., 10–11.
[34] Welsh, *Revolutionärer Wandel auf Befehl?*, 31–43, 73–74; Biddiscombe, *Denazification of Germany*, 128–29.

was directed by the refrain, "hang the big Nazis and let the little ones go."[35]

In the west, Public Safety officials regularly quarreled with local military governors about employing Nazis in influential positions. One American intelligence officer, for example, complained that "they [military government] will employ almost anybody it believes capable of putting a town on a functioning basis."[36] He viewed these decisions as short-sighted and dangerous. The same officer described the reaction of a military governor, after discovering that the former Nazi he had appointed mayor had been removed: "In the doorway, drawn to his full height, his eyes bloodshot, his fists clenched ... He shrieked, 'What the goddam hell is going on here behind my back?' ... 'This is my town, I want you to know. This is my mayor ...' He pounded his chest with both fists as if he were determined to cave it in."[37] Such conflict was perhaps inevitable, as some groups were in Germany to deconstruct the Nazi state in all its vestiges, while others had been ordered to rehabilitate the country.

An even more troublesome relationship existed with the regular army, who really could not be bothered with the screening of doctors, teachers, and engineers. A vocal spokesman of this group was General George S. Patton, the quintessential function-focused soldier, who insisted that far too much fuss was being made about denazifying Germans.[38] The Soviets were no exception, with many documented cases of Red Army commanders going against civil affairs orders by allowing prominent Nazis to continue as mayors, police officers, and teachers.[39] It was common for denazification officials to make major concessions on civil appointments simply because they were in the service of the armed forces and outranked. Recounted in Public Safety reports, war diaries, and memoirs are many stories of frustrated Special Branch agents going to great lengths to sell their chosen non-Nazi candidate to a ranking officer, almost always with no avail.[40]

Even when permitted to do their job and screen for non-leading active Nazis, denazification agents did not always have the resources they needed for their investigation. It was assumed that identification would

---

[35] Noel Matthews, "Memorandum on the Policy and Practice of Denazification in the British Zone - Conference on Some Aspects of the German Problem. Vol. 2, Part 2," March 1948, Chatham House, Cultural Section, Appendix.
[36] Padover, *Experiment in Germany*, 251.   [37] Ibid., 99.
[38] Raymond Daniell, "Patton Belittles Denazification; Holds Rebuilding More Important," *New York Times*, September 22, 1945, p. 26.
[39] Vogt, *Denazification in Soviet-Occupied Germany*, 39.
[40] See, for example, Padover, *Experiment in Germany*, 332.

be a straightforward task, achieved by comparing completed Fragebögen with seized government and party records. But hard intelligence was not readily available in the field, as many archives had been destroyed or remained unaccounted for and existing intelligence reports were often outdated and inaccurate.[41] In fact, the central repository of NSDAP records – which included all 11 million party membership cards – had not yet been located. At best, information provided by the CIC, OSS, Sûreté, NKVD (People's Commissariat for Internal Affairs, USSR), and other intelligence groups, helped agents screen only the highest-level bureaucrats. This was a monumental problem. Denazification officials had no reliable way of identifying who was a Nazi and therefore their coordinated screening system could not function. One American investigator recalled the "impossibility to accurately investigate most of these [Fragebogen] cases."[42] It was because of this early absence of Nazi records, as well as the mounting pressure to restore a basic level of government and economic functionality, that officials increasingly came to rely on voluntary denunciations.[43] An informal whispering campaign of rumors and accusations quickly developed, while stacks of blank Fragebögen remained untouched in military government offices.

The use of questionnaires, and likewise adherence to screening procedures, seldom occurred during the first few weeks of the occupation. Most Western armies did not distribute Fragebögen until March 1945, and there is little evidence that Soviet detachments did so prior to April.[44] In fact, during the initial invasion, the content of the form, as well as the general scope of the project, were still being debated at SHAEF headquarters. Some G-5 officers demanded that a much shorter Fragebogen be drafted immediately. This was met with protest by key US officials, including O. W. Wilson, who argued that a revised form would seriously undermine the purpose of the denazification campaign. As the debate grew, dozens of German towns were being occupied and field detachment offices, already handicapped by a lack of reliable intelligence, received conflicting orders about political screening. The first assessment of denazification activities was conducted by the OSS in March 1945. The report concluded that: "It is evident that no consistent attempt at denazification has yet been undertaken in western

---

[41] Taylor, *Exorcising Hitler*, 248.
[42] "Fragebogen Clearance," February 20, 1946, NARA, RG 260, OMGB, ID, Box 144.
[43] See, for example, Counter Intelligence Corps, *Counter Intelligence Corps History and Mission in World War II*, 47–48.
[44] "Survey of Operations and Policy, Military Government-Berlin," July 21, 1945, NARA, RG 220, USGCC, AG, General Correspondence, 1944–45, Box 15.

Germany ... the decision to what extent the Nazis are to be used apparently rests with the individual MG [military government] officer."[45]

Occasionally, an ambitious unit commander or military government official distributed Fragebögen immediately upon coming into contact with a defeated population. This was more common in cities where the occupation bureaucracy was larger, but only if relevant Nazi records were accessible. For example, by early March, the US Military Government in Aachen had already processed 754 Fragebögen.[46] In Cologne, during the first week of April, 136 Fragebögen were received and 81 evaluated.[47] The 16th Infantry Regiment was distributing questionnaires in Bonn only a few hours after the city fell.[48] In fact, even during these early weeks, efforts were made to standardized Fragebogen activities across the SHAEF territories. Beginning on February 26, 1945, experts from the German Country Unit, including M. K. Wilson, visited dozens of military government detachments and tactical units to assist in the "correct evaluation of the Fragebogen."[49] In mid-April, on the eve of the German surrender, both SHAEF and the Red Army began using questionnaires more widely. The fighting had then become isolated, which allowed room to build screening apparatuses and train fresh recruits. Furthermore, locally sourced records were being accumulated at "collections points" throughout the country.

The move toward institutionalizing the Fragebogen program was initiated by the Americans. As their armies fought eastward, the USGCC implemented two important policy directives, both of which ordered the use of questionnaires. The first was a single coordinating denazification plan, outlined in Annex XXXIII of the "Basic Preliminary Plan: Allied Control and Occupation of Germany."[50] All previous denazification policies were integrated into this decree and the Fragebogen was presented as the cornerstone of the screening campaign. The directive included detailed instructions for evaluating the form, sample documents, and a workflow chart. American vetting agents were further

---

[45] OSS, "European Political Report," March 2, 1945, Vol. II, No. 9, pp. 6–7, NARA, RG 331, SHAEF, GS, G-5, IB, HS, Box 110.
[46] CA Weekly Summary No. 38, March 3, 1945, NARA, RG 331, SHAEF, GS, G-5, Secretariat, Box 29.
[47] MG Daily Report No. 53 (Cologne), April 9, 1945, NARA, RG 498, ETO/USFET, CAD, Container 2952.
[48] Leßau, *Entnazifizierungsgeschichten*, 64.
[49] CA Weekly Summary No. 38, March 3, 1945, NARA, RG 331, SHAEF, GS, G-5, Secretariat, Box 29; "Public Safety Position Descriptions," NARA, RG 260, OMGUS, PSB, Box 332.
[50] Its full text can be found here: "Annex XXXIII (Public Safety)," March 15, 1945, NARA, RG 260, USGCC, Box 32.

supported by the April 26 issuing of policy directive JCS 1067, which included guiding principles for the military occupation and treatment of Nazis. This decree demanded that "all members of the Nazi Party who have been more than nominal participants in its activities, all active supporters of Nazism or militarism and all persons hostile to Allied purposes will be removed and excluded from public office and from positions of importance in quasi-public and private enterprises."[51] Further on in the document, it was clarified that "more than nominal" Nazis included Germans who had held office of any kind or who "believed in Nazism." These individuals were to be identified through Fragebogen screening and removed from virtually every office and agency that provided a civil service or influential bearing, including government, commerce, industry, agriculture, and education.

This hardening of denazification policy was ultimately rejected by the British and French, who considered it too severe. Instead, the CCG(BE) drafted its own more conciliatory directive, while the French offered no policy revision at all. This resulted in a further splintering of the Western Allied denazification campaign. By the end of April 1945, SHAEF was governing three independent occupation directives, each with its own program and scope for the eradication of Nazism. But while JCS 1067 created a major policy rift between the members of the western command, the basic mechanics of the political purge remained the same.

In the weeks following the German surrender, the distribution of questionnaires increased rapidly. In Frankfurt am Main, for example, over a six-day period, nearly 2,000 residents were forced to fill out the American survey, 431 of whom were dismissed from municipal offices.[52] Special Branch in nearby Neustadt reported that "detachments are giving more attention to the screening of German public officials."[53] In late June, the HQ commander for Bavaria, Col. Charles E. Keegan, bragged that in just four weeks his office had processed some 3,816 Fragebögen and that new forms were being printed at a faster rate than ever.[54] Meanwhile, the British established a "Fragebogen Department" in its Berlin office, and the *Cinquième Bureau* ordered all civil servants in its

---

[51] The full text of JCS 1067 is printed in US Department of State, *Foreign Relations of the United States. Diplomatic Papers. 1945. Volume III: European Advisory Commissions, Austria, Germany* (Washington, DC: United States Government Printing Office, 1968), 485–503.
[52] MG Daily Report, June 9, 1945, NARA, RG 331, SHAEF, GS, G-5, Secretariat, Box 28.
[53] MG Weekly Summary No. 11, June 1, 1945, NARA, RG 331, SHAEF, GS, G-5, Secretariat, Box 28.
[54] MG Weekly Report No. 7, June 29, 1945, NARA, RG 331, SHAEF, GS, G-5, Secretariat, Box 28.

administered territory to complete the survey within five days.[55] Likewise, a field report from the civil affairs detachment in Stuttgart announced that "denazification is in full swing" and that American and French officers in the city had processed thousands of questionnaires, resulting in more than 500 dismissals.[56] Even clergy were forced to complete Fragebögen, although some British officials revised the questions so as "not to offend the sensibilities of the Churches."[57]

Public Safety offices, which sometimes employed just one or two Special Branch agents, soon realized that they were not equipped to process so many questionnaires. The CCG(BE) asked for an additional 276 investigators, but the War Office denied the request, as it was dealing with its own personnel shortages.[58] To remedy this problem, neighboring districts often pooled their resources, and in some American-controlled *Kreise*, trusted Germans were hired to assist in searching records and even evaluating Fragebögen.[59]

Mayors, police chiefs, and industry managers were ordered to distribute the survey to men and women who wished to be employed in their respective office. It was their responsibility to ensure that the forms were completed on time – usually between three to five days – and then delivered to the nearest military government building for processing. More common, however, was having groups of employees complete the questionnaire while under the direct supervision of soldiers, either at a military government building, the workplace itself, or in a large public space. When US troops entered Marburg in early May 1945, all residents who had been a member of a Nazi affiliated organization were required to meet in the town's main square to complete the questionnaire.[60] They were also ordered to list the names and addresses of anyone they knew had been a party member. Some weeks earlier, in Karlsruhe and Baden Baden, French authorities demanded the entire male population between the ages of eighteen and sixty-five be registered, distributing

---

[55] "Responsibilities and Organization of Special Branch in Berlin," April 27, 1945, TNA, FO 1050/335; Grohnert, *Die Entnazifizierung in Baden*, 20–26.
[56] MG Weekly Report No. 54, June 23, 1945, NARA, RG 331, SHAEF, GS, G-5, IB, HS, Box 218; Memorandum, May 4, 1945, ADMAE, HC72.
[57] JonDavid K. Wyneken, "Driving out the Demons: German Churches, the Western Allies, and the Internationalization of the Nazi Past, 1945–1952" (PhD diss., Ohio University, 2007), 238.
[58] Jones, "Eradicating Nazism," 155.
[59] MG Weekly Summary No. 11, June 1, 1945, NARA, RG 331, SHAEF, GS, G-5, Secretariat, Box 28; Joseph R. Starr, *Denazification, Occupation and Control of Germany, March–July 1945* (Salisbury, NC: Documentary Publications, 1977), 13.
[60] Gimbel, *A German Community under American Occupation*, 48.

more than 10,000 questionnaires over the course of one day.[61] Germans who wished to work for military government as translators, clerks, or secretaries also completed a Fragebogen and were instructed to register with the local labor office.[62]

Nearly all surveys distributed in the spring of 1945 were the original 72-question SHAEF form.[63] Beginning in June, US detachments received the updated 131-point sheet, while French and Soviet soldiers continued to use the SHAEF version or issued new temporary surveys, drafted and printed in the field.[64] The circulation of these ad hoc questionnaires was common due to shortages of the official forms and because of a general propensity on the part of local military governors to formulate their own procedures.

In SHAEF-administered territories, after a Fragebogen was filled out it was forwarded by a soldier or German manager to the nearest Public Safety office. In rural districts, it sometimes ended up on the desk of a lone civil affairs agent who had no denazification training. It was their responsibility to conduct an investigation that would either confirm or refute the applicant's answers. First, each form was checked against available "black lists" and the mandatory arrest categories. The names of any implicated persons were forwarded to the relevant counterintelligence agency or to the local army detachment for investigation and possible arrest. Special Branch then began its evaluation of the remaining cases. This involved inspecting questionnaire responses for any citation of Nazi organizations, offices, or political backgrounds that required mandatory dismissal or non-appointment. Here, the *Public Safety Manual* acted as the primary reference guide. The categories listed were broad and included those who had been a member of any police or paramilitary group (including the SA and SS), nearly all ranked officials in the Nazi Party and in its dozens of axillary groups (including the Hitler Youth and Reich Labor Service), and all senior civil servants in the state bureaucracy. If an applicant had joined the NSDAP prior to 1933, they were barred from working in civil administration.

Questionnaire answers were then cross-checked against available NSDAP and police records, counterintelligence reports, civil service certificates, archived newspapers, and written statements by local

---

[61] Starr, *Denazification, Occupation and Control of Germany*, 39.
[62] Bianka J. Adams, "Between Idealism and Pragmatism: The Administration and Denazification of Bremen, United States Enclave in the Context of Anglo-American Governments in the Second World War" (PhD diss., The Catholic University of America, 1998), 330.
[63] Griffith, "The Denazification Program in the United States Zone of Germany," 44n.
[64] Julius Posener, *In Deutschland, 1945 bis 1946* (Berlin: Siedler, 2001), 65.

informants. Proven cases of falsification were sent to the military government main office.[65] After an investigation was completed and its findings recorded in a worksheet, the denazification agent submitted a "Fragebogen Action Sheet" to the original inquiring officer. In this document, the investigator's findings were summarized and the applicant placed into one of four categories, which acted as a recommendation for employment eligibility: (a) Removal or no-appointment appears mandatory; (b) Removal or non-appointment to be discretionary; (c) No objection to retention or appointment on the basis of positive evidence of Anti-Nazi activity; (d) Retention or appointment recommended.[66] Upon receipt of this official recommendation, the officer in charge of the inquiring administrative section was expected to carry out the removal or appointment, usually through a German manager intermediate. If the applicant had fallen into a discretionary removal category, the officer was granted authority in deciding their fate. These steps were multiplied and standardized as the number of questionnaires received increased. During this initial phase of the occupation, from February to July 1945, the Soviets rarely used questionnaires, but when they did, the procedures were similar, with SMA using SHAEF-issued manuals and forms.[67]

With the Potsdam Conference in sight, SHAEF was disbanded on July 14, 1945. The combined command had struggled to devise and enforce a shared denazification program in the months before and immediately after the German surrender. Battling for a common policy in a chaotic war-torn environment, the vetting machine never operated as intended. Instead of a coordinated campaign of systematic screening, the eradication of Nazism had begun as a sporadic series of mass arrests and other acts of rough justice directed by local circumstance and discretion. Similarities in the distribution and analysis of questionnaires were not the result of shared policy but practical necessity. It is perhaps because of this lack of uniformity that the Fragebogen program gathered so much momentum in the weeks after VE-Day. When the war in Europe ended, the questionnaire was the only device that occupation armies had at their disposal. Weekly field reports show how the Fragebogen gradually

---

[65] For example, MG Weekly Field Report, No. 54, June 30, 1945, NARA, RG 331, SHAEF, GS, G-5, IB, HS, Box 218.

[66] SHAEF, *Public Safety Manual of Procedures* (September 1944), Section VI, Paragraph 192. In April 1945, after their refusal to accept JCS 1067, the British instituted its own screening categories.

[67] Letter, C. W. Wickersham (US Brigadier General) to N. V. Ivanov (USSR Embassy, London), April 6, 1945, NARA, RG 260, USGCC, AG, General Correspondence, 1944–45, Box 3.

pervaded the bureaucracies of all four military governments. By early July 1945, the word Fragebogen appeared in nearly every American and British civil affairs report. Whether discussing politics, public relations, press and radio, or displaced persons, most conversations concluded with talk of political screening.

The Questionnaires under Military Government Administration, 1945–1946

In late summer 1945, after the dust from the war had settled, the victorious Allied armies divided Germany into four zones of occupation, each ruled by an autonomous military government. The Americans (OMGUS), British (CCG[BE]), French (AMFA), and Soviets (SMA) established their headquarters in Frankfurt am Main, Bad Oeynhausen, Baden Baden, and Berlin, respectively. Under their new designations, these mostly civilian-staffed administrations functioned, with some variation, at the *Land*, *Regierungsbezirk*, and *Kreis* levels. In July 1945, most soldiers withdrew to their designated zones, and while millions of tactical troops were demobilized or redeployed to the Pacific Theater, thousands of specially trained civil affairs recruits began trickling into occupation offices. The smallest detachments had one or two denazification agents, while the largest had around seventy.[68] Each zone was placed under the authority of a military governor, who acted as commanding general of their respective nation's armed forces, as well as representative to the quadripartite ACC, which sought to maintain a certain uniformity in policy across all territories.[69]

The four-power zonal arrangement was confirmed at the Potsdam Conference, in late July. This last major Allied conclave was an important pivot point in the story of denazification because it confirmed the autonomy of the four vetting campaigns. The Potsdam Agreement did not use the term "denazification," but sketched out the broadly conceived measures for the eradication of Nazism: "All members of the Nazi Party who have been more than nominal participants in its activities and all other persons hostile to Allied purposes shall be removed from public

---

[68] Adams, *From Crusade to Hazard*, 42–43.
[69] Only gradually did power shift to these new institutional hierarchies, and all military governments struggled to maintain a sufficient staff of qualified specialists. Due to the vast reduction of tactical troops, it was not uncommon for denazification officers to take on security jobs, such as guarding POW camps. Gimbel, *A German Community under American Occupation*, 39.

and semi-public office, and from positions of responsibility in important private undertakings."[70]

All signatories agreed to these actions. Despite the recent fracturing of Western Allied denazification policy, incited by the JCS 1067 directive, there remained high hopes that a common program would ultimately prevail. In fact, the Americans were confident that the other Allied nations would adopt their own revamped screening program. At the very least, the ACC would ensure the general coordination of denazification policy.

However, interzonal uniformity was never achieved during this second phase of denazification. Instead, screening activities operated in fits and starts, fluctuating between harsh and lenient interpretations of doctrine. Numerous laws were passed at the zonal level, which produced distinct campaigns of differing scope and scale. The Americans consistently cast their net the furthest, conducting a more comprehensive operation, one framed as a moral crusade with a messianic fervor. The British staggered in the opposite direction, gradually building a modest program with less arbitrary application of removal from office orders and with greater mind to economic recovery. The French allowed individual Länder to interpret denazification laws as they liked, and while political screening was widespread, punishments were not so severe. The Soviets also allowed regional administrations to determine their own policy, but only after an initial round of sweeping dismissals.[71] In the end, the Russians were not so concerned with the individual's political past but with their commitment to the future of the "antifascist" state.

It is dizzying to track the policy changes of each military government, but they all faced similar problems. Administrators struggled to distinguish between "active" and "nominal" Nazis and to enforce a punitive curriculum in an environment that longed for rehabilitation. None of the occupiers had the manpower needed to screen the number of people that their directives mandated, and the uncomfortable union of military and civilian worlds was always vulnerable to criticism. The denazification goals of the four military governments proved unrealistic and the scope of their campaigns unmanageable. In this sea of administrative confusion and policy fickleness, the Fragebogen arose as a common denominator.

Following the Potsdam Conference, the questionnaire became more embedded in American, British, and French military government bureaucracies. It had the support of the ACC and was viewed by many politicians as an objective screening tool; the program had the same

---

[70] Potsdam Agreement, Part II, Section A, Paragraph 6. [71] Bessel, *Germany 1945*, 199.

democratic face as the Nuremberg Trials.[72] However, at the ground level, most soldiers and administrators disliked the Fragebogen, believing it to be too rigid and monotonous a device. Nevertheless, whenever the popular press, or any other critic, accused denazification of being lenient, the immediate response from Western armies was to distribute more forms. Quickly, the questionnaire became tethered to the perceived success of denazification.

Another reason for the expanded use of Fragebögen was the gradual accumulation of official Nazi records. As we have learned, denazification officers initially struggled to acquire reliable intelligence for the purpose of identifying Nazis, which made the use of questionnaires difficult. However, after Potsdam, zonal headquarters began compiling large collections of civil service files, newspapers, and other physical intelligence.[73] In November 1945, the intact NSDAP archive was found at a paper-mill outside of Munich; it included the 10.7 million party membership cards.[74] These records were ultimately combined with Gestapo, SS, and other party files in the Berlin Document Center (BDC), a central file repository administered by the Americans but available to any authority that wished to cross-reference Fragebögen (see Figure 3.1).[75] As the BDC collections grew, military governments began to view the Fragebogen as a more reliable screening instrument. Remembered by John W. McDonald, an OMGUS lawyer posted in Frankfurt am Main:

Every scrap of paper that any Nazi had signed or was a part of was carefully stored away in those [BDC] files. So when we would get a case where somebody felt that this person might have falsified their questionnaire, their Fragebogen, we would ask for the file from Berlin and sometimes get back a foot of paper about what this particular person did and how he was in the hierarchy.[76]

The United States carried out the most rigorous denazification campaign and was therefore the greatest consumer of Fragebögen, albeit a rather unenthusiastic one. Its July 7 "Removal of Nazis and Militarists"

---

[72] The defendants and witnesses at the Nuremberg Trials were required to complete a special Fragebogen. See "Fragebogen für den Zeugen," BAK, ALLPROZ 3/175.
[73] For example, see "Organization of Special Branch Section, Detachment HG-307," n.d., NARA, RG 260, OMGB, FOD, Box 800.
[74] Friedlander, *Archives of the Holocaust*, x.
[75] Before they were moved to Berlin, the membership records were taken to Fürstenhagen (near Kassel) and then to Frankfurt am Main, where they were transferred onto index cards. The BDC eventually contained more than four hundred tons of records, including Nazi Party membership files and SS and SA personnel records. Berlin Document Center, *Who Was a Nazi? Facts about the Membership Procedure of the Nazi Party* (7771 Document Center, OMGUS, 1947), 7–9.
[76] John W. McDonald, Interview by Charles Stuart Kennedy (The Association for Diplomatic Studies and Training Foreign Affairs Oral History Project), June 5, 1997.

Figure 3.1 Two civil affairs officers sort through captured Nazi records at the Berlin Document Center, 1946.
Source: Archive Alliierten Museum/US Army Photography

directive launched a uniform denazification program with the questionnaire as its centerpiece. This was the strictest denazification law in any territory, as it broadened the category of "active Nazi" and required all civil servants to complete a screening questionnaire. Appended to the order was a copy of the revised form (identified as MG/PS/G/9a) and a declaration that all Germans occupying a public office or a "position of importance in a quasi-public and private enterprise" must fill one out.[77] The law listed 136 mandatory removal and expulsion categories and stipulated that membership in the NSDAP prior to May 1, 1937, or the holding of any Nazi office, was grounds for removal. A supplementary directive was announced on August 15, which called for even more screening. Public Safety officers circulated leaflets, pinned-up posters, and published notices in newspapers, informing citizens that the completion of a Fragebogen was mandatory for employment in most

---

[77] OMGUS, CAD, *Denazification, Cumulative Review. Report, 1 April 1947–30 April 1948*, pp. 23–36.

professions. When OMGUS took over operations from USFET in late September 1945, additional Special Branch offices were opened, and denazification activities became more systematic and orderly; thousands of completed forms began rolling in.

The same screening procedures were carried out in all Kreise. First, the military government official assigned to the agency or enterprise under supervision reviewed each completed form, using evaluation keys to identify any political affiliations or offices held that warranted mandatory removal or exclusion.[78] For example, answering "Yes" to Question 32 – "Have you ever been a member of the General Staff Corps?" – or Question 44 – "Were you a member of the SS Security Service [Sicherheitsdienst, SD]?" – rendered the applicant automatically ineligible for employment.[79] After this initial evaluation, the remaining questionnaires were delivered to the nearest Public Safety office. Upon arrival, they were arranged in order of importance of position and assigned an index number, which was printed on a "Fragebogen Record Card." Then the formal investigation was initiated, which meant checking questionnaire responses against local Nazi Party, government, and police records, newspapers, and voluntary denunciations, as well as documentary evidence from the BDC. Again, evaluation keys informed investigators, warning of suspicious answers, such as a salary increase after 1933, which might indicate "Nazi favoritism," or ownership of a large, landed estate, which suggested "Junker identity" with "militarist tendencies." Any notes were recorded in a worksheet. After the denazification agent completed the investigation, they filled out a "Fragebogen Action Sheet," which contained a summary of the findings and ultimate ruling on employment eligibility. If the applicant was identified as a "nominal Nazi," and therefore fell into a discretionary removal category, the local Public Safety officer made the final decision for removal or exclusion. The Action Sheet was then routed back to the original official overseeing the relevant agency or enterprise that was under review; he was required to endorse the action and return the documentation for filing.[80]

In rare cases, the occupying army allowed a particular institution to conduct its own internal purge, but screening questionnaires still had to be used. Such was the case at the University of Leipzig, where panels of

---

[78] SHAEF, *Public Safety Manual of Procedures*, Section VI, Paragraph 192.
[79] OMGB-Special Branch, *German Denazification Law and Implementations with American Directives Included*, 165–73.
[80] Fragebogen Record Cards were catalogued using a US propounding apparatus that punched holes into the cards. In some cases, IBM machines were used. Mann, *Comeback*, 64; Griffith, "The Denazification Program in the United States Zone in Germany," 17.

"democratic faculty" evaluated their colleagues and appended a joint recommendation letter to each Fragebogen, which was then forwarded to SMA headquarters.[81] In the British zone, the Evangelical Church in Germany (EKD) was allowed to "clean house" with condition that all clergy submitted a questionnaire for review by an internal denazification panel.[82] The same was true under the Soviets, as long as the Church encouraged its congregations to support the occupying authorities.[83]

It is impossible to know precisely how many Germans omitted incriminating information from their questionnaires or submitted false answers, but thousands of respondents were prosecuted for *Fragebogenfälschung* (Fragebogen falsification).[84] US Military Governor Lucius Clay admitted that while it was "almost impossible to falsify a questionnaire without detection … it was possible for some to escape the screening process."[85] There was no standard punishment for falsification, but prison sentences usually ranged from two to five years.[86] For example, an American-appointed mayor failed to record his membership in the NSDAP, which led to a two-year sentence.[87] According to one soldier, in a typical fortnight the detachment office in Munich recorded ninety-nine cases of false statements and ninety "discrepancies."[88] Across the Western zones, cases of Fragebogen falsification were published in local newspapers and posted in town squares in hopes to reduce future violations,

---

[81] Stephen P. Remy, *The Heidelberg Myth: The Nazification and Denazification of a German University* (Cambridge, MA: Harvard University Press, 2002), 161–63.

[82] "Education Control: Denazification of Clergy," June 3/4, 1946, CCG(BE), Schleswig-Holstein Region, EZA 2/323, Entnazifizierung Bd. IV.

[83] Clemens Vollnhals, "Die evangelische Kirche zwischen Traditionswahrung und Neuorientierung," in *Von Stalingrad zur Währungsreform: zur Sozialgeschichte des Umbruchs in Deutschland*, 3rd ed., eds. Martin Broszat, Klaus-Dietmar Henke, and Hans Woller (Munich: R. Oldenbourg, 1990), here 113–16. There exists a large body of scholarship on the denazification of the Protestant churches, some of the most notable works being, Clemens Vollnhals, *Evangelische Kirche und Entnazifizierung 1945–1949: Die Last der nationalsozialistischen Vergangenheit* (Munich: Deutscher Taschenbuch Verlag, 1991); Matthew D. Hockenos, *A Church Divided: German Protestants Confront the Nazi Past* (Bloomington: Indiana University Press, 2004); and Ernst Klee, *Persilscheine und falsche Pässe: Wie die Kirchen den Nazis halfen* (Frankfurt am Main: Fischer, 1991).

[84] Niethammer, *Entnazifizierung in Bayern*, 573–74. For more on data falsification during denazification proceedings, see Marie-Bénédicte Vincent, "La sanction des falsificateurs de la dénazification ou comment s'élabore une éthique de la fonction publique ouestallemande après 1945, entre héritage weimarien et renouvellement," *Allemagne d'aujourd'hui* 208 (2014): 43–55, and Leßau, *Entnazifizierungsgeschichten*, 101–19.

[85] Clay, *Decision in Germany*, 68.

[86] "Proposed release on Fragebogen procedure," June 29, 1945, BAK, POLAD, 731/15.

[87] Hubert W. Keltner, "Denazification: Problem and Program, U.S. Zone, 1945–1949" (MA thesis, Montana State University, 1954), 56n.

[88] Julian Bach Jr., *America's Germany: An Account of Occupation* (New York: Random House, 1946), 177.

while in the Soviet zone, falsifiers were fined or interned without any public notice.[89] A widely publicized trial was that of Prince Ferdinand, stepson of the deposed Kaiser, who lied in his British form.[90]

Even in cases where the answers were not falsified, investigating Fragebögen was time consuming and a highly mechanical process. Remembered by counterintelligence officer John Kormann, "the paper work entailed, as can readily be surmised, was immense."[91] An army journalist agreed, observing that although necessary, the "Fragebogen obstacle course" was exasperating for denazification officials.[92] The data submitted by each detachment office shows not only the vast scale of the program, but how it impacted nearly all occupation duties. For example, a July 1945 special report on civil administration in the Bremen Enclave is filled with references to the Fragebogen.[93] Officers in the Education, Public Works, and Financial sections of OMGUS all professed their utter reliance on questionnaires, which dictated who they could hire and consequently the ability to fulfill their assignments. Every day, thousands of Fragebögen were submitted in the US zone, often far too many for small, understaffed denazification offices to manage. By September 1945, the Land detachment in Bavaria had already received 324,729 competed forms; two months later, OMGUS reported that a total of 783,045 Fragebögen had been processed, while hundreds of thousands were still waiting for review.[94] Stationed in the Hessian town of Büdingen, Officer Hubert Keltner recalled that, "As time went on the bare walls became decorated with cases of files of Fragebogen."[95] Public Safety was well over its head, but things would soon get much worse.

At a September 22 press conference, four-star US general and district military governor of Bavaria, George S. Patton, voiced a frustration felt by many administrators. He loudly mocked implications of differentiating between "active" and "nominal" Nazis, stating that "Nazism might

[89] Niethammer, *Entnazifizierung in Bayern*, 573–74; Natalia Tsvetkova, *Failure of American and Soviet Cultural Imperialism in German Universities, 1945–1990* (Leiden: Brill, 2013), 244–45.
[90] Some British coverage of the trial: "New Tube for Mass Television," *The Evening Telegraph*, August 26, 1947, p. 4; "Kaiser's Stepson Cleared," *Derby Evening Telegraph*, October 24, 1947, p. 1. The prince's nine-month sentence was quashed by appeal.
[91] John Kormann, *U.S. Denazification Policy in Germany, 1944–1950* (Office of the Historical Division, US High Commissioner for Germany, 1952), 27.
[92] Bach, *America's Germany*, 176.
[93] "Proceedings of a Board of Officers," July 21, 1945, NARA, RG 260, USGCC, AG, General Correspondence, 1944–45, Box 4.
[94] Clemens Vollnhals, *Entnazifizierung: politische Säuberung und Rehabilitierung in den vier Besatzungzonen 1945–1949* (Munich: Deutscher Taschenbuch Verlag, 1991), 13; Griffith, "The Denazification Program in the United States Zone of Germany," 91n.
[95] Keltner, "Denazification," 66.

well be compared to any political parties at home – Republican or Democratic."[96] Patton told reporters that he did not see the need for "this denazification thing," and when asked about the Fragebogen, he sarcastically responded, "Fragebogen ... What the hell's a Fragebogen?"[97] The incident became a scandal, with the American press unleashing an unrelenting attack on denazification practices; the *New York Times* wrote that "General Patton belittles the very purpose for which the war in Europe was fought, namely, the denazification of Germany."[98]

Instead of a restrained and judicious response, American commissioners panicked. General Clay and his Assistant Deputy Major General Clarence Adcock hastily sketched out a more severe denazification law, which they hoped would change public opinion back home. Commonly referred to as Law No. 8, the "Prohibition of Employment of Members of the Nazi Party in Positions in Business other than Ordinary Labor and other Purposes" was rushed through on September 26, 1945. It was drafted in a single day and without the knowledge of any denazification staff.[99] The new directive dramatically intensified the vetting campaign in the American zone. Screening was thereafter extended to the entire economy, except agriculture, and Germans themselves were now criminally liable for failure to remove former Nazis from civil service and managerial positions.[100] With this new decree, hundreds of thousands of additional Germans were brought into the screening campaign and the Fragebogen program nearly doubled in size. Perhaps because it was known that the new prescribed categories of incrimination were problematic, an appeals procedure was created for those who fell into the mandatory removal or exclusion category.[101] However, this only increased the

---

[96] "Eisenhower Calls Patton for Denazification Report," *The Evening Independent*, September 26, 1945, p. 1.
[97] Robert Engler, "The Individual Soldier and the Occupation," *Annals of the American Academy of Political and Social Science* 257 (January 1950): 77.
[98] "General Patton on Policy," *New York Times*, September 24, 1945, p. 18. For more on the "Patton incident," see Caruthers, *The Good Occupation*, 188–89.
[99] Griffith, "The Denazification Program in the United States Zone of Germany," 96. For a copy of the full law, see Report, "Preliminary Report by Working Committee to Denazification Policy Board," December 20, 1945, NARA, RG 260, OMGUS, CAD, PSB, Box 332.
[100] US Army, *Troop I&E Bulletin: Denazification*, vol. 3, no. 15 (April 11, 1948), 10; Report, "Preliminary Report by Working Committee to Denazification Policy Board," December 20, 1945, NARA, RG 260, OMGUS, CAD, PSB, Box 332.
[101] The original draft of the law did not include procedures for appeals, this was added later. LAB, C Rep. 31/1/6, Nr. 310. The July 1945 USFET "Removal of Nazis and Militarists" directive allowed for individual appeal, but this was limited to a small group of Germans. See Niethammer, *Entnazifizierung in Bayern*, 152.

number of questionnaire submissions, as petitioners were required to fill out another survey to request an appeal. Two weeks after Law No. 8 was announced, Patton was relieved of his command; it seems the Fragebogen regime had consolidated power.

The pace of denazification operations increased enormously, as thousands of employees who held positions in the private sector – those who could hire, dismiss, set policy, or supervise others – were forced to fill out the questionnaire. Public Safety officers, who had already been struggling with the high number of Fragebögen, found themselves caught completely off guard. Before Law No. 8, some Special Branch offices were receiving around fifty Fragebögen a day, now they were seeing upward of 300. In the first month alone, more than 600,000 surveys were submitted in the American zone.[102] Army correspondent, Julian Bach Jr., estimated that "tens of thousands of Germans filled out these Fragebogen, or questionnaires, every day."[103] Questionnaires could not be printed fast enough. One civil affairs officer complained that in his detachment office in Hesse, there were only two evaluators and a dozen German clerical employees to process thousands of Fragebögen.[104] Such protest resulted in OMGUS recruiting more German civilians to assist the existing two hundred Special Branch officers in distributing, processing, and in some cases, investigating Fragebögen.[105] The need for personnel was so dire that even former Nazi Party members were hired to assist with denazification.[106]

The reaction to Law No. 8 was just as boisterous as the Patton scandal that produced it. The expanded purge was rejected by nearly everyone involved in denazification at the ground level. All but acknowledging his mistake, Clay created a special Denazification Policy Board to conduct a formal review of the screening campaign. However, the only practical solution offered was to hand over responsibility to the Germans.[107] The French and British had already devolved some power to German ministries and an assembly of civilian-staffed commissions, but the American proposal for transfer was essentially unconditional.

By the time denazification was finally delivered to the Land ministries, in June 1946, Special Branch had received a total of 1,613,000

---

[102] Griffith, "The Denazification Program in the United States Zone of Germany," 109.
[103] Bach, *America's Germany*, 169.   [104] Keltner, "Denazification," 65.
[105] "Employment Policy for OMGUS," n.d., NARA, RG 260, OMGUS, CAD, PSB, Box 442. OMGUS hired some 8,000 German civilians in Berlin alone.
[106] Ibid.
[107] Griffith, "The Denazification Program in the United States Zone of Germany," 142–43.

Table 3.1 *US Special Branch review of Fragebögen in Bavaria, Württemberg-Baden, and Hesse (prior to May 31, 1946)*[108]

Special Branch Findings	Number
Non-employment mandatory	247,193
Employment discretionary (adverse recommendation)	101,077
Employment discretionary (no adverse recommendation)	396,506
No evidence of Nazi activity	770,908
Evidence of anti-Nazi activity	6,148
Total, all findings	1,521,832

*Not included are unprocessed questionnaires and those received in the Bremen Exclave and US Sector of Berlin.

Fragebögen.[109] About 16 percent of these case applicants, or 373,762, were denied employment – it should be noted that this was a far greater turnover of personnel than the one carried out in 1933, when the Nazis came to power.[110] The vast scale of the American screening campaign is depicted in Table 3.1, as well as the sizable portion of Germans who fell into discretionary employment categories.

By enacting Law No. 8 and widening the distribution of its revised long-form questionnaire, OMGUS became typecast as an overly bureaucratic and impractical administrator. On November 6, 1945, American journalist John Dos Passos visited the Military Government office in Bad Wiesse and asked the lead denazification agent how it was possible that so many former Nazis had been screened in such a short period of time. The response was simple: "It's the fragebogen. You don't know about the fragebogen. The fragebogen's the greatest thing in Germany. ... Everybody gets fragebogend sooner or later."[111] Dos Passos's resulting article on the military occupation was appropriately titled, "Land of the Fragebogen."

In the British zone, the denazification campaign was not as enthusiastic or extensive. Most activities were governed by the August 1945, "Directive on Arrest and Removal," which reduced the number of SHAEF mandatory categories and granted more discretionary powers to officers in the field. Still, much like its American counterpart, the CCG(BE) relied on screening questionnaires. All Germans employed or

---

[108] Report of the Military Governor, No. 34, "Denazification (Cumulative Review)," April 1, 1947–April 30, 1948, Office of the Military Government for Germany (US), p. 3.
[109] Plischke, *Denazifying the Reich*, 158.
[110] Zink, *American Military Government in Germany*, 142–43; Bessel, *Germany 1945*, 195.
[111] John Dos Passos, *Tour of Duty* (Boston: Houghton Mifflin, 1946), 254.

seeking employment in public offices and enterprises were required to complete a Fragebogen. Special Branch officers operating under Public Safety collected forms and opened individual investigations by accessing seized party and police records, speaking to informants, and working in conjunction with the BDC. Producing similar outcomes as the Americans, the British instituted its own employment categories. Fragebögen were classified as either "M," removal or non-appointment mandatory; "D," removal or non-appointment within discretion of the military government; "NEG," no objection to appointment or retention; or "R," retention or appointment recommended.[112] For applicants graded into the first two groups, they had the option of petitioning the decision in an appellate court.[113] While OMGUS had expanded "active" Nazi status to include party members who had joined prior to May 1937, the British continued to use the date of January 1933 to differentiate between "active" (removal mandatory) and "nominal" (removal discretionary) Nazis.[114]

The British never fully extended its purge to private industry, there was no equivalent to Law No. 8, and this was for practical reasons. The CCG (BE) governed the largest and most physically devastated zone in Germany, and it feared a wholesale economic collapse. Furthermore, the British government was not as sensitive to criticism from its domestic press, of which there was plenty, or prone to radical policy swings. Still, hundreds of thousands of Germans were subjected to the questionnaire program. By October 1945, around 60,000 questionnaires had been processed just in the city of Hamburg.[115] As explained by Frank Donnison, the official historian of the British occupation, "there was never any attempt to conduct denazification on such a scale [as the Americans] but the operation nevertheless involved the evaluation of several thousand fragebogen daily."[116]

Persons with Nazi affiliations working for local government were screened without clemency. Because there existed little administrative oversight from CCG(BE) headquarters in Bad Oeynhausen, Special Branch sometimes handed out Fragebögen to private sector workers, and not just supervisors. For example, despite the coal industry being granted amnesty from denazification orders, some key managerial and

---

[112] Donnison, *Civil Affairs and Military Government: North-West Europe*, 364.
[113] Stella Moore, "Fragebogen: British Questions to Germans," *The Scotsman*, June 1, 1946, p. 5.
[114] OMGUS, CAD, *Denazification, Cumulative Review. Report, 1 April 1947–30 April 1948*, p. 1.
[115] Report, "The Progress on De-nazification," October 16, 1945, TNA, FO 1050/119.
[116] Donnison, *Civil Affairs and Military Government North-West Europe*, 367.

technical personnel were screened and dismissed.[117] German teachers, doctors, postal and railway workers, and municipal clerks were all required to complete either the SHAEF questionnaire or the revised British form, sometimes with an appended sheet containing additional questions.[118] One German public health officer who assisted in coordinating screening procedures, elaborated on its wide scope, that forms were required by "nursing directors in hospitals, mother-house officials, public health agencies, and to individual midwives."[119] Journalists and artists were also screened en mass. In Hamburg, a prominent actor and film producer was fined 5,000 marks and sentenced to six months in prison for falsifying his Fragebogen.[120] Like OMGUS, the CCG(BE) occasionally tolerated internal purges, but again, only on the condition that questionnaires were used and completed correctly. The Rector of the University of Kiel, for example, was removed when it was discovered he had manipulated the Fragebögen of a number of professors.[121]

On January 12, 1946, the Allied Control Council introduced Directive 24, which required all zonal governments to establish a comprehensive set of removal and exclusion criteria for more than nominal Nazis and to expand their Fragebögen programs.[122] By then, however, the British were already overwhelmed with questionnaires, having accumulated a massive backlog.[123] In an October 1945 report, the Standing Committee on Denazification admitted that "the progress of de-Nazification has inevitably been deliberate rather than speedy owing to the enormous weight of work involved in the examination of thousands of Fragebogen."[124] Rather reluctantly then, the British were forced to involve Germans in the administration of denazification, transferring some responsibility in January 1946, with the enactment of Zonal Policy Instruction 3. Over the next two years, another 2 million questionnaires were filled out; both the German officials and the CCG(BE), who continued to screen for key positions, relied on the instrument.[125] The fundamental importance of the Fragebogen to all authorities

---

[117] Adams, *From Crusade to Hazard*, 47.
[118] "Nachtrag zum Fragebogen," December 31, 1945, BAK, Z 31/274.
[119] Lorraine Setzler, "Nursing and Nursing Education in Germany," *The American Journal of Nursing* 45, no. 12 (December 1945): 994.
[120] "German Film Actor Sentenced; Gave False Information," *The Manchester Guardian*, November 27, 1945, p. 5.
[121] Biddiscombe, *Denazification of Germany*, 97.
[122] For the full text of Directive 24, see "Allied Control Authority: Directive No. 24," NARA, RG 260, OMGUS, OMGBr, Denazification Division, Box 174.
[123] Vollnhals, *Entnazifizierung*, 26.
[124] Report, "The Progress on De-nazification," October 16, 1945, TNA, FO 1050/119.
[125] Vollnhals, *Entnazifizierung*, 28.

The Questionnaires under Military Government Administration   137

operating in the British zone is illustrated by Stella Moore, a reporter for *The Scotsman*, in a June 1946 article: "One of the phrases most frequently met in Germany to-day is the German word 'Fragebogen' – meaning 'questionnaire.' The word is used as if it were English, and an official will ask 'Has this man been Fragebogened?' These questions play, in fact, a most important part in Germany under Allied control."[126]

The French handed over some limited responsibility for political screening to the Germans in September 1945, considerably earlier than the British and Americans. By the time this transition was complete, the AMFA had already become reliant on questionnaires. In August 1945, the long overdue denazification (or *épuration*) policy manual had arrived from Paris, which led to the drafting of a uniquely French Fragebogen. The new form was printed at AMFA headquarters in Baden Baden and distributed to the three Länder, as well as the Saar Region and Berlin. By the end of the month, tens of thousands of forms had arrived at regional military government offices. As we have already learned, the new questionnaire was essentially the same as the American form and screening procedures closely resembled those indicated earlier under SHAEF.[127] In fact, many Sûreté offices, operating at the Kreis level, continued to use the original SHAEF form.[128] Much like the other Allied occupiers, the French took advantage of seized Nazi records housed in the BDC to cross-reference responses.[129]

The screening program expanded quickly in the fall of 1945, even after the decision was made to establish German commissions. In an October memorandum, Administrator General of the French zone, Émile Laffon, reasserted the centrality of the Fragebogen in the screening campaign: "SHAEF's instructions require the use of a questionnaire. It will therefore be necessary in the sphere of private economy to have similar documents drawn up in the shortest possible time ... Questionnaires will begin being processed even before the establishment of the committees."[130]

In all French-occupied regions, civil servants, and some managers in private industry, were subject to screening. Some were forced to fill out a

---

[126] Moore, "Fragebogen."
[127] For example, Fragebogen of H.G., January 19, 1946, ADMAE, ZFO, WH 1298.
[128] For example, Fragebogen of F.W., April 17, 1947, ADMAE, ZFO, RP 11/5.
[129] "Disposition of Special Branch Records," July 28, 1948, ADMAE, ZFO, AP 81/1, 3306/116, État des opérations de dénazification en Zone américaine (1946–1948); Möhler, *Entnazifizierung in Rheinland-Pfalz und im Saarland unter französischer Besatzung*, 187–89.
[130] Memorandum, October 31, 1945, ADMAE, AP 72/2, Dénazification: Dossier général (1946–48), 3902/89.

Fragebogen under direct supervision of occupation soldiers, while others took the form home and returned it within three days. Typically, political leaders were the first to be screened, then the process disseminated downward, from the Kreis and rural district level to municipal governments and then regular civil service offices.[131] The AMFA greatly emphasized the role of education in a denazified Germany and therefore every teacher in the zone was carefully screened. Newspaper and radio staff were also some of the first to submit a questionnaire to the Sûreté for investigation.[132]

At least a dozen new surveys, tailored for specific industries and professions, were published in the French zone. For example, film exhibitors in Freiburg completed two special Fragebögen, which contained questions concerning Nazi business dealings and partnerships.[133] Similarly, a sheet of "Special Questions for the Directorate of the News Office" was appended to questionnaires distributed to journalists and editors in Württemberg-Baden, asking about past employment in "propaganda companies."[134] The Americans, British, and Soviets also produced profession- and industry-specific questionnaires, but many more varieties existed in the French zone. While there were six different versions in the US zone, no fewer than twenty-three were distributed by the French. It seems that the AFMA was more attentive to the nuances of Nazi affiliation and the circumstances of individual respondents. According to an unofficial source, the screened population in the French zone ranged from 8 percent to 57 percent.[135] Plainly stated in an official July 1946 memo circulated in Württemberg-Baden: "Regarding the Fragebogen, we must maintain an incredibly flexible policy."[136]

Allowing for local autonomy does not seem to have come at the cost of a lenient campaign. Unlike in the American, British, and Soviet territories, the French attempted to interrogate all repatriated refugees, returning POWs, and some former members of Nazi youth

---

[131] Biddiscombe, *Denazification of Germany*, 164.
[132] Report, Direction L'Information, "Sur l'oeuvre de demilitarisation, dénazification et de democratisation entreprise par la Direction de l'Information," January 8, 1947, ADMAE, ZFO, AP 141/2, Affaires Politiques, Service Information, Dénazification Épuration, 1945–48.
[133] Campion, "Negotiating Difference," 132.
[134] Fragebogen of J.S., December 12, 1945, ADMAE, AP 141/1a, Affaires Politiques, Service Information, Journalistes allemandes (1), 1945–49.
[135] Biddiscombe, *Denazification of Germany*, 164.
[136] Memo, Director of Division of Justice to the Military Tribunal, Freiburg, July 12, 1946, ADMAE, ZFO, BADE 1303.

organizations.[137] Rudolf Dorner was only fourteen when he was ordered to complete a political survey.[138] In February 1946, members of the German Red Cross were also required to fill out the form, and in the Saar Protectorate, the questionnaire was used to screen citizens for potential expulsion.[139] In all other zones, hundreds of thousands of late-returning POWs were not required to complete a Fragebogen, nor were refugees, who, at least on paper, fell under the administrative purview of the United Nations Relief and Rehabilitation Administration (UNRRA).[140] Despite being significantly smaller in size and population, an estimated 670,000 questionnaires were processed by the AFMA.[141] With a zonal population of only 3,949,000, this represents a greater proportion of Fragebögen than in any other zone.

Like the French, denazification activities under the Soviet Military Administration were carried out unevenly, even after the Potsdam Conference. The Fragebogen was used only sparingly and with little consistency between Länder. From the onset of the occupation, the Russians were more willing to grant denazification powers to German antifascist groups, but a full transfer of screening authority did not come until much later. With little oversight from Berlin, local officials established their own procedures for screening, sometimes circulating questionnaires but more often relying on informal intelligence, especially voluntary denunciations.

The purge moved forward clumsily over the winter of 1945/46, with SMA watching the American campaign with great interest and adopting some of its instruments and procedures. Publicly, the Russians claimed its program was thoroughly independent, going so far as to disregard the American-inspired ACC Directive No. 24, at least initially.[142] Still, screening questionnaires were distributed. In its designated sector of

---

[137] Biddiscombe, *Denazification of Germany*, 178.
[138] Dr. Rudolf Dorner in discussion with the author in Hamburg, July 24, 2013. In the US zone, Germans below the age of eighteen were exempt from political screening, at least during the military government phase. Lutz Niethammer, *Die Mitläuferfabrik: die Entnazifizierung am Beispiel Bayerns* (Berlin: Dietz, 1982), 343–44; OMGUS, *Denazification, Cumulative Review. Report, 1 April 1947–30 April 1948*, p. 3.
[139] Letter, Dr. Pieper to Administrator Governor Laffon, October 22, 1945, ADMAE, AP 72/2, Dénazification: dossier général (1946–48), 3902/89; Bronson Long, *No Easy Occupation: French Control of the German Saar, 1944–1957* (Rochester, NY: Camden House, 2015), 45.
[140] "German Denazification Law and Implementation with American Directives Included," June 15, 46, Institut für Zeitgeschichte, 11/Dk, 090.003.
[141] OMGUS, *Denazification, Cumulative Review. Report, 1 April 1947–30 April 1948*, p. 13; Henke, *Politische Säuberung unter französischer Besatzung*, 171–72; Fürstenau, *Entnazifizierung*, 146–47, 228–30; Biddiscombe, *Denazification of Germany*, 181.
[142] Biddiscombe, *Denazification in Germany*, 138.

Berlin, SMA investigated 12,000 municipal police officers using the SHAEF form, most of whom were dismissed, and in Saxony, all 6,842 former Nazis removed from municipal offices had completed a questionnaire.[143] There are also recorded cases of questionnaires being used to screen healthcare professionals, teachers, Reichsbahn workers, and farmers.[144] Still, the institutionalization of the program did not occur until the early months of 1947, when dozens of district-level commissions, staffed by Germans, began operation. Before then, the use of questionnaires was spontaneous and improvised, much like all denazification activities in the Soviet zone. Common was the drafting of makeshift surveys for use in a specific district, with little coordination from Berlin.[145] When Directive 24 was finally instituted by SMA in early 1947, a new Fragebogen was written for the German-staffed commissions and circulated widely.[146]

Criticism of the questionnaire transcended zonal boundaries. Perhaps no other military government project came under such negative scrutiny. The condemnation was far reaching and profound; military governors, denazification officers, regular soldiers, and journalists reviled the form and the campaign it sustained. The German distaste for the Fragebogen is well known, but what the occupation authorities thought of their flagship strategy to eradicate Nazism is not.

To be fair, there was some subtle approval. Aldo Raffa and O. W. Wilson, the authors of the original questionnaire, were confident that the mistakes made in Italy would not be replicated in Germany, and the occasional soldier marveled in the size of the program and its broad implications.[147] When the denazification machine was working, the Fragebogen was applauded; but it was almost never working. Instead, most parties viewed the questionnaire as the source of many of the problems that plagued military government and as a physical representation of an overly ambitious and painfully bureaucratic denazification campaign. Early criticism was aimed at the mere concept of an ideological cleanse and the belief that a blunt instrument could effectively and fairly evaluate the personal sentiments of Germans. Candidly described

---

[143] Ibid., 129.
[144] Report, "Gesetz über die Reinigung der öffentlichen Verwaltung von Nazi-Elementen vom 23. Juli 1945," October 1, 1945, BAB, DQ 1/1336; "Reinigung vom Nationalsozialismus," July 5, 1945, BAB, DM 1/1494; "Entnazifizierung der Molkerei-Genossenschaften in der Provinz Mark Brandenburg," September 17, 1946, BAB, DY 30-IV, 2/7/291.
[145] For example, Fragebogen of H.P., May 10, 1945, BAB, R 8128/5191.
[146] "Fragebogen und Antrag zur Direktive 24," n.d., BAB, R 8128/5191.
[147] Milton Backer, "Rich Gives AMG Biggest Problem," *New York Times*, April 1, 1945, p. 8; Dos Passos, *Tour of Duty*, 255.

in 1949 by Chief of the OMGUS Denazification Division, Joseph F. Napoli: "We who have been active in denazification have realized from the first days of the occupation that we were swimming against the tide. We have been attacked as Communists, as Jewish *Rächer* [avengers], and as impractical idealists. The attacks on us have come from both German and American sources."[148]

Some administrators recognized that the nuances of living under a totalitarian dictatorship could not be interpreted in a standardized six-page form or captured in rigid categories of political affiliation. Reflected upon by US Military Governor Clay: "Our Public Safety officers had to apply arbitrary definitions to determine the degree of participation which would exclude the individual and frequently this led to injustices which punished the nominal participant as severely as the active one."[149] A similar admission was made by the Legal Advice Branch in Bavaria, that a "great deal of injustice has been done in fragebogen cases."[150] Others believed that far too much emphasis was being placed on removing incriminated Germans from employment and not enough on reorientation.[151] Most administrators agreed that the Fragebogen was far too complicated a document and that the evaluation process was unnecessarily bureaucratic. They argued that Germans did not fully understand the questions being asked of them, or the consequence of their answers, and that evaluators were not qualified to make major discretionary decisions about employment.

After witnessing the questionnaire program in action, Wolfgang Friedman, a British officer, claimed that "almost every German of any prominence has filled out the Fragebogen at least six times" and that this "should have been reduced."[152] Such concern was echoed by Richard Stokes, an elected official in the House of Commons who, during a November 1946 sitting, declared to his peers: "I am told that a great many people have been de-Nazified – it sounds almost like deloused – three times, and that there are still over a million waiting to be de-Nazified, or to answer a ridiculous questionnaire containing 150 ludicrous

---

[148] Joseph F. Napoli, "Denazification from an American's Viewpoint," *Annals of the American Academy of Political and Social Science* 264 (July 1949): 115.
[149] Clay, *Decision in Germany*, 69.
[150] Letter, Dr. Rheinstein to R. L. Guthrie, December 10, 1946, BAK, OMGUS, 15/128–1/18.
[151] Griffith, "The Denazification Program in the United States Zone of Germany," 134.
[152] Wolfgang Friedmann, *The Allied Military Government of Germany* (London: Stevens & Sons, 1947), 116.

questions."[153] John W. McDonald, a lawyer employed by OMGUS admitted that "it was a very complicated questionnaire, and a lot of Nazis filled them out incorrectly."[154] After visiting the Special Branch office in Stuttgart, the Swedish reporter and novelist Stig Dagerman referred to the Fragebogen as a "kind of ideological equivalent of tax returns."[155] Others, including an OSS agent, believed that too much confidence was being placed in investigators who read little German and who knew nothing about the Nazi dictatorship.[156] One American denazification officer confessed:

> We ought to have more preparation ... I just don't have the preparation for this job ... I only had a high school education ... I went to school all right at Charlottesville ... but most of the time I've had to throw the book out the window ... It's surprising we do as well as we do with the conflicting directives we get and the reports...[157]

However, the domestic press was perhaps the greatest critic of all. Inflamed by wartime emotions, journalists aggressively attacked any instance in which denazification was suspected of being implemented leniently or that accommodations were being made to former Nazis. The American liberal press was especially swift to expose half-baked efforts to remove former Nazis from positions of influence. A September 1945 *New York Times* article accused the Military Government of a "lackadaisical attitude" in its enforcement of denazification, citing General Patton's comments about the Fragebogen and claiming that "Nazis Keep the Best Jobs."[158] Writing for the *Associated Press*, Louis P. Lochner explained that the "voluminous 'fragebogen'" was a flawed instrument and that it allowed many Nazis to evade justice.[159] Likewise, the *Montreal Gazette* announced that "Nazis Still Hold Big Jobs in Reich," while *The Scotsman* reported that the Fragebogen produced an enormous amount of work, which forced military governments to cut

---

[153] House of Commons, Sitting, November 27, 1946, "British Administration, Germany," in *Parliamentary Debates, House of Commons Hansard*, 5th Series, Vol. 430, col. 1690–1748, here col. 1724.

[154] John W. McDonald, Interview by Charles Stuart Kennedy (The Association for Diplomatic Studies and Training Foreign Affairs Oral History Project), June 5, 1997.

[155] Dagerman, *German Autumn*, 66.

[156] John H. Herz, "The Fiasco of Denazification in Germany," *Political Science Quarterly* 63, no. 4 (December 1948): 570–71.

[157] Dos Passos, *Tour of Duty*, 261.

[158] Raymond Daniell, "Denazification Hit by U.S. Officers," *New York Times*, September 21, 1945, p. 10.

[159] Louis P. Lochner, "Bavaria's Public Offices Purges, A.M.G. Turns De-Nazification Drive on Business and Industry," *St. Louis Post-Dispatch*, October 26, 1945.

corners.[160] Such reports waxed and waned in synchrony with various scandals, such as those already mentioned in Aachen and Bavaria. Nothing good was ever said of the Fragebogen, only that it was not being used as intended, and that when it was, Germans found ways to manipulate it.[161] Applicants could conceal their pasts by simply changing their name on the form or continuing to operate a private business by transferring ownership to their spouse or a relative, whose political past was clean.[162]

Perhaps the most popular line of criticism, one voiced mainly by denazification officials themselves, was that the Fragebogen program was too broad in its scope and that it demanded an impractical amount of resources. Public Safety reports, military government memorandums, and ACC meeting minutes exhaustively ridiculed the project for this reason. Some critics pointed to the lack of qualified investigators, while others lamented the insufficient manpower, low budgets, and paper shortages. A June 1946 progress report from a detachment office in British-controlled Hannover explained that "denazification is proceeding according to plan though speed has decreased owing to lack of Fragebogen."[163] German authorities voiced similar grievances about the scarcity of questionnaires. For example, city council members for greater Berlin complained regularity to the four-power Kommandatura about a "paper shortage in the denazification commissions."[164] Even finding enough space to store the questionnaires was an issue. Denazification officer Harold Zink described how the forms were "stacked in bundles, more or less as fire wood is stacked, in the hallways, in closets, in cellars, and indeed wherever vacant space could be found."[165] This category of criticism was almost always paired with statistical evidence. That only 25 percent of Fragebögen had been processed or that the BDC could not possibly cross-check hundreds of thousands of forms.[166]

---

[160] Raymond Daniell, "Nazis Still Hold Big Jobs in Reich," *Montreal Gazette*, September 22, 1945, p. 3; "Still Too Many Nazis," *The Scotsman*, March 22, 1946, p. 4.
[161] Biddiscombe, *Denazification of Germany*, 59.
[162] Adams, *From Crusade to Hazard*, 37–38.
[163] "Excerpt from the Ninth Monthly Report HQ Mil HQs, Hannover Region for 1 to 30 June 1946," n.d. TNA, FO 1051/687.
[164] Meeting Minutes, "Achtzehnte Sitzung der Stadtverordnetenversammlung von Groß-Berlin," February 27, 1947, LAB, C Rep. 1, Stadtverordnetenversammlung von Groß-Berlin, Nr. 18.
[165] Zink, *The United States in Germany*, 159.
[166] Fitzgibbon, *Denazification*, 140; Otto Gritschneder, *Dead End "Denazification"* (Munich: Dr. Otto Gritschneder, 1948), 39.

Whatever the specific complaint, the resounding consensus was that while denazification was necessary, the procedures used to achieve it were not realistic or effective. At best, functional officers held an apathetic attitude; most were cynical about the foreseeable outcome of the purge. When Victor Gollancz asked a high-placed British official how long it would take to process the many Fragebögen piling up in his office, he replied "About two years ... but of course, the whole thing will be discontinued before then."[167]

It is remarkable that such a fundamental and widely used instrument of the occupation had practically no support from any level of government or from the military. This emphasizes a point made in the two previous chapters, that the Fragebogen was never a consensus document. Instead, it was accepted out of necessity, and developed haphazardly. Even more interesting is that despite the Fragebogen causing so many administrative problems and being the source of so much criticism, it was continuously offered as a solution. The unchecked expansion of the screening campaign, including reactionary legislation, such as Law No. 8, resulted in more questionnaires, which in turn, led to the collapse of military government denazification efforts and the transfer of authority to the Germans.

The Questionnaires under German Administration, 1946–1949

The Germans inherited responsibility for denazification at different times, stretched out over a fifteen-month period: The French devolved limited authority in September 1945, followed by the British in January 1946, the Americans in March 1946, and the Soviets in December 1946. Within each zone, the transfer occurred unevenly, and the amount of responsibility granted to German institutions varied widely. Still, the reason for this administrative overhaul was the same in Frankfurt am Main, Bad Oeynhausen, Baden Baden, and Berlin. It was meant to relieve military government personnel of the exhaustive task of political screening. For the three Western occupiers, sidestepping an excessively critical domestic press and demobilizing a wearied army were added incentives. Throughout 1946, denazification increasingly became a German problem, which was still dominated by mass screening and categorization, but also included judicial review and sanctions.

---

[167] Gollancz, *In Darkest Germany*, 103.

The ACC hoped to manage the staggered transfer of responsibility. Its Directive No. 24, issued on January 12, 1946, was an attempt to standardize denazification across all zones and install a more rigorous system of screening. The new law introduced a comprehensive criterion for the removal and exclusion of "more than nominal Nazis" from public, semi-public, and important private offices by outlining ninety-nine compulsory removal categories, many of which had previously been classified as discretionary.[168] Every job candidate, without exception, had to complete a Fragebogen. A second order, Directive No. 38, was announced October 12, 1946, introducing five categories of incrimination and quasi-judicial procedures for investigating and punishing Germans.[169] The British, French, and Soviets were resistant to the wide scope and rigidity of this ACC curriculum, which was modeled on the American system, but eventually, both directives were adopted by all the occupiers. Guided by ACC policy, each vetting campaign was now permanently recast to allow Germans to investigate and judge their own people. Thousands of denazification boards – called commissions, committees, councils, or tribunals – were established, scattered throughout the four zones, employing tens of thousands of civilians.

The British and French were the first to entrust authority to denazification boards, although they did so in phases. In late 1945, the CCG (BE) set up Kreis-level German Advisory Councils to assist Special Branch in assessing cases that had landed in the discretionary removal category. Additional authority was transferred in January, with the issuance of Zonal Policy Instruction 3. A German-staffed "Denazification Panel" was created in each district, charged with nominating members to the more numerous "German Review Boards." These two bodies sorted through Fragebögen and made recommendations about job eligibility to the Public Safety Branch.

The French had in fact created a committee system four months earlier, in September 1945, by authority of General Pierre Koenig and his civil administrator, Émile Laffont. Under Directive CAB/C 722, each of the three Land governments, as well as the Saar Protectorate, created a centralized *Säuberungskommissionen* (*Chambres d'épuration*), which received cases from the dozens of *Untersuchungsausschüsse* (*Delegation d'instruction*) that screened job candidates at the Kreis level.[170]

---

[168] Directive, "ACC Draft Directive on the Removal from Office and from Positions of Responsibility of Nazis and of Persons Hostile to Allied Purposes," January 12, 1946, NARA, RG 260, OMGUS, CAD, PSB, Box 441.

[169] Ruhm von Oppen, *Documents on Germany under Occupation*, 168.

[170] Möhler, *Entnazifizierung in Rheinland-Pfalz und im Saarland unter französischer Besatzung*, 76; Grohnert, *Die Entnazifizierung in Baden*, 80–88.

The *Säuberungskommissionen* imposed one of four punishments: transfer, demotion, forced retirement, or dismissal with loss of pension benefits.[171] The French ignored most of the regulations outlined in Directive No. 24, but when Directive No. 38 was announced in October, the AFMA ordered all Länder to implement the five classifications of guilt, much like in the US zone.

The Americans handed denazification over to the Germans in one great swoop, with its March 5, 1946 "Law for Liberation from National Socialism and Militarism" (*Gesetz zur Befreiung von Nationalsozialismus und Militarismus*), or "Liberation Law."[172] This landmark piece of legislation transferred all executive functions for political screening to newly created denazification ministries, one for each of the four Land governments, who administered their portion of a zonal network of 545 *Spruchkammern* (Special Tribunals), as well as supporting *Berufungskammern* (Appellate Tribunals). These nonjudicial commissions began operating at the Kreis level in June 1946 and were staffed by around 22,000 Germans.[173] The Liberation Law also introduced a much shorter screening questionnaire, called a *Meldebogen* (registration form), which every German over the age of eighteen had to complete in order to receive a food rations card. If the form indicated that the respondent was chargeable under the new law, they were required to face a tribunal, where a principle of presumptive guilt was imposed. After reviewing documented evidence and hearing testimony, a four-person tribunal panel determined which category of guilt the subject under review would be placed: *Hauptschuldige* (Major Offender), *Belastete* (Offender), *Minderbelastete* (Lesser Offender), *Mitläufer* (Follower), or *Entlastete* (Exonerated).[174] Each category had a corresponding punishment, from arrest to amnesty. In all zones, most respondents were categorized as Mitläufer or likewise term – accused of being unimpassioned Nazi supporters, one susceptible to peer pressure – which usually only mandated a minor penalty, such as a nominal fine. Famous Mitläufer were Martin Heidegger and Leni Riefenstahl. Around 3.66 million Germans were forced to face one of these US zone denazification tribunals.[175]

---

[171] Biddiscombe, *Denazification of Germany*, 168.
[172] For a full copy of the Liberation Law, see "German Denazification Law and Implementation with American Directives Included," June 15, 1946, Institut für Zeitgeschichte (hereafter, IfZ), 11/Dk, 090.003.
[173] Clay, *Decision in Germany*, 259.
[174] Hermann Weber, *Das Gesetz zur politischen Säuberung vom 5. März 1946* (Karlsruhe: Badenia, 1947).
[175] Norbert Frei, *Adenauer's Germany and the Nazi Past: The Politics of Amnesty and Integration* (New York: Columbia University Press, 2002), 38–39; Montgomery, *Forced to Be Free*, 23.

Early in the occupation, the Soviets allowed some limited German participation, but a complete transfer of responsibility for denazification did not come until late 1946. Finally adhering to ACC Directive No. 24, a network of 2,562 German-staffed commissions was established to screen some 850,000 people for Nazi ties and sympathies.[176] Each Land supervised its own set of district and city commissions, which were chaired by a prominent antifascist, as well as representatives from the SED, CDU, and *Liberal-Demokratische Partei* (LDP), and a single trade unionist.[177] Under the new administrative framework, some local discrepancies continued but political screening was surprisingly consistent across the zone. Further centralization came in August 1947, when SMA issued Order 201, which unified the commission system across the five Länder and brought the political purge firmly under the control of the SED.[178] This much more liberal directive stressed rehabilitation rather than punishment, as the Russians realized that in order to ensure long-term political and economic stability of a socialist government, they would have to reinstate some former Nazis. As a result, thousands of Germans who had previously been denied work in civil service offices and private businesses were permitted to reapply.

It would be wrong to state that denazification was now only a German endeavor, despite this being the common portrayal. All military governments continued to screen for the most senior offices. In fact, OMGUS Special Branch disapproved of the Liberation Law and insisted, with some success, that their organization maintain authority to intervene in the evaluation of some Fragebögen and to block tribunal decisions.[179] Across the four zones, the occupiers continued to screen mayors, police chiefs, and the heads of large private companies. Political parties, universities, performing arts groups, newspapers, and radio broadcasters also remained under the purview of military government.[180] In some special districts, like Berlin and Bremen, civil affairs officers continued to distribute Fragebögen much like they had prior to the establishment of the

---

[176] Steven M. Schroeder, *To Forget It All and Begin Anew: Reconciliation in Occupied Germany, 1944–1954* (Toronto: University of Toronto Press, 2013), 22.
[177] Vogt, *Denazification in Soviet-Occupied Germany*, 116.
[178] Welsh, *Revolutionärer Wandel auf Befehl?*, 187–88.
[179] Griffith, "The Denazification Program in the United States Zone of Germany," 153.
[180] Report, "Sur l'oeuvre de demilitarisation, dénazifictaion, et de democratisation entreprise par la Direction de l'Information," January 8, 1947, ADMAE, ZFO, AP 0141/2, Affaires Politiques, Service Information, Dénazification Épuration, 1945–48; Potter, *Art of Suppression*, 99; Biddiscombe, *Denazification of Germany*, 65; Toby Thacker, *The End of the Third Reich: Defeat, Denazification & Nuremberg, January 1944–November 1946* (Stroud, Gloucestershire: Tempus, 2006), 50.

German commissions.[181] It must also be remembered that the occupation armies still managed the majority of seized Nazi records, including those in the Berlin Document Center, and therefore worked closely with denazification committees to cross-check questionnaire responses. Cases of falsification were also forwarded to the respective military government offices for investigation.[182]

Furthermore, in all zones, Germans who wished to be employed by military government, as clerks, translators, drivers, or assistants, were screened directly by the Allied armies.[183] Tens of thousands of civilians were investigated for this purpose. Employees in German denazification ministries and prosecutors' offices, as well as all board members of the commissions were also required to complete a military government-issued questionnaire.[184] In March 1946, the Special Branch detachment in the British Sector of Berlin estimated that it still received about 5,000 questionnaires per month.[185]

Table 3.2 shows that in a typical one-week period, the US Special Branch in Bavaria not only cross-checked Meldebögen submitted by

Table 3.2 *Questionnaire activities by US Special Branch in Bavaria (August 13–19, 1946)*[186]

Special Investigation Section	
Backlogged Fragebogen	113
Fragebogen received	10
Fragebogen processed	12
Prosecution Section	
Backlogged Fragebogen	280
Cases of Fragebogen falsification received	18
Record Checking	
Meldebogen cross-checked locally	1,864
Number of discrepancies found	19

---

[181] Report, "Durchführungs- und Ausführungsbestimmungen zum Gesetz über die Reinigung der öffentlichen Verwaltung von Nazi-Elementen," July 23, 1945, BAB, DQ 1/1336; Report, "Denazification in Berlin," October 30, 1945, AM, AK 94/10; Adams, *From Crusade to Hazard*, 74.

[182] James Tent, *Mission on the Rhine: Reeducation and Denazification in American-Occupied Germany* (Chicago: University of Chicago Press, 1982), 83.

[183] For example, "Fragebogen Cases," October 4, 1949, FO 1051/110.

[184] "German Denazification Law and Implementation with American Directives Included," June 15, 1946, IfZ, 11/Dk, 090.003.

[185] "Special Branch – Berlin," March 16, 1946, TNA, FO 1050/335.

[186] "Weekly Information Report (for the period 13–19 August 1946)," August 20, 1946, NARA, RG 260, OMGUS, OMGB, CAD, PS, SB, Box 90.

German courts but conducted its own independent investigations using the Fragebogen.

The questionnaire was therefore not simply altered and passed off to the new constellation of German-staffed commissions. Instead, the workload was shared, and everyone used screening surveys. When OMGUS ordered the discontinuation of the Fragebogen in January 1947, Special Branch refused to abide and continued to distribute the form.[187] Even when denazification was abandoned altogether, first by the Russians in March 1948, then in the Western zones in late 1948 and early 1949, the Fragebogen was still being distributed by all four occupation authorities. Konrad Adenauer's first-term government used political surveys to screen for important public positions as late as 1953.[188] A comparable form, called a *Personalbogen*, was used for the same purpose in the early years of the German Democratic Republic.[189]

Nevertheless, from 1946 to 1948, most questionnaires were processed by the approximately 4,000 German denazification committees and public prosecutors' offices. During this phase of the purge, the use of questionnaires was greatly extended, with upward of 16 million people completing the survey in one of its many varieties.[190] Each German ministry adopted the Fragebogen of its respective military government, and although there remained considerable variation between zones, and even Länder, the screening process had the same basic parameters.

Job candidates and accused Nazis completed a questionnaire, which was then investigated by a German agent, usually a public prosecutor. If it was discovered that the respondent had incriminating Nazi ties, they were required to face a civilian court, where the questionnaire was reviewed again, along with any other physical evidence or oral testimony. The commission then made its judgment, or "recommendation" to the military government, and informed the respondent as to which category they had been placed in and what the corresponding punishment was. The proceedings were short, lasting between ten and forty-five minutes. Across the four zones, the commission system produced an incredible amount of paperwork: questionnaires, letters of recommendation,

---

[187] Letter, General Clay to OMGUS directors, January 16, 1947, BAK, OMGUS 17/55–1/9.

[188] Letter, Herrn Bundeskanzler to Villa Schaumburg, January 20, 1953, BAK, B 136/4218.

[189] "An Answer to Every Russian Move," *The Manchester Guardian*, February 13, 1950, p. 7.

[190] Between 1946 and 1948, 13,180,300 Germans in the US zone, 2 million in the British zone, and 669,000 in the French zone completed a questionnaire. Herf, *Divided Memory*, 204.

personal statements, worksheets, etc. Popular was the adage that denazification courts were mere "paper-mills."[191]

Committees in the British zone utilized Fragebögen and made recommendations to Public Safety for either the removal/exclusion or retention/inclusion of individuals. When the CCG(BE) issued ZEI No. 54 in December 1947, German investigators began classifying respondents into one of five prescribed categories of Nazi affiliation. The most serious offenders continued to be investigated by Special Branch. The new apparatus required all Germans working in public and semi-public positions, and in some private offices, to complete a questionnaire. According to one critic, this meant that nearly 1.5 million Germans filled out the survey a second time, for the same position, along with all new applicants, as well as thousands of employees who had never been screened by Military Government during the initial, more lenient, phase of denazification.[192] Furthermore, all former members of the Wehrmacht, regardless of their current employment status, had to register with the local police and complete a questionnaire detailing their past political affiliations.[193] A March 1948 Chatham House report estimated that British zone panels had screened nearly 2.2 million Germans; several thousand Fragebögen were processed every day.[194]

The massive influx of questionnaires put considerable strain on the German investigators and panels and there were many reports of paper shortages. In February 1947, for example, city council members in the British Sector of Berlin discussed at length about problems resulting from a paper shortage in the denazification panels.[195] Around the same time, *The Guardian* reported that some commissions had been forced to temporarily halt their activities because local printing centers could not keep up with the demand for questionnaires.[196]

In the French zone, it was the foremost task of the German-staffed *Untersuchungschüsse* to check the veracity of questionnaires.[197] Individuals

---

[191] For example, see Dagerman, *German Autumn*, 72.
[192] Gollancz, *In Darkest Germany*, 102.
[193] Frank Schlosar in discussion with the author in Calgary, Canada, November 17, 2013.
[194] Noel Matthews, "Memorandum on the Policy and Practice of Denazification in the British Zone - Conference on Some Aspects of the German Problem. Vol. 2, Part 2," March 1948, Chatham House, Cultural Section, p. 5; Donnison, *Civil Affairs and Military Government North-West Europe*, 367.
[195] Meeting Minutes, "Achtzehnter Sitzung der Stadtverordnetenversammlung von Groß-Berlin," February 27, 1947, LAB, C Rep. 1, Stadtverordnetenversammlung von Groß-Berlin, Nr. 18.
[196] *The Guardian*, May 21, 1946. As cited in Marshall, "German Attitudes to British Military Government," 669.
[197] "Der französische Oberkommandierende in Deutschland," October 31, 1945, BAB, BY 1/393.

working in public and semi-public offices, as well as leaders in the private sector, were required to complete a Fragebogen and submit it for review.[198] The survey was then forwarded to the appropriate *Säuberungausschüsse*, where it was again examined and, with thought to other evidence, a decision was made regarding the respondent's employment eligibility.[199] This judgment was then forward to the Political Advisory Council for approval. French provincial governors and *Untersuchungschüsse* were free to adopt their own standards for processing questionnaires, but most chose to distribute them widely.[200] So ubiquitous were questionnaires under the AFMA, that they were sometimes used as scrap paper for notes and folded into makeshift envelopes.[201]

Access to Soviet denazification records from the period prior to August 1947 remain limited, and the case files that are available consist mostly of registration cards.[202] It is no wonder, then, that the role the Fragebogen played in the Russian political purge is largely overlooked. However, evidence suggests that German-staffed commissions in the Soviet zone also relied on questionnaires. In December 1946, SMA ordered a more comprehensive and synchronized screening campaign. The larger Land commissions investigated former party members employed in key offices, including state justice, police ministries, and banks while all other public or private offices, with some notable exceptions, faced a Kreis commission.[203] "Extraordinary denazification commissions" were established for the coal industry, Reichsbahn, and postal service.[204] No matter what commission one faced, some version of the Fragebogen had to be completed, and because all previous investigations were reopened, thousands of Germans had to complete a form for the second time.[205]

The indicted Nazi, called a "petitioner," was required to submit a Fragebogen to a district commission for review, along with a handwritten autobiography (*Lebenslauf*) and personal request to remain employed in their current office.[206] The commission then opened a formal

---

[198] Memorandum, "Dénazification des administrations," September 19, 1945, ADMAE, AP 72/2, Dénazification: dossier général (1946–48), 3902/89; Henke, *Politische Säuberung unter französischer Besatzung*, 39, 48, 73; Biddiscombe, *Denazification of Germany*, 171.
[199] Möhler, *Entnazifizierung in Rheinland-Pfalz und im Saarland unter französischer Besatzung*, 76; Reinhard Grohnert, *Die Entnazifizierung in Baden*, 80–88; Biddiscombe, *Denazification of Germany*, 167.
[200] Willis, *The French in Germany*, 155–58.
[201] For example, see files in ADMAE, AP 75/3.
[202] Timothy Vogt's study of denazification in Brandenburg reveals much about the function of German denazification commissions in the Soviet zone.
[203] Biddiscombe, *Denazification of Germany*, 139.   [204] Ibid., 142.   [205] Ibid., 139.
[206] Vogt, *Denazification in Soviet-Occupied Germany*, 123–24.

investigation, cross-checked answers in the questionnaire, and completed a "Protokoll" sheet, which indicated what employment category the applicant had fallen into.[207] Petitioners waited upward of five months to appear before a commission. Before delivering their verdict, commission members allowed the petitioner to make a formal statement regarding their Nazi affiliations and activities and to submit witness testimony as evidence. However, there existed vast differences in screening procedures between Länder. In Brandenburg, during the fourteen-month commission period, an estimated 28,901 Germans completed a questionnaire, while in Saxony, over a six-month period, more than 170,000 Fragebögen were processed.[208]

The true champion of the Fragebogen, however, was the US zone commissions, or *Spruchkammern*.[209] No other institution in any territory processed more questionnaires. When the Liberation Law was first considered, in late 1945, Major M. K. Wilson, coauthor of the original SHAEF Fragebogen, strongly encouraged the four Land ministries to continue using questionnaires.[210] The Public Safety Branch that he represented believed that the new law should not eliminate this instrument of investigation but simply "obviate the necessity of Special Branch Fragebogen investigations."[211] The Meldebogen that was ultimately adopted by the Spruchkammern was much shorter than its predecessor and meant to act as a means for registering the adult population for denazification screening rather than an instrument for thorough investigation. Still, in many ways, the form served the same purpose as the Fragebogen, and Germans continued to refer to it by the original name.

Under the Liberation Law, every German adult in the American zone, nearly 13.5 million people, was required to complete the Meldebogen.[212] The forms had to be submitted in duplicate to either the local mayor's office or police station by April 28, 1946, six weeks prior to when the tribunals began operating.[213] Upon receival, the Meldebogen was signed

---

[207] For example, "Protokoll," March 17, 1947, BAB, DM 1/165.
[208] Vogt, *Denazification in Soviet-Occupied Germany*, 143; Welsh, *Revolutionärer Wandel auf Befehl?*, 73–74. According to Vogt, tens of thousands of these questionnaires are housed in German archives but remain closed to researchers under the terms of the federal Law for the Protection of Personal Data (*Datenschultzgesetz*). Vogt, *Denazification in Soviet-Occupied Germany*, 285n.
[209] The most thorough investigation on the Spruchkammer system is Niethammer, *Die Mitläuferfabrik*, esp. 335–537.
[210] William E. Griffith, "Denazification in the United States Zone of Germany," *Annals of the American Academy of Political and Social Science* 267 (January 1950): 70.
[211] Report "Special Branch Operations," n.d., NARA, RG 260, OMGUS, CAD, PSB, Box 437.
[212] The Liberation Law was issued in March 1946 but did not come into effect until June.
[213] Niethammer, *Die Mitläuferfabrik*, 343.

and stamped and sent to a designated prosecutor's office. The registrant was given a submission receipt (*Quittung*), torn from the bottom of the questionnaire, which could thereafter be shown to a potential employer or army official upon request. More importantly, the *Quittung* was required by the registrant to obtain a food rations booklet.

With the assistance of OMGUS Special Branch, investigators in the prosecution attorney's office evaluated each questionnaire, cross-checked answers, and tentatively classified registrants into one of the five categories of Nazi affiliation.[214] The questionnaire was the most important, and sometimes only, piece of evidence used by prosecutors to render a decision about a particular case; tribunal instructions stated that the Meldebogen "will form the basis for the proceedings."[215] According to John Herz, a German émigré OSS researcher who advised investigators, "prosecutors were inclined to base the indictment mechanically on what the accused put in his questionnaire."[216]

Much like what their American overseers had experienced prior, German denazification staff spent countless hours investigating potentially chargeable cases. Millions of Meldebögen were submitted in an eight-week period and therefore it took prosecutors months to classify them into chargeable and non-chargeable groups.[217] After an investigation was concluded, the written charge (*Klageschrift*), if there was one, was recorded by the relevant Ministry for Political Liberation, followed by a formal summons sent to the indicted German by the prosecutor's office to a district Spruchkammer. The 3.5 million Germans charged under the Liberation Law were restricted from working in any public or otherwise prominent job until they had faced a tribunal, sometimes having to wait more than a year. In some districts, the names of individuals scheduled to face a review panel were listed, along with their profession and home address, on large court docket posters outside of the town hall.[218]

Each of the 545 tribunal boards consisted of a chairman and four associates, all of whom had been vetted. During a typical Spruchkammer,

---

[214] The Meldebogen evaluation guide can be found here: "Instructions for Officials in Charge of Evaluating the Meldebogen," n.d., NARA, RG 260, OMGUS, CAD, PSB, Box 440.
[215] Ibid.
[216] "Administrative Instructions No. 1 for the Public Prosecutor," n.d., NARA, RG 260, OMGUS, CAD, PSB, Box 440; Herz, "The Fiasco of Denazification in Germany," 572.
[217] OMGUS, CAD, *Denazification, Cumulative Review. Report, 1 April 1947–30 April 1948*, pp. 4–5.
[218] Poster for Denazification in Wilmersdorf, United States Library of Congress, Washington, DC (hereafter, LOC), Third Reich Collection, DD257.2.P687, Folder 10.

the panel reviewed the charges and evidence presented by the prosecutor and allowed the accused to plead their case and present evidence, often in the form of affidavits from known non-Nazis. The board eventually delivered its decision, placing the accused into one of the same five categories of incrimination that the Americans had defined earlier (Major Offender; Offender; Lesser Offender; Follower; Exonerated).[219] Tribunal decisions could be, and often were, petitioned in an appellate court. Taken as a whole, this was a massive bureaucratic apparatus, with thousands of tribunals being convened across the US zone every month.[220]

Special attention must be given to the new Meldebogen questionnaire (Figure 3.2), not only because it was completed by more than 13 million people, but it was also the cornerstone of the Spruchkammer system. The *New York Times* touted it as the "Fragebogen to end all Fragebogen."[221] While the original form had been reserved for individuals who held or hoped to hold a position of authority, every German over the age of eighteen was required to complete a Meldebogen.[222] Unlike the original questionnaire that targeted mostly men, the Meldebogen did not discriminate by gender, resulting in millions of German women coming under denazification screening for the first time.[223]

The Meldebogen was considerably shorter, containing only twenty-six questions, printed on two pages. The same personal information questions were found at the top of the form, while the subsequent section listed fourteen Nazi organizations, instead of fifty-four. In addition to the NSDAP, SA, SS, and Gestapo, registrants were asked to record their affiliation with the *NS-Fliegerkorps* (NS-Flyers Corps), *NS-Kraftfahrkorps* (NS-Motor Corps), *NS-Dozentenbund* (NS-Lecturers' League), *NS-Frauenschaft* (NS-Women's League), and the *NS-Studentenbund* (NS-Students' League), as well as membership in the *Hitlerjugend* (Hitler Youth) and *Bund Deutscher Mädel* (League of German Girls, BDM).

---

[219] Public Safety sent representatives, including Maj. M. K. Wilson, to Stuttgart in April 1945 to assist the German Ministry for Political Liberation in setting up its tribunal system and to draft the new questionnaire. Kristen Dolan, "Isolating Nazism: Civilian Internment in American Occupied Germany, 1944–1950" (PhD diss., University of North Carolina at Chapel Hill, 2013), 123.

[220] OMGUS, *Denazification, Cumulative Review. Report, 1 April 1947–30 April 1948*, p. 4.

[221] Kathleen McLaughlin, "U.S. to Classify Germans in Zone," *New York Times*, March 6, 1946, p. 18.

[222] Niethammer, *Entnazifizierung in Bayern*, 343–44; OMGUS, *Denazification, Cumulative Review. Report, 1 April 1947–30 April 1948*, p. 3.

[223] After the spring of 1947, the Meldebogen was also adopted by some French district commissions. See, for example, Meldebogen of O.G., May 15, 1947, ADMAE, ZFO, BADE 1303.

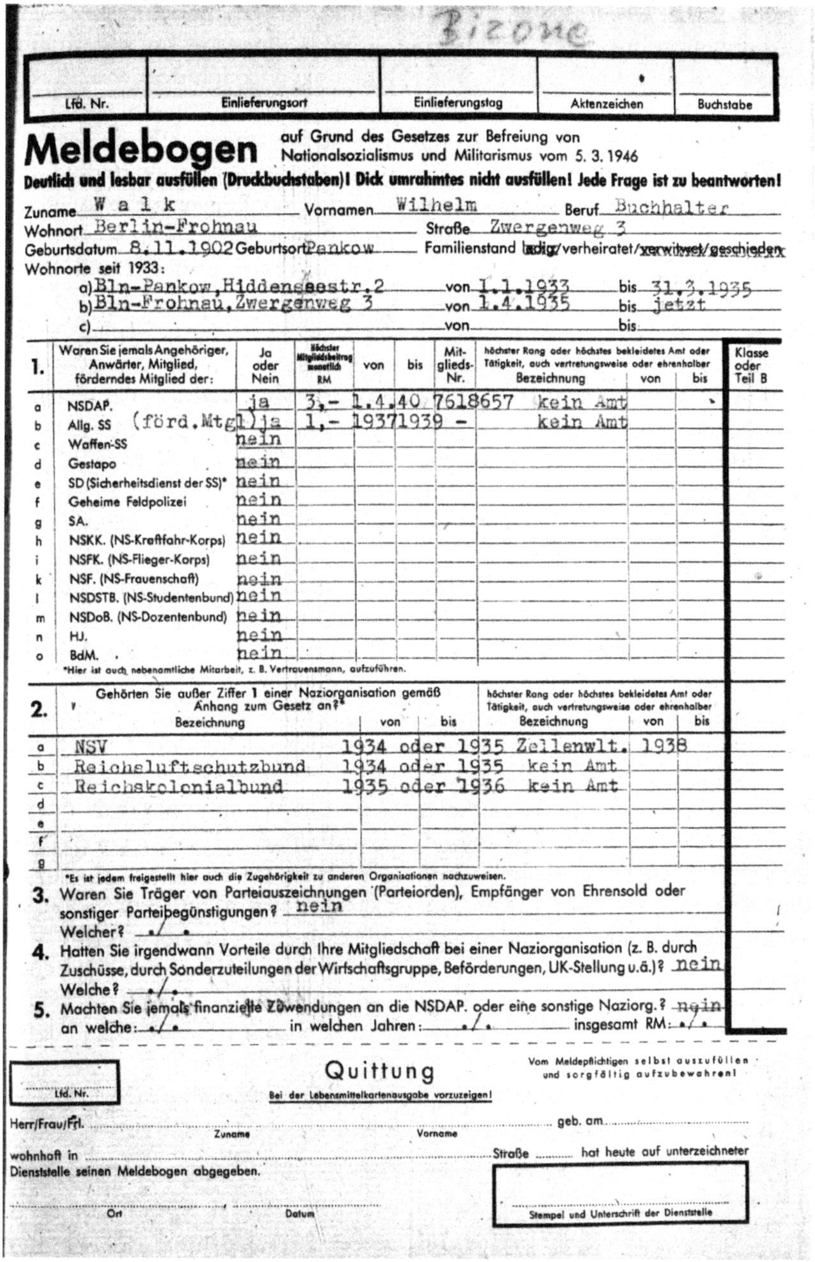

The Questionnaires under German Administration 155

Figure 3.2 First page of the Meldebogen.
Source: US National Archives

This short list was followed by the question, "Have you belonged to any Nazi organizations other than the ones listed in Question 1 in accordance with the [Liberation] Law?" The Meldebogen concluded with three, more specific, questions related the respondent's acquirement of special Nazi titles or decorations and their financial dealings with the regime. Hoping to root out non-party sympathizers, the only question in the form that was not also in the Fragebogen asked, "Did you ever make financial contributions to the NSDAP or any other Nazi organization?"

From June 1946, when the first tribunal convened, until denazification formally ended in the Federal Republic in 1950–51, the Meldebogen was the principal instrument for political screening. It never replaced the longer Fragebogen, as is often claimed, but simply outpaced and overshadowed it.[224] More than 13.5 million Germans filled out the registration form, including 6.7 million in Bavaria.[225] The number of questionnaires processed by commissions in the British, French, and Soviet zones is decidedly lower, simply because there was no attempt to systematically register the entire population, but still, the scale is impressive.

It is no surprise then that each commission system began to unravel only a few months after their establishment. Just like their foreign occupiers, the German denazification ministries became overwhelmed by the volume of cases and the avalanche of paperwork they produced. The commissions were also difficult to control, and despite initial pressure placed on them by the supervising military governments, their unpredictable and lenient judgments were never corrected. The Spruchkammern in the American zone faced the most problems. They had millions of questionnaires to process, which, according to an OMGUS report, would take more than eight years.[226] There was also a shortage of qualified non-Nazi ajudicators and a growing resentment from the population, to the point that tribunal members were being threatened with violence.[227] Local commissions and public prosecutors across the country were responsive to public disapproval, but also to the rising influence of various German political parties, most of whom were willing to compete for the large ex-Nazi vote.

By early 1947, the originally stern mandate of the tribunal system had been loosened considerably. Tens of thousands of exoneration statements,

---

[224] Taylor, *Exorcising Hitler*, 281–82.
[225] Adams, "Between Idealism and Pragmatism," 253; Niethammer, *Die Mitläuferfabrik*, 540.
[226] OMGUS, *Denazification, Cumulative Review. Report, 1 April 1947–30 April 1948*, p. 5.
[227] "Another Nazi Purge Court Bombed," *The Evening Telegraph and Post*, October 28, 1946, p. 1.

referred to colloquially as *Persilscheine* (Persil-certificates), after a popular laundry detergent, had the effect of "washing clean" the political past of former Nazis.[228] Written by known anti-Nazis such as priests, communists, and Jews, sometimes for a fee or favor, tribunal panels usually admitted these statements without question. Such compounded problems created a watered-down and lenient court system. Most defendants, even some prominent Nazis, were routinely classified as Mitläufer and required to pay only a nominal fine. Others were granted amnesty or had their penalty downgraded on appeal. Of the 3.5 million tribunal proceedings in the US zone, only 25,000 Germans (less than 1 percent) were classified in the top two categories of Nazi affiliation, while more than 1 million were branded as Mitläufer.[229] Only 2.5 percent of the zone's population was removed or barred from employment.[230] By the end of the occupation, the tribunals had earned the commonly cited moniker of *Mitläuferfabriken* (follower traveler factories).[231] These same problems, although not as profound, were encountered by commissions in the other three zones.

None of the occupying nations were enthusiastic about revitalizing denazification or prolonging the expensive occupation. By 1947, the divide that had always existed between the Soviet Union and the West had deepened to the point of non-repair. In response, domestic opinions and priorities shifted. It was now felt that German economic recovery was more important in order to fight communism or capitalism. For the Allied army occupiers, attention was no longer fixed on punitive actions, but rehabilitation and the nurturing of German political institutions and economic systems, as such to create Cold War allies. This new tone was set, at least for the West, in a widely disseminated September 6, 1946 speech by US Secretary of State James F. Byrnes: "The American people want to return the government of Germany to the German people. The American people want to help the German people to win their way back to an honorable place among the free and peace-loving nations of the world."[232]

Denazification was cut back accordingly. A Youth Amnesty had already been announced by OMGUS in July 1946, which freed some 900,000 Germans, born after January 1, 1919, from almost all penalties.[233] The Christmas Amnesty that followed pardoned around 1 million

---

[228] Niethammer, *Entnazifizierung in Bayern*, 613; Klee, *Persilscheine und falsche Pässe*.
[229] Frei, *Adenauer's Germany and the Nazi Past*, 38–39.
[230] Montgomery, *Forced to Be Free*, 26.   [231] Niethammer, *Die Mitläuferfabrik*, 617–25.
[232] J. F. Byrnes, "Stuttgart Speech ('Speech of Hope')," reprinted in Ruhm von Oppen, *Documents on Germany under Occupation*, 52–60.
[233] Griffith, "The Denazification Program in the United States Zone of Germany," 384.

low-income and disabled persons.[234] This helped reduce the backlog of questionnaires and dropped the number of chargeable cases in the American zone from 3.5 to 1.8 million.[235] In 1947 and 1948, the Liberation Law was amended twice, giving more authority to German prosecutors and allowing indicted Nazis to continue working while their questionnaires were being processed.

The French enacted similar amnesties and in November 1947, threw out the Mitläufer category altogether, while the Soviets pardoned all "nominal" Nazis under Law No. 201.[236] The British followed the same route, and beginning in January 1948, came close to ending political screening altogether.[237] Gradually, all four campaigns were whittled down and eclipsed by rehabilitation projects. In March 1948, the SMA announced that denazification in its zone had been successful and was therefore over. The Western Allies clambered to catch up, resulting in a wave of expedited and lenient commission hearings. On May 17, 1949, all Germans in the American zone serving prison time for Fragebogen falsification were granted clemency.[238] Denazification had ended with a whimper. The Americans, British, and French publicly admitted their failure; the Russians did so privately.

Conclusion

The denazification questionnaire was an indispensable thorn in the side of the military occupiers, one that pained them at every turn. It was too massive a project, with ill-defined parameters and uncoordinated activities. The armies, military governments, and German commissions who administered the program did not have the expertise, resources, patience, or willingness to see it through to completion. In the end, the pervasive Fragebogen, with its immense but still inadequate resources, could not strike the necessary balance between punishment and rehabilitation. Denazification and reeducation initiatives were designed to act in concert, building a new moral foundation for Germany; this never happened. It was not the deeply genuine reorientation campaign celebrated by politicians and journalists, but an administrative purge of the civil service and of private businesses; in the words of one army correspondent, "just as delousing means getting rid of lice."[239]

---

[234] Boehling, "Transitional Justice?" 72.
[235] OMGUS, *Denazification, Cumulative Review. Report, 1 April 1947–30 April 1948*, pp. 7–9.
[236] Grohnert, *Die Entnazifizierung in Baden*, 201–03.
[237] Marshall, "German Attitudes to British Military Government," 670.
[238] "Clemency for Fragebogen Offenders," May 17, 1949, BAK, OMGUS 17/55–1/9.
[239] Bach, *America's Germany*, 173.

Conclusion

However, denazification was also a hollow shell without the Fragebogen. Most of what was visibly achieved – namely, the removal of thousands of incriminated Nazis from positions of political, economic, and cultural influence – was due to this screening device. Questionnaires were imperative to the occupation regimes. From the moment invasion soldiers entered Germany, no matter what flag they carried, screening instruments were fundamental to interpreting and administering the defeated population. The removal of street signs and swastikas and forced visits to concentration camps were popular public displays, and the international media was ever close by to document them, but denazification, as experienced by soldiers, civil affairs officers, and German prosecutors and commission members, consisted mainly of distributing, collecting, and processing Fragebögen.

The two guiding questions that all administrators were continuously faced with were, *who should we trust?* and *who should we punish?* The answers to both questions began with a questionnaire. Millions of investigations revolved around these forms and sometimes they were the only source of political intelligence available to authorities. The importance of the Fragebogen extended well beyond formal denazification proceedings. The internment of civilians and release of POWs were contingent on the evaluation of questionnaires. The revival of democratic political parties and the appointment of community leaders, as well as food distribution and the renewal of public safety services and basic utilities, were all processed through Fragebögen. Factories, schools, and hospitals were often only allowed to operate after their staff had been investigated.

The total number of completed questionnaires is impossible to calculate. The American and British records are incomplete, while there exist no reliable data for the French and Soviet zones. Due to the ad hoc functioning of screening in many regions, the use of different versions of the form, and the irregular submission of monthly reports, we will never know how many Fragebögen were distributed, collected, or processed in any one zone. Many more questionnaires were filled out than were reviewed. Nevertheless, official and unofficial data drawn from numerous sources suggest that between 1945 and 1949, around 19 million questionnaires were evaluated in the Western zones.[240] Statistics for the Soviet territories are more difficult to locate and interpret, but the commissions established after January 1947 screened as many as 800,000 people.[241] Tens of thousands of additional forms were processed in the two years prior, under the direct administration of SMA.

---

[240] Judt, *Postwar*, 56.   [241] Schroeder, *To Forget It All and Begin Anew*, 22.

Table 3.3 *Questionnaires processed in each zone/sector (1945–1949)*[242]

	US zone/ sector	British zone/ sector	French zone/ sector	Soviet zone/ sector
Fragebögen	2,500,000	2,300,000	669,000	800,000
Meldebögen	13,500,000	–	–	–
Total				19,769,000

The figures presented in Table 3.3 are conservative estimates based on incomplete data, with the actual number of questionnaires likely being much higher. For example, Fragebögen processed in the Soviet zone prior to 1947 are not included, as well as those submitted in the Federal Republic, between 1949 and 1951, when denazification formally ended.[243] Tens of thousands of late-returning POWs completed a revised survey; Bavaria did not stop using the form until 1954.[244] The data are complicated further because many Germans completed two or more questionnaires, sometimes in different zones, and reports often fail to distinguish between the number of Fragebögen "distributed" and those "processed." What is certain, however, is that far more questionnaires were administered in the American zone than in any other, in fact more than the British, French, and Soviet zones combined. Anywhere between 30 percent and 90 percent of the adult population in the American zone filled out at least one form.[245]

The United States invested most heavily in the Fragebogen, and its sensitivity to public opinion resulted in the unchecked expansion of the

---

[242] The figures in Table 3.3 are calculated from several official and unofficial sources: Report, "Denazification Report – 15 February 1946," March 5, 1946, NARA, RG 260, OMGUS, EO, CO, IADC, Box 460; Report, "The Present Status of Denazification in Western Germany and Berlin," April 15, 1948, NARA, RG 94, ASD, OB, Foreign (Occupied) Area Reports, 1945–54, Box 1004; Clay, *Decision in Germany*, 59; Griffith, "The Denazification Program in the United States Zone of Germany," 132; Stefan W. Wiecki, "Professors in Purgatory: The Denazification of Munich University" (PhD diss., Brandeis University, 2009), 172; Adams, *From Crusade to Hazard*, 39, 41; Judt, *Postwar*, 56; Turner, "Denazification in the British Zone," 249, 263; Vollnhals, *Entnazifizierung*, 13, 28, 35; Henke, *Politische Säuberung unter französischer Besatzung*, 171–72; Fürstenau, *Entnazifizierung*, 146–47, 228–30; Biddiscombe, *Denazification of Germany*, 181; Borgstedt, "Der Fragebogen," 166–71. For another attempted calculation of total questionnaires processed, see Leßau, *Entnazifizierungsgeschichten*, 56, 79.

[243] "Politischer Fragebogen," May 9, 1949, BAK, Z 11/382.

[244] Fitzgibbon, *Denazification*, 133; Adams, *From Crusade to Hazard*, 41.

[245] Friedmann, *Allied Military Government of Germany*, 114n; Robert Stephens, "The Great Purge in Germany," *The Globe and Mail*, March 5, 1948, p. 6.

Conclusion

program. It was because of its majority influence in the ACC, and a determination to export its denazification curriculum to other territories, that the American paper occupation eventually consumed all of Germany. The American, British, French, and Soviet authorities used the same mechanics for screening; the same instruments, formulas, and methods of evaluating an individual's past. Recognizing the unifying potential of this shared screening instrument, the ACC drafted its own "quadripartite questionnaire" in April 1947.[246] The 92-point form was intended to screen candidates for positions in a Central German Administration, through which the ACC organs would operate, as more responsibilities were passed to the Germans. The four-power Kommandatura in Berlin also attempted to produce an interzonal form, as did an American-British committee preparing for the Bizone partnership.[247] In the existing scholarship, it is uncommon for researchers to acknowledge these joint-efforts and any uniformity between the denazification campaigns. There especially remains a general discomfort in recognizing similarities between the Soviet programs and those in the West. This chapter's examination of on-the-ground political screening activities has challenged the uniqueness of the individual denazification campaigns.

---

[246] "Screening of Candidates for the Central German Administrations," April 3, 1947, NARA, RG 260, IAC, ACA, DIAC, Box 202.

[247] "Implementation in Berlin of Allied Control Authority Directive 38," March 16, 1948, AM, AK 94/1; "Vetting of Appointments for Bizonal Posts," June 18, 1948, NARA, OMGUS, CAD, PSB, Box 352.

4 The "Little Man's Nuremberg"
Germans and Denazification

> I am questionnaire-sick, I am questionnaire-sick. Do you know this terrible suffering? In my questionnaire, almost everything is correct – thank God! ... Have I filled everything in correctly – how should I know? I dream every night that I was in a [Nazi] group, then I start to shake, trembling and become covered in sweat ... Maybe they secretly put me into a [Nazi] group. It's possible, with all the lies and pressure from above. I asked the doctor. He says he cannot help, I have 'NSDAP persecution paranoia.'[1]
>
> —Just Scheu, Entertainer, 1947

Germans mostly ignored the proclamations made by invading Allied armies about their ideological war against Nazism. Many citizens had already become disillusioned with, and even angered by, the Hitler regime; the government's leadership had sacrificed and abandoned them. They also had more important matters on their minds. When the fighting ended in a particular town or region the violence often continued. Allied soldiers, especially the Soviets, participated in murder, torture, forced expulsion, and historically unprecedented acts of rape.[2] Food was scarce, and millions of people, many of them foreign refugees, crowded into cities. The totality and confusion of defeat and the enduring struggle to survive produced a climate of intense fear and anxiety. Among the defeated was sixteen-year-old Magdalena Estel, who was happy to see the war end, but frightened by the British troops who occupied her hometown of Leopoldshöhe. She recalled that all her neighbors were "very scared" because they "did not know what the peace

---

[1] Just Scheu, "Der Fragebogen," Rheinlandhalle Rüdesheim, 1947, Deutsches Rundfunkarchiv (hereafter, DRA), Frankfurt am Main, Nr. 2600351.
[2] The scale of atrocities in the eastern provinces in the early months of 1945 is particularly horrifying, with as many as 2 million German women raped by Red Army soldiers. Further reading: Norman Naimark, *The Russians in Germany* (Cambridge, MA: Harvard University Press, 1995); J. Robert Lilly, *Taken by Force: Rape and American GIs in Europe during World War II* (Basingstoke, Hampshire: Palgrave Macmillan, 2007); Miriam Gebhardt, *Als die Soldaten kamen. Die Vergewaltigung deutscher Frauen am Ende des Zweiten Weltkriegs* (München: DVA, 2015).

would look like."³ Every day her family struggled to find food and she never went out at night. Amid these conditions, there was little concern for something as superfluous as denazification.

It was also not understood what the invading armies meant by "eradicating Nazism." In fact, as we have learned in Chapter 3, Allied soldiers did not know either. SHAEF never produced a consensus definition. Most Germans assumed that denazification would involve the arrest and punishment of only the regime's leadership, and perhaps local party functionaries, SS officers, and Gestapo agents. Such actions were in fact commended, not in small part because they had the effect of radiating blame upward and exonerating the common German. Other early denazification activities did not impact their lives in the least: liquidating the NSDAP, abrogating Nazi laws, and removing signs and symbols. Being forced to sit through propaganda films or tour concentration camps was disliked but tolerated.⁴

This sentiment changed, however, when the campaign shed its superficial skin and was reformatted to root out Nazism from German society. Actions became individualized and encased in an unapproachable screening bureaucracy. By July 1945, few families were beyond the reach of the political purge, one that changed regularly and with little warning. The consequences could be extraordinary. In a time of considerable desperation, screening threatened what was left of one's livelihood. By the spring of 1949, more than 20 million people had filled out questionnaires, 4 million had faced civilian commissions, and 400,000 had been arrested and interned.⁵

The war against Nazism was never meant to be so mechanical. The OSS and GCU civilian planners who designed the campaign for Western armies wanted to change the hearts and minds of the defeated enemy and to target individuals on a case-by-case basis. However, the enormous task of screening millions and the pressure to produce measurable outcomes led to a complex and rigid system dominated by the continuous calculation of mass data. Understandably, historians have engaged with the subject in the same way. Arrests, dismissals, and amnesty numbers have been calculated and compared, the careers of prominent citizens scrutinized, and opinion polls extrapolated. Dozens of studies have produced a definitive verdict on the eradication of an ideology by evaluating statistics generated by occupation armies, military governments, and German

---

³ Magdalena Estel in discussion with the author in Calgary, Canada, December 15, 2014.
⁴ See, for example, Ulrike Weckel, *Beschämende Bilder: Deutsche Reaktionen auf alliierte Dokumentarfilme über befreite Konzentrationslager* (Stuttgart: Franz Steiner, 2012).
⁵ Beattie, *Allied Internment Camps in Occupied Germany*, 1; Remy, *The Heidelberg Myth*, 178.

ministries. Little attention has been given to how denazification was experienced at the time by regular people.

In this chapter, the second perspective from which this book explores and analyzes denazification is introduced, that of the German civilian. It describes a record of how men and women from different backgrounds and occupied territories experienced the campaign to eradicate Nazism; how it impacted their lives, and what they felt about it. Their stories are imparted through journal entries, private letters, newspapers, published and unpublished memoirs, and interviews. Military government records are also consulted, mainly individual case files. These documents chronicle much of the everyday denazification experience. A critical assessment of the political and ideological achievements is unavoidable, but the purpose of this chapter is to humanize the story of denazification. It interprets the purge not as a top-down punitive campaign, but an individual experience with real and immediate consequences for Germans and their families.

The Everyday Experience of Denazification

Historian Lutz Niethammer described denazification as a "purge of the family father."[6] His 1972 study of US-occupied Bavaria is centered on the civilian-staffed Spruchkammern and the mostly married middle-class men who faced them.[7] However, what is lost in his exhaustive analysis is the fact that only 950,000 Germans, or 17 percent of the zone's population, encountered one of these 545 tribunals. A large number indeed, but far from a collective denazification experience, as it is regularly portrayed. The much more pervasive activity, and not just in the American zone, was the completion of questionnaires. As much as one-third of the occupied population filled out a Fragebogen of some sort; relatively few went on to face a civilian commission.

Still, with this broadened scope of what can be considered routine denazification, the demographics change only slightly; most questionnaire respondents were middle-aged, middle-class men. This constituency shows that screening discriminated along two discernible lines: gender and socioeconomic status. It targeted Nazi Party members and officials – the majority of whom were male – from positions of political, economic, and cultural importance – jobs dominated by educated men. Still, the screened population was not uniform. Some questionnaire

[6] Niethammer, *Entnazifizierung in Bayern*, 561.
[7] Niethammer estimated that around 90 percent of Spruchkammer investigations were of married men, the majority of whom were between the ages of thirty-five and fifty-five.

respondents – 30 percent, as suggested by one recent study – were modest civil servants who fell into the lowest salary class with an income below 2,500 Reichsmark (RM).[8] These were rail workers, miners, foresters, and other laborers employed by government offices.

Relatively few women were civil servants, professionals, or managers of private businesses, but more often housewives or low-status, and low-earning, employees. Therefore, women by and large, comprising upward of 60 percent of the postwar population, remained under the radar of denazification.[9] In a 1947 sample study by OMGUS officials, it was estimated that around 21 percent of questionnaires were completed by women.[10] A similar disparity existed with the hundreds of thousands of "ordinary laborers," who, regardless of their Nazi past, were not screened. In the British zone, students who attended German universities had to complete a questionnaire, while those at non-degree granting *Volkshochschulen* did not.[11] In the American occupied town of Usingen, 392 residents completed a Fragebogen, of which only thirty-seven were designated as "working class."[12]

Millions of displaced persons (DPs) and expellees, mostly from the east, also slipped through the cracks of denazification due to the ease at which they moved across national and zonal boundaries. There existed few records or local knowledge about the Nazi affiliations of these individuals. In the American zone, DPs were not required to submit a Meldebogen to obtain a food rations card, as their care came under the jurisdiction of the UNRRA. Special Branch could only hope that "a

---

[8] Leßau, *Entnazifizierungsgeschichten*, 83–84.
[9] Benita Blessing, *The Antifascist Classroom: Denazification in Soviet-Occupied Germany, 1945–1949* (New York: Palgrave, 2006), 92; Atina Grossmann, "Feminist Debates About Women and National Socialism," *Gender & History* 3, no. 3 (1991): 353. There exist only a handful of monographs on the denazification of women: Ruth Elisabeth Bullinger, *Belastet oder entlastet? Dachauer Frauen im Entnazifizierungsverfahren* (Munich: Utz, 2013); Eva Schöck-Quinteros and Jan-Hauke Ahrens, eds., *"Was verstehen wir Frauen auch von Politik?": Entnazifizierung ganz normaler Frauen in Bremen (1945–1952)* (Bremen: Univ. Inst. für Geschichtswiss., 2011); Jutta Mühlenberg, *Das SS-Helferinnenkorps: Ausbildung, Einsatz und Entnazifizierung der weiblichen Angehörigen der Waffen-SS, 1942–1949* (Hamburg: Hamburger Edition, 2010); Kathrin Meyer, *Entnazifizierung von Frauen: die Internierungslager der US-Zone Deutschlands 1945–1952* (Berlin: Metropol, 2004); and Denise Tscharntke, *Re-educating German Women: The Work of the Women's Affairs Section of the British Military Government 1946–1951* (New York: P. Lang, 2003).
[10] ICD Opinion Survey, "Opinions on Denazification," November 26, 1947, NARA, RG 260, OMGUS, EO, CO, Box 456.
[11] Rosenfeld, "The Anglo-American Encounter in Occupied Hamburg," 85n.
[12] Register, NARA, RG 260, OMGUS, CAD, PSB, Fragebogen Relating to Denazification, 1945–48, Box 252. Thirty-seven residents fell under the Christmas Amnesty, which implies they earned less than 4,500 RM annually.

special registration procedure for such persons will be established later."[13] Most children were also exempt from screening, as were hundreds of thousands of late-returning POWs.[14] There were also those whose application to join the NSDAP, SA, or SS, had been rejected. A respondent could very well have been a radical nationalist, militarist, and anti-Semite but still be overlooked simply because some versions of the Fragebogen did not contain a question pertaining to "applications" to Nazi organizations.[15]

These are considerable shortcomings of the questionnaire program and confirm that denazification was not the comprehensive cultural and ideological cleanse proclaimed by many politicians at the time. Instead, it was a political and economic purge, defined largely by job dismissals. There existed some important differences between zones. For example, more private sector workers were targeted by the Soviets early on, and under the Liberation Law, all German adults in the American zone, regardless of gender and economic status, filled out registration questionnaires. Still, the typical German who went through denazification proceedings was a middle-aged educated man, already employed in an influential position, who was married with children and had belonged to a handful of nominal Nazi organizations. One civil affairs officer estimated that prominent Germans filled out no less than six Fragebögen.[16]

Much is known about how political screening was administered, but what was the typical experience for Germans? For most, it did not impact their life in any significant way, at least in the early months of the occupation. It was more common for people to merely witness or hear stories about denazification activities, such as the arrest of leading Nazis and the erasing of physical remnants of the defunct regime. All that one young resident of Düsseldorf remembered was the whitewashing of swastikas on the walls of buildings, while an elderly woman in Löcknitz

---

[13] "German Denazification Law and Implementation with American Directives Included," June 15, 1946, IfZ, 11/Dk, 090.003.
[14] Niethammer, *Die Mitläuferfabrik*, 343–44; OMGUS, *Denazification, Cumulative Review. Report, 1 April 1947–30 April 1948*, p. 3; "Die Gefallenenlisten fehlen," *Neuer Tageblatt*, March 29, 1950. Children were impacted by denazification in other ways, see Michelle Mouton, "Missing, Lost, and Displaced Children in Postwar Germany: The Great Struggle to Provide for the War's Youngest Victims," *Central European History* 48 (2015): 53–78.
[15] Wiecki, "Professors in Purgatory," 125. It should also be noted that some of the Nazi records salvaged by the Allies were incomplete and therefore it proved difficult to cross-check questionnaires. For example, the NSDAP Master File was 90 percent complete, the SS Officers Service records 85 percent complete, and the NSDAP Membership Applications less than 10 percent complete.
[16] Friedmann, *Allied Military Government of Germany*, 123.

heard a rumor that the local *Gauleiter* (NSDAP regional leader) had been arrested and was awaiting trial.[17] Most citizens supported such activities. One OMGUS opinion survey from late 1945, estimated that only 4 percent of Germans disapproved of the formation of the International Military Tribunal in Nuremberg.[18]

For thousands of senior Nazi officials, there was much to worry about. While some fled the invading armies, others remained and were promptly arrested. In an extreme case, Robert Wagner, the former *Gauleiter* of Baden, was detained by French soldiers and later executed.[19] However, most ended up in a regional internment camp or were deported to a forced labor center in the Soviet Union, sometimes never to return. Known Nazis, whose names were on intelligence "black lists" were usually arrested at home by armed soldiers, in front of their families. Other times, they were detained at work or when applying for a new job. It was not uncommon to be confronted by a neighbor who was a member of an antifascist group or a former patriot who had left Germany before the war and was now a member of an occupying army.[20] In larger towns and in cities, soldiers and civil affairs officials distributed SHAEF Fragebögen to municipal employees, which resulted in the arrest of thousands who fell into automatic arrest categories. Extrajudicial civilian internment was the first mass denazification experience, although less than 1 percent of the adult population was affected.

These early actions caused anxiety within communities, as detention could seem, and sometimes was, indiscriminate. No one knew who was on the "black lists" and whether regular membership in the NSDAP was grounds for arrest. Fears were amplified by the widespread practice of voluntary political denunciation, examined in detail in Chapter 5.[21] Arbitrary arrests were not uncommon, usually due to mistaken identity or the result of the occupiers' still limited understanding of Nazi organizational structures and hierarchies.[22] In some French controlled towns, German men were indiscriminately arrested as a tactic to flush out leading Nazis.[23] A young Rudolf Dorner remembers the day when twenty residents of his hometown were "taken hostage" to ensure that

---

[17] Arthur D. Kahn, *Betrayal: Our Occupation of Germany* (New York: Beacon, 1950), 37.
[18] Anna J. Merritt and Richard L. Merritt, *Public Opinion in Occupied Germany: The OMGUS Surveys, 1945–1949* (Urbana: University of Illinois Press, 1970), 93–94.
[19] Dolan, "Isolating Nazism," 11–12.
[20] Beattie, *Allied Internment Camps in Occupied Germany*, 69.
[21] Report, "Daily Military Government Report, 8 April–9 April 1945," NARA, RG 498, ETO/USFET, CAD, Container 2952.
[22] See, for example, Beattie, *Allied Internment Camps in Occupied Germany*, 124.
[23] Willis, *The French in Germany*, 71.

no violence was inflicted on French soldiers.[24] He also witnessed his father, a former party member, being arrested in the middle of the night. While surprisingly few internees were subject to reeducation measures in the estimated seventy-five civilian camps, the act of physically removing this possibly dangerous segment of the population was an act of denazification.[25]

The number of arrests fluctuated throughout the occupation, but generally decreased by the end of 1945, being replaced by the much more inclusive and bureaucratic experience of completing questionnaires. After the Potsdam Conference, in August 1945, the questionnaire became more difficult for Germans to evade. Nazi monuments, streets signs, and symbols had already been removed, and the NSDAP banned, but now a more ubiquitous denazification curriculum was being implemented.

Germans were familiar with the act of completing questionnaires, as the country had a long history of social surveying, going back to at least the late nineteenth century.[26] The Nazis were particularity fond of using such instruments, and beginning in May 1937, required all new NSDAP applicants to submit a questionnaire detailing family history, citizenship, and any criminal convictions.[27] Nearly every auxiliary group, including the SA and SS, required the completion of a comparable form. For very different purposes, Jews (and their property) were registered using questionnaires. Furthermore, between 1934 and 1939, all party members had to complete a two-page "statistical survey" that contained questions about family, employment, and membership in political groups.[28] The irony was not lost on those who completed the military government Fragebogen. The same young Rudolf Dorner recalled that "the whole Fragebogenaktion [questionnaire program] was new to everyone, but it reminded them of the Nazi times, when the government tried to

---

[24] Dr. Rudolf Dorner in discussion with the author in Hamburg, July 24, 2013.
[25] Beattie, *Allied Internment Camps in Occupied Germany*, 49.
[26] See, Marie-Bénédicte Vincent: "La prise en compte de plusieurs générations dans la méthode prosopographique: L'exemple des hauts fonctionnaires prussiens sous l'Empire et la République de Weimar," *Genèses* 56 (September 2004): 125; Martin Bulmer, ed., *The Social Survey in Historical Perspective, 1880–1940* (Cambridge: Cambridge University Press, 2011); and Jürg Fleischer, *Geschichte, Anlage und Durchführung der Fragebogen-Erhebungen von Georg Wenkers 40 Sätzen. Dokumentation, Entdeckungen und Neubewertungen* (Hildesheim: Georg Olms, 2017).
[27] BDC, *Who Was a Nazi?*, 7–9; Friedlander, *Archives of the Holocaust*, x–xii.
[28] A sample of a completed NSDAP questionnaire can be found here: "Parteistatistische Erhebung 1939," July 1, 1939, NARA, RG 260, OMGUS, Fragebogens, 1945–48, Box 4. To my knowledge, a comparative study of Nazi and denazification questionnaires has not been conducted.

determine your ideological orientation."[29] Ernst von Salomon himself quipped that "this is not by any means the first questionnaire with which I have grappled. I have already filled in many identical Fragebogens ... during the period January 30, 1933, to May 6, 1945 ..."[30] In fact, in March 1946, when one Spruchkammer in Bavaria ran out of Meldebögen, it circulated old copies of the Nazi questionnaire, simply crossing out the swastikas and questions on racial purity.[31]

However, for many respondents, completing a screening questionnaire was a new experience, and none had filled out a form that possessed so much authority and could cost them their job or even result in arrest. The process varied across the occupied territories and changed over time, but usually it began with an office manager handing out Fragebögen to employees with verbal instructions to fill them in honestly and to return them within an allotted time. These directions were sometimes communicated by a military government agent, who visited the workplace with a stack of forms and a translator. During the commission phase, the distribution of questionnaires was unsystematic. The forms were sometimes picked up at a regional military government headquarters, police station, city hall, or a labor or finance office (see Figure 4.1). Others were told by their employer to appear at a designated screening center, prepared to complete the Fragebogen in person, under supervision. Often applicants arriving at these locations supplied records and letters that they claimed confirmed their non- or anti-Nazi status. As observed by one American intelligence office, "The Germans were so police-harried and document-conscious that they continued to be uneasy unless we looked at their personal papers. ... I have never seen a people so paper crazy."[32]

Notices were published in newspapers and posted on public buildings, explaining the purpose of the Fragebogen and disclosing the existence of a "comprehensive" record center full of seized Nazi documents against which responses would be checked.[33] Still, much confusion surrounded the screening campaign, and there were claims of "widespread misunderstanding" about how to fill out the forms correctly and how the categories of incrimination were calculated.[34] With the routine passing

---

[29] Dr. Rudolf Dorner in discussion with the author in Hamburg, July 24, 2013.
[30] von Salomon, *Fragebogen*, 7–8, 650.
[31] For example, Fragebogen of A.U., Bayerisches Hauptstaatsarchiv (hereafter, BHStA), MSo 820.
[32] Padover, *Experiment in Germany*, 35.
[33] "Épuration dans les zones américaine et britannique, 1946–48," ADMAE, ZFO, AP 81/3; Biddiscombe, *Denazification of Germany*, 61.
[34] "Intelligence Summary No. 1," IA&C Division, May 27, 1946, TNA, FO 1050/431.

Figure 4.1 Submitting a denazification questionnaire in Berlin's Steglitz district, 1946.
Source: US National Archives

of new denazification laws, both the Evangelical Church and SPD, as well as many legal experts and local labor offices, published short manuals that contained simplified instructions.[35] But confusion remained, expressed with frustration and nervousness. It was never really known what intelligence the occupiers possessed and how the forms were being evaluated; rumors and theories warned of worst-case scenarios. This encouraged respondents to make every possible effort to dissociate themselves from the Nazi regime and its ideology, no matter how trivial. Military governments were overwhelmed by the amount of written commentary submitted with the standard forms.

In some cases, applicants were required to complete the questionnaire in a large group, while under observation by Public Safety officers. Crowded into the basement of a military government building or

---

[35] Erich Schullze, *Gesetz zur Befreiung von Nationalsozialismus und Militarismus vom 5. März 1946* (München: Biederstein, 1947); Kirchenkanzlei der EKD – Berliner Stelle, November 1945–March 1947, EZA 4/584.

Figure 4.2 A crowd of German citizens filling out questionnaires in Frankfurt am Main.
Source: US National Archives

scattered across a town square, they filled out the form in one sitting (see Figure 4.2). After submitting the document, they were sometimes subject to an on-the-spot interrogation by a denazification agent.[36] The act of filling in a questionnaire, therefore, represented both a private and public experience. The Fragebogen was completed by the individual and involved self-reflection, but it was also often completed in groups, under close supervision. Some respondents were allowed to take the survey home and submit it within three days, as was the case in a majority of districts in the Western zones, or within two weeks in the Soviet zone and in all four sectors of Berlin.[37] Recorded in private journals and letters, respondents complained that they had "spent half the night" completing their form, and that they had sat at their typewriters "for many days

---

[36] "Statement by IA&C Division on Progress of De-Nazification," September 11, 1945, TNA, FO 1050/777.

[37] OMGUS, CAD, *Denazification, Cumulative Review. Report, 1 April 1947–30 April 1948*, p. 35; "Gesetz über die Reinigung des Arzteberufes und des Apothekerberufes von Nazi-Elementenvom 1. Oktober 1945," n.d., BAB, DQ 1/1336, Docs. 242–43; Directive, "Implementation in Berlin of Allied Control Authority Directive 38," March 16, 1948, AlliiertenMuseum Berlin (hereafter, AM), AK 94/10.

finishing the questionnaires and everything related to them, and I'm still not done with them."[38] The American Meldebogen had to be submitted in duplicate within six weeks.[39] Countless conversations were surely had at the family dinner table, office breakroom, and in the street about how to interpret the questions and what information to include (and not include).[40] Ernst Schröder, a former party member from Konstanz, filled out three questionnaires, one at home and two while under observation by French soldiers.[41] Gustav Meyer gave his answers in English, perhaps to please the faceless American official reviewing his case.[42] Observed by a British denazification agent in a Berlin office:

> Tiny men and women standing on the chairs around the big table were bending over it filling in their Fragebogen; another group in the middle of the room agitatedly discussed in squeaky voices whether such questions as 'Did you serve in the general or Waffen SS?' or 'What was the last rank you held in the Wehrmacht?' needed to be answered by them at all ... some were reading their questionnaires lying comfortably on their tummies on the carpet.[43]

If permitted, respondents sometimes included supplementary documents with their Fragebogen. Usually this consisted of a short biographical datasheet (*Lebenslauf*), which was most often typed and used to rationalize membership in Nazi organizations and plead ideological and moral innocence. During the commission phase, prosecutors and denazification panels in all four zones encouraged the submission of such commentaries. Sometimes dozens of appended pages were stapled to a questionnaire and not just *Lebensläufe*, but letters of support, sworn declarations, and denunciation statements. The prominent publisher, Erich Welter, for example, attached a letter written by an American-Jewish business associate that attested to his anti-Nazi beliefs.[44] Respondents in the Soviet zone were required to include a *Lebenslauf*, as well as a formal letter of petition addressed to the Land administration or denazification commission that reviewed their case.[45]

---

[38] As quoted in Leßau, *Entnazifizierungsgeschichten*, 90–91.
[39] Niethammer, *Entnazifizierung in Bayern*, 561; Order of the OMGUS Military Governor, "Law for Liberation from National Socialism and Militarism," April 29, 1946. Accessed at the IfZ, see "German Denazification Law and Implementation with American Directives Included," June 15, 1946, IfZ, 11/Dk, 090.003.
[40] Some of these private conversations are examined by Hanne Leßau in *Entnazifizierungsgeschichten*, esp. 124–33.
[41] Denazification file for O.S., ADMAE, ZFO, BADE 1859 (1050).
[42] Fragebogen of R.D., BAK, N 1748/67.
[43] George Clare, *Berlin Days, 1946–1947* (London: Macmillan, 1989), 148f.
[44] Personal papers of Erich Welter, BAK, N 1314.
[45] Vogt, *Denazification in Soviet-Occupied Germany*, 124.

Many Germans lied in their Fragebogen, and some were caught doing so. Most common was the concealment of membership in certain Nazi groups or falsifying the date of membership. These respondents were obviously aware that if they admitted to joining the NSDAP in 1932, for example, they would be barred from working in any civil administration position. In the American zone, one had to have joined after April 1937 to avoid mandatory dismissal. Such was the case of Paul Krüger, a farmer from Walldorf, who was arrested by the US Military Government for claiming he had joined the party in May 1937, not May 1933.[46] In British-occupied Osnabrück, police chief August Hofmann was sentenced to four years imprisonment for lying about his membership in multiple Nazi organizations.[47] An unnamed woman applying for the position of head of a school district in the Soviet zone was threatened with arrest because she failed to mention that her husband was a high-ranking Nazi and currently interned in a Russian POW camp.[48]

While military government records are full of Fragebogen falsification cases, it is likely that most respondents who omitted or distorted answers were not caught. Still, we cannot assume that most responses were false. Germans were aware of the serious consequences that befell those caught falsifying their questionnaires; in many cases, the punishment was much worse (imprisonment) than if they told the truth (employment restriction). Also, if an individual was worried that the information revealed in their questionnaire might lead to arrest or some other major punishment, they could simply choose not to submit a survey at all, at least in the British, Soviet, and French zones, and instead take up low-profile employment, which did not require screening.

After answering all the questions and appending supplementary sheets, the form was signed and dated. By doing so, the applicant certified that the information included was true and that they understood that omissions or false statements would result in prosecution and punishment.[49] The British and Soviet Fragebögen required the signature of a witness, who, almost always, was a work colleague, spouse, or relative.

---

[46] Denazification file for A.S., NARA, RG 260, OMGUS, CAD, PSB, Fragebogen, Box 349.

[47] Letter, Frau W. to Schumacher, May 12, 1946, AdsD, Bestand Schumacher, Mappe 98.

[48] Eli Nobleman, "United States Military Courts in Germany: Setting an Example and Learning Lessons," in *Americans as Proconsuls: United States Military Government in Germany and Japan, 1944–1952*, ed. Robert Wolfe (Carbondale: Southern Illinois University Press, 1984), 183–84.

[49] SHAEF, *Public Safety Manual of Procedures*, Section VI, Paragraph 190.

The questionnaire was then submitted, usually at the same location where it had been received.

Waiting for a decision about employment eligibility sometimes took months, during which time zonal laws and procedures likely changed, while rumors about screening criteria flourished. Falsifiers worried that they would be caught and suddenly arrested, while admitted Nazis wondered if they would be permitted to keep their jobs at all; everyone else was anxious that their answers would be misinterpreted by a denazification agent, who probably did not read German and did not understand the social nuances of the dictatorship. Perhaps they would be the victim of political denunciation. This produced considerable distress for individuals, who knew very little about where their questionnaires were sent after submission, who reviewed them and against what records, and what criteria mandated dismissal. No effort was made on the part of SMA to conduct any public relations campaign to bolster support for denazification or even to inform Germans about the questionnaire program.[50] OMGUS prohibited applicants from working prior to being cleared by Special Branch.[51] As a result, hundreds of thousands of Germans, many of whom had never been a Nazi Party member, were forced to wait upward of six months before being reinstated in their job. Historian Svenja Goltermann has shown that doctors in the city of Bielefeld repeatedly reported "conflicts in completing the questionnaire" as triggers for mental disorders in their patients.[52]

Many hardened Nazis were processed by the Fragebogen machine. Among them was Ludwig Brandt, an early member of the NSDAP, who completed the American form with hopes of retaining his medical license.[53] His comrade, Johannes Ziegler, who served in the *SS-Totenkopfverbände* at Buchenwald concentration camp, filled out no fewer than three questionnaires.[54] A former agent in the *Kriminalpolizei* (criminal police), Fritz Arnold, submitted dozens of documents with his Fragebögen, which he thought would prove his aversion to Nazism, while a military attaché to Washington, Ltg. Friedrich von Boetticher, wrote at length about his apolitical beliefs.[55]

---

[50] Vogt, *Denazification in Soviet-Occupied Germany*, 78.
[51] "Military Government of Germany, Denazification, Monthly Report of Military Governor, No. 3," October 20, 1945, NARA, RG 94, ASD, OB, Foreign (Occupied) Area Reports, 1945–54, Box 1004.
[52] Svenja Goltermann, *Die Gesellschaft der Überlebenden: Deutsche Kriegsheimkehrer und ihre Gewalterfahrungen im Zweiten Weltkrieg* (Munich: Pantheon, 2009), 72.
[53] Denazification file for O.A., Staatsarchiv Ludwigsburg (hereafter, StAL), EL 902/7.
[54] Denazification file for F.B., Staatsarchiv Nürnberg, B/58.
[55] Denazification file for P.D., BAK, N 12651/9; Denazification file for F.B., Bundesarchiv-Militärarchiv, Freiburg (hereafter, BAF), N 323/170.

However, most of the men and women subjected to screening never held political office or commissioned rank: Kurt Schulte was the director of an appliances company in Soviet-controlled Dessau, Georg Etienne a clerk in a Hamburg municipal office, Sophie Engel a midwife in Ravensburg applying for a secretarial position, and Erwin Horn, who wished to work as a legal advisor for the local Spruchkammer.[56] None of them had been politically active, but they were still required to fill out a Fragebogen.

Denazification generated an immense amount of public and private conversation. During the early months of the occupation, much of the response was in fact positive. Many Germans threw their full support behind the screening campaign, which seemed to target only active party members, which they were not. In fact, some felt that denazification should be extended even further, calling for a more vigilant vetting process and wider distribution of questionnaires. For example, a public prosecutor attached to a Munich Spruchkammer asked if his office could continue using the much more detailed Fragebogen, as he believed the new registration form (Meldebogen) was too short and "inferior."[57] An October 12, 1945 article in the *Schwäbisches Tagblatt*, asked "But is this enough? One gets the feeling that the purge hasn't actually proceeded with the needed vigor."[58] Conservative politicians were publicly shamed for not purging their party offices and demonstrations were held to protest lax denazification, such as one in Berlin on August 10, 1945, that drew more than 70,000 people.[59] This adamant support for political screening, and cries for its expansion, diminished as the campaign dragged on and changed format, but it was never completely silenced. A US Gallup poll found that in September 1946, 55 percent of Munich residents felt that tribunal verdicts were too lenient.[60]

However, in the summer and fall of 1945, as more people came under the political microscope, criticism of denazification increased. Support turned into suspicion and frustration, then anger and resentment. Most

---

[56] Letter, W.M. to "whom it may concern," November 23, 1947, BAB, DC 1/4036; "Notice," January 11, 1946, TNA, FO 1014/165; Fragebogen of A.R., LK Ravensburg, ADMAE, ZFO, WH 1298; Denazification file for A.K., NARA, RG 260, OMGUS, CAD, PSB, Fragebogen, Box 1159.
[57] Report, "Trend: A Weekly Report of Political Affairs and Public Opinion," June 20–26, 1946, NARA, RG 260, OMGUS, BDC Admin. Records/OMGUS MG Records, Box 19.
[58] Karl Sinner, "Die politische Reinigung," *Schwäbisches Tagblatt*, October 12, 1945, p. 4.
[59] KPD poster, "Die Entnazifizierung Rollt.!" November 64, AdsD, 6/FLBL001379; Marshall, "German Attitude to British Military Government," 672.
[60] "Weekly Political Report," December 31, 1946, NARA, RG 260, OMGUS, OMGB, ID, Box 105.

vocal were Germans in the American zone, who, regardless of their political past, were barred from their chosen profession until their Fragebogen had been reviewed. The allowance of local elections in 1946 helped coordinate protest, which was led mainly by the CDU/CSU, *Freie Demokratische Partei* (Free Democratic Party, FDP), and the Evangelical Church. OMGUS polls estimated that by the March 1946, only 54 percent of the zonal population was satisfied with denazification; by December, it had dropped to 34 percent and by November 1947, it stood at only 18 percent.[61] In the British and French zones, unified opposition was slower to develop, perhaps because of the more selective screening programs, but a similarly popular indignation eventually emerged there too. Support within the Soviet-occupied territories appears to have been universal, surely on account of more stringent censorship. In all zones, when political parties realized the value of harnessing the former Nazi vote, denazification settled into a permanent state of near universal condemnation; even the SPD produced anti-denazification rhetoric, while the KPD avoided the topic altogether.[62] In a September 3, 1948 editorial, the *Neuer Westfälischer Kurier* announced what everyone else already knew, that "Denazification has entered its crisis. The paper revolution of the questionnaire has passed its zenith."[63]

Newspaper articles, journal entries, private correspondence, speeches, published pamphlets, and opinion polls indicate that criticism was widely held and expressed openly by nearly all groups and demographics. It was generally argued that denazification was unfair, undemocratic, illegal, and immoral, as well as biased, arbitrary, and analogous to methods used by the Nazis themselves. It was also viewed as seriously hindering economic recovery by dismissing managers, specialists, and skilled workers. The primary point of contention, however, was that the expanded campaign targeted and punished "nominal" Nazis, or Mitläufer. The widely distributed Fragebogen, which brought denazification from the courtroom of Nuremberg into the living room of the German home, epitomized this attack on the "small fry" Nazi; it functioned as the "little man's Nuremberg" (*Nürnberg des kleinen mannes*).[64] Reported by a foreign

---

[61] "Criticism of Denazification, Expert Opinions," June 10, 1947, NARA, RG 260, OMGUS, FODS, RGCO, Box 9; "Opinions on Denazification," November 26, 1947, NARA, RG 260, OMGUS, EO, CO, Box 456.
[62] Griffith, "The Denazification Program in the United States Zone of Germany," 412–13.
[63] "Die Krise der Entnazifizierung," *Neuer Westfälischer Kurier*, September 3, 1948, clipping in BAK, Z 42-I/51.
[64] As quoted in Caspar von Schrenck-Notzing, *Charakterwäsche: Die Re-education der Deutschen und ihre bleibenden Auswirkungen* (Graz: Ares, 2015), 154.

journalist in March 1948, "Fragebogen ... this word, probably the most hated in the German language today."[65]

By far the most popular accusation brought against denazification in the Western zones was that it was simply unfair. First, that the "Fragebogen-Formula," namely its evaluation criteria, was ill-conceived.[66] The public often condemned the form as a naïve instrument, with misguided and superficial questions. Dozens of letters addressed to the Denazification Minister in Bavaria decried that the survey was ignorant of the Nazi system and that its vague questions led respondents to make unintentional mistakes.[67] A series of public lectures were broadcast throughout Hesse in February 1946, which concluded that "Only a German who lived through the twelve years of National Socialism in Germany can judge who is a Nazi."[68] Foreign correspondent for the *Frankfurter Zeitung* and Nazi collaborationist Margret Boveri, wrote that it is impossible to "determine the exact degree of affinity with National Socialism via questionnaires, since they could not estimate the reasons for certain behavior."[69] Political parties joined in the chorus of criticism. The eastern zone Liberal Democratic Party published pamphlets that claimed the occupiers could never understand the German psyche, while the FDP leader and future president of West Germany, Theodor Heuss, published a complaint about the limits of the "eternal questionnaire."[70] After being dismissed from his job, a former Nazi party member submitted a letter of resentment to the *Frankfurter Presse*, writing that "in the place of the purifying revolution there was the Fragebogen, which shows there is nothing harder really than to understand a foreign people."[71]

While prominent Nazis remained silent, it was the millions of nominal party members, and their families and colleagues, who drove the engine of protest. They argued that the screening system placed far too much

---

[65] Robert Stephens, "The Great Purge in Germany," *The Globe and Mail*, March 5, 1948, p. 6.
[66] Letter, Professor Dr. H.J.M. to Frau E.D.S., January 13, 1950, LAB, B Rep. 014, Nr. 1947.
[67] Various letters, BHStA, MSo 1957.
[68] Karl Heinrich Knappstein, "Öffentlicher Vortrag über Probleme der Entnazifizierung," February 2, 1946, DRA, X130, 2753303.
[69] Sollors, "'Everybody Gets Fragebogened Sooner or Later,'" 148. Boveri never joined the NSDAP, but she publicly defended the regime's foreign policy and regarded herself a "German patriot." She also held strong anti-Slavic beliefs. Several studies explore her professional and private life, including Heike B. Görtemaker, *Ein deutsches Leben: Die Geschichte der Margret Boveri 1900–1975* (München: C.H. Beck Verlag, 2005).
[70] "Interview with Dr. Kolb," May 29, 1946, NARA, OMGUS, OMGB, ID, Box 128; Sollors, "'Everybody Gets Fragebogened Sooner or Later,'" 148.
[71] As quoted in Harold J. Hurwitz, *Military Government in Germany: Press Reorientation* (Karlsruhe: Historical Division, European Command, 1950), 67.

emphasis on membership, while disregarding individual circumstances. Attention was often drawn to middle-class citizens who held strong nationalist beliefs, but never joined the NSDAP because their independent social and economic status protected them from a reliance on the party system. A Hamburg journalist protested that, "We find people who can produce a beautiful and innocent questionnaire, but who in fact were fanatical Nazis, and they acted as such. ... You can't look into a man's heart."[72] American and British records contain thousands of handwritten and typed letters, submitted by frustrated citizens who professed to being "kleine Nazis."[73] Well known but unconfirmed was the story of Kurt M., an anti-Nazi radio broadcaster who was prohibited to work for two years simply because his Fragebogen was being processed.[74] A similar story circulated about a former concentration camp inmate who filled out twenty-four questionnaires to keep his job.[75]

Whether these cases are in fact true, and they very well could be, they do not represent the typical German experience. It was instead the millions of party members who did not considered themselves "real" Nazis that most loudly protested denazification. Their opinions were recorded in newspapers throughout the Western zones, in letters sent to military government offices, and spoken aloud during commission hearings. One municipal administrator in the town of Bruchsal pleaded with the US Military Government to reinstate his staff, explaining that, "Although 65 percent of my workers were NSDAP members, not one of them is or ever was actually a Nazi."[76] The CDU was perhaps the greatest defender of the Mitläufer. Konrad Adenauer knew that the nominal Nazi vote could propel his party to national government and therefore demanded that the "followers" be left alone.[77]

Common also was the claim that denazification was autocratic and illegal. The hypocrisy of the occupation regimes' messianic claim to have brought democracy to the Germans was regularly put on display. Again, it was the questionnaire that was delivered as tangible proof of this offense – that its content, scope, and categories of guilt were unjust. During the commission phase, letters poured into administrator offices, asking why such a discriminatory form was still being used.[78] Criticizing the Western zones' campaigns, an SPD newspaper in Berlin plainly

---

[72] "Der Fragebogen," FO 1051/689.
[73] For example, NARA, RG 260, OMGUS, OMGB, ID, Box 105.
[74] Louis P. Loachner, "The Idiocy of Our De-nazification Policy," *Reader's Digest* (June 1948): 132.
[75] Ibid., 133.
[76] IA&CD Intelligence Summary No. 52, January 24, 1947, TNA, FO 1050/431.
[77] Judt, *Postwar*, 56.   [78] For example, see various letters, BHStA, MSo 1957.

declared that "Denazification is unjust, and the Fragebogen is the problem."[79] Victor Gollancz wrote that, "A free and law-abiding society cannot be fostered by ticketing millions of people on the score of what they have done, said, or even thought, in the past, and penalizing them accordingly. These are totalitarian methods."[80] Even an American denazification officer wondered "if the Gestapo or the MVD [Soviet interior ministry] have ever developed so all-embracing a political purge machinery."[81] Specific questions in the form were deemed undemocratic, among them, "For what political party did you vote in the election of November 1932?," which appeared in most versions of the survey.[82] Journalist Ursula von Kardorff believed this question to be absurd, recording in her diary that, "I had previously imagined that the secrecy of the ballot was one of the fundamental laws of democracy."[83]

Finally, denazification was criticized for being immoral. Unsurprisingly, this argument was steered by leaders in the Protestant churches, including Bishop Wurm of Stuttgart, who knew that many members of his congregation had been dedicated Nazis. The Church was a silent and divided institution under Nazism. Far more Christians had supported the regime than had resisted it. At the August 1945 Treysa Conference, where the EKD was constituted as a federation, the Fragebogen was condemned outright. The delegates asserted that the screening device "promoted denunciations" by citizens against their neighbors.[84] This opinion was anointed one year later in the EKD's official statement on denazification: "Experience has shown that the questions asked in the questionnaires seduce you in some places and promote inaccuracy. This cannot be conducive to the moral recovery of the people."[85] Such a critique was picked up by church members across the four zones, some going as far as likening the Fragebogen system to the Nazis' registration of Jews.[86]

---

[79] "Wer wird im Westen entnazifiziert?" August 28, 1947, *Vorwärts*, BAB, DO 2/99.
[80] As quoted in Arthur Sträter, "Denazification," *Annals of the American Academy of Political and Social Science* 260 (November 1948): 48–49.
[81] Griffith, "The Denazification Program in the United States Zone in Germany," 17.
[82] Letters to the editor, *Rheinische Zeitung*, October 5, 1946, p. 4.
[83] As quoted in Leßau, *Entnazifizierungsgeschichten*, 86–87.
[84] Letter, Bishop Wurm to General Clay, April 26, 1946, EZA 7/10761; Professor Dr. Emil Brunner, "Deutschland Not," *Neue Zürcher Zeitung*, May 25, 1947.
[85] "Erklärung des Rates der EKD zur Durchführung der Entnazifizierung im deutschen Volk," in *Kundgebungen: Worte und Erklärungen der Evangelischen Kirche in Deutschland, 1945–1959*, ed. Friedrich Merzyn (Hannover: Verlag des Amtsblattes der Evangelischen Kirche in Deutschland, 1959), 35–37.
[86] "Intelligence Report No. 6 [readers of *Neue Zeitung*]," April 1, 1946, NARA, RG 260, OMGUS, OMGB, ID, Box 105.

A common interpretation in the existing scholarship is that denazification, and especially the questionnaire, was not taken seriously by Germans; that it was mocked and belittled as an overly bureaucratic and ridiculous system that temporarily burdened their lives. Newspapers referred to the "comedy of denazification" and military governments reported that the Fragebogen was viewed as a "mockery" and "cabaret joke."[87] The humorous song "Fragebogenkrank" (questionnaire sick) was performed at the Rheinlandhalle in Rüdesheim in 1947, by the celebrated entertainer Just Scheu, and broadcasted throughout the country.[88] Many jokes circulated: "The PG's [party members] are out, the Nazis are in"; "What has the color of my eyes got to do with my political opinions?"[89] Ernst von Salomon allegedly "performed" his questionnaire answers to fellow POWs in the barracks of his camp.[90]

While comedic relief may have helped citizens endure the occupation, denazification was not a comedy; the jokes were drowned out by frustration for something that was out of the individual's control. Evidence shows that Germans took political screening seriously, that they were overwhelmingly critical of the process, and that the focus of their disparagement was the Fragebogen, as it was the gatekeeper to receiving a clean bill of political health. One Berlin resident recalled that the survey was valued so much for its power as a job producer that whenever the British announced a paper shortage, blank Fragebögen were sold illegally on the black market for 25 RM.[91]

Passing or Failing: The Consequences of Political Screening

Denazification was meant to permanently upset existing political and economic systems and root out fascist and militarist attitudes. So, what then was its impact? How did the campaign affect the lives of those it targeted? Surprisingly, this question is rarely asked, and when it is, the response is usually delivered as a statistical calculation of arrests, dismissals, and amnesties.

---

[87] *Tägliche Rundschau*, quoted in "Information Control Weekly Review, No. 68," NARA, RG 498, HQ ETOUSA, HD, Box 4104; CCG(BE), Public Safety Report, "Public Order Special Committee," August 25, 1947, TNA, FO 1056/93; Balfour, *Four-Power Control in Germany and Austria*, 175.
[88] Scheu, "Der Fragebogen," 1947, DRA, X130, 2600351.
[89] Adams, *From Crusade to Hazard*, 66; "Daily Brief," April 30, 1946, NARA, RG 260, OMGB, ID, ICD, Box 128; MacDonogh, *After the Reich*, 146–47.
[90] Parkinson, *An Emotional State*, 87.   [91] Posener, *In Deutschland*, 65.

Passing or Failing

Germans spoke informally about "passing" and "failing" denazification, which almost always referred to employment eligibility. However, the consequences were more complex than this and they impacted every individual differently. There were many potential outcomes to screening procedures – internment, employment, dismissal, monetary penalty, loss of pension, confiscation of property, travel restrictions. In the British zone, proof of "successful" denazification was required to join a political party, to obtain a hunting license, and to enroll in university.[92] It was also common for an applicant to initially be denied a job by military government and then later approved for the same position by a German commission. Some were merely demoted, while others permanently barred. There were ways to circumvent punishment, such as simply changing one's job title or moving to another zone where denazification was more lax. Perhaps more significant is that reward and punishment meant different things to different people. Permission to work might be considered "passing" denazification but being labeled a "Mitläufer" viewed as a mark of shame. Furthermore, what was there to celebrate if a non-Nazi applicant had to endure months of unemployment while waiting for their questionnaire to be processed? The effects of denazification were therefore complicated. What is clear is that the purge had immediate and meaningful consequences for Germans, and that in large part, these were decided by the Fragebogen.

Most Germans "passed" their political screening. They were placed in the *Entlastete* (exonerated) category or designated a Mitläufer or "nominal Nazi," which almost always meant they could be employed in their desired job. Usually, the individual was informed by a supervisor or potential employer that they were permitted to continue or begin work, or by letter from a public prospector's office that they were not required to face a commission. Sometimes, this news only brought temporary relief. Employment policy in all four zones was always changing and many feared that their answers in the Fragebogen would suddenly be reassessed. Job security did not exist, turnover was high, and designations often changed, which resulted in filling out new questionnaires. Applicants in the American zone were held hostage by their questionnaires, as they were not permitted to work until the form had been processed. Many referred to living within the "Fragebogen system."[93]

Nevertheless, Germans were happy to hear that they were permitted to work, whether in their current profession or in a new public or private

---

[92] Leßau, *Entnazifizierungsgeschichten*, 82.
[93] "U.S. Civil Censorship Submission," July 24, 1946, NARA, RG 260, OMGB, ID, IR, Box 105.

office, or for military government. They were relieved that they could earn an income to support their families, maintain their professional credentials and social status, and perhaps receive other employment perks, such as having access to items they could barter on the black market. There was also a mental peace that came with a clean bill of health. They were not, in a sense, among the defeated enemy, nor were they war criminals. Instead, "passing" the Fragebogen allowed many to mentally distance themselves from the regime and its crimes and, in some cases, to confirm an already strong sense of their own victim status, an expression explored in Chapter 5.

Josef Müller, a postal worker from Münchberg, worried he would lose his job due to membership in the NSDAP and *Reichsbund der Deutschen Beamten* (Reich Federation of German Civil Servants).[94] Despite these affiliations, he retained his position. A midwife from French-occupied Weingarten, Alice Stein, joined the *Deutsches Frauenwerk* (German Women's Welfare Organization) in 1938, but this was not enough to condemn her to unemployment.[95] The French-zone *Untersuchungsausschuss* quickly read the Fragebogen and permitted her to "*verbleiben im Amt*" (remain in office). Twenty-three-year-old Reinhold Jahn had joined the party in early 1933 and was therefore dismissed as a warehouse worker for a British military hospital. His Fragebogen, however, included a statement about his "juvenile ignorance," which convinced the Spandau commission to grant him a clean bill of health.[96]

More typical is the story of Karl Vogt, who, prior to the occupation, held a number of odd jobs in and around the Swabian village of Weisingen.[97] He repaired bicycles, worked in the forestry industry, acted as a farmhand, and during the final two years of the war, was a reserve police officer. Shortly after the German surrender, he applied for a cashier position at a local bank and therefore was required to fill out the US Fragebogen. Apart from his membership in the *NS-Kriegsopferversorgung* (National Socialist War Victims Care) and the *NS-Reichskriegerbund* (National Socialist Veterans' Association), Vogt had no Nazi affiliations, and as a result, Special Branch permitted his employment. When the Liberation Law was announced in March 1946, Vogt was again required to complete a questionnaire, this time the Meldebogen. He was now the elected mayor of Weisingen, and therefore

---

[94] Denazification file for F.J., NARA, RG 260, OMGUS, CAD, PSB, Fragebogen, Box 587.
[95] Denazification file for A.H., ADMAE, ZFO, WH 1298.
[96] Fragebogen of T.S., TNA, FO 1050/356.
[97] Fragebogen of J.A., NARA, RG 260, OMGUS, CAD, PSB, Fragebogen, Box 1158.

wondered if his history as a police officer would jeopardize his political career. To his relief, three weeks after submitting his questionnaire, the local prosecutor's office informed him that he was not chargeable under the Liberation Law. Hence, for Karl Vogt, denazification was limited to the completion of two questionnaires, both of which he "passed."

For a relatively small group, denazification granted opportunities that would otherwise not be available. If an applicant effectively used the questionnaire to prove their anti-Nazi status, many different jobs opened up. It helped if the respondent had suffered at the hands of the regime or, especially in the Soviet zone, had participated in political resistance. Kurt Schumacher was known to carry around a copy of his Fragebogen as proof of his anti-Nazi status.[98] These men and women were essentially guaranteed employment. In industries which had been thoroughly Nazified, such as education and healthcare, anti-Nazi applicants, some of whom were underqualified, were rapidly promoted to managerial positions. Such was the case of Ulrich Haas, who, because of his proven distain for Nazism, was appointed manager of a bank in French-occupied Worms.[99] The celebrated anti-Nazi activities of journalist Greta Kuckhoff helped her gain several influential positions, including head of the Berlin Bureau of Denazified and Ownerless Businesses (*Amtsstelle für die entnazifizierten und herrenlosen Betriebe*).[100] There is evidence that all four military governments used the questionnaire as a recruitment tool for their own offices.[101] For example, every version of the form asked about the language proficiencies of the respondent, which sometimes resulted in an unexpected and much desired job as a translator or clerk. The potential benefits of political screening were expounded on in a March 1946 newspaper editorial by Wilhelm Beisel, who explained that the questionnaire was an "oppressive form but only for the burdened; it's liberating and instructive for the others."[102]

Internment was the most consequential of denazification's collective fates, affecting some 400,000 people across the four zones, mostly middle-aged men.[103] Already outlined, this usually occurred after review of a Fragebogen, which landed the respondent in an automatic arrest category. For example, Alexander Heinrich, a schoolteacher from the

---

[98] Fragebogen of Kurt Schumacher, TNA, FO 1050/363.
[99] Fragebogen of R.S., BAK, B 332/110.
[100] Fragebogen of Maria Greta Kuckhoff, BAB, N 2506/197.
[101] See, for example, Meeting Minutes, ACC/DIAC/PSC, September 30, 1947, NARA, RG 260, ACA, DIAC, Box 204.
[102] Wilhelm Beisel, "Der Fragebogen," *Badische Neueste Nachrichten*, March 14, 1946, p. 2.
[103] Biddiscombe, *Denazification of Germany*, 9.

Hessian town of Eisenroth, was arrested at his home on September 18, 1945 after his questionnaire revealed he had been an *Ortsgruppenleiter* (regional party leader).[104] He was interned at Camp 93 in Schwarzenborn for an unknown period of time. Similarly, Felix Ebenau, a city-employed laborer from Berlin-Schöneberg, was detained on June 2, 1947, after submitting a questionnaire that revealed his *Waffen SS* rank of *Scharführer* (troop leader).[105]

Arrest not only resulted in a loss of one's freedom, but also income, usually the only money available to support a spouse or family in already impoverished times. While those dismissed still had the option to work as an "ordinary laborer" or to appeal the decision, internment offered no alternatives. Arrests sometimes occurred suddenly and with little knowledge of why the accused was being detained, where they would be incarcerated, and for how long, evoking feelings of helplessness and uncertainty. The conditions in each camp varied considerably, even within zones, but prisoners usually lived in crowded barracks, some of them in former Nazi concentration camps, anywhere from a few weeks to several years.[106] If arrested by the Russians in the early months of the occupation, one was likely deported to a labor camp in the Soviet Union. The mortality rate was much higher in Soviet "special camps," with an estimated one-third of detainees dying from starvation or disease.[107]

The removal of husbands and fathers fragmented families. Upon arrest, many did not get the chance to notify their next of kin, and family members were kept in the dark for weeks and even months about the whereabouts of their loved ones.[108] Some families struggled to continue a small business or maintain a farm, while others lost all of their income. Children were left without a father, while women sometimes found themselves in a dangerous place, especially in the Soviet zone, where rape and other acts of physical abuse were commonplace. Furthermore, during a time of extreme distress, women were left in a prolonged state of singlehood; their husband's absence deprived them of a close companion to share in emotional recovery from traumatic experiences endured during the war. Whether these conditions resulted in the forced emancipation of women or their economic bondage is arguable. However, what is certain is that denazification required women to fundamentally change

---

[104] Fragebogen of K.E., NARA, RG 260, OMGUS, Fragebogens, Box 11.
[105] Fragebogen of D.G., NARA, RG 260, OMGUS, CAD, PSB, Box 1268.
[106] Plischke, *Denazifying the Reich*, 156–57. For a description of living conditions in civilian internment camps, see Beattie, *Allied Internment Camps in Occupied Germany*, 103–89.
[107] Bettina Greiner, *Verdrängter Terror: Geschichte und Wahrnehmung sowjetischer Speziallager in Deutschland* (Hamburg: Hamburger Edition, 2010), 10.
[108] Elizabeth D. Heineman, *What Difference Does a Husband Make?* (Berkeley: University of California Press, 1999), 113.

the way they lived their lives and, as Elizabeth Heineman has noted, they were forced to learn "a remarkable degree of self-sufficiency."[109]

For both men and women, the more pronounced threat of denazification was unemployment. Prior to the widescale amnesties, the watered-down commission systems, and popular turn toward reorientation, political screening in each zone revolved around a system of punishment by exclusion. After submitting their Fragebogen, the hopeful employee waited anywhere from a month to over a year for the relevant military government to render a decision about their work eligibility. During the early weeks of the occupation, they were informed in person, by a soldier, civil affairs officer, or appointed German official, that they were no longer permitted to work in a particular office or to practice their trade. Exceptions were sometimes made, and temporary employment allowed because of the need for certain technical or administrative expertise. Still, most employees were immediately escorted from their office or had their licenses revoked. In the Soviet and American zones, small business owners lost all legal control of their assets.[110] Usually, the bad news was delivered in writing. For example, in British-occupied Hamburg, civil servants received a letter from the city's senate office that declared: "By order of the Bürgermeister you are here within informed that by virtue of Law No. 6 of Military Government ... you are dismissed from your position ... you are not entitled to any further claims on salary, temporary dues, pension or similar service."[111]

During the military government phase, 1,252,364 Fragebögen were reviewed by the US Special Branch, resulting in the dismissal of more than 308,000 people.[112] In the same period, the British processed some 870,000 questionnaires and removed or excluded 172,615 people, mostly civil servants.[113] French denazification panels dismissed one-third of Germans employed in public office during the first six months of the occupation. It is estimated that some 520,000 former Nazis were fired from their jobs in the Soviet zone, representing around 3 percent of the zone's population.[114] Related numbers are calculated in Table 4.1.

---

[109] Ibid., 106, 114. See also Rebecca Boehling, "Gender Roles in Ruins: German Women and Local Politics under American Occupation, 1945–1955," in *Gender and the Long Postwar: The United States and the Two Germanys, 1945–1989*, eds. Karen Hageman and Sonya Michel (Washington, DC: Woodrow Wilson Center Press, 2014), 51–72.
[110] Vogt, *Denazification in Soviet-Occupied Germany*, 89.
[111] Letter, Verwaltung der Hansestadt Hamburg Personalamt to Rudolf Jürgensen, January 22, 1946, TNA, FO 1014/165.
[112] OMGUS, CAD, *Denazification, Cumulative Review. Report, 1 April 1947–30 April 1948*, p. 3.
[113] Biddiscombe, *Denazification of Germany*, 114.
[114] Jon Elster, *Retribution and Reparation in the Transition to Democracy* (Cambridge: Cambridge University Press, 2006), 79; Herf, *Divided Memory*, 72.

Table 4.1 *Removal and exclusion from public office and private business in each zone/sector*[115]

	From Beginning of Occupation		From January 1, 1946	
	American zone/ sector	Soviet zone/ sector	British zone/ sector	French zone/ sector
Removed	292,089	307,370	112,557	55,054
Excluded	126,218	83,108	56,565	8,515
Total	418,307	390,478	169,122	63,569

Most detrimental to the forfeiture of employment was, of course, the loss of income. Removal or exclusion led to an immediate termination of salary, which many families relied on. Granted, for some, dismissal did not mean unemployment. If physically fit and fortunate enough to find work, they were free to take up "ordinary labor," while others were simply demoted in their same office. Some found loopholes in the denazification bureaucracy, but for thousands of Germans there was no alternative. They were temporarily forced to surrender a lifelong profession, along with a hard-earned salary. Thousands of young professionals and civil servants could easily, albeit begrudgingly, take up some form of menial work, but for elderly professionals – doctors, lawyers, bureaucrats, and teachers, for example – construction or other physical trades were not viable options. Many could not find any work and instead relied on the black-market economy and aid services to survive. Within the postwar economy, cash income was not as lucrative as it once had been, but it was also far from worthless. A salary still bought food and clothes and paid for housing. Furthermore, employment brought other material benefits and privileges, especially if one worked for the military government or in an essential service industry. Depending on what job they once held, a loss of income also came with a loss of pension, which, for some, was needed now more than ever.

Dr. Richard Groß, a thirty-seven-year-old physician from the town of Schönau, did not have to wait long to hear back from US authorities

---

[115] These data do not include the total number dismissed or excluded, as it covers only the 1945–47 period in the American and Soviet zones and 1946–47 in the British and French zones. They also do not account for applicants denied employment on more than one occasion or the much larger number of public officials, professionals, and private industry workers who were reinstated or amnestied during the later phases of denazification. OMGUS, CAD, *Denazification, Cumulative Review. Report, 1 April 1947–30 April 1948*, p. 13.

about his employment eligibility.[116] His early membership in the NSDAP and SA led to his immediate dismissal from the hospital and revoking of his medical license and pension. Groß was told he would never again work in the medicine profession, and he remained unemployed, with no source of income, for several months until a Spruchkammer reclassified him as a Mitläufer. In the Soviet sector of Berlin, Emil Krause completed two questionnaires, hoping to gain work in the Central Administration Office for Transportation.[117] He was initially hired and allotted a sizable income to support his five children. However, when it was later discovered that Krause had falsified his Fragebogen, he was promptly dismissed and made to appear before a Soviet military tribunal. Thousands of similar stories fill the denazification records of the occupation armies. Some are dramatic, but most seemingly trivial and part of standard vetting procedures. In every town and district, residents were stripped of their salaries, pensions, and work prospects. They did not know what the future would bring.

Forced removal also brought a loss of professional status and social standing. High profile bureaucrats, endowed university professors, and small-town doctors were stripped of prestige and privilege. They had spent a lifetime of preparation for their position and now suddenly had it taken away, in their minds permanently, and forced to struggle with so many others on the margins of society. This represented a personal defeat, conjuring emotions of embarrassment and resentment. The psychological shock was even more profound if the individual was arrested. As conveyed by historian Jonathan Wiesen, "to the businessman whose self-image was a proper bourgeois gentleman, arrest and imprisonment represented an unimaginable turn of events."[118] Such was the case of Georg Möller, a successful international merchant living outside Stuttgart, who reacted with "astonishment" about his unemployment and the blocking of his assets.[119] Similarly, Theodor Beck, a well-respected master craftsman, who, despite membership in the NSDAP and SS, was surprised by his routine dismissal from a Babelsberg

---

[116] Denazification file for Dr. G.W., NARA, RG 260, OMGUS, CAD, PSB, Box 350.
[117] Letter, Rechstabteilung to Personalbteilung, Deutsche Zentralverwaltung des Verkehrs in der sowjetischen Besatzungszone, March 17, 1947, BAB, DM 1/165.
[118] S. Jonathan Wiesen, "Overcoming Nazism: Big Business, Public Relations, and the Politics of Memory, 1945–1949," *Central European History* 29, no. 2 (1996): 225. See also Michael R. Hayse, *Recasting West German Elites: Higher Civil Servants, Business Leaders, and Physicians in Hessen between Nazim and Democracy, 1945–1955* (New York: Berghahn, 2003).
[119] Letter, F.S. to F.U. (Landesdirektor des Innern), August 30, 1945, NARA, RG 260, Box 297.

workshop.[120] Dr. Walter Birnbaum lost his University of Göttingen professorship and pension when the British learned he had been a dedicated member of the *Glaubensbewegung Deutsche Christen* (German Christian movement).[121]

The psychological effects of denazification extend even further than this. Former Nazis who "passed" the Fragebogen were relieved about their employment status but ashamed of the political category in which they had been placed. Some of those classified as Mitläufer believed that the label distinguished them as weak-willed and susceptible to peer pressure. They were embarrassed, especially around neighbors and coworkers, who proudly announced their "Non-Nazi" or "Exonerated" status. Of the 3,660,648 Germans who faced a commission in one of the three Western zones between 1946 and 1948, more than a million (27 percent) were classified as some sort of "nominal Nazis."[122] As the number of designated "followers" grew, the category's stigma diminished. With the revived political party system and active canvassing for the ex-Nazi vote, a new popular identity emerged. The Mitläufer was depicted as being victimized twice, first by the manipulative Hitler regime and then by the unjust military government.

At the community level, denazification had both direct and indirect consequences. Civil leadership changed, sometimes prominent businesspeople and local clergy were removed from their positions. Often the town's sole industry, a factory or mill, for example, was acquired by the military government or by a shell company, from which reparations were extracted. In the east, entire municipal administrations were purged, radiating downward from the mayor's office. A new and often inexperienced cast of community leaders was introduced, all members of the KPD and SPD and friendly with the Soviets. Some had returned to the community that had once expelled them.

As we have already seen, gender played a meaningful role in the denazification experience. Men were targeted disproportionally, and punishment was experienced by men and women in different ways. Forced dismissal disrupted traditional economic structures within the family, resulting in other members of the household having to find work. Granted, many women were already employed, and when they lost their jobs due to political screening, the financial impact was no less profound than what their male counterparts experienced. Sometimes, those dismissed were single and lacking in any other financial provisions, or they themselves were supporting elderly parents or children whose fathers had

---

[120] Denazification file of K.P., NARA, RG 260, CAD, PSB, Fragebogen, Box 1273.
[121] Walter Birnbaum Papers, EZA, 745/11.   [122] Remy, *The Heidelberg Myth*, 178.

died during the war or remained missing. "Ordinary labor" was not always an option for the same reasons as men, and work as a *Trümmerfrau* (rubble woman) did not put much food on the table. It also cannot be overlooked that denazification, just like the military occupation more generally, was a highly patriarchal system. Women were subjected to screening and punishment by men who had absolute authority over their public and private lives. As such, life proved exceedingly difficult for those who needed to work but were not permitted to.

Hundreds of thousands of women sought employment after the war.[123] Some reapplied for their existing position, while others took up paid work for the first time in their lives and sometimes in jobs traditionally held by men, a mass movement that threatened to recast gender roles. Margaretha Hartmann, for example, submitted a Fragebogen for a postal assistant position in Münchberg, a line of work that she had no previous experience in, because her husband had been barred from a similar job.[124] In a single district, the French detachment office received hundreds of applications from women who wished to work as secretaries and midwives; only a handful had past experience.[125] These new realities undoubtedly upset gender norms and challenged the difficult postwar process of reconstructing the family.[126] Elizabeth Heinemann tells us that some men who were dismissed or barred from paid employment refused to contribute to the housework.[127] This inevitably challenged marital relations and many women were physically and emotionally overtaxed.

For many men, denazification took away their authority as breadwinners and ability to contribute to society in their chosen profession. It also stripped them of the roles they expected to assume after the war. The urge to master one's environment, physically and spiritually, and assert dominance over others to achieve success was much less available to them now. The loss of career and income, along with military defeat and internment, occupation by a foreign army, and, for some, a recently sustained permanent disability, only added to this crisis of masculinity and to feelings of humiliation and impotency. Some men became passive, uncompetitive, lacking physical and mental willpower, and unwilling to pursue new career goals. Frank Biess has argued that "postwar

---

[123] For an overview of women's labor during the occupation, see Heineman, *What Difference Does a Husband Make?*, 76–95.
[124] Denazification file for B.T., NARA, RG 260, CAD, PSB, Fragebogen, Box 588.
[125] Landkreis Ravensburg, ADMAE, ZFO, WH 1298.
[126] Biess, *Homecomings*, 120–21.
[127] Heineman, *What Difference Does a Husband Make?*, 121. See also Blessing, *The Antifascist Classroom*, 157.

ideals of masculinity did not draw on the front experience but rather on survival under conditions of extreme adversity."[128] For many German men, survival in the immediate postwar years seemed exceedingly bleak. As one US journalist commented in the summer of 1945, "American soldiers pay no attention to German men ... and why should they?"[129] With the war lost, millions of dead, cities in ruin, and the surviving population traumatized, mass disseminated punishment only heightened the psychological shock.

In his celebrated 1961 study of the American occupation of Marburg, John Gimbel argues that denazification did not have a substantial impact on the economic or social lives of residents because most of them were eventually reinstated in their jobs.[130] This retrospective interpretation has prevailed in subsequent scholarship, fueled by a consensus verdict that the eradication of Nazism failed in all regards. By lack of interest, researchers agreed that any immediate consequences of the purge were quickly expunged by the successive wave of exonerations and lenient commission decisions. Through this lens, the completion of the Fragebogen is regularly depicted as a silly compulsory exercise. As one historian describes it: "For most Germans, the obligation to fill out a questionnaire was this: an annoying duty."[131]

As shown above, this interpretation is problematic, and for two reasons. First, it assumes that the only meaningful outcome of denazification was material based, that only income, assets, and employment should be evaluated. However, the campaign uprooted millions of already desperate lives and forced radical changes for the individual, whether economic, social, familial, or otherwise. Reaching well beyond the financial burden of losing employment, denazification inflicted a deep emotional casualty and challenged social norms.

The second assumption made by Gimbel is more transparent, as he uses historical retrospect to minimize meaningful human experience. German citizens are depicted as having maintained an extraordinary degree of sensibility during the occupation and that they were comforted in the apparent knowledge that the purge would be short-lived, and its penalties ultimately reversed. There is indeed evidence to suggest that people suspected they would be reinstated in their jobs, but the ruling emotion was not that of hope. The firsthand accounts do not depict a

---

[128] Biess, *Homecomings*, 102.
[129] Petra Goedde, *GIs and Germans: Culture, Gender, and Foreign Relations, 1945–1949* (New Haven: Yale University Press, 2003), 80.
[130] Gimbel, *A German Community Under American Occupation*, 147.
[131] Frederick Taylor, *Zwischen Krieg und Frieden: Die Besetzung und Entnazifizierung Deutschlands 1944–1946* (Berlin: Berlin Verlag, 2011), 333.

population simply waiting for denazification to collapse, but a deeply embedded fear and feeling of helplessness. Germans did not know, as we do now, about the forthcoming amnesties, and even if they did, such knowledge did not put food on the table. It was also not known what would happen to the workers who had been hired and promoted to replace them or how long the occupation itself would last. Reflected in a popular joke exchanged by Germans until at least 1947: "Hitler declared that the Third Reich would last a thousand years. He survived the first twelve years. De-nazification will easily occupy the remaining 988. He was correct in his forecast."[132] There was far too much uncertainty and accompanying apprehension to deny individual agency.

Case Study: Kreis Hersfeld (Hesse), 1945–1949

Sitting quietly in the northeast suburbs of Hesse, the mostly rural district (Kreis) of Hersfeld-Rotenburg is easy to overlook. The rolling hills of Waldhessen meet the Rhön mountains to the east, while the Fulda River valley winds its way north, toward Kassel. Twenty municipalities dot the landscape, but the region pivots around its largest town and capital, Bad Hersfeld. Hersfeld-Rotenburg has a population of around 120,000 and borders the eastern state of Thuringia, which made it a strategically important region during the Cold War.[133] Older residents remember the large US army garrison, which acted as the first line of defense against a potential Soviet invasion. However, the American presence began as an invasion itself, in early April 1945, during the closing weeks of the war. Back then, the Kreis was half the size and population and simply called Hersfeld.[134]

There are several characteristics that make Kreis Hersfeld a representative case study. For the duration of the occupation, it was part of the US zone, where denazification had its greatest reach. The region was primarily rural, with one sizable urban center, and a diversified economy and corresponding socioeconomic makeup. Although National Socialism found early resonance here, it was never a Nazi stronghold. A majority of the population identified as Protestant, but the district also maintained a sizable Catholic community. There are also methodological reasons for choosing Hersfeld. The American denazification records for the district are fully intact and accessible at the US National Archives.

---

[132] IA&CD Intelligence Summary No. 51, January 10, 1947, TNA, FO 1050/431
[133] "Bevölkerungsstand am 31.12.2018," *Hessisches Statistisches Landesamt* (July 2019).
[134] Hans-Otto Kurz, "Leben an und mit der Grenze im Kreis Hersfeld-Rotenburg," *Hersfelder Geschichtsblätter* 4 (2010): 2.

Corresponding records in Germany are also available, housed mostly at the *Interkommunales Kreisarchiv Nordhessen* and *Louis-Demme-Stadtarchiv* in Bad Hersfeld and the *Hessisches Hauptstaatsarchiv* in Wiesbaden.[135]

Under review are 118 denazification case files compiled by OMGUS between June 1945 and March 1946, with some appended documents extending to as late as August 1948.[136] Subsequent investigations, originating under the Liberation Law and coordinated entirely by the Minister for Political Liberation of Greater Hessen, are incomplete and therefore not included in this study. Also unavailable are records related to improvised screening during the initial weeks of the occupation. Within each case folder there exists an average of eighteen pages of documents, which collectively chart, often in incredible detail, the lifespan of denazification proceedings for each individual who came under review. In addition to Fragebögen and Meldebögen, these folders include arrest reports, work- and action sheets, tribunal decisions, Lebensläufe, sworn statements, character reference letters (*Leumundszeugnisse*), Persilscheine, and denunciations. Most documents were generated by the Hersfeld Military Government and Spruchkammer-Hersfeld, but much of their recorded content comes from the specific individual under investigation. These are biased sources, often sanitized and written with intention, but their historical value should not be overlooked. The records compose a rich collection of quantitative and qualitative data for the interpretation of everyday denazification activities and their consequences. They help to answer the questions already asked in this chapter, namely, how was denazification experienced by regular Germans and how did it impact their lives?

Prior to the Nazi ascendency, residents of Kreis Hersfeld, much like the rest of Hesse, voted overwhelmingly for the SPD. However, in the early 1930s, the upstart NSDAP gained much political ground. In the July 1932 federal election, it won 37 percent of the national vote, becoming the largest party in the Reichstag. In Hersfeld, the party did even better, with more than half of the *Landrat* seats going to Nazi candidates. After Hitler was appointed Chancellor, the NSDAP moved quickly to consolidate its control of the Kreis. KPD and SPD supporters were dismissed from their jobs, some were arrested, non-Nazi newspapers were banned, Jewish shops closed, and a special Hersfeld *Kreispolizei*

---

[135] I am deeply indebted to several archivists and historians in Hesse who assisted with my research, especially Sebastian Hild, Treasurer of the Hersfeld Historical Association. Furthermore, two former students of mine, Declan Gallagher and Matthew Headley, were instrumental in processing the denazification data analyzed in this section.

[136] All OMGUS denazification files for Hersfeld are found here: NARA, RG 260, OMGUS, CAD, PSB, Fragebogen, Boxes 317–19.

was created as an auxiliary organ of the *Staatspolizeistelle* (later Gestapo) in Kassel.[137] On March 5th, the NSDAP established a regional headquarters in the town of Hersfeld. That very night, the *Hersfelder Zeitung* reported on a large torchlit procession in town "... led by a SA band, the powerful train of individual formations of the NSDAP, SA, SS, and other party comrades, filled the streets ... police officers, who wore swastika armbands and carried the SA flag, were particularly noticeable."[138]

By the end of May 1933, forty-eight democratically elected mayors had been removed and replaced by Nazi commissioners.[139] The *Kreisleiter*, Richard Bienert, was appointed district administrator, beating out future president of the notorious *Volksgerichtshof* (People's Court), Roland Freisler.[140] Moderate economic revival in the region followed, spurred by the construction of the Autobahn and the national remilitarization program, which resulted in the building of a large army barracks, all of which increased local support for the regime.[141] On the eve of war, the Kreis could boast a population of nearly 50,000.[142]

Many young men from Hersfeld were killed in combat during the war, but the physical damage to the district itself was relatively minor. The town of Hersfeld was completely spared, supposedly because a single Wehrmacht officer, having been taken prisoner by the Americans, had brokered its peaceful handover.[143] On April 6, 1945, the entire region was occupied by the US Third Army and placed under martial law.[144] The Americans enforced a strict curfew, collected weapons, and threatened to destroy entire towns if their soldiers were attacked by snipers; some rapes were reported.[145] Pockets of violent resistance continued over the following weeks, carried out mainly by members of the *Volkssturm*, until the final capitulation, on May 8th.[146]

In June 1945, the Hersfeld Military Government was officially formed, its headquarters set up in the district court building in downtown

---

[137] Ursula Braasch-Schwersmann et al., *Hessischer Städteatlas* (Dieburg: Philipp Schmidt, 2016), 45–46; Hans-Otto Kurz, "Hersfeld unter dem Hakenkreuz," *Hersfelder Zeitung*, January 29, 2013.
[138] Hans-Otto Kurz, "Hersfeld unter dem Hakenkreuz," *Hersfelder Zeitung*, January 29, 2013.
[139] Ibid.   [140] Ibid.   [141] Braasch-Schwersmann, *Hessischer Städteatlas*, 30.
[142] Kurz, "Leben an und mit der Grenze im Kreis Hersfeld-Rotenburg," 2.
[143] The incredible story of the surrender of Hersfeld is documented by the same officer in his denazification case file. Denazification file for K.G., NARA, RG 260, OMGUS, CAD, PSB, Fragebogen, Box 317. Braasch-Schwersmann, *Hessischer Städteatlas*, 30.
[144] Hans-Otto Kurz, "Der Kreis Hersfeld 1945/1946," *Hersfelder Geschichtsblätter* 7 (2015): 9–11.
[145] Ibid., 12.   [146] Ibid., 10.

Hersfeld, across the street from the former NSDAP office.[147] The commander for the district was Captain George S. Iredell, of the 67th Calvary Division.[148] The estimated 6,000–8,000 American soldiers who remained in the region were housed in confiscated hotels, restaurants, and private apartments, before being demobilized or moved into the former Wehrmacht barracks.[149] During the first six months, the relatively small Military Government office, which governed some 68,319 people, had its hands full.[150] In addition to rebuilding bridges and railroads, reviving the local economy, which included a decimated textile industry, and maintaining soldier discipline, Hersfeld was flooded with refugees from the east, many of whom required housing and medical care.[151] Hospitals and DP camps operated beyond capacity.[152] On September 19, 1945, the newly amalgamated state of Groß-Hessen was created; Hersfeld constituted one of its forty-eight districts.[153] Captain Iredell appointed August Martin Euler, a well-known anti-Nazi but also former legal advisor to the I.G. Farben Chemical Cartel, as the district administrator (*Landrat*).[154]

Denazification activities in Hersfeld began immediately but were not carried out with consistency. Many of the regional government records had been destroyed prior to the arrival of soldiers and therefore early civil affairs agents relied on interrogation and voluntary denunciation to identity active Nazis.[155] First, the district's administrator, Dr. Wilhelm Gerhard, was removed from office, followed by dozens of other leading officials. Within a few days, fifty of the district's eighty-two mayors had been removed and replaced by "untainted" people.[156] Exemptions were made, however, and when a qualified replacement could not be found, Nazi sympathizers retained their position.[157] During these early weeks, the SHAEF Fragebogen was distributed on occasion, but most

---

[147] "Verwaltung des Kreises Hersfeld under Aufsicht der Milit.-Reg., Hess.," StAMRm Best. 180/LA Hersfeld, A 3824, as referenced in, Kurz, "Der Kreis Hersfeld 1945/1946," 10.
[148] Ibid., 30.
[149] Kurz, "Leben an und mit der Grenze im Kreis Hersfeld-Rotenburg," 18; Braasch-Schwersmann, *Hessischer Städteatlas*, 30.
[150] Kurz, "Der Kreis Hersfeld 1945/1946," 81.
[151] Braasch-Schwersmann, *Hessischer Städteatlas*, 30.
[152] Kurz, "Der Kreis Hersfeld 1945/1946," 21, 31–32.
[153] The new district contained 39 Landkreisen and 9 Kreisfreien (independent towns).
[154] Kurz, "Der Kreis Hersfeld 1945/1946," 34. OMGUS, CAD, "Political Parties in Western Germany" (August 1949), 29–30.
[155] Kurz, "Der Kreis Hersfeld 1945/1946," 15.
[156] Hans-Otto Kurz, "1945: Chaos, Not und Neubeginn," *Mein Heimatland* 8, no. 54 (August 2015): 30.
[157] Kurz, "Der Kreis Hersfeld 1945/1946," 16.

employment screening was carried out informally. Municipal offices and large businesses were simply ordered to report all employees who had been a party functionary or member of the SS, SA, or Gestapo.[158] Meanwhile, the NSDAP and sixty auxiliary organizations were banned, Nazi laws abolished, and street names changed. In the town of Hersfeld, Adolf-Hitler-Allee was changed to Am Kurpark and Hermann-Göring-Straße to Stresemannallee.[159]

In August 1945, one week after the Potsdam Conference, the Fragebogen program was inaugurated in Hersfeld. By order of USFET, all civil servants, as well as bank staff, were required to fill out the questionnaire. The written order was circulated to public offices and published in the district's weekly periodical, the *Hersfelder Bekanntmachungen*.[160] Captain Iredell confirmed the *Fragebogenaktion* at a November conference, attended by *Landrat* Euler and all Kreis mayors.[161] On November 9, Euler formally endorsed the screening program, writing to his constituents in the US Military Government Gazette: "Denazification should not be a means of punishing Nazis; its only purpose is to prevent the active Nazis from continuing to exert influence anywhere in the new community ... it was their party that ruined Germany.[162]

In March 1946, the Liberation Law was enacted, and denazification administration transferred to the Minister for Political Liberation of Greater Hessen. The Land set up more than a hundred *Spruchkammern* across its territory, but there existed only one for Kreis Hersfeld's 68,319 residents.[163] Located two doors down from the Military Government office, the tribunal began reviewing cases on July 5, 1946. Thereafter, denazification proceedings were carried out with little disruption and in accordance with various laws enacted at the Land and zone levels. Meldebögen were processed by the tens of thousands and hundreds of citizens were forced to face the tribunal.

Our sample study consists of 118 Hersfelders who went through denazification proceedings between 1945 and 1948. The first formal investigation was opened on June 5, 1945 and was of Christian Gesing, director of the regional Reichsbank.[164] Nearly every person under review (86 percent) lived in the district's largest namesake town of Hersfeld.[165] The remainder, including Hersfeld's own mayor, resided in neighboring

---

[158] Ibid., 25.   [159] Ibid., 23.   [160] Ibid., 13.   [161] Ibid., 39–40.
[162] Kurz, "1945: Chaos, Not und Neubeginn," 32.
[163] Braasch-Schwersmann, *Hessischer Städteatlas*, 36.
[164] Denazification file for O.G., NARA, RG 260, OMGUS, CAD, PSB, Fragebogen, Box 318.
[165] Unless indicated, all percentages have been rounded to the nearest full decimal point.

communities, such as Heringen and Philippsthal. This is unsurprising considering most of the civil servant jobs that required screening, as well as all major businesses, were in Hersfeld. Also anticipated is that most people screened by Military Government were applying to retain employment in an existing position. Only 13 percent of applicants were seeking a new job, most of them with the Military Government, as a secretary or translator, or with the Hersfeld Spruchkammer.

The employment category that endured the most scrutiny was civil administration, which included many different positions in the *Landrat* and *Bürgermeister* offices, such as town councilor and director of a public works. Fritz Imhoff, for example, was a district official who applied to keep his job as a bylaw inspector.[166] Owners and managers of private businesses were also targeted, but not until September 1945, when Law No. 8 was enacted. In Kreis Hersfeld, this meant mostly owners and managers of textile factories and potash mines, as well as merchants in associated businesses. Many of these local businesspeople were wealthy and exerted influence in the community. Carl Ronge, for example, owned and operated a large clothing factory and Hans Randel was chief engineer of a competing company.[167]

Denazification in Hersfeld overwhelmingly targeted men. In fact, of the 118 people screened for employment, only three were women. They were Magdalena Bourdin, a high school history teacher, Elisabeth Bräuer, a war widow and landowner, and Maria Dierksen, who was head of the Hersfeld Red Cross.[168] The average age of the 115 men was forty-two. The youngest applicant was Ulrich Henne, a twenty-four-year-old clerk in the *Landrat* office, and the oldest Dr. Friedrich Böttner, a seventy-two-year-old physician who specialized in internal medicine.[169] Questionnaire respondents were required to disclose their earned annual income between 1931 and 1945. Although this data is incomplete, the members of our sample group did extremely well financially. The average annual income was close to 4,800 RM – much higher than the estimated prewar national average of 1,800 RM.[170] Only thirteen people earned

---

[166] Denazification file for J.H.B., NARA, RG 260, OMGUS, CAD, PSB, Fragebogen, Box 317.
[167] Denazification files for B.R. and O.K., NARA, RG 260, OMGUS, CAD, PSB, Fragebogen, Box 317.
[168] Denazification files for K.S., H.F., and E.C., NARA, RG 260, OMGUS, CAD, PSB, Fragebogen, Boxes 317, 318, 319.
[169] Denazification files for H.H. and H.R., NARA, RG 260, OMGUS, CAD, PSB, Fragebogen, Boxes 317, 319.
[170] This general estimate is for 1937 real wages. Stephen Broadberry and Carsten Burhop, "Real Wages and Labor Productivity in Britain and Germany, 1871–1938: A Unified Approach to the International Comparison of Living Standards," *The Journal of*

less than 1,850 RM, while fifteen made more than 10,000 RM. Heinrich Kirschbaum, coowner of a large lumber company and undoubtedly Hersfeld's wealthiest resident, claimed to have earned 1.47 million RM in 1937 alone.[171] Approximately 77 percent of Fragebogen respondents received an education beyond *Volksschule* (primary school), while 40 percent attended university or other postsecondary institution. The highlevel of education is reflected in the fact that more than a third of those screened spoke a foreign language, usually French or English, or read Latin or Ancient Greek.

Some of the men and women investigated were born in faraway towns, but most lived their whole lives in Hesse; all were German nationals. Among those who recorded a religious affiliation, 78 percent claimed membership in Protestant churches (Lutheran, Reformed, or United) and 17 percent in the Catholic Church. The remaining few identified as atheist or agnostic. The much-liked Lutheran priest in Hersfeld, Johannes Langen, was among the first to be screened for employment.[172]

About 13 percent of applicants had rendered some sort of military service, fighting on the western and eastern fronts. Karl Bohnacker, for example, participated in the spring 1940 invasion of France, while Georg Hermann, later appointed second Chairman of the Hersfeld Spruchkammer, had been a military driver in Poland.[173] Likely believing that denazification officers could not access voting records from a secret ballot election, only half of the applicants responded to the question: "For what political party did you vote in the election of November 1932?" For those who did, not one confessed to voting for the NSDAP, despite the Nazis winning most of the seats in the district that year. Instead, they claimed political allegiance mainly to the SPD and *Deutsche Volkspartei* (DVP). Wilhelm Müller, a small business owner, simply wrote: "Nicht NSDAP."[174]

Economic History 70, no. 2 (June 2010): 408; Walther G. Hoffmann, *Das Wachstum der deutschen Wirtschaft seit der Mitte des 19. Jahrhunderts* (Berlin: Springer, 1965).

[171] For reasons unknown, 1937 was a particularly profitable year for Kirschbaum, perhaps due to the procurement of a large government contract or the sale of assets. His recorded annual income dropped considerably the following year to 397,195 RM. Kirschbaum income is not included in the calculated average for the sample group. Denazification file for L.B., NARA, RG 260, OMGUS, CAD, PSB, Fragebogen, Box 317.

[172] Denazification file for L.H., NARA, RG 260, OMGUS, CAD, PSB, Fragebogen, Box 319.

[173] Denazification files for K.G. and W.B., NARA, RG 260, OMGUS, CAD, PSB, Fragebogen, Box 317.

[174] Denazification file for H.R., NARA, RG 260, OMGUS, CAD, PSB, Fragebogen, Box 318.

But Hersfeld was full of Nazis. Some had fled the region prior to the arrival of the Americans, and many had already been identified and arrested, long before formal screening proceedings began. Still, 37 of the 118 applicants (31 percent) admitted to being members of the NSDAP. Most had joined the party in 1933, shortly after the March election, or in 1937, when the membership rolls were reopened, after a four-year hiatus. This number is higher than the estimated 10–12 percent national rate, but we must consider who populates our sample group.[175] Denazification targeted mostly working professionals, civil administrators, and business leaders, careers with higher membership rates. In Hersfeld, there were undoubtedly some committed Nazis, such as Hans Fastabend, who joined the party in February 1931 and the SA in 1933, but more common were people like city inspector, Otto Köth, who signed up in early 1942, supposedly under duress by the former Nazi mayor of Hersfeld.[176] Dr. Franz Braun joined in 1937, with hopes that his medical practice would be viewed more favorably by the accreditation-granting health ministry.[177]

Thirteen (11 percent) people in our sample group had been members of the SA and three (2.5 percent) of the SS, both higher than the national percentage.[178] All of the SA members joined in 1933 and 1934, after Hitler's appointment as Chancellor, but before the Röhm Purge. The three SS were local businessmen. Factory owner Carl Ronge had been a low-ranking officer in the *Allgemeine* (General) SS, while bank manager Christian Gesing and company director Oskar Staab were "financial patrons" (*Förderndes Mitglied*).[179] Interestingly, Staab was discharged in 1938, when it was discovered he had "non-Aryan" ancestry.

More in accordance with national trends was membership in professional, economic, and social groups. Unsurprising of the mostly middle-aged applicants, only four (3 percent) had been members of the *Hitlerjugend* or *Bund Deutscher Mädel* and three (2.5 percent) of the *NS-Studentenbund*. Better represented were the *Reichskolonialbund*

---

[175] William Brustein, *The Logic of Evil: The Social Origins of the Nazi Party, 1925–1933* (New Haven, CT: Yale University Press, 1998), 13–17.

[176] Denazification files for G.E. and E.K., NARA, RG 260, OMGUS, CAD, PSB, Fragebogen, Box 317.

[177] Denazification file for W.S.H., NARA, RG 260, OMGUS, CAD, PSB, Fragebogen, Box 319.

[178] One study estimates that 2 percent of Germans were in the SS (mostly Waffen-SS) and 6.5 percent in the SA. Matthias Blum and Alan de Bromhead, "Rise and Fall in the Third Reich Social Advancement and Nazi Membership," *European Economic Review* 120 (November 2019): 5.

[179] Denazification files for B.R. and O.G., NARA, RG 260, OMGUS, CAD, PSB, Fragebogen, Box 318.

(10 percent), *NS-Reichskriegerbund* (7 percent), and *NS-Altherrenbund* (7 percent). Reflecting the high number of home front civil administrators, seventeen (14 percent) individuals belonged to the *Reichsbund der deutschen Beamten* and fourteen (12 percent) to the *Reichsluftschutzbund*. All three women who underwent screening had been members of the *NS-Frauenschaft*. Five of the ten teachers, two of the five doctors, and all three lawyers had been members of their respective profession's Nazi group. Still, most applicants did not have any ties to a major Nazi organization. While 80 percent belonged to some auxiliary group – a rate consistent with the rest of the country – most were merely members of the *Nationalsozialistische Volkswohlfahrt* (NSV), the regime's social welfare service, and the *Deutsche Arbeitsfront* (DAF), the national labor organization. A typical membership record was that of Heinrich Burk, manager of a brickyard, who had belonged to the NSV, DAF, and the Reich Labor Service.[180]

The Hersfeld case files not only provide us with a clearer picture of who went through denazification, but how political screening was experienced. Again, not all activities are captured within our sample group – hundreds of Hersfelders were arrested prior to formal vetting procedures and thousands more completed political Meldebögen after March 1946. Still, these 118 cases – which include Nazis, non-Nazis, and anti-Nazis – document many facets of the denazification process and illustrate much of what has already been argued in this chapter.

Only a handful of those screened for employment were arrested. While many Hersfelders, mainly Nazi functionaries, were interned in the early months of the occupation, only two from our group were among them. Several others were held in POW camps and released shortly after the surrender. In fact, OMGUS records indicate that after November 1945, no more than fifty people were arrested in the entire Kreis, all of whom had either fallen into an automatic arrest category or been caught falsifying their Fragebogen.[181] Such was the case for two of our subjects, Hans Fastabend, a woodworker, and Karl Bohnacker, a youth leader, both of whom lied about their membership in the NSDAP. Fastabend claimed to have joined the party in 1933, not February 1931, and Bohnacker denied being a member at all.[182] They were both detained at the

---

[180] Denazification file for K.R., NARA, RG 260, OMGUS, CAD, PSB, Fragebogen, Box 317.
[181] Kurz, "Der Kreis Hersfeld 1945/1946," 52.
[182] Denazification files for G.E. and K.G, NARA, RG 260, OMGUS, CAD, PSB, Fragebogen, Box 317. By the end of 1946, seven mayors had been charged with Fragebogenfälschung. Kurz, "Der Kreis Hersfeld 1945/1946," 58.

Internierungslager Darmstadt, the largest camp of its kind in the American zone, before facing a military court.

However, for the overwhelming majority of Hersfelders, denazification was defined in its entirety by filling out questionnaires. Facing the civilian staffed Spruchkammer was required only if prior screening demanded it. All 118 applicants filled in at least one Fragebogen, as well as a Meldebogen, while only forty-two were found "chargeable" and made to face the commission. Our group filled out at least 340 questionnaires, an average of 2.8 for each individual.

The Fragebogen program officially began in August 1945, when, by order of Captain Iredell, soldiers distributed the SHAEF form to the Landrat and municipal offices.[183] It was the responsibility of local administrators to ensure that all civil servants completed it. Respondents were allowed ten days to return the completed questionnaires, in duplicate, either to their immediate supervisor or directly to the Military Government office in Hersfeld. Most citizens chose to fill out the form by typewriter, which suggests applicants completed them at home or perhaps at work, on their own time. Hersfelders were well informed of the required procedures, as they were printed in the district newsletter and posted outside public buildings. In June 1945, Hersfeld's eighty-two mayors received additional instructions about the screening process, which they, in turn, disseminated to their respective residents.[184] Landrat August Euler went further, announcing in the Military Government newsletter:

On order of the Hersfeld Military Government, all men and women in the city and district of Hersfeld, who at any time held an office in the NSDAP or in one of its affiliated organizations, have 10 days after the publication of this Military Government Gazette to submit the questionnaire. Failure to follow this command will lead to punishment.[185]

In our sample group, 74 of the 118 respondents appended documents to the standardized form. Most common was a one- or two-page *Lebenslauf*, in which the individual reflected on their professional and political life. Many included an emotional recounting of how they had been deceived or coerced to join a specific Nazi organization. Some respondents chose to record their cries of political and moral innocence at the end of their Fragebogen, under the section title "Remarks." For example, Fritz Fettel, a lawyer and member of the *NS-Rechtswahrerbund* (NS-Association of Legal Professionals) wrote: "I have always expressed my opinion regardless of the government or party in power in Germany.

---

[183] Kurz, "Der Kreis Hersfeld 1945/1946," 51.   [184] Ibid., 25.   [185] Ibid., 58.

The politics of the last decades are incomprehensible to me ..."[186] Other supplementary documents included sworn personal statements and letters written by neighbors and coworkers, which again, usually professed to the ideological innocence of the applicant. Several respondents voluntarily added a denunciation statement to their Fragebogen. One was from city inspector, Emil Heinz, who accused the local KPD leader of speaking ill of the American occupiers. Perhaps unsurprisingly, Heinz himself had been denounced at an earlier date by the same person, who claimed that his home was "always decorated with the Nazi flag."[187]

On June 1, 1946, all previously granted employment permits in Kreis Hersfeld were revoked. The Liberation Law required every citizen over the age of eighteen to fill out a Meldebogen, even if they had already delivered a Fragebogen. Thereafter, while denazification agents continued to process the original form, the Hersfeld Public Prosecutor's office received new questionnaires. An estimated 55,000 were submitted in just six weeks; 3.1 million forms were received by offices throughout Hesse.[188]

The district's lone Spruchkammer was located in the town of Hersfeld and chaired by Dr. Eberhard Fahrenhorst, a proven anti-Nazi of "Jewish descent" and member of the LDP. Representatives from each of the other three major political parties – SPD, CDU, and KPD – rounded out the committee.[189] It reviewed its first case on July 5, 1946, which was presented by Public Prosecutor Johannes Salm, head of the Hersfeld SPD.[190] The names of those found chargeable under the Liberation Law were published in the Military Government Gazette and posted outside Hersfeld's townhall.[191]

About a third of our sample group faced the Spruchkammer. This is a relatively high number, but again, not a surprising one, considering the cast of influential civil administrators and professionals who were screened, many of them former party members. Still, most Hersfelders never stepped foot in the courthouse. Every adult resident of the district was required to fill out a Meldebogen, but only 3,500 faced a commission.[192] For those who did, the experience was undoubtedly

---

[186] Denazification file for W.T., NARA, RG 260, OMGUS, CAD, PSB, Fragebogen, Box 317.
[187] Denazification file for H.S., NARA, RG 260, OMGUS, CAD, PSB, Fragebogen, Box 317.
[188] Kurz, "Der Kreis Hersfeld 1945/1946," 81; Dolan, "Isolating Nazism," 281–82.
[189] Denazification file for E.F., NARA, RG 260, OMGUS, CAD, PSB, Fragebogen, Box 318; Kurz, "Der Kreis Hersfeld 1945/1946," 58.
[190] Denazification file for J.S., NARA, RG 260, OMGUS, CAD, PSB, Fragebogen, Box 319. Salm was later replaced by fellow SPD member, Erwin Schellner.
[191] Kurz, "Der Kreis Hersfeld 1945/1946," 60.   [192] Ibid., 63.

stressful, but it usually ended with a positive result. It was well known that Dr. Fahrenhort rarely handed out harsh penalties and that most defendants left their hearing with a mere slap on the wrist and a downgraded category of incrimination. Nearly every individual in our sample group had their Persilscheine accepted by the panel.[193] In this sense, the Hersfeld tribunal was not so much a civilian court to be feared, but an opportunity for defendants to reverse or downgrade a previous penalty suffered under the Fragebogen system. Such a tone was set early on, in July 1946, when Dr. Fahrenhorst declared: "The procedures serve to establish the guilty as well as exonerate the innocent."[194] Examining the personal stories of Hersfelders who went through denazification, it is clear that while the Fragebogen program was punitive and detrimental, the tribunals were not.

Maria Dierksen was head of the district branch of the *Deutsches Rotes Kreuz* (German Red Cross).[195] The fifty-seven-year-old lost her husband in the war and since the surrender had become active in local politics, joining the newly formed LDP. In March 1946, she announced her intention to serve on the Hersfeld town council, and as such was subject to screening. Dierksen had recently completed the mandatory Meldebogen, which allotted her a rations booklet, but because of her political aspirations, also filled out a Fragebogen; she did so at her home on April 10, 1946. Dierksen worried that her membership in the *Deutsches Frauenwerk* would raise unwanted questions and therefore included a note at the end of her form that read: "As head of the Red Cross, I was forced to join the women's organization in October'42, but I refused to join the NSDAP and the NSV." She also remarked that her husband had been a Freemason, and as a result, she herself was "exposed to hostility." Dierksen was not required to face a Spruchkammer, and her denazification experience ended after her two questionnaires had been reviewed.

An NSDAP member since 1933, Ludwig Schüssler's screening lasted much longer and was more consequential.[196] Hersfeld's forestry superintendent and father of two young children filled out four questionnaires over an eight-month period. The first was in September 1945, after which he waited two months to learn he would not be reinstated in his job. He claimed to have struggled after his dismissal to provide for his

---

[193] Ibid., 59.   [194] Ibid.
[195] Denazification file for E.C., NARA, RG 260, OMGUS, CAD, PSB, Fragebogen, Box 319.
[196] Denazification file for W.S., NARA, RG 260, OMGUS, CAD, PSB, Fragebogen, Box 318.

family. The following year, Schüssler's Meldebogen was reviewed by the Public Prosecutor, who categorized him as a *Minderbelastete* (Lesser Offender), which nearly landed him in prison. However, the tribunal he faced in November 1946, was more lenient, designating Schüssler as a Mitläufer and allowing him to be reinstated in his profession after paying a 1,200 RM fine. Schüssler's neighbor and municipal chief clerk, Adam Grossmann, was not as fortunate.[197] The former NSDAP and ranking SA member filled out multiple questionnaires, before being handed a two-year probation sentence and restricted to "ordinary labor." Frustrated and exhausted, in the weeks leading up to his dismissal, Grossmann wrote to the district's commander that "this is the fourth questionnaire I have sent to the Military Government office ... I respectfully ask when will my employment be decided?"[198]

More representative was the case of Johannes Heil, who never faced a civilian court.[199] The trade union leader had only been a member of the DAF and NSV, but because of his important position in the labor market and the ever-changing denazification bureaucracy, was required to fill out five Fragebögen. The self-characterized anti-Nazi received no punishment, but nevertheless went through extensive screening. The same can be said for Alfred Herzog, an actor and artist originally from Hamburg, whose military service and membership in the *Reichstheaterkammer* did not raise any eyebrows, but still required him to complete multiple questionnaires.[200]

Most Hersfelders kept their jobs; they "passed" the Fragebogen. Of the 104 applicants from our sample group on whom we have reliable information, 68 (65 percent) were hired or retained employment. Table 4.2 shows the high approval rate by the Military Government and overwhelming leniency of the Spruchkammer. Of the thirty-six individuals who were denied employment by the Americans, twenty-two were later exonerated by the tribunal. In only one instance did the Public Prosecutor upgrade the charges, but this case was later thrown out.[201] Only three defendants filed an appeal, and the civilian court rarely challenged the authenticity of Persilscheine, designating nearly all

---

[197] Denazification file for F.T., NARA, RG 260, OMGUS, CAD, PSB, Fragebogen, Box 317.
[198] Denazification file for F.T., NARA, RG 260, OMGUS, CAD, PSB, Fragebogens, 1945–48, Box 317.
[199] Denazification file for C.I., NARA, RG 260, OMGUS, CAD, PSB, Fragebogen, Box 317.
[200] Denazification file for C.R., NARA, RG 260, OMGUS, CAD, PSB, Fragebogen, Box 318.
[201] Denazification file for H.R., NARA, RG 260, OMGUS, CAD, PSB, Fragebogen, Box 319.

Table 4.2 *Hersfeld Military Government and Spruchkammer rulings, sample group*[202]

	Military Government	Spruchkammer
	118	43
Retained/hired	68	38
Dismissed/barred	36	4
Monetary fine	–	28
Other punishment	2	2
Outcome unknown	14	1

defendants (86 percent) as Mitläufer and imposing an average fine of around 1,000 RM.

Living within these data is Franz Hinkel, who, despite membership in the SA and a handful of Nazi auxiliary groups, was allowed to continue as director of a large potash mining company.[203] The eighteen pages of supplemental sheets he appended to the Fragebogen elaborated on his political and professional history, likely helped his case. Most applicants removed from employment were again eligible for rehire after appearing before the Spruchkammer or they fell under the terms of an OMGUS amnesty. In fact, around 27 percent of Hersfelders found chargeable under the Liberation Law were pardoned.[204] Dr. Peter Kadel, for example, lost his medical license in October 1945, after a questionnaire revealed his NSDAP membership and that he had worked at a concentration camp.[205] Eight months later, the tribunal downgraded his status to Mitläufer and allowed for his reinstatement in the medical profession. In another case, twenty-six-year-old Dieter Kirschbaum, after five months without work, became employable under the August 1946 Youth Amnesty.[206]

---

[202] Punishment dispersed under the two denazification systems was remarkably different. In Table 4.2, regarding Spruchkammer cases, "retained/hired" means the defendant was permitted to pursue the employment of his or her choice, while "dismissed/barred" means the US Military Government's previous decision to restrict employment to "ordinary labor" was upheld. The Military Government did not dispense monetary fines.
[203] Denazification file for U.F., NARA, RG 260, OMGUS, CAD, PSB, Fragebogen, Box 318.
[204] Kurz, "Der Kreis Hersfeld 1945/1946," 63.
[205] Denazification file for F.C., NARA, RG 260, OMGUS, CAD, PSB, Fragebogen, Box 319.
[206] Denazification file for D.K., NARA, RG 260, OMGUS, CAD, PSB, Fragebogen, Box 317.

However, being reclassified into an incrimination category was not the same as being reemployed. This important distinction is overlooked in most studies that evaluate the effects of denazification. For example, Otto Jäger was initially dismissed as director of a chemical factory, but then, after a drawn-out appeal process and subsequent tribunal hearing, was allowed to reapply.[207] Despite glowing recommendations from several former colleagues, Jäger was not reinstated in his job; instead, he was hired to a subservient position. Similarly, Hugo Rutloh was chief of the Hersfeld finance office, but due to his NSDAP membership, was dismissed.[208] Providing proof that he had carried out anti-Nazi activities during the war, Rutloh was permitted to reapply, but by then, the position had already been filled.

Even those Hersfelders who were fortunate enough to regain their former job struggled in the interim. Any duration of unemployment could have major consequences for individuals and their families. While various welfare organizations operating in Hersfeld did much to assist the impoverished population, and the black market acted as an alternative means for subsistence, the loss of work could be catastrophic. The civil servant, Fritz Imhoff, had his 4,000 RM annual income and pension taken away suddenly in September 1945.[209] In a letter to the Hersfeld Spruchkammer, he decried his Nazi past and recounted in detail the tremendous hardship suffered by not working the previous ten months. Imhoff explained that he and his wife and teenage daughter had no savings to support themselves.

Military Government worksheets show that the ruling on employment hinged almost entirely on the content of the Fragebogen. Of the 104 cases where the verdict is known, only twelve investigations deviated from the standard evaluation procedures outlined in the SHAEF Public Safety Manual. Beyond mandatory removal, denazification agents did possess some discretionary powers, but again, the recommended punishment listed in the Manual for each particular Nazi affiliation was almost always applied.

We do not know the personal impacts that denazification had on Hersfelders who lost their jobs, but still, much can be deduced by the information that is available. Dozens of public officials, certified professionals, and self-made businesspeople had their careers abruptly ended.

---

[207] Denazification file for H.H., NARA, RG 260, OMGUS, CAD, PSB, Fragebogen, Box 317.
[208] Denazification file for F.L., NARA, RG 260, OMGUS, CAD, PSB, Fragebogen, Box 317.
[209] Denazification file for H.B., NARA, RG 260, OMGUS, CAD, PSB, Fragebogen, Box 317.

Nearly all were in leadership positions, at the very top of their professions, and with hundreds of years of collective experience. With one brief review of a screening questionnaire, they were forced out of a career that they had dedicated much of their life to. For example, Jakob Orth was Hersfeld's most successful and revered lawyer.[210] He owned the largest firm in the district and sat on several municipal and regional boards. He was also the *Gruppenführer* of the local *NS-Rechtswahrerbund* branch and an NSDAP and SA member and therefore his law license was revoked by the Americans. He appealed the decision and was denied. Similarly, Dr. Wilhelm Lood was a high school teacher with more than twenty years of experience, with a joint doctorate from the Universities of Göttingen and Berlin; he spoke five languages.[211] However, due to his Nazi affiliations and an accusation that claimed he had been a "propaganda-speaker" for fascist groups, he was fired. When he was amnestied some months later, the school refused to hire him back.

There were 118 Hersfelders who were subject to the first formal round of denazification screening. A close examination of their identity, as well as the experiences and consequences of the vetting process, has revealed much. Denazification mainly involved the screening of already employed middle-class, middle-aged men for influential positions. It was a purge of civil administrators, managers, business owners, and professionals who lived in mainly urban centers. Significant portions of the population were not targeted, namely, women, laborers, displaced peoples, and youth. Some faced a civilian tribunal, that almost always benefited their case, but most Hersfelders only filled out questionnaires and related forms. They took their screening process seriously, submitting supplementary documents and emotion-driven statements. Denazification affected both their financial and mental well-being.

Conclusion

The collective condemnation of political screening activities by German politicians, journalists, and regular citizens has done much to obscure the story of denazification. The amnesty laws of the early 1950s, enacted by the Adenauer and Ulbricht governments, abruptly ended civic discussion about the Nazi past and redirected public concern to the economic and political uncertainties of the future. Within a short generation, the

---

[210] Denazification file for F.G., NARA, RG 260, OMGUS, CAD, PSB, Fragebogens, Box 318.
[211] Denazification file for J.B., NARA, RG 260, OMGUS, CAD, PSB, Fragebogens, Box 318.

Conclusion 207

memories of mass arrests and job dismissals disappeared from public dialogue. Similarly, each occupying power's acknowledgment of its policy failures discouraged the writing of a comprehensive history of denazification. For decades, researchers carried out investigations as to why the purge failed, relying solely on Allied measurements, such as arrest, dismissal, retention, and exoneration. Crowded by statistics and silenced by a loud determination to produce a definitive verdict, the everyday and immediate experiences of denazification are seldom depicted.

This chapter has sought to humanize the political purge by shifting focus to the common German citizen, or at least the common denazified citizen. We are reminded that the ideological war was not experienced by "Germany" or by a designated category of Germans, but by individual men and women and their families.

An examination of on-the-ground activities has revealed that the eradication of Nazism was tethered to employment. The typical encounter consisted of completing questionnaires and submitting them for review in order to attain or retain a job. Despite wide scholarly interest in civilian commissions, especially the American-zone Spruchkammern, facing a review panel was not as common as one might think.[212] Hearings were mostly carried out in the public realm and therefore have always been fairly visible to researchers. The abundance of commission records, accessible in German archives for decades (and in the German language), has also contributed to high scholarly interest in the subject. However, if a shared denazification experience exists it was not the Spruchkammer, or the production of Persilscheine, or even Mitläufer designation. In the American zone, the *Fragebogenaktion* was experienced by twelve times as many Germans and was often more consequential to their lives.[213] The questionnaires were everywhere, in all zones; they simply could not be avoided. They were the symbolic document of administrative denazification and nearly synonymous with the process of political cleansing. As observed by a British officer in 1947, commissioned by the ACC to survey denazification efforts across the four zones: "Throughout Germany the 'Fragebogen' became the most important document in the life of an average German."[214]

This chapter has also shown that the consequences of the screening process were more severe than what is often suggested. Instead of a

---

[212] As has been argued by Fulbrook, *German National Identity after the Holocaust*, 51, and Gerhardt, "Ritualprozeß Entnazifizierung," 75–76.
[213] Dr. Adolf Arndt, "Die Evangelische Kirche und das Gesetz zur Befreiung von Nationalsozialismus und Militarismus," *Frankfurter Hefte*, Nr. 5, October 23, 1946, EZA 2/321; Vollnhals, *Entnazifizierung*, 262–72.
[214] Friedmann, *Allied Military Government of Germany*, 114.

bureaucratic nuisance, Germans recognized that the questionnaire wielded an immense power. Depending on how the answers in the form were evaluated, the respondent could find themself unemployed and impoverished. Completing the survey was a necessary task to achieve financial security in the devastated postwar years and therefore the stakes were high. The form had the potential of permanently altering one's material security, as well as professional and community status. Going through political screening was emotionally exhausting. There is good reason why the questionnaire lay at the center of the anti-denazification movement in the late 1940s. Politicians spoke regularly about the "tragedy of the Fragebogen," and even the KPD called for an end to the "Fragebogen War."[215] Although Ernst von Salomon claimed that the Fragebogen became "quite a joke," it took more than 800 pages for him to deliver the punchline.[216] His emotional condemnation suggests that the questionnaire was significant to him, and to the millions of Germans who read his book.

---

[215] Niethammer, *Entnazifizierung in Bayern*, 289; Willis, *The French in Germany*, 162.
[216] von Salomon, *Fragebogen*, 595.

5 Writing Away Culpability
The Unintended Outcomes of Denazification

> For professional reasons I entered the Party late in 1937 in order to avoid serious difficulties ... I never wore the Party uniform or even owned one. I never took part in the political life of the NSDAP.[1]
> —Werner Hartmann, Judicial Chief Inspector

> My medical practice was suspended in November 1945 on account of my "active membership in the NSDAP"... but I was never interested at all in politics ... in fact, in May 1940 I resigned from the Nazi Party on political and religious grounds.[2]
> —Hans Meyer, Doctor

In late April 1944, Otto Kirchheimer reviewed the most recent draft of an OSS report on the influence of Nazism on the German civil service. He aggressively crossed out several paragraphs of the document and at the bottom of the final page wrote that public officials "must participate in emancipation!"[3] The Fragebogen that the GCU wrote the following month was much to Kirchheimer's liking. The form's instructions, questions, and allowances presented political screening as a conversation, not an interrogation. Respondents were granted the space to recount, in their own words, the events of their recent past, to explain the circumstances of their political decisions, and to comment on anything else they thought relevant. The same allowances were made by denazification commissions, to whom Germans submitted sworn statements, personal notes, and letters that defended their political standing and moral character. Mandatory screening therefore had an element of democratic enrollment and it inspired introspection, giving a clear and uninterrupted voice to the questionnaire respondent.

---

[1] Letter, A.S. to USFET, June 28, 1946, NARA, RG 260, OMGUS, OMGH, CAD, DB, Box 1117, Doc. 17318.
[2] Letter, G.W. to MG Heidelberg, April 29, 1946, NARA, RG 260, OMGUS, CAD, PSB, Fragebogen, Box 350.
[3] "General Principles of Administration and Civil Service in Germany," NARA, RG 226, OSS, R&A, EAD, Container 2. It is unclear when Kirchheimer added this comment, but the draft document is dated April 17, 1944.

We have already assessed the financial, professional, and emotional consequences of the denazification experience, in so much as they relate to arrest and dismissal. What follows here, in the book's final chapter, is a more nuanced study of how political vetting engaged with and transformed German memory, identity, and community. The Fragebogen was a malleable instrument and many respondents, especially those complicit with Nazism, actively used it for their own benefit. This perspective adds to an expanding body of scholarship that recognizes that the shortcomings of denazification allowed Germans an opportunity to reinvent themselves after the war, or at least to tailor their own history, sometimes at the expense of others, in order to whitewash their past.[4]

My research challenges the traditional single-frame interpretation of the Fragebogen. It views the form not only as a screening device, but a rich and revealing record of autobiography. Respondents submitted numerous pages of written commentary, which, for many, was the first time they had seriously reflected on their relationship with the Nazi dictatorship. The millions of processed questionnaires have led to the accumulation of an enormous archival repository that is likely one of the largest collections of ego-documents related to the National Socialist period.[5] These emotional and survival-motivated annotations are a window into the mind of the common German citizen and a means to understand individual mental processing of the Nazi era. This chapter argues that men and women undergoing political investigation were not merely the passive subjects of a mandatory denazification program, but active participants who used the questionnaire, consciously and subconsciously, for their own benefit.

Under review are hundreds of personal stories written by Germans, as well as accusations made against them, across the occupied territories, but predominantly in the American zone. In the first section of this chapter, it is shown how the Fragebogen program, with its many

---

[4] Among them is Helen Roche, who concludes that denazification encouraged the formation of "evasive selective memory" among former pupils of Nazi elite schools, as well as Michael Hayse, who maintains that civil servants, doctors, and business leaders used the screening campaign to cast themselves as victims of the regime. Helen Roche, "Surviving Stunde Null: Narrating the Fate of Nazi Elite-School Pupils during the Collapse of the Third Reich," *German History* 33, no. 4 (2015): 570–87; Michael Hayse, *Recasting West German Elites: Higher Civil Servants, Business Leaders, and Physicians in Hesse between Nazism and Democracy, 1945–1955* (Oxford: Oxford University Press, 2003). See also Blessing, *The Antifascist Classroom*, 121–40 and Leßau, *Entnazifizierungsgeschichten*, 199–267.

[5] On the historical value of ego-documents, see Mary Fulbrook and Ulinka Rublack, "In Relation: The 'Social Self' and Ego-Documents," *German History* 28, no. 3 (September 2010): 263–72.

allowances, encouraged respondents to denounce their fellow citizens. Already familiar with the practice of accusation, many people embraced the opportunity, perpetuating a denunciatory culture and delaying community healing. The second and lengthier section reveals how the questionnaire allowed millions of Germans to reflect on their past and to convince the authorities, and perhaps themselves, that their actions and beliefs were politically and morally acceptable. The Fragebogen was used to build whitewashed identities with accompanying narratives. Completing the questionnaire was a unique opportunity for vulnerable people to reflect on their past with conscious intention, performance, and a deep willingness to survive the postwar years. Modern psychology has fully acknowledged the mental process by which distorted and invented stories, when documented, memorized, and defended, can acquire self-perceived truth.

Resorting to "Gestapo Methods": Denunciation and Denazification

In 1843, August Heinrich Hoffmann wrote with great distain that "the denouncer is, and remains, the biggest scoundrel in the entire country."[6] The celebrated literary figure and author of the *Deutschlandlied* had recently lost his professorship at the University of Breslau on account of an informant who exposed his writings on liberal freedoms to the Prussian authorities. Despite the resounding echo of his condemnation – it has been applauded by those on the political left and right, including Nazi officials – Germans have remained receptive to the act of accusation.[7] Whether voluntarily reporting a "racial crime" or detailing the social activities of a neighbor, denunciation features prominently in the history of the modern state. The study of denunciation is focused overwhelmingly, and understandably, on the National Socialist and East German regimes, that is to say the Gestapo (*Geheime Staatspolizei*) and Stasi (*Ministerium für Staatssicherheit*). Overlooked, however, is the period that lay between them, during the Allied military occupation, when informing was prevalent and even extended beyond Nazi practices. It was the denazification campaigns, especially the Fragebogen program,

---

[6] Original German: "Der größte Lump im ganzen Land. Das ist und bleibt der Denunziant." Horst Luther, "Denunziation als soziales und strafrechtliches Problem in Deutschland in den Jahren 1945–1990," in Günter Jerouschek, Inge Marßolek, and Hedwig Röckelein, eds., *Denunziation: Historische, juristische und psychologische Aspekte* (Tübingen: Edition Diskord, 1997), 258.

[7] Heinz Boberach et al., *Richterbriefe: Dokumente zur Beeinflussung der deutschen Rechtsprechung, 1942–1944* (Boppard am Rhein: H. Boldt, 1975), 171.

that encouraged political denunciation and allowed for a continuation of the tradition. Countless informants submitted statements in different forms and under varying degrees of complicity to American, British, French, and Soviet military government offices, as well as German-staffed commissions.

As stated previously, the massive bureaucratic undertaking of screening millions of civilians and returning soldiers was dependent on the salvaging of reliable sources of political intelligence, mainly Nazi Party and government records. The problem was that by early 1945, most of these files did not exist; they had been lost in the bombing campaigns or deliberately destroyed by party officials. The central repository of NSDAP membership files was not discovered and catalogued until January 1946.[8] Such intelligence was needed much earlier, when soldiers first occupied hundreds of villages and towns throughout the country. Due to a lack of reliable information, and under considerable pressure to quickly restore a basic level of government and economic functionality, denazification officers in all four armies increasingly came to rely on denunciations.

In weekly field reports, Public Safety units wrote cryptically about the use of informants: "Additional intelligence has been gathered ..." and "It has been revealed that ..."[9] The American detachment in Cologne was more forthright, admitting its "reliance on locals" and how their investigators followed up diligently on all received denunciations.[10] Prisoners-of-war were also interrogated, which led to drawing up lists of known party members and collaborators.[11] This early reliance on informants is captured in the official history of the US Counter Intelligence Corps:

> As the Divisions moved rapidly from one area to the next ... informants in each area were developed and leads were secured which led to the arrest of many persons of high rank and position in the Nazi regime ... it was almost impossible to ferret these people out without the aid of the native informant who worked undercover.[12]

American, British, and French denazification authorities hurriedly rewrote screening procedures to recognize the use of local informants for unofficial intelligence. Even OSS researcher Herbert Marcuse, who

---

[8] Taylor, *Exorcising Hitler*, 248–52.
[9] CA Weekly Reports (various), NARA, RG 331, SHAEF, GS, G-5, IB, HS, Box 218.
[10] "Daily MG Report, No. 32," April 9–10, 1945, NARA, RG 498, ETO/USFET, CAD, Box 2952.
[11] Counter Intelligence Corps, *Counter Intelligence Corps History and Mission in World War II*, 46.
[12] Ibid., 46–48.

worried that anonymous denunciations could be used for personal revenge, admitted that "occupation authorities can hardly avoid following them [denunciations] up ... the detection of active Nazis not identified by their official positions is difficult and can eventually be made only with the help of the local population."[13] By late April 1945, on the eve of the German military surrender, all three Western armies had created denunciation units, or "Special Investigation Sections," who were tasked with the interrogation of citizens and processing denunciation statements.[14] The British went further, setting up "advisory boards" composed of trusted Germans, who submitted lists of names of former Nazis.[15] In the eastern territories, the Red Army and SMA granted considerable authority to local communists, who incriminated neighbors and colleagues in their hometowns.[16] The Interior Minister for Brandenburg, Bernhard Bechler, declared that it was the "special task and duty" of all citizens to report information regarding "the guilty" in their communities.[17]

However, it was the Americans who relied the most on informants, mainly because their screening campaign was more ambitious and far-reaching. In a village outside of Aachen, the newly appointed mayor produced a long list of individuals who he recommended the Americans investigate.[18] In Hersfeld, the Military Government Gazette announced: "All persons and departments that are able to provide useful information about the persons concerned are requested to submit them in writing, or orally, to the Hersfeld Chamber."[19] By early 1946, denazification procedures had been redrafted to recognize informants as acceptable sources of political intelligence. Workflow instructions for Special Branch ordered all detachment offices to maintain a "denunciation file."[20] These repositories were usually catalogued under the title "Other Information" or "Rumors."[21] Investigators did not rely solely on denunciations, nor was the intelligence gathered always trusted. Reports suggest that it was extremely rare for someone to be arrested

---

[13] Neumann, *Secret Reports on Nazi Germany*, 261.
[14] "Daily Summary, Cologne," April 23–24, 1945, NARA, RG 498, ETO/USFET, CAD, Box 2952.
[15] "Instructions and Orders for Denazification in British Zone," TNA, FO 1014/397.
[16] Vogt, *Denazification in Soviet-Occupied Germany*, 29–39.   [17] Ibid., 191.
[18] Padover, *Experiment in Germany*, 79.
[19] Kurz, "Der Kreis Hersfeld 1945/1946," 60. In this section, to ensure anonymity, pseudonyms are used for both the accusers and accused.
[20] "Introduction to the New Special Branch Workflow," NARA, RG 260, OMGUS, OMGB, FOD, Box 800.
[21] See, for example, "Rumors, 1946," NARA, RG 260, OMGUS, Bremen, Denazi. Div., Box 167.

or dismissed from employment simply because an informant had identified them as a Nazi; investigators understood that many denunciations stemmed from jealousies and personal vendettas.[22] In some cases, denazification agents detained the denouncer until their investigation was over.[23] Still, official investigations into the identification of Nazis and war criminals often began with an informal accusation.

After the Potsdam Conference, denunciation continued to feature prominently in the intelligence-gathering practices of all four military governments. In fact, the Fragebogen itself institutionalized the act, as all versions demanded that the respondent inform on others. The original SHAEF questionnaire asked: "Have you any close relatives who have occupied any of the [Nazi] positions named above? If yes, give the name and address and a description of the position."[24] The revised American form extended this question to membership in all fifty-four of the listed Nazi auxiliary groups, even asking respondents how committed their children were to National Socialism. The British and French forms did the same and also asked for the title of nobility, education, income, and assets of relatives. Using different language than their Western counterparts – "fascist" instead of "Nazi" – the Soviet questionnaire demanded that respondents list the names and addresses of all relatives who were members of a "fascist party organization" and to describe their "political attitude." A special survey distributed to residents of the Soviet Sector of Berlin asked about "known acquaintances" who had carried out fascist activities or inflicted suffering on others in the name of the regime and its ideology.[25] Ironically, another version of the Russian Fragebogen asked if the applicant knew anyone who had denounced non-Nazi dissenters during the Third Reich.[26] In all cases, the questionnaires asked the respondent, under duress, to provide incriminating information about the people in their lives. Refusing to do so could result in a five-year prison sentence.[27] Such was the ruling of a woman in

---

[22] Wiecki, "Professors in Purgatory," 119, 382. Prior to the military surrender, denunciations did often possess absolute authority. See, for example, Gisela Schwarze, *Eine Region in demokratischen Aufbau. Der Regierungsbezirk Münster 1945/46* (Düsseldorf: Schwann, 1984), 199–200.
[23] Dolan, "Isolating Nazism," 101.
[24] SHAEF Fragebogen, Question 3(i), SHAEF, *Public Safety Manual of Procedures, Military Government of Germany*, Appendices V.
[25] "Personalfragebogen," LAB, C. Rep. 120, Magistrat der Stadt Berlin, Volksbildung.
[26] "Fragebogen," BAB, DM 1/11494.
[27] Letter, Robert Murphy to U.S. Secretary of State, July 7, 1945, published in U.S. Department of State, *Foreign Relations of the United States: Diplomatic Papers, 1945, European Advisory Commission, Austria, Germany*, vol. III (Washington, DC: U.S. Government Printing Office, 1945), 497.

Thuringia, who was arrested in June 1945 for not incriminating her husband in her own Fragebogen.[28]

Although they did not necessarily determine the character of a denazification investigation, denunciations acted as a starting point, and they were taken seriously by officers when deliberating the employment eligibility of applicants. For example, American agents operating in the city of Nuremberg testified that all Fragebögen were verified by "obtaining voluntary denunciations from citizens who willingly informed."[29] Reliance on denunciations was extended further because the BDC could not process all the forms they received from detachment offices.[30] When this formal channel of intelligence was unavailable, as limited as its abilities already were, local sources became ever-more important to investigations. In fact, the Fragebogen worksheet used by American, British, and French officers contained a dedicated section for the evaluation of denunciations.[31]

In all zones, civilian-staffed commissions inherited the mainstay practice of using informants from their respective occupier. Nearly 4 million Germans faced a special denazification panel between 1946 and 1948, to defend their political past in the face of accusation.[32] Public prosecutors and their army overseers encouraged citizens to come forward with information, blurring the line between judicial evidence and reward-based accusation. Throughout the US zone, notices posted on municipal buildings read: "Whoever has incriminating information will contact the Public Prosecutor."[33] The four-power Berlin Kommandatura permitted the city's prosecutor to "carry out his investigation informally or he may arrange for the interrogation of one or more witnesses ..."[34] Historians Timothy Vogt and Frank Biess have shown the unconcealed hypocrisy of the commissions in the Soviet zone. While SMA publicly condemned political denunciation and even convicted Nazi informers, it still solicited denunciations from the occupied population.[35] These witness testimonies bore much influence. In one case, a Yugoslav citizen and former

---

[28] "Arrest Report: Herr E.A.," June 26, 1945, NARA, RG 498, ETO/USFET, CAD, Box 2950.

[29] Dastrup, *Crusade in Nuremberg*, 30.   [30] BDC, *Who Was a Nazi?*, 9–12.

[31] For example, see LAB, B Rep. 031/03/02, Nr. 984. Fragebogen Worksheet, ADMAE, ZFO, BADE 1303.

[32] Remy, *The Heidelberg Myth*, 178.   [33] Gritschneder, *Dead End "Denazification"*, 40.

[34] Allied Kommandatura, "Procedures for Denazification Commissions," June 29, 1946, AM, ACC, AK 94, BK/21.003, p. 3.

[35] Vogt, *Denazification in Soviet-Occupied Germany*, 191–97; Biess, *Homecomings*, 154–67. The most famous Soviet trial of a Nazi informant was that of office worker Helene Schwärzel, who in 1947 was sentenced to six years' imprisonment for having denounced a prominent member of the Nazi resistance in 1944.

slave laborer came forward with a sworn testimony that Herr Krause, mayor of the Bavarian town of Vohenstrauß, had allowed the SS to murder two Russian workers. Based largely on this lone accusation, the commission categorized the defendant as a Major Offender and forwarded his file to the ACC's war crimes division.[36]

In some cases, the commission members themselves can be perceived as kinds of informants. Many of these hand-picked anti-Nazis lived in the towns or regions that they arbitrated over and were given the opportunity to punish the very neighbors who had driven them into exile or landed them in a concentration camp. In French-occupied Friedrichshafen, for example, the newly appointed mayor complained to the Landrat that the local denazification committee, full of Nazi-persecuted town residents, had conducted an informal purge campaign, arresting and dismissing whoever they pleased.[37] In the Soviet zone, in particular, liberated communists often acted as both judge and jury in denazification cases.[38]

Reminiscence of this style of investigation was not lost on the occupied population. In his literary critique of the Fragebogen, Ernst von Salomon casted the CIC as an "American Gestapo-type organization."[39] Similarly, the CDU politician, Dr. Paul Binder, after being dismissed from his administrative post on account of an anonymous denunciation, likened French investigators to the Gestapo.[40] In a published protest of the American Liberation Law, Munich attorney Otto Gritschneder protested, "it is grotesque that, on the one hand informing committed during the Third Reich is punished as a crime against humanity and that to-day on the other hand, informants are encouraged ..."[41] Furthermore, the CIC's official history documents instances when its offices received letters addressed to the "American Gestapo" and "American SD."[42] Some agents interpreted this, perhaps wrongly, as a "clear token of German respect for the Americans' authority."

---

[36] "Information for Spruchkammer Trial," December 4, 1947, BHStA, MSo 1947.
[37] Biddiscombe, *Denazification of Germany*, 162.
[38] Vogt, *Denazification in Soviet-Occupied Germany*, 31–39, 114–15.
[39] von Salomon, *Fragebogen (The Questionnaire)*, 423; Interrogation Rpt., Screening Center (Provisional), Civilian Internment Camp No. 5 to HQ USFET AC of G-2, "Von Salomon, Ernst, Case No. 5-2492," NARA RG 498, ETO/USFET, Box 66, F: Misc. Interrog. Rpts. 1945–46. A similar comparison was made by the children's book author Erich Kästner, who had been arrested twice by the Gestapo. See Erich Kästner, *Notabene 45: ein Tagebuch* (Berlin: Atrium, 1961).
[40] Dr. Paul Binder, "Demontage der Demokratie," Archiv für Christlich-Demokratische Politik (hereafter, ACDP), 01/105/002/001.
[41] Gritschneder, *Dead End "Denazification"*, 40.
[42] Dolan, "Isolating Nazism," 101. It is unnerving, but also not altogether surprising, that this depiction of intelligence officers immediately preceded the onset of the Red Scare and the era of McCarthyism in the United States.

As we have already learned, the Evangelical Church was particularly vocal in its condemnation of the Fragebogen program, claiming that it encouraged denunciations that tore at the social fabric of recovering communities. This outspoken criticism was in no small part a defensive maneuver inspired by the Church's own record of Nazi collaboration. An official statement published in May 1946 read: "The questions in the questionnaire, in some places, encourage seduction, lies, and denunciation. This is immoral and does not help with the rehabilitation."[43] According to the Church, denazification "encouraged a wave of denunciation followed by mutual distrust and hatred among the people" and that the purge had "deteriorated into a program of revenge."[44]

Similar criticism rang out from the occupiers themselves. For example, OSS officer John Herz, who witnessed the daily functioning of the commission panels, wrote at length about the high degree of community intimidation involved in their proceedings.[45] Similarly, a British analyst explained in a December 1946 report that, "Now that they have been handed over to German panels confusion has been worse confounded because opportunity is provided for settling old scores and political heresy-hunting."[46] In a rare case, the hypocrisy of some Fragebogen questions was realized. In a June 1947 meeting, the ACC agreed to omit Question 88 from its proposed four-zone questionnaire, which required respondents to list the names and addresses of any Nazi sympathizers in their family.[47] However, none of the criticism voiced by members of the occupying forces led to a change in policy; the intelligence provided by informants was far too valuable.

The truth is that many Germans did not need encouragement to realize the utility of denunciation. When Allied armies entered the Reich, citizens were quick to volunteer incriminating information about their neighbors and colleagues. One British intelligence officer stationed in Hamburg recalled such enthusiasm, writing that, "The process of turning in Nazis was continuing all the time. There was plenty of evidence, in fact, too much. In this situation, denunciation was rife as ever. As soon as people realized I could speak German, I was flooded with

---

[43] Report, Council of the Evangelical Church in Germany (Bielefeld), May 4, 1946, Archiv des Diakonischen Werkes, Bestand Johannes Kunze, ADW, JK 63.
[44] Wyneken, "Driving out the Demons," 229.
[45] Herz, "The Fiasco of Denazification in Germany," 572.
[46] M.Z., "The British Zone in Germany," *The World Today* 2, no. 12 (December 1946): 579.
[47] "Screening of Candidates for the Central German Administration," June 23, 1947, BAK, OMGUS 15/122-1/7.

information."[48] A similar account comes from an American soldier, who remembered that "detachment officers were deluged by Germans who denounced their compatriots, and by denouncers who denounced the denouncers."[49] Possibly inspired by the questions in the survey itself, many respondents decided on their own accord to append denunciation statements to their forms. They wrote detailed accounts in which they accused others of being "Hitler supporters" and "big time Nazis," who had somehow managed to evade screening and avoid punishment.[50] The American civil affairs unit stationed in Aachen received thirty-six voluntary denunciations on the first day of the occupation alone.[51] The records of both the American and British military governments are filled with denunciation statements, as are German commission files. For example, the *Sonderministerium* collection at the *Bayerisches Hauptstaatsarchiv* has at least 2,000 handwritten or typed letters, while the OMGUS files at the US National Archives contains, perhaps, 10,000.[52]

The immediate and widespread practice of condemning fellow citizens should not be met with surprise. By the war's end, the defeated population already had twelve years of experience with a state surveillance system based around denunciation. The Gestapo relied heavily on informants to initiate its cases and hundreds of thousands of men and women voluntarily submitted statements. They denounced neighbors for hiding Jews, coworkers for obstructing the war effort, and family members for criticizing the government. Robert Gellately estimates that at least 80 percent of Gestapo cases originated from intelligence outside the ranks of the police.[53] Citizens had come to appreciate the ideological and moral reward of supporting the regime, as well as material benefits, such as preferential treatment in the workplace and professional promotion. They had also grown accustomed to strict government censorship, mass arrests and internment, and a ubiquitous military presence.

While most denunciations were voluntary, it is possible that some citizens were motivated by the fear of punishment and looked for ways to ingratiate themselves with the power bearers. They had come to learn of the dangers associated with remaining silent about political dissent.

---

[48] Eyck, *A Historian's Pilgrimage*, 299.
[49] Gimbel, *A German Community under Occupation*, 8.
[50] Letter, M.S. to MG Zwiesel, NARA, OMGB, FOD, Box 800.
[51] "Civil Affairs Weekly Summary No. 38," February 24–March 3, 1945, NARA, RG 331, SHAEF, GS, G-5, Secretariat, Doc. 20/557, Box 29.
[52] BHStA, MSo 1946, 1947, 1949, 1951, 1956, 1957; NARA, RG 260, OMGUS, Boxes 1–1275.
[53] Robert Gellately, "Denunciations in Twentieth-Century Germany: Aspects of Self-Policing in the Third Reich and the German Democratic Republic," *The Journal of Modern History* 68, no. 4 (December 1996): 942.

Still, this does not satisfy interest in or explain fully the widespread practice of informing during the postwar years. What we do know is that, whether motivated by fear, material advantage, ideological conviction, or personal revenge, denunciation had become commonplace and socially accepted long before the denazification campaigns. Reflecting on his time as an American army correspondent, Julian Bach wondered why the Germans have a "national habit for squealing."[54]

There does not seem to be any discernible pattern to the act of denunciation. Some statements were submitted under threat of punishment, but many more were sent voluntarily to local military government offices, attached to Fragebögen, or to public prosecutors, commissions, political party headquarters, police stations, and newspapers. They also arrived in different forms – handwritten, typed, or scribbled on scraps of paper. Some were signed, others were submitted anonymously. It is likely that most statements were delivered verbally at military government offices, police stations, or POW and civilian internment camps, and are therefore undocumented.

Hundreds of thousands of *Leumundszeugnisse* (character references) were also submitted with questionnaires or to denazification commissions. These Persilschein-generating documents were written in support of the individual undergoing screening, recognizing them as a non- or anti-Nazi. In other cases, letters were written to exonerate those who had been denounced. While these affirmative statements do not constitute denunciation, they stand as voluntary acts of informing and are part of the postwar intelligence from below activities and what could be called participatory justice.

Denunciation: A Sample Study

Thousands of denunciation statements are unevenly filed in the denazification collections of archives in Germany, Great Britain, France, and the United States; I have catalogued a little over one hundred for this sample study. Most were submitted directly to the American detachment office in Landkreis Regen (Bavaria), beginning in March 1945.[55] This is but one sample group chosen at random from dozens of Kreis collections in the US National Archives, some of which contain entire folders of denunciation statements. The remaining statements were drawn from German, British, and French archives, and other American collections, having been originally submitted to military government and public

---

[54] Bach, *America's Germany*, 145–46.
[55] All the LK Regen documents can be found in, NARA, OMGB, FOD, Box 800.

prosecutor offices, commissions, and German police stations, between 1945 and 1950. Almost all statements were submitted voluntarily, with no obvious act of coercion or promise of reward by any authority and usually appended to the accuser's Fragebogen or delivered directly to a civil affairs or prosecutor's office.

Most statements include the accuser's name. Among them is a letter from a local government minister in Kirchberg im Wald, who incriminated the town's current mayor for being a "committed Nazi since early years."[56] A similar statement came from Tobias Berger in the village of Zwiesel, who accused a neighbor and his wife of denouncing community members during the war and calling the local Volkssturm soldiers "cowards" for surrendering to the Americans. Berger signed his statement, which was typed on monogrammed stationery.[57] Others provided their home address and even a list of townspeople who could corroborate their claim. For example, a group of disgruntled farmers in the Bavarian town of Schlag submitted a damning letter about a fellow, much wealthier, farmer. The accused "active Nazi" was remembered as having once said that "National Socialism means everything to my life."[58] Seven men signed the letter and listed their addresses. Other informants were not so transparent and did not wish for their accusation to be made public. For example, a woman who had recently left a DP camp appended a denunciation to her questionnaire but asked the Military Government, "please do not tell my name!"[59]

In cases where the identity of the accuser is known, two trends are noteworthy. The first is that while men constitute the largest group of accusers, a disproportional number of women submitted written denunciations, despite filling out far fewer questionnaires, which was the principal channel for informing.[60] It is estimated that less than 5 percent of denazification cases were of women, but they comprise more than a third of the informants catalogued for this study. Among them is Monika Wolff, who accused neighbors in the alpine town of Bischofsmais of various infractions, including the mayor, who she claimed had unfairly distributed firewood. She wrote that "he only gave wood to those who

---

[56] Letter, P.K. to MG Regen, n.d., NARA, OMGB, FOD, Box 800.
[57] Letter, F.K. to MG Regen, November 3, 1945, NARA, OMGB, FOD, Box 800.
[58] Letter, L.S. to MG Regen, December 20, 1945, NARA, OMGB, FOD, Box 800.
[59] Letter, H.S. to MG Regen, January 16, 1946, NARA, OMGB, FOD, Box 800.
[60] Much has been written on the role of gender in voluntary denunciations during the Nazi period. While informing is still often depicted as a "female crime," it has been estimated that only 20 percent of known denouncers in Nazi Germany were women. See Eric A. Johnson, "German Women and Nazi Justice: Their Role in the Process from Denunciation to Death," *Historical Social Research* 20, no. 1 (73) (1995): 33–69.

did not sympathize with the Americans. Besides, the former NSV nurse is a guest in his house every day."[61] Anke Decker filed a much more serious accusation against two former neighbors in Munich, who she claimed had denounced her to the Gestapo in 1940.[62] In our sample group, most men denounced coworkers, while women incriminated neighbors and family members, likely the result of fewer women being employed in offices. More interesting is that denunciations made by men were usually of a political or ideological nature, accusing others of hiding Nazi affiliations or nationalist sentiments, while those made by women were more personalized, alleging that others were exhibiting immoral behavior that, in their minds, was harmful to the community.

The second noticeable trend related to identity is that many accusers were themselves members of the NSDAP or an elite auxiliary group. For example, at least five volunteers sent letters or testified in front of the Bensheim Spruchkammer, accusing local teacher Hans Huber of being a devoted Nazi; all were party members themselves.[63] Ena Möller, a teacher from Kirchdorf im Wald, who wrote a long incriminating letter about a neighbor, was a leader in the NS-Frauenschaft.[64] Civilian courts in the Soviet zone heard from hundreds of former Nazis who now accused others of denouncing fellow citizens to the Gestapo during the war.[65] It is likely that these informants had their own political affiliations in mind. Attaching the statement to their questionnaire, they perhaps believed that by exhibiting a willingness to assist the authorities in identifying "real" Nazis, their own case would be reviewed with some leniency, despite there being little indication that respondents in fact received preferential treatment for assisting authorities. To the contrary, there are documented incidences where denazification agents expressed suspicion of those Germans who volunteered incriminating information about a neighbor.[66]

Scrutinizing the content of denunciations provides some clues as to the motivation for informing. There were many different kinds of indictment – political, ideological, professional, economic, moral, and sexual – but most informers accused others of association with the NSDAP or an

---

[61] Letter, M.S. to MG Regen, November 11, 1945, NARA, OMGB, FOD, Box 800.
[62] Letter, D.A. to MG Regen, November 3, 1945, NARA, OMGB, FOD, Box 800.
[63] Denazification file for H.K., NARA, OMGUS, Fragebogen, Box 4.
[64] Letter, K.D. to MG Regen, December 1946, NARA, OMGB, FOD, Box 800.
[65] Some of these cases are explored in Andrew Szanajda, "The Prosecution of Informers in Eastern Germany, 1945–51," *The International History Review* 34, no. 1 (March 2012): 139–60.
[66] Hugh Gordon, "Cheers and Tears: Relations between Canadian Soldiers and German Civilians" (PhD diss., University of Victoria, 2010), 124.

affiliated group, such as the SS. They claimed that the individual had successfully concealed political affiliations, either by falsifying their questionnaire or removing themselves from any profession that mandated screening. For example, Robert Thomas, a schoolteacher from Bayreuth, attached a letter to his form that read: "The town clerk, [K.S.], still has her job, though she is a Party Member and the daughter of the innkeeper [J.S.] who himself was an ardent Nazi."[67]

Popular also was accusing others of supporting the regime without having formally joined any Nazi organization. Citizens were aware that denazification screened for membership not ideology and therefore many nationalists and militarists escaped punishment. Especially popular was the denunciation of profiteers, men and women who were not necessarily Nazis, but who had collaborated with the regime and as a result, benefited in some way, usually by expanding a business or receiving luxury items. In a letter to the French governor in Baden Baden, a woman petitioned the release of her husband, a special official in the German Red Cross, who she claimed had been wrongfully denounced as a Nazi profiteer and sympathizer.[68] Such accusations were usually levied by individuals who worked in the same profession or industry as the accused, perhaps an intimation that their claims were motivated by jealousy, resentment, and material benefit. It should be noted that none of the denunciations reviewed for this study accused others of holding anti-Semitic beliefs or as having committed offenses against Jews.

While it is difficult to determine the motivation of any individual informant, it is evident that personal grievances inspired many denunciations. Sometimes, the accusation had nothing to do with the regime; instead, it simply contained a critical summary of what the informant considered inappropriate behavior. Coworkers were accused of cheating the food rationing program and neighbors identified as being a threat to the moral integrity of the community. Lawyer Otto Gritschneder, who criticized the occupiers' encouragement of denunciations on moral and ethical grounds, observed that:

Mostly it [informing] is malicious joy, hatred, greed, vindictiveness or class hatred which induce this type to bring about the fall of a commercial, professional or political opponent.[69]

---

[67] Letter, L.L. to MG Regen, August 4, 1945, NARA, RG 260, OMGUS, OMGB, FOD, Box 800.
[68] Letter, Frau P. to MG, October 10, 1945, ADMAE, ZFO, AP 72/2.
[69] Gritschneder, *Dead End "Denazification"*, 40.

Rudolf Dorner, a retired doctor whose early teenage years were spent in French occupied Riedlingen, explained that denazification, and the questionnaires specifically, led to a flourishing of voluntary denunciations and that this was how "old debts were settled."[70]

Informants expressed their distaste for a neighbor or family member by identifying a particular incident where they had been mistreated or the accused displayed behavior, they considered inappropriate. In the town of Zwiesel, for example, in November 1945, the US Special Branch office received a letter attached to the Fragebogen of a candidate for a civil service position that stated:

My son-in-law [A.G.], has treated me badly. He promised to behave decently to my wife and me. We gave him our house, arable land, and 500 Marks. No sooner was he in the house when he began to act violent against me. My son-in-law was a strong supporter of the Nazi-Party, he collected much money and had the function of a Blockleiter. ... I cannot stand these maltreatments any longer. ... I have heard that the American Court of Justice has settled several such cases.[71]

In a similar tone, a woman in a village near Dessau wrote a word of warning in her Fragebogen: "Don't let that housekeeper fool you. She has plenty of everything. This is the richest farm in the region, and it supplies the neighboring towns with most of their milk and butter. That woman is just a damn Nazi."[72]

While it is clear that unprovoked accusations were motivated by personal distress, informants made sure to include a political component to their accusation. Presumably, they knew that for the individual they denounced to be investigated by the authorities, a Nazi connection had to be formulated. For example, Anita Koch accused three women in her hometown of fornicating with American soldiers.[73] While the alleged behavior of these women was clearly the source of her grievance, she seems to scramble at the end of her letter to also include a political accusation. Written as a sort of postscript, she reported that some of the women had been "married to former SS officers."

---

[70] Herr Dr. Rudolf Dorner in discussion with the author in Hamburg, July 24, 2013.
[71] Letter exchange, J.H. and American Court of Justice, November 5, 1945, NARA, RG 260, OMGB, FOD, Box 800. A *Blockleiter* was a party member responsible for the political supervision of a neighborhood or city block.
[72] As quoted in Padover, *Experiment in Germany*, 367.
[73] Letter, M.S. to MG Regen, NARA, OMGB, FOD, Box 800. It was common for women to be denounced for fraternizing with occupation soldiers. See Andrea O'Brien, "American–German Encounters and U.S. Foreign Policy in Occupied Germany, 1945-1949" (PhD diss., University of California, Berkeley, 2012), 105.

The occupation armies were well aware of personal vendettas and many units attempted to isolate them during investigations. In a widely circulated May 1946 CCG(BE) memorandum, a request was made of the Standing Committee on Denazification to discourage political denunciations. An anxious letter from the Chief of the British Legal Division expressed his concern about the "malicious denunciations" being made within the German legal community. He explained that "civil servants appointed with the approval of the Military Government were suffering from a feeling of insecurity as a result of the fear of denunciations made against them" and that "this practice of denunciation, which now threatens under the guise of denazification, is strongly reminiscent of Nazi methods."[74] Suspecting a wide prevalence of false denunciations, the officer concluded that "there is fear that similar feelings are rife in other fields of German administrative business and industrial life." Nothing came of this complaint, however, as denazification agents knew of no better way to acquire the much-needed local intelligence for their screening campaign, for which Germans seemed so willing to volunteer.

Recognition that there existed a prosperous postwar denunciatory culture and that denazification preserved and expanded the act of informing, conjures two important conclusions. The first is that there exists a degree of continuity in the German tradition of denunciation. The popular act of informing within Germany's two dictatorships – the Gestapo and Stasi regimes – are usually studied in isolation, and rightfully so. Like other familiar features of dictatorial society, denunciation is heavily dependent on local conditions and contexts. However, such propensity to respect historical specificity distracts from the fact that voluntary denunciation was subject to continuity. Civilian denunciations did not disappear with the collapse of the Nazi dictatorship, there was no accusatory pause. In fact, with the invasion of Allied armies, acts of denunciation likely increased. During the Third Reich, denunciations flowed from below, initiated by the people, and in the GDR, they flowed from above, initiated by the government. During the interim postwar military occupation, denunciations moved in both directions. Allied authorities encouraged denunciations from the population, while at the same time, many citizens, unprovoked by any authority, submitted incriminating information. Denunciation was institutionalized and mandatory but also sporadic and voluntary. This discovery refutes Martin

---

[74] "Denunciations of Officials and other persons approved by Military Government," May 24, 1946, TNA, FO 937/134; "Denunciation of Legal Officials," April 9, 1946, TNA, FO 1005/1387.

Broszat's eminent claim that the democratic culture promoted during the Allied occupation discouraged the act of informing.[75]

The second conclusion is that the widespread practice of denunciation allowed for the cultivation of social distrust and anxiety and in the most intimate of environments – neighborhoods, workplaces, and homes. It is true that the reforging of emotional relationships, what historian Barbara Rosenwein calls "emotional communities," also occurred, mainly as a consequence of the collective experiences of violence and loss and shared feelings of humiliation and helplessness.[76] However, such mental solace was undercut by the widespread and accepted practice of denunciation. As prescribed by leading theorists of mental health, strong communal bonds and personal feelings of trust and autonomy are essential to post-conflict rehabilitation.[77] Denazification activities, especially the completion of Fragebögen, fragmented relationships within local communities and weakened bonds that were necessary for recovery from war trauma. Trapped within an environment of wholesale destruction and military occupation, financial insecurity, and emotional anxiety, there existed little social cohesion in some communities. The Evangelical Church condemned denazification for this very reason.

In spite of the likely negative consequences that sanctioned denunciation had on community healing, informing did in fact benefit the denazification campaign. Locally sourced political intelligence assisted Allied armies and German authorities in identifying and punishing former party members. It is also probable that some denunciations were honest attempts to clear the nation of known Nazis, who were blamed by many for the country's devastation. Furthermore, the well-warranted fear of being denounced by a neighbor or coworker no doubt discouraged many Germans from publicly exhibiting any latent sympathies for National Socialism. Denunciation increased the risk of Nazi incrimination, as it moved the threat of exposure beyond the parameters of formal screening activities. An individual could hide or obscure their Nazi affiliations by falsifying a Fragebogen or by simply choosing employment in a profession that did not require screening. Voluntary denunciation,

---

[75] Martin Broszat, "Politische Denunziationen in der NS-Zeit. Aus Forschungserfahrungen im Staatsarchiv München," *Archivalische Zeitschrift* 73 (1977): 221f.

[76] Barbara H. Rosenwein, *Emotional Communities in the Early Middle Ages* (Ithaca: Cornell University Press, 2006). See also Frank Biess, "Feelings in the Aftermath," in *Histories of the Aftermath: The Legacies of the Second World War*, eds. Frank Biess and Robert G. Moeller (New York: Berghahn, 2010), 41.

[77] See, for example, Steven M. Weine et al., "Guidelines for International Training in Mental Health and Psychosocial Interventions for Trauma Exposed Populations in Clinical and Community Settings," *Psychiatry* 65, no. 2 (2002): 156–64.

on the other hand, did not possess bureaucratic loopholes, nor was it confined to exposing only registered members of Nazi organizations; sympathizers and profiteers who had never joined the party were not protected. The fear of denunciation likely kept many Germans quiet about their past support for the regime and perhaps even encouraged a public presentation of non- and anti-Nazi attitudes. In an extended military occupation, even insincere ideological conversion can find some psychological permanence. If this is true, the practice of denunciation had a varied effect on the postwar German population, both fragmenting communities and discrediting the Hitler regime.

Tailoring Truth: Memory Construction and Whitewashing the Nazi Past

Wilhelm Becker rushed to join the Nazi Party. In February 1933, not three weeks after Hitler was appointed chancellor, the thirty-four-year-old schoolteacher from Mannheim, and father of four, visited the local recruitment office and completed the required paperwork. In the membership questionnaire, he wrote: "National Socialism has penetrated my flesh and blood. ... I am excited about the future of Hitler's Germany."[78] Soon after, he also joined the NS-Lehrerbund and the SA-Reserve. Thirteen years later, following the collapse of the regime, Becker filled out another questionnaire, this one for the US Military Government as part of denazification proceedings. In this form, his language and tone were much different. He disclosed no fascist sentiments and denied collaboration with the dictatorship. In fact, Becker claimed he had been "coerced" (*gezwungen*) into joining the party, and that for the entirety of the twelve-year Reich, he had acted as a "political and spiritual resister" because he continued to teach the subject of religion to his students.[79] "I lived in a constant state of fear," he wrote, "afraid the Gestapo would arrest me at any time." It seems he convinced the American officer who reviewed his application, as he was permitted to continue teaching and did so for another twenty years.

Becker's story is far from unique; there are hundreds of thousands of cases like his in the records of the Allied occupation armies. Once enthusiastic Nazis were now adamantly denouncing the failed dictatorship and

---

[78] NSDAP Questionnaire of T.S., February 24, 1933, NARA, RG 260, OMGUS, OMGWB, GAD, Box 297. A version of this section of Chapter 5 was previously published in the Spring 2021 issue of *German Politics and Society*.

[79] Fragebogen of T.S., March 12, 1946, NARA, RG 260, OMGUS, OMGWB, GAD, Box 297.

downplaying or "forgetting" memories of support and collaboration, while emphasizing, and perhaps fabricating, stories of resistance and suffering. Whether they had been a card-carrying party member, SA thug, Wehrmacht soldier, factory worker, or office secretary, Germans attempted to publicly distance themselves from the regime. This was exhibited in different ways: by assisting military government in its civil administration, joining a revived democratic political party, or publicly cursing the Nazi criminals and their destructive wars. However, such actions were usually not enough to convince the authorities that a mental reorientation had occurred. Screening proceedings required Germans to thoughtfully revisit the Nazi years and to record their personal account of living under the Third Reich.

While the act of narrative distancing needed no added incentive, it was given voice and consequence by mandatory activities of denazification. The Fragebogen, along with its appended autobiographies, sworn statements, denunciations, and letters, allowed millions of men and women to rationalize, in writing, their past Nazi affiliations and to emphasize alleged non- and anti-Nazi behavior and beliefs. Many made a similar defense of political and moral innocence when facing a denazification commission. They recounted their distressed relationship with the party and distaste for Nazi politics and social policies, and how they had suffered during the war. The influence of written narrative on individual memory is substantial and enduring, and many Germans embraced the opportunity to rewrite or recreate their own history. Such an abundance of politically charged personal commentary raises the question, how did denazification affect Germans, especially those complicit with Nazism?

In order to answer this question, the Fragebogen needs to be interpreted in a much different way than has been done in previous chapters of this book. It must be viewed not simply as an investigation tool of the occupying armies, but a self-reflective ego-document in which respondents constructed a tailored identity and performed it, on paper, and possibly in person at a commission hearing. Political screening was intimate and extremely consequential for the individual and hence, the questionnaire program contributed much to how Germans remembered National Socialism.

Denazification as a Memory Device

The act of self-reflection that denazification demanded has led to the accumulation of a massive repository of emotion-driven and survival-motivated commentaries, or *Selbstzeugnisse*, a largely overlooked collection of autobiographical writings about the Third Reich. While most other methods of repudiating Nazi ties were impersonal and voluntary, completing the Fragebogen was, for most, intimate and compulsory, as it required personal information and private stories in written form. For most respondents, this was the first and perhaps only instance when they seriously reflected on their relationship with National Socialism and recorded memories and opinions of the Hitler regime.

Many denazification activities were predicated on a system that discouraged honest recollection. Respondents recorded their histories with great concern for their readership, namely, a faceless civil affairs officer, and they considered what answers would support a ruling of retention or hire. Regardless of whether the stories they communicated had been distorted, this was the relationship with the regime that the respondents chose to "remember" (while other stories they chose to "forget") and that could be subsequently built into family histories and inherited by future generations. Therefore, despite their uncertain veracity, these sources act as a window into the mind of the common German citizen during the immediate postwar years, and as a means to understand internal interactions, whether real or imagined, between the individual and the regime. This is how I interpret these records, as written acts of forced remembrance and as ego-documents with performative features.[80]

My analysis draws largely from narrative psychology, which emphasizes the value and function of storytelling in shaping individual identity. The social psychologist Theodore R. Sarbin maintained that our beliefs, behaviors, and self-identity stem from the stories that we have about ourselves, others, and the world – that we integrate our life experiences by constructing stories.[81] Sarbin argued that humans are naturally inclined to organize their experiences into definable categories of interpretation and to create identities according to "narrative plots." Recording one's experiences in written form is an act by which meaningful identity is constructed and communicated.[82] Even if the written words are deliberately inauthentic, they can be extremely convincing to the author, so much so that they cause the narrative and the historical action itself to act as one and the same semantic structure.

---

[80] Hanne Leßau puts forward a similar interpretation but comes to a slightly different conclusion. See Leßau, *Entnazifizierungsgeschichten*, esp. 475–89.

[81] Theodore R. Sarbin, "Believed-In Imaginings: A Narrative Approach," in *Believed–In Imaginings: The Narrative Construction of Reality*, eds. Theodore Sarbin and Joseph de Rivera (Washington, DC: American Psychological Association, 1998), 15; Theodore R. Sarbin, ed., *Narrative Psychology: The Storied Nature of Human Conduct* (New York: Praeger, 1986), 7.

[82] Sarbin, *Narrative Psychology*, 15, 29.

The transformative and self-affirming nature of written language is also recognized by cognitive sociologists and psycholinguists, who argue that it establishes and reinforces individual and group identities. Sociologist Erving Goffman, for example, argued that the individual exists only within the narrative one tells oneself and the narratives one is told about oneself.[83] Language practices – be they speech, reading, or writing – shape and limit cognitive capabilities and solidify self-constructed narratives about ourselves in order to make sense of our perceived environment. A story expressed verbally or in writing, while being told, begins to "recognize itself" and to establish a purposeful context and a comprehensive, personal meaning.[84] Furthermore, when an individual omits or distorts memories, for whatever motive, a new coherent story begins to be constructed, one that can quickly acquire self-perceived truth and even replace actual events.[85]

Cognitive research supports the claim that an imagined autobiographical past can be just as memorable as a real one. In a 2016 study, neuroscientist Kentaro Oba found that when induced by the prospect of compensation, subjects were more likely to turn an artificial experience into something perceived as real.[86] If it could assure material recovery and financial security, civilians and returning soldiers in postwar Germany would have been highly motivated to mentally validate distorted memories. Even if reward-based motivation was absent, the individual surely experienced emotional discomfort about the conflicting content of "real" and "false" memories, which in turn, could lead to an unconscious alteration in their attitude in order to reduce anxiety, also known as cognitive dissonance. Written commentaries therefore played a significant role in the construction of postwar narratives. Within an

---

[83] Erving Goffman, *The Presentation of Self in Everyday Life* (New York: Doubleday, 1959), 152–62.

[84] Frederick Wyatt, "The Narrative in Psychoanalysis: Psychoanalytic Notes on Storytelling, Listening, and Interpreting," in *Narrative Psychology: The Storied Nature of Human Conduct*, ed. Theodore R. Sarbin (New York: Praeger, 1986), here 204.

[85] Robert S. Steele, "Deconstructing Histories: Toward a Systematic Criticism of Psychological Narrative," in Sarbin ed., *Narrative Psychology*, here 268–71. Similar arguments about the pervasive influences of false and manipulated memories, especially as they relate to the construction of a "narrative self," can be found in Jens Brockmeier, *Beyond the Archive: Memory, Narrative, and the Autobiographical Process* (Oxford: Oxford University Press, 2015), and Amia Lieblich, Dan P. McAdams, and Ruthellen Josselson, eds., *Identity and Story: Creating Self in Narrative* (Washington, DC: American Psychological Association Press, 2006).

[86] Kentaro Oba et al., "Memory and Reward Systems Coproduce 'Nostalgic' Experiences in the Brain," *Social Cognitive and Affective Neuroscience* 11, no. 7 (July 2016): 1069–77. See also Erica G. Hepper et al., "Pancultural Nostalgia: Prototypical Conceptions across Cultures," *Emotions* 14, no. 4 (August 2014): 733–47. These two studies are concerned specifically with the creation of false nostalgia.

environment of unprecedented destruction, many Germans were disillusioned and emotionally traumatized. They sought a meaningful representation of the past twelve years and an explanation for the political collapse, military defeat, and extensive devastation of their lives.

Meanwhile, the entire process of denazification blocked honest soul-searching and encouraged a nonlinear process of remembering. Germans were preoccupied with fulfilling their basic needs for survival and in reinventing themselves in the postwar world in order to secure employment. Instead of an ideological transformation, denazification was simply a means to an end. My analysis is mindful of both realities, recognizing them as mutually compatible. Denazification presented an opportunity for the individual to actively construct politically approved and morally acceptable narratives in order to secure employment. However, it also encouraged them to passively reconceptualize their identity according to these new narratives, replacing individual memories of support and collaboration with those of resistance and suffering. Verbal self-reflection no doubt continued after denazification ended, but it was during this initial mental interrogation that a narrative foundation was built and the line between fictional and autobiographical realms became blurred.

The subsequent sharing of transformed memories with family members, friends, and colleagues would only reinforce these whitewashed identities. Family narratives are especially prone to omissions and distortions of the past, largely because of familial loyalties, a trend that has been shown to increase with each successive generation.[87] Sociologist Harold Welzer's study of intergenerational family memory, for example, concluded that third-generation Germans (born after 1970) showed a much more pronounced dissociation between real and perceived memories than their parents.[88] More recent studies on the discrepancies between German private and public memories have made similar findings. A 2018 representative study of one thousand participants found that the two most frequent family representations were

---

[87] See Friederike Eigler, *Gedächtnis und Geschichte in Generationenromanen seit der Wende* (Berlin: Erich Schmidt, 2005), and Christian Gudehus, *Dem Gedächtnis zuhören: Erzählungen über NS-Verbrechen und ihre Repräsentation in deutschen Gedenkstätten* (Essen: Klartext, 2006).

[88] In this study, 2,000 stories told by three generations of Germans from forty different families were analyzed. Harald Welzer, Sabine Moller, and Karoline Tschuggnall, *"Opa war kein Nazi": Nationalsozialismus und Holocaust im Familienfedächtnis* (Frankfurt am Main: Fischer Taschenbuch, 2002). An associated investigation had similar findings: Olaf Jensen, *Geschichte machen: Strukturmerkmale des intergenerationellen Sprechens über die NS-Vergangenheit in deutschen Familien* (Tübingen: Edition Diskord, 2004). See also Meik Zülsdorf-Kersting, *Sechzig Jahre danach: Jugendliche und Holocaust: Eine Studie zur geschichtskulturellen Sozialisation* (Münster: Lit., 2007).

"victims" and "helpers."[89] Representations of "perpetrators" were the least frequent. Not only does this suggest that whitewashed stories are inherited by family members, but that future generations themselves participate in the mental process of narrative distancing by further distorting these stories. Anti-Nazi family stories have had, and continue to have, a defining expression on the autobiographical memories of Germans today.[90]

The common forum in which new identities were built, or at least in which they gained legitimacy, is exhibited in the recorded responses of a sample group. For this section, I have analyzed a simple random sample of 200 denazification case files, mostly comprised of handwritten and typed statements appended to Fragebögen. Partially depicted in Table 5.1, the demographic of the sample group is diverse – men, women, former Nazis, communists, concentration camp survivors, politicians, businesspersons, and laborers – living in different occupations zones between 1945 and 1948.

Table 5.1 *Denazification case files, sample group*[91]

	American zone/sector	British zone/sector	French zone/sector	Soviet zone/sector
Men	73	38	27	17
Women	25	4	4	9
Total number	98	42	31	26
NSDAP, SS, and/or SA members	33	18	16	8

---

[89] Jonas H. Rees, Michael Papendick, and Andreas Zick, "This Ain't No Place for No Hero: Prevalence and Correlates of Representations of Victims, Helpers, and Perpetrators during the Time of National Socialism in German Families," *Journal of Pacific Rim Psychology* 15 (2021): 1–12. See also Anke Fiedler, "Defying Memory? Tracing the Power of Hegemonic Memory in Everyday Discourse Using the Example of National Socialism in Germany," *International Journal of Communication* 15 (2021): 3379–96.

[90] A similar argument is made by narrative psychologist Robyn Fivush in *Family Narratives and the Development of an Autobiographical Self: Social and Cultural Perspectives on Autobiographical Memory* (New York: Routledge, 2019).

[91] These records were selected from a larger catalogue of scanned denazification files, collected at government, political party, and church archives in Germany, the United States, Great Britain, and France. Every fifth folder was chosen from a database of approximately 1,000 denazification case files, ordered alphabetically. There is a disproportionate number of Germans in the US zone because this is where denazification activities were the most extensive and American archival records are easier to access.

Within this group, there exist some clear qualitative trends in how Germans responded to their screening, despite demographic diversity and the fact that these men and women lived under four different military governments, thus suggesting a measure of representativeness. No matter what their background or who administered their screening, respondents applied similar strategies and built analogous stories to convince others, and perhaps themselves, that they existed in certain isolation from the ideology and politics of the Nazi regime.

This general proposition, that Allied army measures impacted the way in which Germans confronted their Nazi past, is not original. A growing number of scholars have made similar claims, including Hanne Leßau, who argues that the biographical storytelling of denazification processes assisted individuals in distancing themselves from National Socialism.[92] Donald Bloxham accuses Allied reeducation policies of inadvertently enabling Germans to absolve themselves of feelings of guilt and to accommodate fixation on one's own victimhood.[93] Similarly, Helen Roche maintains that former administrators of Nazi elite schools utilized denazification to reformulate unusable pasts and develop a politically acceptable collective memory about their profession.[94]

We cannot expect the questionnaires to provide an entirely honest account of the political life of citizens during the Third Reich due to the simple fact that respondents were attempting to keep their jobs or gain employment and therefore were motivated to embellish or exclude particular events and experiences. Respondents considered what answers would support a verdict of retention or hire. However, we also cannot assume that most of the written responses were fabricated or even exaggerated. Viewed in this light, the recording of past political transgressions can be interpreted as an act of confession. Ernst von Salomon wrote that, "The deeper I plunge into this Fragebogen, the more I find myself compelled, against my will, to make unpleasant

---

[92] Leßau, *Entnazifizierungsgeschichten*, 199–267.
[93] Donald Bloxham, "The Genocidal Past in Western Germany and the Experience of Occupation, 1945–6," *European History Quarterly* 34, no. 3 (2004): 306–07.
[94] Helen Roche, *The Third Reich's Elite Schools: A History of the Napolas* (Oxford: Oxford University Press, 2021), 394–410. See also Dominic Detzen and Sebastian Hoffmann, "Stigma Management and Justifications of the Self in Denazification Accounts," *Accounting, Auditing & Accountability Journal* 31, no. 1 (2018): 141–65; Stefanie Rausch, "Good Bets, Bad Bets and Dark Horses: Allied Intelligence Officers' Encounters with German Civilians, 1944–1945," *Central European History* 53 (2020): 120–45; and Jan Erik Schulte, "Wiege apologetischer Narrative. Die Organisationsverfahren gegen SS, Gestapo und SD vor dem Internationalen Militärgerichtshof in Nürnberg 1945/46," in Jan Erik Schulte and Michael Wildt, eds., *Die SS nach 1945: Entschuldungsnarrative, populäre Mythen, europäische Erinnerungsdiskurse* (Göttingen: V&R Unipress, 2018), 29–55.

confessions."[95] Furthermore, it cannot be forgotten that if individuals were worried that the information recorded in the questionnaire might lead to their arrest or other serious punishment, they could simply choose not to submit a survey at all, at least in the British, Soviet, and French zones, and instead take up low-profile employment, which required no political screening.

The questionnaire, like all autobiographical materials, is not an objective source, but the recorded narratives do represent real historical value. Not only can many truths still be gathered, although with considerable caution, regarding political, social, and cultural life during the Third Reich, but so too can insight be gained into postwar German memory and how individuals chose to remember the National Socialist years and their personal relationship with the regime.

Memories of Resistance

In the 200 denazification case files reviewed for this section, which include questionnaires, appended Lebensläufe, and other personal testimonies, it is shown that regardless of their past political affiliations and activities, Germans went to great lengths to demonstrate their nonsupport for the Nazi government. Considering the potential consequences of political screening, it is unsurprising that most applicants recorded a personal condemnation of National Socialism. However, many in the sample group – forty-eight (24 percent) – also described themselves as dedicated anti-Nazis and resisters of the regime. These individuals wrote at length about their political, ideological, and moral opposition to the Nazi Party and the ways in which they had undermined the government.

The definition of "resister" and what qualified as "resistance" varied considerably in the recorded statements. For a select few, their resister status is undeniable, as evidence of physical opposition was submitted or there is some record that the respective military government confirmed the validity of their stories. For example, future GDR politician, Greta Kuckhoff, recorded in a Soviet Fragebogen her activities in the underground antifascist group *Die Rote Kapelle*, and denazification agents found records of her 1942 internment in a labor camp.[96] Similarly, US Special Branch added documented proof to the file of a machine operator in Cologne who described his anti-Nazi political activities in his questionnaire.[97] Although not a member of our sample group, Social

---

[95] von Salomon, *Der Fragebogen*, 128.
[96] Nachlass of Greta Kuckhoff, BAB, N 2506/021 and /197.
[97] Interrogation of "Wilhelm," December 16, 1944, NARA, RG 331, SHAEF, G-5, IB, HS, Doc. 5674/55.

Democratic Party leader Kurt Schumacher appended copies of anti-Nazi writings to his British Fragebogen and listed the many concentration camps he had been interned in before and during the war.[98] These written commentaries remind us that while claiming resister status was a popular tactic to avoid punishment, some Germans had in fact risked their lives opposing the regime. Still, such acts of resistance were extremely rare. Within our sample group of 200 cases, only three people, including Kuckhoff, provided evidence of active resistance.

There were many more who made an unfounded claim of having carried out physical resistance. For example, Bremen resident Hermann Seidel recorded in his Lebenslauf that as soon as the Nazis came to power in 1933, he began writing political leaflets that opposed the new government, an act that eventually landed him in the custody of the Gestapo.[99] Seidel offered no evidence, and it was noted in an investigation sheet that he was "likely falsifying these claims." Konrad Laun of Bad Wiessee wrote in his questionnaire that he and four friends had published a series of leaflets in April 1945 that condemned the "fascist terror" and therefore had committed an act of high treason.[100] In a French Fragebogen, Emil Werner claimed to have been a member of a Nazi opposition group in France, *the Ligue des droits de l'Homme*.[101] Werner refused to list the names of his collaborators, out of supposed fear that they might be targeted by "dangerous fascists" in their hometown. In a few cases, the respondents claimed to have joined the party to carry out anti-Nazi activities. For example, one applicant attached a letter to his Fragebogen, explaining that he had joined to get away from the SA and to allow for "better opportunities for passive resistance under the cover of party membership."[102] Most of these respondents were Nazi Party members themselves, and none offered original copies of the publications they referred to or the names of others who could corroborate their stories. American intelligence officer, Saul Padover, interviewed hundreds of Germans during the early months of the occupation, nearly all of whom claimed to be anti-Nazis; only two had actually physically resisted the regime.[103]

---

[98] Fragebogen of Kurt Schumacher, TNA, FO 1050/363.
[99] Fragebogen of H.G., NARA, RG 260, OMGUS, OMGBr, Box 174.
[100] Fragebogen of G.G, IfZ, Z S/A 4, Band 4.
[101] Fragebogen of R.P., BAK, B 332/110; William D. Irvine, *Between Justice and Politics: The Ligue des droits de l'homme, 1898–1945* (Stanford: Stanford University Press, 2007), 1–4.
[102] Letter, P.S. to President of the Review Board (Biedenkopf), December 27, 1945, NARA, RG 260, OMGUS, Fragebogen, Box 11.
[103] Padover, *Experiment in Germany*, 62, 115.

However, for the majority of Germans, "resistance" came in the form of subtle acts of defiance, non-conformity, and passive anti-Nazi attitude and behavior. One example is Kurt Otto, who submitted a handwritten statement to an American detachment office in October 1945, in which he recalled an instance when he had refused to employ an SA member at the factory he managed in Heringen, despite extreme pressure from local party functionaries.[104] Otto was ultimately classified as a "nominal Nazi" by a denazification tribunal and permitted to keep his job. He expressed thanks in a subsequent letter addressed to the same office, celebrating that he could continue to provide for his children and that his family was "absolved of National Socialism."[105]

In another case, a rail worker in Wiesloch recorded in his Lebenslauf that he had resisted the regime by disrupting train schedules at the height of the war.[106] Two former Wehrmacht soldiers described themselves as resisters, writing that they had refused to obey orders from their superiors during the defense of Berlin.[107] Others maintained that the reason they had been dismissed from their civil service position was because of their "anti-Nazi attitude" or "national untrustworthiness."[108] The only SS officer in our sample group wrote: "Yes, I was a member of the SS-Sturm, but never in the service of the National Socialists. ... I was a devout Catholic and doctor of women and children who resisted the regime."[109]

Even if these self-described acts of defiance are taken at face value, one cannot help but question whether they qualify as resistance toward the regime. Such a consideration will no doubt feed into the long and somewhat contentious scholarly discussion about how to accurately define *Widerstand* during the Third Reich. If a widened definition is adopted, such as the one offered by the Institut für Zeitgeschichte, which accounts for "every form of active or passive behavior," then many questionnaire respondents had in fact resisted the regime – again, assuming that the activities they recorded were true.[110] But while most

---

[104] Fragebogen of R.B., NARA, RG 260, OMGUS, CAD, PSB, Fragebogen, Box 318.
[105] Denazification file for R.B., NARA, RG 260, OMGUS, CAD, PSB, Fragebogen, Box 318.
[106] Fragebogen of R.B., NARA, RG 260, OMGUS, CAD, PSB, Fragebogen, Box 349.
[107] For example, Fragebogen of F.B., BAF, N 323/170.
[108] Denazification file for H.S., NARA, RG 260, OMGUS, CAD, PSB, Fragebogen, Box 317.
[109] Lebenslauf of O.A., July 27, 1948, StAL EL 902/7-131.
[110] The Institut für Zeitgeschichte views resistance as "every form of active or passive behavior that allows recognition of the rejection of the National Socialist regime or a partial area of National Socialist ideology." The 1973 research project, "Persecution and Resistance in Bavaria 1933–1945," and its results are summarized in Harald Jaeger

Germans became disillusioned by the Nazis during the final months of the war, it is unlikely that they self-identified as either active or passive resisters. This distinct identity developed only after the invasion and was in large part given definition and credibility by denazification activities.

The surveys themselves muddled the definition of resistance and allowed room for creative interpretation. Specific questions in Fragebögen distributed in the American, British, and French zones asked applicants to elaborate on personal experiences from their past that could be considered acts of resistance against the regime. The questionnaire asked, "Have you ever been a member of any anti-Nazi underground party or groups since 1933?" and "Have you ever been dismissed from the civil service, the teaching profession or ecclesiastical positions or any other employment for active or passive resistance to the Nazis or their ideology?"[111] The Soviet Fragebogen contained a similar question, asking, "Did you take part in any illegal antifascist activities between 1933 and 1945?"[112] These questions are undoubtedly vague and allowed respondents to determine for themselves what was meant by "anti-fascist activities" (*antifaschistisch Aktivitäten*) and "passive resistance" (*passiver Widerstand*). What resulted were broad and flexible interpretations.

It was common for individuals to identify themselves specifically as "passive resisters," a term seemingly introduced in the questionnaire.[113] For example, a secretary at the Reichsbahn office in French-occupied Riedlingen claimed to have carried out "passive resistance" by forbidding her children from attending Hitler Youth events.[114] In a personal statement attached to his Soviet-issued questionnaire, a clerk in the Stralsund mayor's office wrote that he had continuously exercised "passive opposition" toward his SA comrades by disagreeing with them about the failings of socialism.[115] One version of the French Fragebogen asked if the applicant had carried out any acts of "spiritual resistance"; again, this language was adopted.[116] A teacher in Koblenz repudiated his Nazi ties by attesting to "spiritual resistance" as a faithful member of the local Catholic congregation.[117] Another respondent, originally from Austria,

---

and Hermann Rumschöttel, "Das Forschungsprojekt 'Widerstand und Verfolgung in Bayern 1933–1945'," *Archivalische Zeitschrift* 73, no. 1 (1977): 209–20.

[111] "Military Government of Germany Fragebogen," August 22, 1947, BAK, Z 6II/25, p. 9.
[112] See, for example, "Personalfragebogen," August 28, 1946, BAB, DO 105/19028, p. 3.
[113] See, for example, "Military Government of Germany Fragebogen – W.K.," September 19, 1945, NARA, RG 260, Box 317.
[114] Fragebogen of G.S., January 19, 1946, ADMAE, ZFO, WH 1298.
[115] Fragebogen of R.S., March 12, 1946, BAB, DO 1/25069.
[116] Fragebogen, ADMAE, ZFO, BAD 1303/494.
[117] Fragebogen of M.G., October 2, 1945, ADMAE, ZFO, BAD 1835/1050.

Tailoring Truth 237

explained how he was an antifascist and "spiritual enemy" of the state because he had been active in the Dollfuss movement in Vienna.[118] In total, twenty-two of the forty-eight questionnaire respondents who claimed resister status recited the precise language presented to them in the questionnaires.

All versions of the Fragebogen emphasized political opposition. The Soviet questionnaire, for example, asked about party membership prior to the Nazi consolidation of power, specifically the respondent's association with the KPD and SPD.[119] The American form required a list of "democratic affiliations," including the political party that the applicant had voted for in the November 1932 national election.[120] In response, Germans wrote at length about their pre-Nazi political past. Former party members claimed to have "always belonged" to the SPD or that they had been "raised with christian democratic beliefs."[121] Some also listed non-party democratic organizations that they had been affiliated with before the seizure of power.[122] Within these written dialogues, respondents rejected National Socialism, fascism, and militarism. A tax inspector and former party member in Bremen wrote that he had been a "fighter for democracy before 1933," and a banker in the British zone maintained he had always been a "staunch liberal."[123] When asked what his religious preferences had been prior to the war, Oldenburg resident Hans Ronge simply wrote, "FREETHINKER!"[124]

Of course, most claims of resistance were difficult, if not impossible, for denazification officers to verify. The records of underground anti-Nazi organizations were either nonexistent or unattainable, and while many employment records had been destroyed during the war, those that did survive gave little indication as to why the individual had been dismissed. Even if these records did contain such information, denazification agents did not have the resources to investigate all cases in such detail. Furthermore, many respondents claimed they had carried out undisclosed resistance or experienced unreported persecution, and that they had subverted political or ideological beliefs during their "inner migration"; therefore, no documentation or witnesses could provide

---

[118] Fragebogen of E.K., February 13, 1946, ADMAE, ZFO, WH 1298. See also Padover, *Experiment in Germany*, 231.
[119] "Personalfragebogen," August 28, 1946, BAB, DO 105/19028.
[120] Fitzgibbon, *Denazification*, 185–94.
[121] Letter, W.H. to Herr Dr. Schumacher, May 27, 1946, AdsD, Bestand Schumacher, Mappe 90; Fragebogen of F.E., NARA, OMGUS, CAD, PSB, Fragebogen, Box 356.
[122] Fragebogen of S.P., AdsD, Bestand Schumacher, Mappe 98.
[123] Letter, S.P. to Regierungspräsident, March 9, 1945, AdsD, Bestand Schumacher, Mappe 98; Letter, R.G.B. to Erich Welter, August 14, 1947, BAK, N 1314/78.
[124] Fragebogen of R.D., BAK, N 1748/67.

confirmation.[125] One American intelligence officer recalled that interrogations often began with an enthusiastic denunciation of Hitler, but that "it did not take us long to realize that 'anti-Nazi' was a gag ... we have asked questions of so many people, and they were all anti-Nazis!"[126] The commonality of such responses is evidenced in a 1946 US Special Branch manual on denazification law, which provided instructions for the evaluation of questionnaires: "Questions 110 to 116: These questions are intended to reveal those who remained in active or passive resistance to the Nazis. It should be borne in mind that almost everyone now claims to have been against the Nazis and to have joined the NSDAP under compulsion."[127]

By asking open-ended and ambiguous questions about individual acts of resistance, the military governments not only made political classification exceedingly difficult for their administrations, but also encouraged varying interpretations of the term "resister." Germans may not have considered themselves formal opponents of the regime prior to completing a questionnaire, but after being introduced to the concept of "passive resistance" and permitted to elaborate on any activities or beliefs that could be construed as anti-Nazi, the interpretation of their own political past could have changed. Furthermore, distorted memories were validated if the respondent was permitted to work, in a sense giving the new narrative an official stamp of approval (see Figure 5.1). Denazification either provided an opportunity for Germans who had in fact opposed the Nazis to document their activities and confirm their resister status or it allowed respondents to actively falsify or exaggerate past experiences and build a new anti-Nazi identity.

The profound influence and endurance that this identity had on both the individual and the family is demonstrated in a 1953 written statement by Detlev Glismann, a small business owner and former party member. When accused by a West German welfare office of having been a Nazi profiteer, he declared: "Myself and my family were cleared of all wrongdoing by the [British] military government and by a civilian court. I was targeted by the Hitler government and suffered tremendously."[128] It is not surprising that despite the near absence of physical resistance to the Nazis, a 2002 survey suggests that as many as half of third-generation Germans believe that their relatives had firmly disapproved of Nazism.[129]

[125] See, for example, Letter, M.M. to Denazification Committee of the Municipality of Dortmund, May 28, 1946, ACDP, CDU Parteigremien, 03/002/001/1.
[126] Padover, *Experiment in Germany*, 36, 62.
[127] OMGB-Special Branch, *German Denazification Law and Implementations with American Directives Included*, 171.
[128] Denazification file for R.S., TNA, FO 1050/363.
[129] Harald Welzer et al., *"Opa war kein Nazi."* 246.

Tailoring Truth 239

DIE BRÜCKE ZUR FREIHEIT.......

Figure 5.1 "The Bridge to Freedom," by former Nazi caricaturist Walter Hofmann ("Waldl"), 1946.
Source: Staatsarchiv Ludwigsburg

Memories of Suffering

Denazification also allowed and encouraged Germans to report stories of personal suffering endured at the hands of the Nazi dictatorship. In fact, hardship was the most popular memory recorded in, or appended to, questionnaires, appearing in eighty-two (41 percent) of the case files. Specific people were usually identified as the source of the respondent's distress – an intolerant boss, an intimidating relative, an unknown Gestapo officer, or Hitler himself. Economic and social conditions were also recognized as sources of oppression – wartime bombings or the burden of an unfed family. Common was the claim that one joined the Nazi Party, or an auxiliary group, out of fear. In all cases, respondents presented themselves as the victim of deceit, suffering, violence, or prejudice. How could one possibly support a regime that had inflicted so much pain on oneself and one's family? Regardless of their past political affiliations, respondents felt that these experiences stood as proof of their non- or anti-Nazi status, and that in turn, they deserved a clean bill of health and clearance to be employed in their chosen profession.

Post–World War II representations of German suffering have received considerable attention from researchers across disciplines and generations.[130] The subject has always been fraught with debate, in and

---

[130] It is mainly historians, psychologists, literary scholars, and novelists who occupy this field of study. Nearly all of them argue that wartime suffering was used by Germans, in various ways, to minimize, ignore, and/or deny their previous support for the Nazi

outside of Germany, and for good reason. Resilient and firm opposition is faced when discussing German victims in relation to, or in isolation from, the Holocaust, or when any attempt it made to define as victims those who may themselves have acted, in one way or another, as perpetrators, or perhaps supporters, benefactors, or complicit bystanders. At the center of this problematic victim–perpetrator dichotomy is the implicit assumption that the German people have no moral right to claim ownership of suffering; that the violence they collectively inflicted on others outweighs any possible claim to sympathy.

Nevertheless, most Germans were exposed to extreme and prolonged violence and multiple trauma-inducing experiences during and immediately after the war.[131] They were severely impacted by the unprecedented human loss and physical destruction produced by nearly six years of industrial warfare. By the time the armistice was announced, approximately 5.3 million German soldiers had been killed, another 4.4 million had incurred injuries, and more than a million had died, or soon would die, in prisoner-of-war camps.[132] During the Allied bombing campaign, an estimated 600,000 German civilians perished and 7.5 million rendered homeless.[133] As many as 1.5 million refugees and expellees died as a result of their migration from Eastern Europe and hundreds of thousands of women were the victims of rape by invasion and occupation

---

regime and as a measure for moral evasiveness. Some notable works that make this claim are Robert G. Moeller, *War Stories: The Search for a Usable Past in the Federal Republic of Germany* (Berkeley: University of California Press, 2001); W. G. Sebald, *Luftkrieg und Literatur* (Frankfurt am Main: Fischer, 2002); Lothar Kettenacker, ed., *Ein Volk von Opfern. Die neue Debatte um den Bombenkrieg 1940–1945* (Berlin: Rowohlt, 2003); Aleida Assmann, *Der lange Schatten der Vergangenheit. Erinnerungskultur und Geschichtspolitik* (Munish: Beck, 2006); Bill Niven, ed., *Germans as Victims* (Basingstoke, Hampshire: Palgrave Macmillan, 2006); Helmut Schmitz, *A Nation of Victims? Representations of German Wartime Suffering from 1945 to the Present* (Amsterdam: Rodopi, 2007). Susan Carruthers convincingly argues that many American military personnel also came to regard themselves as victims – as displaced soldiers, far from home with no war to fight in. Carruthers, *The Good Occupation*, 189–90.

[131] Discussion of German wartime suffering has remained centered on World War II and its aftermath, specifically the Allied bombing campaign, the rape of women at the hands of invasion and occupation soldiers, and the flight and expulsion of ethnic Germans from Eastern Europe.

[132] Rüdiger Overmans, *Deutsche militärische Verluste im Zeiten Weltkrieg* (Munich: R. Oldenbourg, 1999), 246, 292, 336; Percy E. Schramm, *Kriegstagebuch des Oberkommandos der Wehrmacht: 1940–1945* (Frankfurt am Main: Bernard & Graefe, 1961), 1508–11.

[133] Alice Förster and Birgit Beck, "Post-Traumatic Stress Disorder and World War II," in *Life after Death: Approaches to a Cultural and Social History of Europe during the 1940s and 1950s*, eds. Richard Bessel and Dirk Schumann (Cambridge: Cambridge University Press, 2003), 28.

soldiers.[134] Recognizing the scale of German suffering is one thing, but to contextualize these experiences and integrate them into conversation about guilt and accountability and victim hierarchy is explicably problematic.

The scope of interpretation within this large body of scholarship is diverse, but one point most scholars agree on is that the hardships of the war and the immediate postwar years allowed ordinary German citizens to view themselves as victims.[135] It is also generally acknowledged that many used their acquired victim status to create a psychological disconnect between themselves and the regime, a narrative that remembered the Nazis only as a criminal organization that had taken advantage of and manipulated the German people, dragging them into a long and destructive war. Therefore, it comes as no surprise that after the war, in the words of historian Robert Moeller, "the past about which Germans talked most was that of their own loss and suffering."[136]

Within our sample of denazification case files, the perceived definition of Nazi "victim," much like Nazi "resister," varies greatly. Some questionnaire respondents maintained, and rightfully so, that they had been victims of the regime, evidenced by time spent in a labor or concentration camp. In some cases, such claims were accompanied by a piece of irrefutable evidence or a reliable reference letter. For example, Rudolph Kress, who had survived three concentration camps since 1938, appended two letters to his Soviet Fragebogen, written by well-known local members of the KPD.[137] Thousands of survivors underwent denazification screening after the war, some in employment offices, others in displaced persons camps.[138] Few were Jewish, as less than 10,000 had survived the genocide and returned to their hometowns in

---

[134] Ray M. Douglas, *Orderly and Humane: The Expulsion of the Germans after the Second World War* (New Haven, CT: Yale University Press, 2012), 1.

[135] See, for example, Kettenacker, ed., *Ein Volk von Opfern*.

[136] Robert G. Moeller, "Winning the Peace at the Movies: Suffering, Loss, and Redemption in Postwar German Cinema," in *Histories of the Aftermath: The Legacies of the Second World War*, eds. Frank Biess and Robert G. Moeller (New York: Berghahn, 2010), here 139.

[137] Personalfragebogen of R.K., July 28, 1946, BAB, DO 1/25577.

[138] SHAEF also issued a "Concentration Camp Inmates Questionnaire," which asked survivors about the abuses they had endured while incarcerated, as well as information on political affiliations, military service, employment history, and anti-Nazi attitudes. See SHAEF, *Public Safety Manual of Procedures, Military Government of Germany*, 1st ed. (September 1944), Appendix CC. A similar form was distributed in some Soviet-occupied regions. See, for example, questionnaires for liberated prisoners at Hohenstein-Ernstthal Subcamp, BAB, DO1/32513.

Germany, about 2 percent of the pre-1933 community.[139] Instead, most unequivocal cases of physical suffering came from political victims who were reapplying to their former jobs. Among them was Wilhelm Gerhard, a union leader from Hersfeld, who appended a typewritten page to his American questionnaire.[140] After being dismissed from a labor office in March 1933 for "speeches made against the national socialists," Gerhard was continually monitored by the local police battalion before being arrested in August 1944 and sent to Sachsenhausen. His neighbor, Heinrich Fenner, wrote about losing a long-standing job with the Reichspost on account of his membership in the Freemasons.[141] The Fragebogen was the first opportunity for these persecuted people to formally document their sufferings, a fact that is sure to attract future research by scholars of Nazi violence.

However, in our sample group, of those respondents who chose to record memories of suffering, few were members of a recognized Nazi-targeted group. Instead, they were largely middle-class Germans, who self-identified as social democrats or conservatives. About half of them were Nazi Party members themselves. In their Fragebogen, these applicants usually recalled a particular incident in which they had experienced hardship at the hands of a government agent or due to the enactment of a particular Nazi law. Small business owners wrote at length on how government industry contracts had bankrupted them, civil servants lamented losing their jobs to members of the SS, and factory workers remembered how their trade unions were disbanded under the oppressive measures of the regime. A laborer in Aachen, for example, complained that the "fascists" had overtaxed him and made his family suffer, while a former journalist recalled how he was socially ostracized at his workplace because of his pro-American opinions.[142] Respondents were vague on the details, writing only a line or two about the incident, seldom providing names, dates, or references to confirm their stories. For example, a high-ranking official in the Ministry of Transportation wrote in a French questionnaire, "I was continuously monitored by the Gestapo for my political beliefs," but provided no further information.[143]

---

[139] In January 1946, there were approximately 85,000 displaced persons in the US, British, and French zones registered as "Jewish," but relatively few were originally from Germany. See The American Jewish Committee, "Statistics on Jews," *Thirty-Ninth Annual Report* (1946): 606.
[140] Fragebogen of G.G., NARA, RG 260, OMGUS, CAD, PSB, Fragebogen, Box 317.
[141] Fragebogen of W.S., NARA, RG 260, OMGUS, CAD, PSB, Fragebogen, Box 317.
[142] Fragebogen of O.R., NARA, RG 498, USFET, CAD, Box 2950; Letter, E.K.W. to ISCS (U.S. HQ Berlin), n.d., AM, AMG, HQBD, ICS.
[143] Fragebogen of E.B., EZA, 655/10.

It was common for these stories to be immediately followed by claims of political and moral innocence – that the respondents were the furthest thing from a Nazi enthusiast and the only "real" victims in their respective workplaces. An American denazification officer remembered that "nearly all those who are hostile to the Nazi regime complain of their personal sufferings. They overflow with self-pity."[144] He concluded that these expressions were "more or less conscious techniques of justifying an acceptance and toleration of Nazism."

A common story recorded in denazification documents came from former Nazis who claimed they had joined the party out of fear of the authorities and that they had been threatened with physical force. These individuals were not so much afraid of losing their jobs as they were their lives. Some argued they would have been arrested, incarcerated, and possibly murdered had they refused to join the party or attempted to leave its ranks. For example, when expanding on Question 116 of his Fragebogen, Wilhelm Hagen, a prominent doctor and social hygienist who had overseen health services in the Warsaw Ghetto, wrote that he was forced to join the NSDAP in May 1938, and that when he tried to leave the party, his life was threatened. He wrote that "a later exit was not possible, not unless I was willing to put my whole existence on the line and land in a concentration camp."[145] Despite some postwar controversy surrounding Hagen's case – Martin Broszat wrote about the doctor's "stubborn resistance" against the SS – there is no question about his commitment to the regime.[146]

Another government official admitted to joining the party in August 1937, but only after he discovered that a colleague in the same office who had publicly opposed the regime had been murdered.[147] Other respondents feared for their lives because they were members of a persecuted political or religious minority, maintaining that they joined to conceal their identity and to avoid physical violence. Writing to the Soviet

---

[144] Padover, *Experiment in Germany*, 115–16.
[145] Fragebogen of W.H., IfZ, ED 66/1/5, Band 1. In his questionnaire, Hagen claimed he had not acted as an accomplice in the extermination of Jews but had worked tirelessly to improve living conditions in the Warsaw Ghetto. It was revealed in the 1960s that Hagen, then a senior official in the West German Ministry of Health, had in fact held anti-Semitic views during the war. For more on the "Hagen-Affäre," see David Bankier and Dan Michman, eds., *Holocaust Historiography in Context: Emergence, Challenges, Polemics and Achievements* (New York: Berghahn, 2009), here 188–89.
[146] During a typhus epidemic in the Warsaw Ghetto, Hagen called for "Jews who are wandering around to be shot." See Benjamin Carter Hett, "The Story Is about Something Fundamental: Nazi Criminals, History, Memory, and the Reichstag Fire," *Central European History* 48, no. 2 (June 2015): 219.
[147] Fragebogen of E.B., EZA, 655/10.

authorities, Kurt Meier claimed he had been "denounced as a former socialist" by a coworker and that he joined the NSDAP to dispel the rumor and avoid exposure.[148] In all such cases, focus remained distinctly on the individual having been victimized by the regime and its agents. We now know that refusal to join the Nazi Party or the voluntary termination of membership rarely resulted in physical punishment. Nevertheless, the culture of fear that the regime generated could have surely impacted the decisions of those Germans reluctant to conform to party standards.[149]

An even larger number of respondents justified joining Nazi organizations by explaining the dire financial consequences that would have accompanied any other decision. The threat of being unemployed and not being able to support one's family was depicted as an overwhelming burden, one which produced mental hardship. In a British Fragebogen, Gerhard Huber explained that his decision to join the party was made after several days of "painful consideration" and that he eventually signed up only because he had six children to support.[150] Weiner Engel, an engineer from the Hessian village of Wilhelmshütte, defended his membership by writing: "[B]esides my family of 4 persons, I had to provide, as sole supporter, for the living and care of my blind, ill father and a severely ill and unmarried sister."[151] It was common for respondents to claim they joined the NSDAP for the good of others. For example, in his appended Lebenslauf, Gustav Pfeiffer, a schoolteacher from Wiesloch, stated that he joined "to avoid inconveniences for the young people" and to spare his students the Nazi teachings of his likely replacement.[152]

Some applicants went to great lengths to implicate others, usually a work manager, claiming they had been forced to become involved in politics under threat of dismissal. The headmaster of a Catholic school in Heidelberg wrote that he had joined the NSDAP upon "insistence by the local [Nazi] group leader."[153] According to a character reference letter written on behalf of Paul Sauer, a businessman from Alsfeld, the applicant had always been opposed to the Nazis and joined only "under extreme pressure" from his superiors and with the threat of losing a large government work contract.[154] Similarly emphasizing the emotional anxieties felt within the workplace, a Munich University law professor wrote in a Fragebogen supplement:

---

[148] "Protokoll" of E.G., November 18, 1946, BAB, DM 1/165.
[149] OMGUS, "Are There 'Good' Nazis?" NARA, RG 260, Box 782, p. 6.
[150] Fragebogen of E.G., EZA, 655/10.
[151] Letter, P.S. to President of the Review Board (Biedenkopf), December 27, 1945, NARA, RG 260, OMGUS, Fragebogen, Box 11.
[152] Fragebogen of R.B., NARA, RG 260, OMGUS, CAD, PSB, Fragebogen, Box 349.
[153] Ibid.   [154] Statement of W.M., NARA, RG 260, OMGUS, Fragebogen, Box 1.

I joined in 1942 only because of the threat that my refusal to become a member of the Party would be seen as open opposition and that I would have to fear for my job, if not worse. Because I have a serious nerve condition – due to which I was unable to serve in both wars – I could not bear the consequences of an open conflict with the Party.[155]

The comments written by denazification agents in Fragebogen worksheets reveal that most of these stories were interpreted as simple instances of opportunism. Still, the written narratives never focused on financial gain or professional promotion, just the threat and resounding fear of dismissal from office and the great hardship that *could* have prevailed.

The outpouring of self-pity was not necessarily initiated by the individual. Here, again, denazification instruments and procedures encouraged the respondent to build a politically approved identity. Questionnaires that were circulated in all four occupation zones asked about personal instances of Nazi persecution. The American, British, and French forms, for example, all asked, "Have you ever been a member of any trade union or professional or business organization which was dissolved or forbidden [*aufgelösten oder verboten*] since 1933?" Similarly, the Soviet Fragebogen, asked, "Have you ever been subjected to a Nazi court?" When reading these questions, respondents surely searched their memories for specific experiences that could qualify as acts of discrimination and adopted the same language that appeared on the printed form. Tobias Scholz, for example, a banker's assistant in the US zone, wrote that when he was a teenager, his Catholic youth group had been "dissolved and forbidden," an event that led him into a deep state of depression.[156] In a British form, Greta Winkler reiterated the events leading up to her forced participation in the NS-Frauenschaft, explaining that she had been "forbidden" to join any other social or political organization.[157]

The Fragebogen program itself was predicated on an uncompromising system of classification, one in which respondents, after having their questionnaires reviewed, were placed into explicit categories of Nazi affiliation. After reviewing a completed form, American and British officers, for example, placed the applicant into one of four categories,

---

[155] Fragebogen of A.H., BHStA, Spruchkammerakten K 784. The denazification of this individual is also investigated in Wiecki, "Professors in Purgatory," 261–62.
[156] Fragebogen of P.D., April 12, 1945, NARA, RG 260, OMGUS, CAD, PSB, Fragebogen, Box 582.
[157] Fragebogen of S.P., TNA, Special Branch Progress Reports, FO 1050/249.

either "active Nazi," "nominal Nazi," "non-Nazi," or "anti-Nazi."[158] When denazification administration was handed over to the Germans, respondents were classified as either *Hauptschuldige* (Major Offender), *Belastete* (Offender), *Minderbelastete* (Minor Offender), *Mitläufer* (Follower), or *Entlastete* (Exonerated).[159] The only category that did not mandate some form of punishment or sanction was *Entlastete*, which required individuals to have "not only showed a passive attitude but also actively resisted the National Socialistic tyranny to the extent of their powers and thereby suffered disadvantages."[160]

These categories of incrimination and their corresponding punishments were well known to Germans; they were printed in local newspapers and posted outside public offices. Applicants thus understood that if they wanted to retain their civil service position, or whatever job they were pursuing, either they had to fall into the category of *Entlastete*, and therefore demonstrate they had experienced personal hardship, or gamble on the next category of *Mitläufer*, which could result in some form of punishment that would likely be minimal but was still unknown to them. Within this strict systematic procedure of categorization, one that emphasized the utility of personal suffering, Fragebogen respondents were encouraged to make clear distinctions as to their identity and to define themselves as anti-Nazis.

Many took advantage of the opportunity to add a personal commentary or other written note to their form. The American questionnaire included a blank section entitled *Bemerkungen* (Remarks), where respondents could expand on any of the answers previously given and explain the professional and social contexts in which they had become affiliated with the Nazi apparatus. When applicants made use of this section, their comments evoked memories of deceit and persecution. For example, a former party member hoping to retain his job as a municipal tax inspector wrote: "In 1943, I was considered an enemy of the State, charged with disseminating information and was constantly threatened to be punished in a concentration camp."[161] The US Special Branch investigator assigned to this case could not find any evidence of such a charge. Another applicant explained that although he had been a member of the SS, he had once held "communistic views," and therefore the threat of exposure was an everyday burden he was forced to live

---

[158] OMGUS, CAD, *Denazification, Cumulative Review. Report, 1 April 1947–30 April 1948* (Adjutant General, OMGUS, 1948), p. 2. All four military governments used a similar classification system.
[159] Ibid., 54.   [160] Ibid., 59.
[161] Fragebogen of E.K., January 16, 1946, NARA, RG 260, OMGUS, CAD, PSB, Fragebogen, Box 317.

with.[162] Still another respondent thought it relevant to share a family story in the remarks section of his Fragebogen, one in which his sister had died in the Lodz Ghetto, as she had accompanied her Jewish husband there in 1941.[163]

In some districts, Soviet denazification agents used the information recorded in Fragebögen to identify Nazi victims and categorize them into what was essentially a two-tier compensation system.[164] First-class victims were labeled "Fighters Against Fascism" and deemed eligible for monetary reparation and preferential employment opportunities, followed by "Victims of Fascism," which including Jewish and Roma survivors. Here, screening questionnaires were used to build a discernable hierarchy of victimhood, one that promised the respondent a chance at material reward.

Many more Germans reserved their emotional recounting for the allowable supplementary documents, such as biographical summaries, personal testimonies, and denunciation statements. Nearly half of the case files of the sample group include lengthy annotations that proclaim the respondent's political and ideological innocence, and in some cases acts of resistance, but also severe hardships perpetuated by others. For example, in March 1946, an employee of the district court in the Franconian town of Münchberg appended a statement to his questionnaire declaring that despite extreme pressure from his superiors, he had refused to join the NSDAP and was therefore labeled a "traitor" by his colleagues.[165] He maintained that the only reason he eventually joined the party, and later the SA, was to retain his job and feed his family and because he feared harassment by the Gestapo. Furthermore, he claimed that his wife had been denounced by party members within the NS-Frauenschaft and forced to work under horrific conditions in an armaments factory. Another civil servant, this one in Hamburg, wrote that his four underage children had suffered during the war and that any past Nazi affiliations were now "more than compensated" by the pain endured by his family, which included the loss of their home.[166] Similarly, an applicant from Heidelberg wrote a long letter to the local

---

[162] Fragebogen of O.G., June 5, 1945, NARA, RG 260, OMGUS, CAD, PSB, Fragebogen, Box 318.
[163] Fragebogen of W.K., September 19, 1945, NARA, RG 260, OMGUS, CAD, PSB, Fragebogen, Box 317.
[164] Schroeder, *To Forget It All and Begin Again*, 31.
[165] "Permission for Reinstatement as Employee of Justice at the District Court (Amtsgericht) Münchberg," March 21, 1946, NARA, RG 260, OMGUS, CAD, PSB, Fragebogen, Box 588.
[166] Letter, S.P. and Regierungspräsidium, March 12, 1945, AdsD, Schumacher Bestand, Mappe 98.

American detachment office, describing the hardships his family had faced during the war: "My wife and children have been displaced to Gartow on account of the air raids. Our house and its surroundings were destroyed during battles between the 9th American Army and German troops here. They were forced to spend eight days in the woods, where my child contracted dysentery."[167]

Victimhood was a commodity during the postwar; a valued means to solicit sympathy from the occupying forces, to dissociate oneself from the Nazi regime, and to evade punishment for political transgressions. The currency of suffering undoubtedly had an emotional impact on the individual, who had been, in all likelihood, traumatized by the war. Employment screening and commission hearings encouraged Germans to generate stories of violence, extreme anxiety, and posttraumatic stress. Leading theories of trauma recovery suggest that it is only after the honest characterization of traumatic experiences that mental recovery can occur.[168] Instead of sincere self-reflection, many Germans retreated into their trauma and commodified their suffering, a process inadvertently facilitated by the occupation authorities.[169] However, it is also possible that for those who recorded authentic stories, the mere documentation of traumatic events had a therapeutic effect. Cathy Caruth interprets this as the respondent "asking to be seen and heard," and it is in this display that the profound story of traumatic experience would be externalized and in sense, confronted.[170]

Whatever the effect on mental health and community rehabilitation, it is certain that written and verbal self-reflection influenced what the individual chose to remember about the Nazi regime and how they personally associated with these memories. The Fragebogen was a catalyst in the construction of narratives and the formation of identities for millions of Germans. While it is unclear if the memories of personal suffering were fabricated in order to improve the chance of obtaining

---

[167] "Application," June 19, 1945, NARA, RG 260, OMGUS, CAD, PSB, Box 356.
[168] Judith Herman, *Trauma and Recovery: The Aftermath of Violence – from Domestic Abuse to Political Terror* (New York: Basic Books, 1992), 133–36, 155; Kai T. Erikson, *Everything in Its Path: Destruction of Community in the Buffalo Creek Flood* (New York: Simon and Schuster, 1971), 216, 234, 240, 255–59.
[169] An investigation into such consequences is conducted in Dack, "Retreating into Trauma," 143–70.
[170] Cathy Caruth, *Unclaimed Experience: Trauma, Narrative, and History* (Baltimore, MD: Johns Hopkins University Press, 1996), 9. A similar argument is made by Mary Cosgrove, "Narrating German Suffering in the Shadow of Holocaust Victimology: W.G. Sebald, Contemporary Trauma Theory and Dieter Forte's Air Raid Epic," in *Germans as Victims: In the Literary Fiction of the Berlin Republic*, eds. Stuart Taberner and Karina Berger (Rochester, NY: Camden House, 2009), 169–70.

employment, we do know that thousands of Germans were arrested for Fragebogen falsification. Even if we avoid making assumptions about the validity of these stories, it can be inferred, according to the tenets of narrative psychology, that the mere documentation of personal sufferings, the identification of specific oppressors, and the creation of a victim–victimizer dichotomy greatly contributed to self-narratives.

The Fragebogen allowed room for, and even encouraged Germans toward, stories of loss and hardship. Denazification, therefore, inadvertently perpetuated a culture of victimhood that already had begun to develop prior to the arrival of Allied armies, and which continued to flourish during the occupation within families and local communities. Germans had already recreated themselves as a people deprived of their rights and deceived by a violent regime, but it was denazification that allowed them to confirm and expand upon this narrative and to establish partner identities. This builds on Mary Fulbrook's conclusion that the verbal testimonies at denazification commissions "helped to shape at least the outlines of a (sometimes overstated) 'community of the oppressed.'"[171]

Other Memories

Resisters and victims were not the only personas assumed by the men and women in our sample group. Popular also was the claim that one had been a rescuer, or sympathetic associate, of a recognized Nazi-persecuted group. Some wrote about how they came to the aid of a Jewish or communist neighbor, or that they had simply remained silent about their identity. For example, Herman Seidel explained that "for a long time past I have been in friendly relations with non-Aryans and have received them in my private dwelling."[172] The practice of victim association is perhaps most apparent in the submission of exonerating letters written by persecuted peoples. Such letters all but guaranteed amnesty and they flooded the denazification commission systems in all four zones, even being sold on the black market.[173] Ernst von Salomon himself reflected on the prevalence of Persilscheine, satirically writing that "each has his own rescued Jew."[174] Once again, the questionnaires coached the

---

[171] Fulbrook, *German National Identity after the Holocaust*, 51.
[172] Letter, H.S. to MG, October 17, 1945, OMGUS, CAD, PSB, Fragebogen, Box 317.
[173] Posener, *In Deutschland*, 65.
[174] Ido de Haan, "Paths of Normalization after the Persecution of the Jews: The Netherlands, France, and West Germany in the 1950s," in *Life after Death: Approaches to a Cultural and Social History of Europe during the 1940s and 1950s*, eds. Richard Bessel and Dirk Schumann (Cambridge: Cambridge University Press, 2003), 83.

respondent, as they emphasized the plight of certain persecuted groups, while denazification commissions placed a high value on character letters.

A smaller number of applicants constructed a self-image in which they were ideological and cultural disciples of the occupying nations. They elaborated on pre-1933 political affiliations, fluency in foreign languages, international travel, and relationships with naturalized citizens.[175] Any sort of association with the United States, Britain, France, or the Soviet Union, no matter how trivial, was included in questionnaires. For example, the German military attaché Friedrich von Boetticher wrote about his time living in Washington DC and how he respected American military history and culture.[176] One respondent cited membership in an American-based academic organization and another recounted fond memories of a summer vacation in southern France.[177]

Regardless of the stories solicited by the individual undergoing screening, it is clear that the Fragebogen exercise allowed an opportunity to tailor the truth about the past. Memories could be revived and manipulated, stories reworked and retold, and identities confirmed and constructed. No one confessed to be a hardened National Socialist. Instead, respondents cast themselves as either resisters or victims of the regime, oftentimes both, and as friends of Nazi victims and of the occupation nations. It is likely that many of the stories were manufactured or at least distorted in some way, but they still gained a degree of truth for the respondent as a learned memory through the act of documentation. Individual memories are formed through a complex interplay of external stimuli and mental representations, none of which can be completely controlled by a written document. However, the questionnaire facilitated memory work, mainly by introducing ambiguous terms and asking flexible questions relating to anti-Nazi activities. The form's unreliability as a source of intelligence had the effect of turning denazification into an invitation to create and disseminate myths. In effect, screening activities laid the groundwork for individuals to build whitewashed self-images and to bury their compromised pasts.

We cannot say with certainty if the claims of political and moral innocence made by the two hundred people of our sample group had a lasting impact on individual identity, or if they were incorporated into a

---

[175] For example, see Letter, W.H. to Herr Dr. Schumacher, May 27, 1946, AdsD, Bestand Schumacher, Mappe 90; Fragebogen of F.E., NARA, OMGUS, CAD, PSB, Fragebogen, Box 356.
[176] Fragebogen of F.B., BAF, N 323/170.
[177] Fragebogen of D.O., NARA, OMGUS, CAD, PSB, Fragebogen, Box 1162; Fragebogen of V.S., ADMAE, ZFO, WH 1298.

larger national narrative. However, knowing the transformative power of the written word, especially for vulnerable people during desperate times, it is likely that these myths were carried forward into the post-occupation years, eventually inherited, and perhaps embellished upon, by family members. The proud declaration made by many Germans is a familiar one, that "*Opa war kein Nazi*" (Grandpa was not a Nazi); he was instead a notable resister and a certain victim of the dictatorship.

Conclusion

The Fragebogen was not simply a bureaucratic screening instrument of the occupying armies. It was also an unintended emancipatory device that gave voice to many Germans, inviting them to participate in the determination of their own fate. In a postwar environment where the defeated people were monitored, harassed, and threatened with violence, screening procedures allowed some degree of independence. This was a consequence of the unrealistic objectives and limitations of denazification. Germans enthusiastically embraced the unusual opportunity. They used the Fragebogen to incriminate others, settle old debts, and to justify, diminish, and conceal Nazi pasts to improve their chance of postwar recovery. The form was a versatile and opportune device. It acted as a denunciation slip and an ego document, a canvas upon which a new more acceptable (and employable) citizen could be conceived. It was also an appliance of introspection and confession. Perhaps for some, it had a therapeutic function, assisting in the processing of past traumas and to mentally grapple with memories of war and dictatorship.

What were the implications of these varied effects of denazification? While the questionnaire helped the authorities identify Nazis, some of whom were attempting to conceal their political past, the screening program came at a social and psychological cost. The Fragebogen encouraged the practice of denunciation, pitting Germans against one another and further fragmenting relationships and local communities. It may have also allowed individuals and families to avoid honest confrontation with their past and with it a sense of accountability. Using their own suffering as commodity, citizens retreated into trauma, thus strengthening the postwar culture of victimhood and for some, delaying genuine mental recovery.

Still, while confrontation with the Nazi past was mandatory and enforced from above, and it likely generated a mostly superficial reorientation, the Fragebogen drove a massive wedge between the individual German and National Socialism. With hopes to retain or secure employment, avoid a fine or having to face a review commission, respondents went to great lengths to distance themselves from the regime. The substantiated fear of being denounced, whether for real or fictitious offences, further pushed the individual into a defensive position. Any accusation of Nazi affiliation was ardently denied. Screening procedures may have contributed to converting millions of citizens into self-imagined resisters and victims, but they also forced them to dig in their heels and stand firmly behind their written claims. Memories were expressed within an approved antifascist framework. This may not have been what the OSS and GCU planners had in mind when they mapped out their denazification project, but the effect was analogous. Genuine anti-Nazi opinions ran shallow, but they were declared loudly and publicly. In small groups and within families, these beliefs and associated personas were celebrated. By the end of the occupation, being identified as a Nazi or continuing to sympathize with the collapsed regime was unmistakably taboo and offensive. Whatever the result, this chapter has shown that the screening campaigns of the occupation governments not only affected the physical livelihood of the German citizen, but played a powerful role in how they, especially former party members, interpreted and remembered the Nazi regime.

The question remains, however, did the popularity and enthusiasm of refuting National Socialism have a lasting influence? Soon after the creation of the two Germanys, tens of thousands of former Nazis were rehabilitated in their jobs. In both countries, a comprehensive program of exoneration and reintegration was instituted. But while the amnesty laws have been presented as clear proof that denazification failed, this measure of evaluation overlooks the public, and even more importantly private, discrediting of Nazism that occurred during the occupation. Despite vast policy differences between zones, it is inconceivable that the exhaustive four-year denazification enterprise, which affected nearly every citizen, did not have a lasting influence on larger communities. It is unquestionable that the shared experience of documenting prescribed stories of political and moral innocence had a collective result. Barbara Rosenwein and Ute Frevert have both emphasized the power and identity-forming function and endurance of emotional bonds within communities.[178] While loss and suffering perhaps acted as the strongest bond, the shared condemnation of Nazism and widespread identification as antifascists also contributed to a larger national narrative.

---

[178] Rosenwein, *Emotional Communities in the Early Middle Ages*, esp. 20–29; Frevert, *Emotions in History*, 3–18.

Conclusion
Everyday Denazification

In his first formal parliamentary address, on September 20, 1949, West German chancellor Konrad Adenauer condemned the denazification measures of the previous five years:

> Much unhappiness and damage has been caused by denazification ... we should no longer distinguish between two classes of people in Germany: the politically reliable and the politically unreliable. This distinction must disappear as soon as possible ... the Federal Government is determined wherever possible, to put the past behind us.[1]

The following day, the CDU/CSU leader in the Bundestag, Heinrich von Brentano, continued the eulogy, declaring to his fellow parliamentarians that, "The system of evaluating questionnaires has failed dismally, as had been foreseen from the very beginning."[2]

In the months following these inaugural speeches, a series of legislative acts were passed, at different levels of government, that nullified what was left of the political screening system in Germany and amnestied hundreds of thousands of politically tainted citizens. According to historian Norbert Frei, this legal "liquidation" of denazification was directed by the solitary goal of enlarging the electoral base of the major political parties.[3] The April 10, 1951 *Entnazifizierungsschlussgesetz* (Law to End Denazification), amended retrospectively as Article 131 of the Federal Republic's constitution, permitted the reemployment of public servants and other workers who had been previously dismissed. In fact, state governments were required to employ these individuals, who the

---

[1] Konrad Adenauer, "Policy Statement of the German Federal Republic...," September 20, 1949, in Office of the U.S. High Commissioner for Germany, *Germany's Parliament in Action: The September 1949 Debate on the Government's Statement of Policy* (Washington, DC: Office of Political Affairs, 1950), 20–28.

[2] Dr. Heinrich von Brentano, "Policy Statement of the German Federal Republic...," September 21, 1949, in *Germany's Parliament in Action*, 39.

[3] Frei, *Vergangenheitspolitik*, 68f.

media affectionally called "131ers."[4] Few recognized the subtle irony that Law 131 rehabilitated those punished by the 131 questions of the most reviled version of the Fragebogen.[5] The following year, the German Democratic Republic's *Volkskammer* enacted a similar piece of legislation, removing all employment restrictions on former Nazi Party members. Politicians across the party landscape, in both Germanys, celebrated the end of what was viewed as an antiquated and misguided campaign, going so far as to integrate its failure into a story of homegrown political and economic revival.[6] With denazification thrown out, so it went, Germans could collectively embrace democracy and pursue shared economic prosperity.

It would seem then that the denazification era was finally over; its policies had been discontinued and proscriptions reversed. This is how the story has been told for decades. The massive screening campaign of the Allied armies had collapsed under its own weight and was then unequivocally eradicated by the two German successor states. Denazification failed and its effects were negligible.

This book has challenged this traditional interpretation by recounting a more comprehensive history of denazification, one of mid-level planners, civil affairs soldiers, and regular German men and women. It has attempted to move the analytical gaze away from the Allied dictates of Potsdam, the verdicts of Nuremberg, and the amnesties of Bonn to focus on how the eradication of Nazism was experienced by ordinary people.

This study has shown that denazification was an enormous paper project. At the ground level, the ideological war waged against fascism was fought largely by screening individuals for employment through the evaluation of forms, letters, and written statements. The Fragebogen was at the center of this bureaucracy and in many ways determined what the occupying authorities could and could not achieve during their administration. If a narrow definition of denazification is adopted, then the questionnaire program is nearly synonymous with the larger campaign. It was not the only initiative to cleanse the German political consciousness, but it was by far the largest and most influential.

The Fragebogen was an ambitious experiment, one that mobilized social scientists, academics, and other civilian experts. However, the project never fully satisfied the many groups involved in its functioning,

---

[4] With some exceptions, the law stipulated that at least 20 percent of state administrations' staff had to be from this group of formally dismissed employees.

[5] Another irony was that in early 1950, the government began distributing questionnaires to assist lawmakers in determining how many people had been dismissed and not reinstated since 1945.

[6] Frei, *Adenauer's Germany and the Nazi Past*, 5–39.

as they all desired different approaches and outcomes for denazification. It began as an idealistic endeavor with an equivocal vision, before colliding with the practical realities of military government and postwar politics. All four major Allied nations believed that a new strategy had to be pursued to prevent another world war, but none possessed the time, patience, or foresight to successfully chart its course. It was easy for them to consent to high-policy objectives, but much more difficult to produce an agreed upon pragmatic program. The questionnaire had many inherent problems, not least of which was that the form possessed contradictory components. It was both malleable and rigid, it contained sympathetic questions and allowances but was also predicated on uncompromising categories of incrimination. The screening system failed to strike a balance between rehabilitation and punishment. Nevertheless, the Fragebogen was the engine that drove the denazification machine; it was all the occupiers could come up with in the disorderedly final months of the war – how else could they interrogate millions of people? This adds credence to the popular turn of phrase heard at the time, that the project was "impossible but necessary."[7] Denazification stumbled forward, moving from one reactionary directive to the next. The questionnaire was continuously reconceptualized and rewritten.

This book has also shown that the mechanics of denazification were remarkably similar across occupation zones. The Fragebogen is often depicted as an American invention and failure, but the form was in fact a joint-Allied venture that all four military governments participated in. The British, French, and Soviets relied on the same ubiquitous instrument for their vetting campaigns, and thousands of local German commissions inherited it. There were significant differences in the scale and scope of the individual programs, but the underlying function was the same.

For many Germans, the completion of questionnaires defined their denazification experience. "Ideological reorientation" was confined to filling out one or more of these forms – honestly or not – adding desired supplementary sheets and waiting for the relevant military government or German office to evaluate their responses and either allow or refuse employment. The denazification commissions, especially those in the American zone, have been the topic of much research and are often portrayed as the principal activity of denazification, even though only

---

[7] Patricia Meehan, *A Strange Enemy People: Germans under the British, 1945–1950* (London: Peter Owens, 2001), 111.

5 percent of Germans faced one of these special courts.[8] As much as one-third of the postwar population completed a questionnaire, making it the closest thing to a shared denazification experience.

The questionnaire held immense authority, influencing the financial and emotional well-being of millions of citizens. The occupation years were characterized by widespread impoverishment and for many, a positive Fragebogen was the only path to material recovery. Furthermore, the form disrupted social hierarchies by threatening the standing of privileged community members who may have cooperated with the Nazis. Completing a questionnaire and waiting on its evaluation was a trying experience, generating a wide range of emotions. Respondents recognized the authority that the document possessed; the act of filling it out was not trivialized.

The Fragebogen encouraged the practice of denunciation, as it demanded incriminating information about family members and Allied army investigators diligently followed up on accusations brought against neighbors and coworkers. This encumbered the emotional recovery of already fractured communities. For millions of Germans, the questionnaire was the first instance in which they had reflected in depth on the National Socialist years and on their participation in the dictatorship. The resulting personal narratives, written by emotionally vulnerable and anxiety-ridden people, convey much about how Germans remembered and interpreted the Third Reich. Respondents went to great lengths to distance themselves from the regime and to confirm non-Nazi identities and create new ones. They depicted themselves as resisters and victims, as well as friends and rescuers of persecuted minorities and supporters of the Allied nations. With all its ambiguities and allowances, the questionnaire provided respondents an opportunity, and for many an imperative, to rewrite their personal history. The confirmative memory-creating power of written language is considerable, and Germans sometimes exploited their own screening to build functional identities to absolve themselves of moral guilt.

Existing scholarship on postwar memory maintains that the ease with which Germans broke from their Nazi past can be attributed to lenient denazification commissions, a preoccupation with economic recovery, and the popular political agenda of the 1950s that promoted reintegration. I have suggested that the whitewashing process began earlier and that it was instigated, in part, by the Allied armies and their political screening programs. More broadly, this study has argued that the

---

[8] Remy, *The Heidelberg Myth*, 178.

Conclusion: Everyday Denazification

occupiers had an intimate and lasting influence on how Germans remembered, interpreted, and recorded their own past. In the same breath, it has also granted agency to the Germans themselves, recognizing that they were active players in their own denazification, and that political screening aided in their mental as well as economic recovery.

However, we are left asking, was the Fragebogen an effective approach to eradicating Nazism from German society? While it has not been the intention of this study to generate a definitive answer, or provide a recipe for a successful reorientation campaign, an evaluation is unavoidable and important. As we have seen, the success of the questionnaire project is difficult to measure for many reasons. The form's purpose and application varied between and within zones and it regularly changed during the occupation. There is also the fundamental question of whose standards of success should we use? The bullet-point goals listed in the SHAEF Handbook? Perhaps the objectives published in JCS1067 or the Potsdam Agreement, or one of the ACC directives? They all somewhat differed in their interpretation of successful denazification. Most studies defer to one of these Allied criteria and an evaluation of arrests, dismissals, and exonerations. Such an investigation usually concludes with an account of Adenauer's amnesty laws and hence a verdict of failure.

The more difficult inquiry is determining how individual Germans and their communities responded to and were affected by denazification. One method of evaluation, that of affirmed Allied policy, is concerned with physical manifestations – removal and exclusion of Nazis from public life and the drafting of new constitutions, laws, and textbooks – while the other, that of ideological reorientation, considers long-lasting abstract outcomes – discreditation of National Socialism and markable change in German discourse and behavior toward democratic reforms. But how do we evaluate changes that are mostly personal, internal, and invisible? Should we confine our assessment to the years of occupation or allow the effects of denazification more time to permeate German society?

A comprehensive quantitative analysis of the Fragebogen as an Allied program is relatively straightforward and has been conducted in this book. The instrument was not successful in its original mandate, which was to screen for all positions of influence and exclude every active Nazi and militarist from democratic life. The SHAEF planners who set these goals knew they were unrealistic. Most Nazis who lost their jobs were eventually reinstated and reintegrated into the democratic party landscape (or communist dictatorship). The form itself was not an ideal instrument for political investigation, as it contained vague and sometimes contradictory questions, plenty of bureaucratic loopholes for deceit, and failed to interpret the social nuances of the Nazi dictatorship. The program suffered from a lack of resources, including adequate political intelligence. It was poorly coordinated, especially in the French and Soviet zones, and evaluation procedures were governed by rigid categories of incrimination, which relied on the respondent's membership record and not individual actions. As a professional employment screening device, the Fragebogen allowed many Germans, especially women, laborers, and displaced persons, to circumvent denazification.

Still, there were notable achievements. The questionnaire system successfully identified and removed hundreds of thousands of former Nazis from influential employment; they were replaced by non- or lesser Nazis. Many of these individuals were later rehabilitated, but not before being denied a role in the rebuilding of postwar society. Also, it should not be assumed that political amnesty guaranteed reemployment. While most former Nazis – civil servants, doctors, lawyers, managers – were reinstated in their jobs, others could not find work or discovered that their position had been filled during their absence.[9] Some were not permitted to work until the 1954 Amnesty Law had passed, and by then, they were no longer professionally competitive. Research on the postoccupation continuity of Nazi careers has only recently been conducted, but the blanket assumption that reintegration into the workforce in the early 1950s was a seamless process is questionable to say the least.[10] There was certainly not a process of "re-nazification."

Recognition must also be given to the extraordinary size and scope of the Fragebogen program. Attempting to change how 70 million citizens think and behave was absurdly ambitious and so too was the mass distribution of self-administered surveys to identify who had to be punished. Marveling in the project as it unfolded, a journalist in Karlsruhe wrote, "[F]or the first time in history ... [we] comprehensively examine

---

[9] This false assumption is emphasized in Armin Schuster, *Die Entnazifizierung in Hessen 1945–1954: Vergangenheitspolitik in der Nachkriegszeit* (Wiesbaden: Historische Kommission für Nassau, 1999), and Norbert Frei, "Nach der Tat: die Ahnung deutscher Kriegs- und NS-Verbrechen in Europa – eine Bilanz," in *Transnationale Vergangenheitspolitik: der Umgang mit deutschen Kriegsverbrechern in Europa nach dem Zweiten Weltkrieg*, ed. Norbert Frei (Göttingen: Wallstein, 2006).

[10] See Thomas Schlemmer and Susanna Schrafstetter, eds., "After Nazism: Relaunching Careers in Germany and Austria," *German Yearbook of Contemporary History* 5 (2021). This special issue includes research on the postwar careers of *Funktionseliten* (professional elites), with contributions by Axel Schildt, Mary Fulbrook, Hans-Hennig Kortüm, Margit Reiter, Thomas Schlemmer, Gerald Steinacher, and Andreas Wirsching. Other relevant works include Ulrich Brochhagen, *Nach Nürnberg: Vergangenheitsbewältigung und Westintegration in der Ära Adenauer* (Hamburg: Junius, 1994) and Wilfried Loth and Bernd-A. Rusinek, eds., *Verwandlungspolitik: NS-Eliten in der westdeutschen Nachkriegsgesellschaft* (Frankfurt am Main: Campus Verlag, 1998).

political behavior by asking questions and examining the answers."[11] One of the more interesting reasons given by researchers for the failure of the project was its determination to provide Germans with a fair and democratic due process, one defined by individual evaluation, physical evidence, civilian commissions, and appellate hearings. Considering the logistical requirements of such a massive undertaking, one that was administered by multiple governments over five years in a war-devastated country, it is nothing less than remarkable that millions of forms were processed. Remembered by a senior civilian advisor in the American zone, the Fragebogen was a "bureaucratic masterpiece."[12]

The evaluation of the Fragebogen as an eradicator of Nazism is much more difficult, but also more important given that the issues facing the world eighty years later have ideological rather than economic roots. The screening program clearly created animosity among the German public, so much so that political parties canvased for election on the promise of eliminating the "Fragebogen regime."[13] Its limitations forced the Allies to rely on denunciations, which hindered community cohesion and rehabilitation. More relevant is that the questionnaires allowed respondents to focus, and perhaps invent, memories of resistance and suffering and to build whitewashed narratives that would keep them employed.

Despite this, the questionnaire turned denazification into an individual act of reflection. It forced Germans to critically evaluate their past affiliations, beliefs, and life decisions. Respondents spent millions of collective hours arguing that they had never been Nazi supporters and that they wished Adolf Hitler had not come to rule the country. Their answers may have been distorted, but Germans used the questionnaire to write Nazism out of their lives. It was hard work to prove one's innocence, completing the form and appending documents was a meaningful psychological commitment. This shared rite of passage had the effect of discrediting the regime and its ideology and removing Nazism from all respectable political and social discourses.[14] The fact that there was never a serious resurgence of Nazism, and that today's Federal Republic is a world leader in democracy, is not incidental. Just because denazification did not unfold in accordance with the task-based

---

[11] Wilhelm Beisel, "Der Fragebogen," *Badische Neueste Nachrichten*, May 14, 1946, p. 2.
[12] Walter L. Dorn, "The Unfinished Purge," unfinished manuscript, IfZ, ED127, B.3, p. 18.
[13] For example, Poster, "Schluss mit der Entnazifizierung!," ACDP, 07/001/3457.
[14] The post-occupation resilience and influence of these denazification stories is difficult to measure. A first attempt has been made by Hanne Leßau, but a more systematic investigation is needed. See Leßau, *Entnazifizierungsgeschichten*, here 399–473.

objectives of the occupying armies does not mean the goals of the vetting campaign were not achieved.

Where does this leave us? It is impossible to say for certain if the Fragebogen failed or succeeded, just as it is to measure the outcome of any large-scale government program. In 1945, "successful" denazification was measured differently than it is today, when supplied with historical hindsight. Any evaluation of long-term ideological change is further obscured by the influence of larger events and experiences, some of them very consequential to Germans. It could be argued that the *Wirtschaftswunder* (economic miracle) and the physical division brought by the Cold War were the most effective deterrents of Nazism. However, it remains clear that denazification contributed much to the collective condemnation and discrediting of National Socialism and that the Fragebogen played a central role at a very early point.

Whatever the calculation, in more recent decades, screening questionnaires have become popular instruments of transitional justice, used by both domestic governments and foreign agencies in post-conflict environments. In addition to the Allied campaigns in post–World War II Italy, Germany, Austria, and Japan, self-administered surveys have been distributed to public officials in Greece (1974), Rwanda (1995), Bosnia and Herzegovina (1999), Kosovo (1999), Democratic Republic of the Congo (2003, 2013), and Afghanistan (2003).[15] The United Nations Mission in Bosnia and Herzegovina processed 24,000 surveys, which asked police and judicial personnel about their professional and military background and required the names of three persons who could corroborate their answers.[16] After civil wars in El Salvador (1980–92) and Liberia (1999–2003), senior security officials were required to complete registration forms similar to the Meldebogen.[17] The content and scale of distribution of these questionnaires vary greatly, a reflection of each country's unique political and cultural circumstance. However, administrators

---

[15] Some of these cases are explored in Alexander Mayer-Rieckh and Pablo de Greiff, eds., *Justice as Prevention: Vetting Public Employees in Transitional Societies* (New York: Social Science Research Council, 2007).

[16] Serge Rumin, "Gathering and Managing Information in Vetting Processes," in *Justice as Prevention: Vetting Public Employees in Transitional Societies*, eds. Alexander Mayer-Rieckh and Pablo de Greiff (New York: Social Science Research Council, 2007), 417–20.

[17] Rumin, "Gathering and Managing Information in Vetting Processes," 439; Deniz Kocak, "Security Sector Reconstruction in Post-Conflict: The Lessons from Timor-Leste," in *Impunity: Confronting Illicit Power Structures in War and Transition*, eds. Michael Miklaucic and Michelle Hughes (Washington, DC: National Defense University, 2016), 350. The United Nations has established guidelines for vetting processes, see United Nations Development Programme, "Vetting Public Employees in Post-conflict Settings: Operational Guidelines" (2006).

struggled with the same issues as their German predecessor: lack of dependable political intelligence, overreliance on civilian denunciation, inadequate definitions of targeted groups, poor coordination, and the human capital cost of mass dismissals.

All of the post-Soviet governments in Eastern Europe carried out vetting (or "lustration") processes in the early 1990s.[18] However, instead of using screening surveys and civilian commissions, most administrations simply released the employment (and informant) files of the deposed authoritarian regime to the public, which allowed vetting to unfold at the discretion of individual offices.[19] The only exception, perhaps unsurprisingly, was in Germany after the dissolution of the GDR. Here, vetting was carried out in a decentralized manner, but usually it required employees to fill out a questionnaire that detailed their political function in the GDR and association with the Stasi.[20] Emphasis was placed on the identification of civilian informants, mainly because the Stasi files was the largest (mostly) intact record collection and the abuses of the state secret service had been at the center of the 1989 revolution. Special commissions were set up to review submitted questionnaires and make recommendations about the employment eligibility of candidates. It is intriguing that decades earlier, some of these civil servants had completed a similar form for both the Nazi Party and an Allied army occupier. A comparative study of denazification and de-Stasification is overdue.

One important exception where questionnaires were not used was during the de-Baathification campaign in Iraq, which began in 2003 as an initiative of the US-directed Coalition Provision Authority. The American public was told that the process "borrows from the 'de-Nazification' program," but politicians seemed to have liked the analogy

---

[18] Kieran Williams, Brigid Fowler, and Aleks Szczebiak, "Explaining Lustration in Central Europe: A 'Post-Communist Politics' Approach," *Democratization* 12, no. 1 (2005): 22–54.

[19] Mayer-Rieckh and de Greiff, *Justice as Prevention*, 260–347.

[20] Christiane Wilke, "The Shield, the Sword, and the Party: Vetting the East German Public Sector," in *Justice as Prevention: Vetting Public Employees in Transitional Societies*, eds. Alexander Mayer-Rieckh and Pablo de Greiff (New York: Social Science Research Council, 2007), 348–400. On de-Stasification, see John O. Koehler, "East Germany: The Stasi and De-Stasification," in *Dismantling Tyranny: Transitioning Between Totalitarian Regimes*, eds. Ilan Berman and J. Michael Waller (Lanham, MD: Rowman & Littlefield, 2015), 43–74; James McAdams, *Judging the Past in Unified Germany* (Cambridge: Cambridge University Press, 2001); Anne Sa'adah, *Germany's Second Chance: Trust, Justice, and Democratization* (Cambridge, MA: Harvard University Press, 1998); Peter Quint, *The Imperfect Union* (Princeton: Princeton University Press, 1997); and Inga Markovits, *Imperfect Justice: An East-West German Diary* (Oxford: Oxford University Press, 1995).

more than the lessons, making many of the same mistakes, while ignoring denazification's successful elements.[21] For example, instead of enrolling the defeated population in its own screening, blanket dismissals based on rank-and-file membership in the Ba'ath Party were carried out. The Iraqi military was completely dissolved, resulting in the unemployment of around half a million armed soldiers.[22] Most analysts agree that de-Baathification was a comprehensive failure and ultimately became a tool for escalating political conflict between ethnic groups, facilitating the rise of terrorism in the region.[23] Such critics attest that the candidate vetting process should have been more democratic and focused on the assessment of individual actions rather than group membership.[24]

An informal review of more recent questionnaire-based screening methodologies confirms many of the conclusions already made regarding the effectiveness of denazification, some of which should be considered when developing future vetting campaigns. While there does not exist a "one-size-fits-all" mechanism, political screening should never rely entirely on group association but also assess individual actions and integrity to the extent possible – as the Fragebogen attempted. Program policy must be practical and extend only as far as the available intelligence allows, and definitions should be clearly interpreted before screening begins – something denazification agents did not achieve. Collaboration between military and civilian groups should be valued and pursued and appropriate resources allocated. Also, vetting systems should incorporate due process guarantees, such as the right to an appeal. However, perhaps the greatest lesson from the Fragebogen experiment is that individuals and communities should be enrolled in their own screening; political reorientation cannot be achieved without the active participation of the population.

Germans complained explicitly about this very process – forced self-reflection and the painstaking investigation of their private lives. Adenauer regularly spoke of citizens who had been "damaged by

---

[21] Karen DeYoung and Peter Slevin, "Full U.S. Control Planned for Iraq," *Washington Post*, February 21, 2003. For a succinct comparison of the purges in Germany and Iraq, see Aysegul Keskin Zeren, "From De-Nazification of Germany to De-Baathification of Iraq," *Political Science Quarterly* 132, no. 2 (2017): 259–91.

[22] Zeren, "From De-Nazification of Germany to De-Baathification of Iraq," 282.

[23] For an overview of de-Baathification, see Miranda Sissons and Abdulrazzaq Al-Saiedi, "A Bitter Legacy: Lessons of De-Baathification in Iraq," *International Center for Transitional Justice* (March 2013). On the failures of Iraq's vetting processes, see Amal Hamdan, "Collective Guilt, Selective Exclusion: Iraq's Candidate Screening Process," *International Foundation for Electoral Systems* (March 2020): 1–31.

[24] For example, Sissons and Al-Saiedi, "A Bitter Legacy," 31–38.

denazification" (*Entnazifizierungsgeschädigte*).[25] He was referring not just to those who had lost their jobs, but everyone whose lives were disrupted by the invasive screening campaign. Interestingly enough, this is precisely the denazification experience that Franz Neumann and the other OSS researchers had wanted. Their vision of how political screening could heal German society was driven by a belief that individual introspection and self-interrogation were the only effective tools to build a genuine Nazi-free society. They had demanded that denazification be personalized and emotional; that it make the individual uncomfortable.

Postwar political screening was not merely a mechanical data-collecting program with a massive bureaucracy. It was also an unprecedented experiment that had enduring consequences for Germans. The Fragebogen brought denazification into the homes of millions of citizens, requiring them to seriously reflect on their past decisions and affiliations, and to assert their current beliefs, including political and moral positions. Most importantly, it forced respondents to prove they were not Nazis. In fact, the questionnaire provided Germans with a forum in which to create and rehearse non-Nazi and anti-Nazi identities. Respondents were compelled to revise their personal history if they wanted to work. These edited memories and attitudes, having been declared publicly and in writing, were the first crucial step toward individual transformation.

In the April 1948 issue of a widely published GI magazine, an anonymous US soldier delivered an honest reflection of what was then a crumbling denazification system.[26] He explained to his readers that permanent political reorientation required both the removal of active Nazis from influential employment and the elimination of the "seed of Nazism" from the minds of the German people. He argued that "we want to denazify Germany in spirit as well as in fact." While there were many problems with the Fragebogen screening program, it is difficult to imagine a different process that would have been more effective in achieving both these ends – the removal of Nazism as a practical political force *and* the transformation of the beliefs of individual Germans.

[25] Frei, *Adenauer's Germany and the Nazi Past*, 3–4.
[26] U.S. Army, *Troop I&E Bulletin: Denazification*, 3, no. 15 (April 11, 1948): 19.

Appendix   The Fragebogen Questions

English text of the United States questionnaire (published May 15, 1945)

MG/PS/G/9a

MILITARY GOVERNMENT OF GERMANY

Fragebogen

WARNING: Read the entire Fragebogen carefully before you start to fill it out. The English language will prevail if discrepancies exist between it and the German translation. Answers must be typewritten or printed clearly in block letters. Every question must be answered precisely and conscientiously and no space is to be left blank. If a question is to be answered by either "yes" or "no", print the word "yes" or "no" in the appropriate space. If the question is inapplicable, so indicate by some appropriate word or phrase such as "none" or "not applicable". Add supplementary sheets if there is not enough space in the questionaire [*sic*]. **Omissions or false or incomplete statements are offenses against Military Government and will result in prosecution and punishment.**

A.   PERSONAL

1. List position for which you are under consideration (include agency or firm).
2. Name (Surname) (Fore Names).
3. Other names which you have used or by which you have been known.
4. Date of birth.
5. Place of birth.
6. Height.
7. Weight.

Appendix

8. Color of hair.
9. Color of eyes.
10. Scars, marks, or deformities.
11. Present address (City, street, and house number).
12. Permanent residence (City, street, and house number).
13. Identy [sic] card type and Number.
14. Wehrpaß No.
15. Passport No.
16. Citizenship.
17. If a naturalized citizen, give date and place of naturalization.
18. List any titles of nobility ever held by you or your wife or by the parents or grandparents of either of you.
19. Religion.
20. With what church are you affiliated?
21. Have you ever severed your connection with any church, officially or unofficially?
22. If so, give particulars and reasons.
23. What religious preference did you give in the census of 1939?
24. List any crimes of which you have been convicted, giving dates, locations and nature of the crimes.

B. SECONDARY AND HIGHER EDUCATION

Name & Type of School (If a special Nazi school or military academy, so specify)	Location	Dates of Attendance	Certificate, Diploma or Degree	Did Abritur permit University matriculation?	Date

25. List any German University Student Corps to which you have ever belonged.
26. List (giving locations and dates) any Napola, Adolph [sic] Hitler School, Nazi Leaders College or military academy in which you have ever been a teacher.
27. Have your children ever attended any of such schools? Which ones, where and when?
28. List (giving location and dates) any school in which you have ever been a Vertrauenslehrer (formerly Jugendwalter).

C. PROFESSIONAL OR TRADE EXAMINATIONS

Name of Examination	Place Taken	Result	Date

D. CHRONOLOGICAL RECORD OF FULL TIME EMPLOYMENT AND MILITARY SERVICE

29. Give a chronological history of your employment and military service beginning with 1st of January 1931, accounting for all promotions or demotions, transfers, periods of unemployment, attendance at educational institutions (other than those covered in Section B) or training schools and full-time service with para military organizations. (Part time employment is to be recorded in Section F.) Use a separate line for each change in your position or rank or to indicate periods of unemployment or attendance at training schools or transfers from one military or para military organization to anohter [sic].

From	To	Employer and Address or Military Unit	Name and Title of Immediate Superior or C.O.	Position or Rank	Duties and Responsibilities	Reasons for Change of Status or Cessation of Service

30. Were you deferred from Military Service?
31. If so, explain circumstances completely.
32. Have you ever been a member of the General Staff Corps?
33. When?
34. Have you ever been a Nazi Military Leadership Officer?
35. When and in what unit?
36. Did you serve as part of the Military Government or Wehrkreis administration in any country occupied by Germany including Austria and Sudetenland?
37. If so, give particulars of offices held, duites [sic] performed, location and period of service.
38. Do you have any military orders or other military honors?
39. If so, state what was awarded you, the date, reasons and occasion for its bestowal.

E. MEMBERSHIP IN ORGANIZATIONS

40. Indicate on the following chart whether or not you were a member of and any offices you have held in the organizations listed below. Use lines 96 to 98 to specify any other associations, society, fraternity, union, syndicate, chamber, institute, group, corporation, club or other organization of any kind, whether social, political, professional, educational, cultural, industrial, commercial or honorary, with which you have ever been connected or associated.

> Column 1: Insert either "yes" or "no" on each line to indicate whether or not you have ever been a member of the organization listed. If you were a candidate, disregard the columns and write in the word "candidate" followed by the date of your application for membership.
> Column 2: Insert date on which you joined.
> Column 3: Insert date your membership ceased if you are no longer a member. Insert the word "Date" if you are still a member.
> Column 4: Insert your membership number in the organization.
> Column 5: Insert the highest office, rank or other post of authority which you have held at any time. If you have never held an office, rank or post of authority, insert the word "none" in Columns 5 and 6.
> Column 6: Insert date of your appointment to the office, rank or post of authority listed in Column 5.

1 Yes or No	2 From	3 To	4 Number	5 Highest Office or rank held	6 Date Appointed

41. NSDAP
42. General-SS
43. Waffen-SS
44. SS-Security Service
45. SA
46. Hitler Youth / League of German Girls
47. NS-German Students' League
48. NS-Association of University Lecturers
49. NS-Women's League
50. NS-Motor Corps
51. NS-Flying Corps

Appendix

(cont.)

	1 Yes or No	2 From	3 To	4 Number	5 Highest Office or rank held	6 Date Appointed
52. Reich Federation of German Civil Servants						
53. German Labor Front						
54. Strength Through Joy						
55. NS-Public Welfare Organization						
56. NS-Association of German Nurses						
57. NS-Organization for War Victims						
58. NS-Association of German Technology						
59. NS-Physicians' League						
60. NS-Teachers' League						
61. NS-Association of Legal Professionals						
62. German Women's Welfare Organization						
63. Reich Association of German Families						
64. NS-Sport Association						
65. NS-Alumni Association						
66. German Students' Union						
67. German Council of Municipal Governments						
68. NS-Veterans' Association						
69. Reich Lecturers League						
70. Reich Chamber of Culture						
71. Reich Chamber of Literature						
72. Reich Chamber of Press						
73. Reich Chamber of Radio						
74. Reich Chamber of Theatre						
75. Reich Chamber of Music						
76. Reich Chamber of Fine Arts						
77. Reich Chamber of Film						
78. American Institute						
79. German Academy of Munich						
80. German Institute for Foreign Affairs						
81. German Christian Movement						
82. German Faith Movement						
83. German Fichte Federation						
84. German Hunting Society						
85. German Red Cross						

(*cont.*)

	1 Yes or No	2 From	3 To	4 Number	5 Highest Office or rank held	6 Date Appointed
86. Ibero-American Institute						
87. Institute for Research on the Jewish Question						
88. USA Fellowship						
89. East European Institute						
90. Reich Labor Service						
91. Reich Colonial League						
92. Reich Air Raid Protection League						
93. State Academy for the Maintenance of Racial Health						
94. Association for German Cultural Relations Abroad						
95. Advertising Council of German Industry						
Others (Specify):						
96.						
97.						
98.						

99. Have you ever sworn an oath of secrecy to any organization?
100. If so, list the organizations and give particulars.
101. Have you any relatives who have held office, rank or post of authority in any of the organizations listed from 41 to 95 above?
102. If so, give their names and addresses, their relationships to you and a description of the position and organizations.
103. With the exception of minor contributions to the Winterhilfe and regular membership dues, list and give details of any contributions of money or property which you have made, directly or indirectly, to the NSDAP or any of the other organizations listed above, including any contributions made by any natural or juridical person or legal entity through your solicitation or influence.
104. Have you ever been the recipient of any titles, ranks, medals, testimonials or other honors from any of the above organizations?
105. If so, state the nature of the honor, the date conferred, and the reason and occasion for its bestowal.
106. Were you a member of a political paty [*sic*] before 1933?
107. If so, which one?
108. For what political party did you vote in the election of November 1932?
109. And in March 1933?

110. Have you ever been a member of any anti-Nazi underground party or groups since 1933?
111. Which one?
112. Since when?
113. Have you ever been a member of any trade union or professional or business organization which was dissolved or forbidden since 1933?
114. Have you ever been dismissed from the civil service, the teaching profession or ecclesiastical positions or any other employment for active or passive resistance to the Nazis or their ideology?
115. Have you ever been imprisoned or have restrictions of movement, residence or freedom to practice your trade or profession been imposed on you for racial or religious reasons or because of active or passive resistance to the Nazis?
116. If you have answered yes to any of the questions from 110 to 115, give particulars and the names and addresses of two persons who can confirm the truth of your statements.

F. PART TIME SERVICE WITH ORGANIZATIONS

117. With the exception of those you have specifically mentioned in Sections D and E above, list: a. Any part time, unpaid or honorary position of authority or trust you have held as a representative of any Reich Ministry or the Office of the Four Year Plan or similar central control agency; b. Any office, rank or post of authority you have held with any economic self-administration organization such as the Reich Food Estate, the Bauernschaften, the Central Marketing Associations, the Reichswirtschaftskammer, the Gauwirtschaftskammern, the Reichsgruppen, the Wirtschaftsgruppen, the Verkehrsgruppen, the Reichsvereinigungen, the Hauptausschüsse, the Industrieringe and similar organizations, as well as their subordinate or affiliated organizations and field offices; c. Any service of any kind you have rendered in any military, paramilitary, police, law enforcement, protection, intelligence or civil defense organization such as Organisation Todt, Technische Nothilfe, Stoßtruppen, Werkscharen, Bahnschutz, Postschutz, Funkshutz, Werkschutz, Land- und Stadtwacht, Abwehr, SD, Gestapo and similar organizations.

From	To	Name and type of organization	Highest office or rank you held	Date of your Appointment	Duties

G. WRITINGS AND SPEECHES

118. List on a separate sheet the titles and publishers of all publications from 1923 to the present which were written in whole or in part, or compiled or edited by you, and all public addresses made by you, giving subject, date, and circulation or audience. If they were sponsored by any organization, give its name. If no speeches or publications write "none" in this space.

H. INCOME AND ASSETS

119. Show the sources and amount of your annual income from January 1, 1931 to date. If records are not available, give approximate amounts.

Year	Soureos [sic] of Income	Amount
1931		
...		
1945		

120. List any land or buildings owned by you or any immediate member of your family, giving locations, dates of acquisition, from whom acquired, nature and description of buildings, the number of hectares and the use to wich [sic] the property is commonly put.
121. Have you or any immediate members of your family ever acquired property which had been seized from others for political religious or raciag [sic] reasons or expropriated from others in the course of occupation of foreign countries or in furtherance of the settling of Germans or Volksdeutsche in countries occupied by Germany?
122. If so give particulars, including dates and locations, and the names and whereabouts of the original title holders.
123. Have you ever acted as an administrator or trustee of Jewish property in furtherance of Aryanization decrees or ordinances?
124. If so, give particulars.

I. TRAVEL OR RESIDENCE ABROAD

125. List all journeys or residence outside of Germany including military campaigns.

Countries Visited	Dates	Purpose of Journey

126. Was the journey made at your own expense?
127. If not at whose expense was the journey made?
128. Persons or organizations visited.
129. Did you ever serve in any capacity as part of the civil administration of any territory annexed to or occupied by the Reich?
130. If so, give particulars of office held, duties performed, location and period of service.
131. List foreign languages you speak, indicating degree of fluency.

REMARKS

The statements on this form are true and I understand that any omissions or false incomplete statements are offenses against Military Government and will subject me to prosecution and punishment.

Singed *Date*

CERTIFICATION OF IMMEDIATE SUPERIOR

I certify that the above is the true name and signature of the individual concerned and that, with the exceptions noted below, the answers made on this questionnaire are true to the best of my knowledge and belief and the information available to me. Exceptions (if no exceptions, write "none"):

Signed *Official Position* *Date*

Bibliography

Archives Consulted

Alliiertenmuseum (AM), Berlin.
Archiv der sozialen Demokratie (AdsD), Bonn.
Archiv des Diakonischen Werkes (ADW), Berlin.
Archiv für Christlich-Demokratische Politik (ACDP), Sankt Augustin.
Archives Diplomatiques, Ministère des Affaires Étrangères (ADMAE), Paris-La Courneuve.
Bayerisches Hauptstaatsarchiv (BHStA), Munich.
Bundesarchiv, Berlin (BAB).
Bundesarchiv, Koblenz (BAK).
Bundesarchiv-Militärarchiv, Freiburg (BAF).
Deutsches Rundfunkarchiv (DRA), Frankfurt.
Evangelisches Zentralarchiv (EZA), Berlin.
Imperial War Museum (IWM), London.
Institut für Zeitgeschichte (IfZ), Munich.
Landesarchiv Berlin (LAB).
Library of Congress (LOC), Washington, DC.
National Archives and Records Administration (NARA), College Park, MD.
Staatsarchiv Ludwigsburg (StAL).
Staatsarchiv Nürnberg (StAN).
The National Archives of the United Kingdom (TNA), Kew.

Newspapers and Magazines

Badische Neueste Nachrichten.
Chicago Tribune.
Evening Independent.
Evening Telegraph and Post.
Globe and Mail.
Hersfelder Zeitung.
Manchester Guardian.
Neue Zürcher Zeitung.
New York Times.
Press and Journal.
Reader's Digest.

Rheinische Zeitung.
Saturday Review.
Schwäbisches Tagblatt.
St. Louis Post-Dispatch.

Interviews

Dr. Rudolf Dorner. Interview by author. Hamburg, Germany. July 24, 2013.
Andy Estel. Interview by author. Calgary, Canada. December 15, 2014.
Magdalena Estel. Interview by author. Calgary, Canada. December 15, 2014.
Frank Schlosar. Interview by author. Calgary, Canada. November 17, 2014.

Published Documents, Official Histories, Contemporary Accounts, and Memoirs

Bach Jr., Julian. *America's Germany: An Account of the Occupation.* New York: Random House, 1946.
Berlin Document Center. "Who Was a Nazi? Facts about the Membership Procedure of the Nazi Party." Berlin: 7771 Document Center, OMGUS, 1947.
Boveri, Margaret. "Hollerith-Maschinen oder: Der Weg zum Fragebogen." In *Amerikafibel für erwachsene Deutsche*, edited by Margret Boveri, Heike B. Görtemaker, and Theodor Heuss, 41–61. Berlin: Landtverlag, 1946.
Buchwitz, Otto. *Brüder, in eins nun die Hände.* Berlin: Dietz, 1956.
Clay, Lucius. *Decision in Germany.* Garden City, NY: Doubleday, 1950.
Coles, Harry Lewis, and Albert Katz Weinberg, eds. *Civil Affairs: Soldiers Become Governors*, United States Army in WWII Series. Washington, DC: United States Army Center of Military History, 1964.
Control Commission for Germany (British Element). "I.A. and C. Division, Public Safety Branch. Technical Instructions Nos. 1 to 28." August 5, 1946.
Counter Intelligence Corps. "Counter Intelligence Corps History and Mission in World War II." Baltimore, MD: Counter Intelligence Corps School, 1951.
Dagerman, Stig. *German Autumn*, 2nd ed., translated by Robin Fulton Macpherson. Minneapolis: University of Minnesota Press, 2011.
Davidson, David. *The Steeper Cliff.* New York: Random House, 1947.
Diem, Hermann. *Kirche und Entnazifizierung: Denkschrift der Kirchlich-theologischen Sozietät in Württemberg.* Stuttgart: W. Kohlhammer, 1946.
Dombois, Hans. *Politische Gerichtsbarkeit: der Irrweg der Entnazifizierung und die Frage des Verfassungsschutzes.* Gütersloh: Kirche und Mann, 1950.
Donnison, Frank Siegfried Vernon. *Civil Affairs and Military Government North-West Europe 1944–1946.* London: His Majesty's Stationery Office, 1966.
Engler, Robert. "The Individual Soldier and the Occupation." *Annals of the American Academy of Political and Social Science* 267 (January 1950): 77–86.
Eyck, Frank. *A Historians Pilgrimage: Memoirs and Reflections.* Calgary: Detselig, 2009.

Friedlander, Henry, and Sybil Milton, eds. *Archives of the Holocaust, Vol. 11: Berlin Document Center, Part I*. New York: Garland Publishing, 1992.
Friedman, Wolfgang. *The Allied Military Government in Germany*. London: Stevens & Sons, 1947.
Friedrich, Carl J., ed. *American Experiences in Military Government in World War II*. New York: Rinehart, 1948.
Gallup, George, and Claude Robinson. "American Institute for Public Opinion Surveys, 1935–38." *Public Opinion Quarterly* 2, no. 3 (July 1938): 373–98.
Gaskill, Gordon, ed. "Leaves from the Diary of a Military Commander." *American Magazine* (1947): 32–33, 108–11.
Gollancz, Victor. *In Darkest Germany*. London: Victor Gollancz, 1947.
Griffith, William E. "The Denazification Program in the United States Zone of Germany." PhD diss., Harvard University, 1950.
"Denazification in the United States Zone of Germany." *Annals of the American Academy of Political and Social Science* 267, no. 1 (January 1950): 68–76.
Gritschneder, Otto. *Dead End "Denazification."* Munich: Dr. Otto Gritschneder, 1948.
Harris, Charles Reginald Schiller. *Allied Military Administration of Italy, 1943–1945*. London: H. M. Stationery Office, 1957.
Harris, Joseph P. "Selection and Training of Civil Affairs Officers." *American Political Science Review* 38, no. 2 (April 1944): 694–706.
Heberle, Rudolf. Review of *Der Fragebogen* by Ernst von Salomon. *Social Forces* 31, no. 3 (March 1953): 286–87.
Herz, John. "The Fiasco of Denazification in Germany." *Political Science Quarterly* 63, no. 4 (December 1948): 569–94.
Hill, Russell. *Struggle for Germany*. New York: Harper, 1947.
Holborn, Hajo. *American Military Government: Its Organization and Policies*. Washington, DC: Infantry Journal Press, 1947.
Horkheimer, Max, and Theodor W. Adorno. *Dialektik der Aufklärung*. Amsterdam: Querido, 1947.
House of Commons. *Parliamentary Debates (Hansard)*. 5th Series, Vol. 430. London, 1946.
Hunt, Irwin L. "American Military Government of Occupied Germany, 1918–1920: Report of the Officer in Charge of Civil Affairs Third Army and American Forces in Germany," March 4, 1920. Washington DC: U.S. Government Printing Office, 1943.
Hurwitz, Harold J. "Military Government in Germany: Press Reorientation." Karlsruhe: Historical Division, European Command, 1950.
Hyneman, Charles S. "The Army's Civil Affairs Training Program." *The American Political Science Review* 38, no. 2 (April 1944): 342–53.
Jaspers, Karl. *Die Schuldfrage*. Heidelberg: Lambert Schneider, 1946.
Kahn, Arthur D. *Betrayal: Our Occupation of German*. New York: Beacon, 1950.
Kesaris, Paul, ed. *A Guide to O.S.S./State Department Intelligence and Research Reports – Germany and Its Occupied Territories during World War II*. Washington, DC: University Publications of America, 1977.

Kesaris, Paul, ed. *A Guide to O.S.S./State Department Intelligence and Research Reports: Japan and Its Occupied Territories during World War II.* Washington, DC: University Publications of America, 1977.

Lange, Irmgard. *Entnazifizierung in Nordrhein-Westfalen: Richtlinien Anweisungen, Organisation.* Siegburg: Respublica-Verlag, 1976.

Lingg, Anton. *Die Verwaltung der Nationalsozialistischen deutschen Arbeiterpartei.* Munich: Zentralverlag der NSDAP. Munich: Franz Eher, 1941.

Loachner, Louis P. "'The Idiocy of Our De-Nazification Policy.'" *Reader's Digest* (June 1948): 130–36.

Longmire, Robert A., and Kenneth C. Walker. "Herald of a Noisy World – Interpreting the News of All Nations, the Research and Analysis Department of the Foreign and Commonwealth Office: A History." *Foreign Policy Document Series No. 263.* London: Foreign and Commonwealth Office, 1995.

M.Z. "The British Zone in Germany." *The World Today* 2, no. 12 (December 1946): 567–80.

Marcus, Alan. *Straw to Make Brick.* Boston, MA: Atlantic Little Brown, 1948.

Mason, John Brown. "Lessons of Wartime Military Government Training." *The Annals of the American Academy of Political and Social Science* 267, no. 1 (January 1950): 183–92.

Matthews, Noel. "Memorandum on the Policy and Practice of Denazification in the British Zone - Conference on Some Aspects of the German Problem. Vol. 2, Part 2." Chatham House, Cultural Section, March 1948.

Merritt, Anna J., and Richard L. Merritt. *Public Opinion in Occupied Germany: The OMGUS Surveys, 1945–1949.* Urbana: University of Illinois Press, 1970.

Merzyn, Friedrich, ed. *Kundgebungen: Worte und Erklärungen der Evangelischen Kirche in Deutschland, 1945–1959.* Hannover: Verlag des Amtsblattes der Evangelischen Kirche in Deutschland, 1959.

Morton, Frederic. "One Prussian's Story." Review of *Fragebogen (The Questionnaire). The Saturday Review* (January 1, 1955): 54.

Müller-Meiningen, Ernst. *Die Parteigenossen.* Munich: Kurt Desch, 1946.

Napoli, Joseph F. "Denazification from an American's Viewpoint." *Annals of the American Academy of Political and Social Science* 264 (July 1949): 115–23.

Neumann, Franz L., Herbert Marcuse, and Otto Kirchheimer. *Secret Reports on Nazi Germany: The Frankfurt School Contribution to the War Effort.* Edited by Raffaele Laudani. Princeton, NJ: Princeton University Press, 2013.

Office of Military Government for Bavaria, Special Branch. "German Denazification Law and Implementation with American Directives Included." June 15, 1946.

Office of Military Government for Germany, Civil Administration Division. *Denazification, Cumulative Review. Report, 1 April 1947–30 April 1948.* Adjutant General, OMGUS, 1948.

Office of the U.S. High Commissioner for Germany. *Germany's Parliament in Action: The September 1949 Debate on the Government's Statement of Policy.* Washington, DC: Office of Political Affairs, 1950.

Padover, Saul K. *Experiment in Germany: The Story of an American Intelligence Office*. New York: Duell, Sloan and Pearce, 1946.
Passos, John Dos. *Das Land des Fragebogens: 1945: Reportagen aus dem Besiegten Deutschland*. Frankfurt: Rowohlt, 1945.
Tour of Duty. Boston: Houghton Mifflin, 1946.
Pick, Robert. "En Route to De-Nazification." Review of *Furlough*, by Franz Hoellering. *Saturday Review of Literature* (August 19, 1944): 10.
Plischke, Elmer. "Denazifying the Reich." *The Review of Politics* 9, no. 2 (August 1947): 153–72.
Pogue, Forrest C. *The Supreme Command*. Washington, DC: Office of the Chief of Military History, Department of the Army, 1954.
Pollock, James, and James H. Meisel. *Germany under Occupation: Illustrative Materials and Documents*. Ann Arbor, MI: George Wahr, 1949.
Popkin, Zelda. *Small Victory*. Bridgewater, NJ: Replica Books, 1947.
Posener, Julius. *In Deutschland: 1945 bis 1946*. Berlin: Siedler, 2001.
Reichsorganisationsleiter der NSDAP, ed. *Partei-Statistik der NSDAP 1935*. Munich: Zentralverlag der NSDAP, 1935.
Reid, A. K. "Canadian Participation in Civil Affairs – Military Government. Part I: Background and Beginnings." CMHQ Report No. 140 (July 10, 1945).
Rey, W. H. Review of *Der Fragebogen* by Ernst von Salomon. *Books Abroad* 27, no. 1 (1953): 47–48.
Rohowsky, Margarete. *Gleichschaltung und Ausschaltung: Beiträge zum Problem der Entnazifizierung*. Berlin: Der Neue Geist, 1947.
Ruhm von Oppen, Beate. *Documents on Germany under Occupation 1945–1954*. London: Oxford University Press, 1955.
Salinger, Margaret. *Dream Catcher: A Memoir*. New York: Washington Square Press, 2000.
Salomon, Ernst von. *The Answers of Ernst Von Salomon*. Translated by Constantine Fitzgibbon. London: Putnam, 1954.
Der Fragebogen. Reinbeck: Rowohlt, 1951.
Fragebogen (The Questionnaire). Translated by Constantine Fitzgibbon. New York: Doubleday, 1955.
Schullze, Erich. *Gesetz zur Befreiung von Nationalsozialismus und Militarismus vom 5. März 1946*. Munich: Biederstein, 1947.
Schultz, Johannes. *Abschluss der Entnazifizierung und Durchführung des Gesetzes zu Art. 131 GG in Niedersachsen. Bd. 1*. Göttingen: Schwartz, 1952.
Setzler, Lorraine. "Nursing and Nursing Education in Germany." *The American Journal of Nursing* 45, no. 12 (December 1945): 993–95.
Starr, Joseph R. *Denazification, Occupation and Control of Germany, March–July 1945*. Salisbury, NC: Documentary Publications, 1977.
Supreme Headquarters, Allied Expeditionary Force. *Handbook for Military Government in Germany: Prior to Defeat or Surrender*. December 1944.
Military Government Gazette Germany / Sixth Army Group (Twelfth Army Group and 21st Army Group) Area of Control. 1944.
Public Safety Manual of Procedures, Military Government of Germany. First Edition, September 1944. Second Edition, February 1945.

The American Jewish Committee. "Statistics on Jews." *Thirty-Ninth Annual Report* (1946).
United States Army. "Troop I&E Bulletin: Denazification." 3, no. 15 (April 11, 1948).
United States Department of Labor. "Establishment of Foreign Economic Administration." *Monthly Labor Review* 57 (November 1943): 936–37.
United States Department of State. *A Decade of American Foreign Policy: Basic Documents, 1941–49*. Washington, DC: U.S. Government Printing Office, 1950.
Foreign Relations of the United States: Conferences at Malta and Yalta, 1945. Washington, DC: U.S. Government Printing Office, 1945.
Foreign Relations of the United States: Diplomatic Papers, 1945, European Advisory Committee, Austria and Germany, vol. III. Washington, DC: U.S. Government Printing Office, 1968.
Vansittart, Robert Gilbert. *Black Record: Germans Past and Present*. London: H. Hamilton, 1941.
Vollnhals, Clements. *Entnazifizierung: Politische Säuberung und Rehabilitierung in den vier Besatzungszonen 1945–1949*. Munich: Deutscher Taschenbuch Verlag, 1991.
Entnazifizierung und Selbstreinigung im Urteil der evangelischen Kirche: Dokumente und Reflexionen, 1945–1949. Munich: Kaiser, 1989.
Weber, Hermann. *Das Gesetz zur Politischen Säuberung vom 5. März 1946*. Karlsruhe: Badenia, 1947.
Zink, Harold. *American Military Government in Germany*. New York: Macmillan, 1947.
The United States in Germany, 1944–1955. New York: Van Nostrand, 1957.

Secondary Sources

Abel, Theodore F. *Why Hitler Came into Power*. Cambridge, MA: Harvard University Press, 1986.
Adams, Bianka J. "Between Idealism and Pragmatism: The Administration and Denazification of Bremen, United States Enclave in the Context of Anglo-American Governments in the Second World War." PhD diss., The Catholic University of America, 1998.
From Crusade to Hazard: The Denazification of Bremen Germany. Lanham, MD: Scarecrow Press, 2009.
Alsen, Eberhard. *J.D. Salinger and the Nazis*. Madison: University of Wisconsin Press, 2018.
Andrew, Christopher. "F.H. Hinsley and the Cambridge Moles: Two Patterns of Intelligence Recruitment." In *Diplomacy and Intelligence: Essays in Honour of F.H. Hinsley*, edited by Richard Langhorne, 22–40. Cambridge: Cambridge University Press, 1985.
Assmann, Aleida. *Der lange Schatten der Vergangenheit. Erinnerungskultur und Geschichtspolitik*. Munich: Beck, 2006.
Backhouse, Roger, and Philippe Fontaine, eds. *The History of the Modern Social Sciences*. Cambridge: Cambridge University Press, 2010.

Baerwald, Hans H. *The Purge of Japanese Leaders under the Occupation.* Berkeley: University of California Press, 1959.
Balfour, Michael, and John Mair. *Four Power Control in Germany and Austria, 1945–1946.* London: Oxford University Press, 1956.
Bankier, David, and Dan Michman. *Holocaust Historiography in Context: Emergence, Challenges, Polemics and Achievements.* New York: Berghahn Books, 2009.
Barnes, Trevor J. "Geographical Intelligence: American Geographers and Research and Analysis in the Office of Strategic Services 1941–1945." *Journal of Historical Geography* 32, no. 1 (2006): 149–68.
Battini, Michele. *The Missing Italian Nuremberg: Cultural Amnesia and Postwar Politics.* New York: Palgrave Macmillan, 2007.
  Peccati di memoria. La mancata Norimberga italiana. Rome: Laterza, 2003.
Baumeister, Roy F., and Leonard S. Newman. "How Stories Make Sense of Personal Experiences: Motives that Shape Autobiographical Narratives." *Personality and Social Psychology Bulletin* 20, no. 6 (1994): 676–90.
Beattie, Andrew H. *Allied Internment Camps in Occupied Germany: Extrajudicial Detention in the Name of Denazification, 1945–1950.* Cambridge: Cambridge University Press, 2020.
Beniger, James R. *The Control Revolution: Technological and Economic Origins of the Information Society.* Cambridge, MA: Harvard University Press, 1986.
Berman, Ilan, and J. Michael Waller, eds. *Dismantling Tyranny: Transitioning Between Totalitarian Regimes.* Lanham, MD: Rowman & Littlefield, 2015.
Bessel, Richard. *Germany 1945: From War to Peace.* New York: HarperCollins, 2009.
  Nazism and War. New York: Weidenfeld & Nicolson, 2004.
Bessel, Richard, and Dirk Schumann, eds. *Life after Death: Approaches to a Cultural and Social History of Europe during the 1940s and 1950s.* Cambridge: Cambridge University Press, 2003.
Bessière, Céline et al. "L'enquête par questionnaire." *Genèses* 29 (December 1997): 99–122.
Biddiscombe, Perry. *The Denazification of Germany: A History 1945–1950.* Stroud, Gloucestershire: Tempus, 2007.
Biess, Frank. *Homecomings: Returning POWs and the Legacies of Defeat in Postwar Germany.* Princeton, NJ: Princeton University Press, 2006.
Biess, Frank, and Robert Moeller. *Histories of the Aftermath: The Legacies of the Second World War in Europe.* New York: Berghahn Books, 2010.
  et al. "Forum: History of Emotions." *German History* 28, no. 1 (2010): 67–80.
Blessing, Benita. *The Antifascist Classroom: Denazification in Soviet-Occupied Germany, 1945–1949.* New York: Palgrave Macmillan, 2006.
Bloxham, Donald. "The Genocidal Past in Western Germany and the Experience of Occupation, 1945–6." *European History Quarterly* 34, no. 3 (2004): 305–35.
Blum, Matthias, and Alan de Bromhead. "Rise and Fall in the Third Reich: Social Advancement and Nazi Membership." *European Economic Review* 120 (November 2019): 1–40.

Blumer, Martin, Kevin Bales, and Kathryn Kish Sklar, eds. *The Social Survey in Historical Perspective, 1880–1940*. Cambridge: Cambridge University Press, 1991.

Boberach, Heinz et al. *Richterbriefe: Dokumente zur Beeinflussung der deutschen Rechtsprechung, 1942–1944*. Boppard am Rhein: H. Boldt, 1975.

Boehling, Rebecca L. "Sociopolitical Democratization and Economic Recovery: The Development of German Self-Government under U. S. Military Occupation: Frankfurt, Munich and Stuttgart, 1945–1949." PhD diss., University of Wisconsin-Madison, 1990.

Bohman, Eric James. "Rehearsals for Victory: The War Department and the Planning and Direction of Civil Affairs, 1940–1943." PhD diss., Yale University, 1984.

Bopp, William J. "In Quest of a Police Profession: A Biography of Orlando W. Wilson." PhD diss., Florida Atlantic University, 1975.

Borgstedt, Angela. "Der Fragebogen. Zur Wahrnehmung eines Symbols politischer Säuberung nach 1945." *Der Bürger im Staat* 56 (2006): 166–71.

Botzenhart-Viehe, Verena. "The German Reaction to the American Occupation, 1944–1947." PhD diss., University of California, Santa Barbara, 1980.

Bower, Tom. *Blind Eye to Murder: Britain, America and the Purging of Nazi Germany – A Pledge Betrayed*. London: Andre Deutsch, 1981.

The Pledge Betrayed: America and Britain and the Denazification of Postwar Germany. Garden City, NY: Doubleday, 1982.

Braasch-Schwersmann, Ursula et al. *Hessischer Städteatlas, Bd. 30*. Dieburg: Philipp Schmidt, 2016.

Brain, Robert Michael. "The Ontology of the Questionnaire: Max Weber on Measurement and Mass Investigation." *Studies in the History and Philosophy of Science* 32, no. 4 (2001): 647–84.

Broadberry, Stephen, and Carsten Burhop. "Real Wages and Labor Productivity in Britain and Germany, 1871–1938: A Unified Approach to the International Comparison of Living Standards." *The Journal of Economic History* 70, no. 2 (June 2010): 400–27.

Brochhagen, Ulrich. *Nach Nürnberg: Vergangenheitsbewältigung und Westintegration in der Ära Adenauer*. Hamburg: Junius, 1994.

Brockmeier, Jens, and Donal Carbaugh, eds. *Narrative and Identity Studies in Autobiography, Self and Culture*. Philadelphia: John Benjamins, 2001.

Brogi, Alessandro. *A Question of Self-Esteem the United States and the Cold War Choices in France and Italy, 1944–1958*. Westport, CT: Praeger, 2002.

Broszat, Martin. *German National Socialism, 1919–1945*. Translated by Kurt Rosenbaum and Inge Böhm. Santa Barbara: Clio Press, 1966.

"Politische Denunziationen in der NS-Zeit. Aus Forschungserfahrungen im Staatsarchiv München." *Archivalische Zeitschrift* 73 (1977): 221–38.

Brückweh, Kerstin et al., eds. *Engineering Society: the Role of the Human and Social Sciences in Modern Societies, 1880–1980*. Basingstoke, Hampshire: Palgrave Macmillan, 2012.

Brustein, William. *The Logic of Evil: the Social Origins of the Nazi Party, 1925–1933*. New Haven, CT: Yale University Press, 1996.

Buchanan, Andrew. "'Good Morning, Pupil!' American Representations of Italianness and the Occupation of Italy, 1943–1945." *Journal of Contemporary History* 43, no. 2 (2008): 217–40.
Bullinger, Ruth Elisabeth. *Belastet oder entlastet? Dachauer Frauen im Entnazifizierungsverfahren.* Munich: Utz, 2013.
Bulmer, Martin, Kevin Bales, and Kathryn Kish Sklar, eds. *The Social Survey in Historical Perspective, 1880–1940.* Cambridge: Cambridge University Press, 2011.
Campion, Corey J. "Negotiating Difference: French and American Cultural Occupation Policies and German Expectations, 1945–1949." PhD diss., Georgetown University, 2010.
Canosa, Romano. *Storia dell'epurazione in Italia.* Milan: Baldini e Castoldi, 1999.
Capshew, James H. *Psychologists on the March: Science, Practice, and Professional Identity in America, 1929–1969.* Cambridge: Cambridge University Press, 1999.
Carruthers, Susan L. *The Good Occupation: American Soldiers and the Hazards of Peace.* Cambridge, MA: Harvard University Press, 2016.
Chalou, George C., ed. *The Secrets War: The Office of Strategic Services in World War II.* Washington, DC: National Archives and Records Administration, 1992.
Chauffour, Sébastien et al., eds. *La France et la dénazification de l'Allemagne après 1945.* Brussels: Peter Lang, 2019.
Childers, Thomas. *The Nazi Voter: The Social Foundations of Fascism in Germany, 1919–1933.* Chapel Hill: University of North Carolina Press, 1983.
Clare. George. *Berlin Days, 1946–1947.* London: Macmillan, 1989.
Cointet, Jean-Paul. *Expier Vichy: l'Épuration en France, 1943–1958.* Paris: Perrin, 2008.
Connelly, John. *Captive University: The Sovietization of East German, Czech and Polish Higher Education, 1945–1956.* Chapel Hill: University of North Carolina Press, 2000.
Converse, Jean M. *Survey Research in the United States: Roots and Emergence, 1890–1960.* Berkeley: University of California Press, 1987.
Creuzberger, Stefan. *Die sowjetische Besatzungsmacht und das politische System der SBZ.* Weimar: Böhlau, 1996.
Cross, Gary S. *Worktowners at Blackpool: Mass-Observation and Popular Leisure in the 1930s.* London: Routledge, 1990.
Cuomo, Glenn R. "The NSDAP's Enduring Shadow: Putting in Perspective the Recent Outing of Brown Octogenarians." *German Studies Review* 35, no. 2 (2012): 265–88.
Dack, Mikkel. "A Comparative Study of French Denazification: Instruments and Procedures in Allied Occupied Germany." In *La France et la dénazification de l'Allemagne après 1945*, edited by Sébastien Chauffour et al., 109–127. Brussels: Peter Lang, 2019.
"Die Entnazifizierung einer „Tätergesellschaft": Bestrafung und Reintegration im besetzten Deutschland und Österreich." In *NS-Täterinnen und –Täter in der Nachkriegszeit*, 59–72. Wien: KZ-Gedenkstätte Mauthausen, 2017.

"Retreating into Trauma: The Fragebogen, Denazification, and Victimhood in Postwar Germany." In *Traumatic Memories of the Second World War and After*, edited by Peter Leese and Jason Crouthamel, 143–70. London: Palgrave Macmillan, 2016.

"Tailoring Truth: Political Amnesia, Memory Construction, and Whitewashing the Nazi Past from Below." *German Politics and Society* 39, no. 1 (Spring 2021): 15–36.

Dastrup, Boyd. *Crusade in Nuremberg: Military Occupation, 1945–1949*. Westport, CT: Greenwood Press, 1985.

De Rivera, Joseph, and Theodore R. Sarbin, eds. *Believed-in Imaginings: The Narrative Construction of Reality*. Washington, DC: American Psychological Association, 1998.

Desch, Michael. *Cult of the Irrelevant: The Waning Influence of Social Science on National Security*. Princeton, NJ: Princeton University Press, 2019.

Detzen, Dominic, and Sebastian Hoffmann. "Stigma Management and Justifications of the Self in Denazification Accounts." *Accounting, Auditing & Accountability Journal* 31, no. 1 (2018): 141–65.

Dolan, Kristen. "Isolating Nazism: Civilian Internment in American Occupied Germany, 1944–1950." PhD diss., University of North Carolina at Chapel Hill, 2013.

Domenico, Roy Palmer. *Italian Fascists on Trial, 1943–1948*. Chapel Hill: University of North Carolina Press, 1991.

Douglas, Ray M. *Orderly and Humane: The Expulsion of the Germans after the Second World War*. New Haven, CT: Yale University Press, 2012.

Drechsel, Wiltrud. *"Denazification": zur Entnazifizierung in Bremen*. Bremen: Edition Temmen, 1992.

Dudman, Helga. *Letters Home to San Francisco from Occupied Germany, 1945–1946*. Jerusalem: Carta, 2007.

Dussault, Éric. *La dénazification de l'Autriche par la France: la politique culturelle de la France dans sa zone d'occupation, 1945–1955*. Quebec City: Presses de l'Université Laval, 2005.

Düwell, Kurt, and Michael Matheus, eds. *Kriegsende und Neubeginn: Westdeutschland und Luxemburg zwischen 1944 und 1947*. Stuttgart: Steiner, 1997.

Ebsworth, Raymond. *Restoring Democracy in Germany: The British Contribution*. London: Stevens Praeger, 1961.

Eigler, Friederike. *Gedächtnis und Geschichte in Generationenromanen seit der Wende*. Berlin: Erich Schmidt, 2005.

Eisenberg, Carolyn. *Drawing the Line: The American Decision to Divide Germany, 1944–1949*. Cambridge: Cambridge University Press, 1996.

Elster, Jon. *Retribution and Reparation in the Transition to Democracy*. Cambridge: Cambridge University Press, 2006.

Erikson, Kai T. *Everything in Its Path: Destruction of Community in the Buffalo Creek Flood*. New York: Simon and Schuster, 1971.

Ericksen, Robert P. *Theologians under Hitler*. New Haven, CT: Yale University Press, 1985.

Erlichman, Camilo, and Christopher Knowles, eds. *Transforming Occupation in the Western Zones of Germany: Politics, Everyday Life and Social Interactions, 1945–55.* London: Bloomsbury, 2018.

Ettle, Elmar. *Die Entnazifizierung in Eichstätt: Probleme der politischen Säuberung nach 1945.* Frankfurt: Lang, 1985.

Falter, Jürgen W., Thomas Lindenberger, and Siegfried Schumann. *Wahlen und Abstimmungen in der Weimarer Republik: Materialien zum Wahlverhalten, 1919–1933.* Munich: Beck, 1986.

Ferguson, Niall. *Kissinger, Vol. 1, 1923–1968: The Idealist.* New York: Penguin, 2015.

Fervert, Ute. *Emotions in History: Lost and Found.* Budapest: Central European University Press, 2011.

Fiedler, Anke. "Defying Memory? Tracing the Power of Hegemonic Memory in Everyday Discourse Using the Example of National Socialism in Germany." *International Journal of Communication* 15 (2021): 3379–96.

Fireman, Gary, Ted McVay, and Owen Flanagan. *Narrative and Consciousness Literature, Psychology, and the Brain.* Oxford: Oxford University Press, 2003.

Fisher, Donald. "The Role of Philanthropic Foundations in the Reproduction and Production of Hegemony: Rockefeller Foundations and the Social Sciences." *Sociology* 17, no. 2 (May 1983): 206–33.

Fitzgibbon, Constantine. *Denazification.* New York: Norton, 1969.

Fivush, Robyn, and Catherine A. Haden, eds. *Autobiographical Memory and the Construction of a Narrative Self: Developmental and Cultural Perspectives.* Mahwah, NJ: Erlbaum, 2003.

Fleischer, Jürg. *Geschichte, Anlage und Durchführung der Fragebogen-Erhebungen von Georg Wenkers 40 Sätzen. Dokumentation, Entdeckungen und Neubewertungen.* Hildesheim: Georg Olms, 2017.

Franck, Dieter. *Jahre unseres Lebens 1945–1949.* Reinbek bei Hamburg: Rowohlt, 1980.

Frankel, Martin R., and Lester R. Frankel. "Fifty Years of Survey Sampling in the United States." *The Public Opinion Quarterly* 51, no. 2 (1987): 127–38.

Freeman, Mark Philip. *Hindsight: The Promise and Peril of Looking Backward.* Oxford: Oxford University Press, 2010.

Frei, Norbert. *Adenauer's Germany and the Nazi Past: The Politics of Amnesty and Integration.* New York: Columbia University Press, 2002.

ed. *Transnationale Vergangenheitspolitik: der Umgang mit deutschen Kriegsverbrechern in Europa nach dem Zweiten Weltkrieg.* Göttingen: Wallstein, 2006.

Vergangenheitspolitik: die Anfänge der Bundesrepublik und die NS-Vergangenheit. Munich: Beck, 1996.

Fritzsche, Peter. *Germans into Nazis.* Cambridge, MA: Harvard University Press, 1998.

Fry, Helen. *Denazification: Britain's Enemy Aliens, Nazi War Criminals and the Reconstruction of Post-War Europe.* Stroud, Gloucestershire: The History Press, 2010.

Fulbrook, Mary. *German National Identity after the Holocaust.* Cambridge: Polity Press, 2002.

Fulbrook, Mary, and Ulinka Rublack. "In Relation: The 'Social Self' and Ego-Documents." *German History* 28, no. 3 (September 2010): 263–72.
Fürstenau, Justus. *Entnazifizierung. ein Kapitel deutscher Nachkriegspolitik.* Neuwied: Luchterhand, 1969.
Galimi, Valeria. "Circulation of Models of Épuration after the Second World War: From France to Italy." In *Dealing with Wars and Dictatorships: Legal Concepts and Categories in Action*, edited by Liora Israël and Guillaume Mouralis, 197–208. The Hague: TMC Asser, 2014.
Gebhardt, Miriam. *Als die Soldaten kamen. Die Vergewaltigung deutscher Frauen am Ende des Zweiten Weltkriegs.* Munich: DVA, 2015.
Gehrz, Christopher Allan. "The Reeducation of Germany and the Education of the West, 1945–1949." PhD diss., Yale University, 2002.
Gellately, Robert. "Denunciations in Twentieth-Century Germany: Aspects of Self-policing in the Third Reich and the German Democratic Republic." *The Journal of Modern History* 68, no. 4 (December 1996): 931–67.
Gerhardt, Uta, and Gösta Gantner. "Ritualprozeß Entnazifizierung: eine These zur gesellschaftlichen Transformation der Nachkriegszeit." *Forum Ritualdynamik* 7 (July 2004): 1–80.
Gimbel, John. *A German Community under American Occupation: Marburg, 1945–52.* Stanford: Stanford University Press, 1961.
Goedde, Petra. *GIs and Germans: Culture, Gender, and Foreign Relations, 1945–1949.* New Haven, CT: Yale University Press, 2003.
Goffman, Erving. *The Presentation of Self in Everyday Life.* Garden City, NY: Doubleday, 1959.
Goltermann, Svenja. *Die Gesellschaft der Überlebenden: Deutsche Kriegsheimkehrer und ihre Gewalterfahrungen im Zweiten Weltkrieg.* Munich: Pantheon, 2009.
Gordon, Hugh. "Cheers and Tears: Relations between Canadian Soldiers and German Civilians." PhD diss., University of Victoria, 2010.
Görtemaker, Heike B. *Ein deutsches Leben: Die Geschichte der Margret Boveri 1900–1975.* Munich: C.H. Beck, 2005.
Gramer, Regina Ursula. "The Socialist Revolutionary Dilemma in Emigration: Franz L. Neumann's Passage Toward and Through the Office of Strategic Services." MA thesis, University of Arizona, 1989.
Greiner, Bettina. *Verdrängter Terror: Geschichte und Wahrnehmung sowjetischer Speziallager in Deutschland.* Hamburg: Hamburger Edition, 2010.
Grimm, Friedrich. *Nun aber Schluss mit Rache und Vergeltung!: eine ernste Betrachtung, 10 Jahre nach d. Zusammenbruch.* Göttingen: Göttinger Verlagsanstalt, 1955.
Grohnert, Reinhard. *Die Entnazifizierung in Baden, 1945–1949: Konzeptionen und Praxis der "Epuration" am Beispiel eines Landes der französischen Besatzungszone.* Stuttgart: Kohlhammer, 1991.
Grossmann, Atina. "Feminist Debates about Women and National Socialism." *Gender & History* 3, no. 3 (1991): 350–58.
Jews, Germans, and Allies: Close Encounters in Occupied Germany. Princeton, NJ: Princeton University Press, 2007.
Gudehus, Christian. *Dem Gedächtnis zuhören: Erzählungen über NS-Verbrechen und ihre Repräsentation in deutschen Gedenkstätten.* Essen: Klartext, 2006.

Guglielmo, Mark. "The Contribution of Economists to Military Intelligence during World War II." *The Journal of Economic History* 68, no. 1 (2008): 109–50.
Hamdan, Amal. "Collective Guilt, Selective Exclusion: Iraq's Candidate Screening Process." *International Foundation for Electoral Systems* (March 2020): 1–31.
Hamilton, Richard. *Who Voted for Hitler?* Princeton, NJ: Princeton University Press, 1982.
Hageman, Karen, and Sonya Michel, eds. *Gender and the Long Postwar: The United States and the Two Germanys, 1945–1989*. Washington, DC: Woodrow Wilson Center Press, 2014.
Hayse, Michael. *Recasting West German Elites: Higher Civil Servants, Business Leaders, and Physicians in Hessen, 1945–1955*. New York: Berghahn, 2003.
Hearst, Joseph Albert. "The Evolution of Allied Military Government Policy in Italy." PhD diss., Columbia University, 1960.
Heinemann, Elizabeth. *What Difference Does a Husband Make? Women and Marital Status in Nazi and Postwar Germany*. Berkeley: University of California Press, 1999.
Henke, Klaus-Dietmar. *Die amerikanische Besetzung Deutschlands*. Munich: R. Oldenbourg, 1995.
Politik der Widersprüche: zur Charakteristik der französischen Militärregierung in Deutschland nach dem Zweiten Weltkrieg. Stuttgart: Deutsche Verlags-Anstalt, 1982.
Politische Säuberung unter französischer Besatzung: die Entnazifizierung in Württemberg-Hohenzollern. Stuttgart: Deutsche Verlags-Anstalt, 1981.
Hepper, Erica G. et al. "Pancultural Nostalgia: Prototypical Conceptions Across Cultures." *Emotions* 14, no. 4 (August 2014): 733–47.
Herf, Jeffrey. *Divided Memory: The Nazi Past in the Two Germanys*. Cambridge, MA: Harvard University Press, 1997.
Herman, Judith. *Trauma and Recovery: The Aftermath of Violence – From Domestic Abuse to Political Terror*. New York: Basic Books, 1992.
Hermand, Jost. *Ernst von Salomon. Wandlungen eines Nationalrevolutionärs*. Leipzig: Hirzel, 2002.
Hett, Benjamin Carter. "The Story Is about Something Fundamental: Nazi Criminals, History, Memory, and the Reichstag Fire." *Central European History* 48, no. 2 (June 2015): 199–224.
Hockenos, Matthew D. *A Church Divided: German Protestants Confront the Nazi Past*. Bloomington, IN: Indiana University Press, 2004.
Hoffmann, Peter. *Widerstand, Staatsstreich Attentat: der Kampf der Opposition gegen Hitler*. Munich: Piper, 1970.
Hoffmann, Walther G. *Das Wachstum der deutschen Wirtschaft seit der Mitte des 19. Jahrhunderts*. Berlin: Springer, 1965.
Höhn, Maria. *GIs and Fräuleins: The German-American Encounter in 1950s West Germany*. Chapel Hill: University of North Carolina Press, 2002.
Horkheimer, Max. *Critical Theory: Selected Essays*. Translated by Matthew J. O'Connell. New York: Herder and Herder, 1972.

Horowitz, Joseph. *Artists in Exile: How Refugees from Twentieth-Century War and Revolution Transformed the American Performing Arts.* New York: HarperCollins, 2008.

Hydén, Lars-Christer, and Jens Brockmeier. *Health, Illness and Culture: Broken Narratives.* New York: Routledge, 2008.

Igo, Sarah E. *The Average American: Surveys, Citizens, and the Making of a Mass Public.* Cambridge, MA: Harvard University Press, 2008.

Irvine, William D. *Between Justice and Politics: The Ligue des Droits de L'homme, 1898–1945.* Stanford: Stanford University Press, 2007.

Israël, Liora, and Guillaume Mouralis, eds. *Dealing with Wars and Dictatorships: Legal Concepts and Categories in Action.* The Hague: TMC Asser, 2014.

Jaeger, Harald, and Hermann Rumschöttel. "Das Forschungsprojekt 'Widerstand und Verfolgung in Bayern 1933–1945.'" *Archivalische Zeitschrift* 73, no. 1 (1977): 209–20.

Jähner, Harald. *Aftermath: Life in the Fallout of the Third Reich, 1945–1955.* Translated by Shaun Whiteside. New York: Knopf, 2022.

Jarausch, Konrad. *After Hitler: Recivilizing Germans, 1945–1995.* Oxford: Oxford University Press, 2006.

Jeffery, Keith. *MI6: The History of the Secret Intelligence Service, 1909–1949.* London: Bloomsbury, 2010.

Jensen, Olaf. *Geschichte machen: Strukturmerkmale des intergenerationellen Sprechens über die NS-Vergangneheit in deutschen Familien.* Tübingen: Edition Diskord, 2004.

Jerouschek, Günter, Inge Marßolek, and Hedwig Röckelein, eds. *Denunziation: Historische, juristische und psychologische Aspekte.* Tübingen: Edition Diskord, 1997.

Johnson, Eric A. "German Women and Nazi Justice: Their Role in the Process from Denunciation to Death." *Historical Social Research* 20, no. 1 (73) (1995): 33–69.

Jones, Jill. "Eradicating Nazism from the British Zone of Germany: Early Policy and Practice." *German History* 8, no. 2 (June 1990): 145–62.

———. *Preparations for Denazification in the British Zone of Germany.* PhD diss. University of Manchester, 1988.

Judt, Tony. *Postwar: A History of Europe since 1945.* New York: Penguin Press, 2005.

Jürgensen, Kurt. "British Occupation Policy after 1945 and the Problem of Re-educating Germany." *History* 68 (1983): 225–44.

Jurt, Joseph, ed. *Von der Besatzungszeit zur deutsch-französischen Kooperation.* Freiburg: Rombach, 1993.

Justice, Benjamin. "When the Army Got Progressive: The Civil Affairs Training School at Stanford University, 1943–1945." *History of Education Quarterly* 51, no. 3 (August 2011): 330–61.

Kanig, Christian. "Reeducation through Soviet Culture: Soviet Cultural Policy in Occupied Germany, 1945–1949." PhD diss., Indiana University, 2011.

Kater, Michael H. *The Nazi Party: A Social Profile of Members and Leaders, 1919–1945.* Cambridge, MA: Harvard University Press, 1983.

Keltner, Hubert W. "Denazification: Problem and Program, U.S. Zone, 1945–1949." MA thesis, Montana State University, 1954.
Kershaw, Ian. *The Nazi Dictatorship: Problems and Perspectives of Interpretation*, 4th ed. London: Bloomsbury, 2015.
Kettenacker, Lothar, ed. *Ein Volk von Opfern. Die neue Debatte um den Bombenkrieg 1940–1945*. Berlin: Rowohlt, 2003.
Keyserlingk, Robert H. "Arnold Toynbee's Foreign Research and Press Service, 1939–43 and Its Post-War Plans for South-East Europe." *Journal of Contemporary History* 21, no. 4 (October 1986): 539–58.
Klee, Ernst. *Persilscheine und falsche Pässe. wie die Kirchen den Nazis halfen*. Frankfurt: Fischer, 1991.
Klein, Markus Josef. *Ernst von Salomon: Eine politische Biographie mit einer vollständigen Bibliographie*. Limburg: San Casciano, 1994.
Knafla, Louis A. *Policing and War in Europe*. Westport, CT: Greenwood Press, 2002.
Knight, Robert. *Denazification and Integration in the Austrian Province of Carinthia*. Chicago: University of Chicago, 2007.
Koellreutter, Otto. *Das Wesen der Spruchkammern und der durch sie durchgeführten Entnazifizierung: ein Rechtsgutsachten*. Göttingen: Göttinger Verlagsanstalt, 1954.
Kurz, Hans-Otto. "1945: Chaos, Not und Neubeginn." *Mein Heimatland* 8, no. 54 (August 2015): 29–32.
"Der Kreis Hersfeld 1945/1946." *Hersfelder Geschichtsblätter* 7 (2015): 7–77.
"Leben an und mit der Grenze im Kreis Hersfeld-Rotenburg." *Hersfelder Geschichtsblätter* 4 (2010): 1–50.
Kyre, Martin, and Joan Kyre. *Military Occupation and National Security*. Washington, DC: Public Affairs Press, 1968.
Langhorne, Richard, ed. *Diplomacy and Intelligence during the Second World War: Essays in Honour of F.H. Hinsley*. Cambridge: Cambridge University Press, 1985.
Laschitza, Horst. *Kämpferische Demokratie gegen Faschismus*. Berlin: Deutscher Militärverlag, 1969.
Leese, Peter, and Jason Crouthamel, eds. *Traumatic Memories of the Second World War and After*. London: Palgrave Macmillan, 2016.
Leßau, Hanne. *Entnazifizierungsgeschichten. Die Auseinandersetzung mit der eigenen NS-Vergangenheit in der frühen Nachkriegszeit*. Göttingen: Wallstein, 2020.
Leiby, Richard A. "Public Health in Occupied Germany 1945–1949." PhD diss., University of Delaware, 1984.
Lilly, J. Robert. *Taken by Force: Rape and American GIs in Europe during World War II*. Basingstoke, Hampshire: Palgrave Macmillan, 2007.
Link, Fabian. "Cooperation and Competition: Re-establishing the Institute of Social Research and the Emergence of the 'Frankfurt School.'" *NTM Zeitschrift für Geschichte der Wissenschaften, Technik und Medizin* 24, no. 2 (2016): 225–49.
Long, Bronson. *No Easy Occupation: French Control of the German Saar, 1944–1957*. Rochester: Camden House, 2015.
Longerich, Peter. *Die braunen Bataillone: Geschichte der SA*. Munich: Beck, 1989.

Loth, Wilfried, and Bernd-A. Rusinek, eds. *Verwandlungspolitik: NS-Eliten in der westdeutschen Nachkriegsgesellschaft*. Frankfurt: Campus Verlag, 1998.

Lowe, Keith. *Savage Continent: Europe in the Aftermath of World War II*. New York: Picador, 2013.

Lupo, Salvatore. *History of the Mafia*. Translated by Antony Shugaar. New York: Columbia University Press, 2009.

MacDonogh, Giles. *After the Reich: The Brutal History of the Allied Occupation*. New York: Basic Books, 2007.

MacPherson, Nelson. *American Intelligence in War-Time London: The Story of the OSS*. London: Frank Cass Publishers, 2003.

―――. *Kings and Desperate Men: The United States Office of Strategic Services in London and the Anglo-American Relationship, 1941–1946*. Toronto: University of Toronto Press, 1995.

―――. "Reductio Ad Absurdum: The R&A Branch of OSS/London." *International Journal of Intelligence and Counter Intelligence* 15, no. 3 (November 2002): 390–414.

Mann, Anthony. *Comeback: Germany, 1945–1952*. London: Macmillan, 1980.

Markovits, Inga. *Imperfect Justice: An East-West German Diary*. Oxford: Oxford University Press, 1995.

Marquardt-Bigman, Petra. *Amerikanische Geheimdienstanalysen über Deutschland 1942–1949*. Berlin: De Gruyter Oldenbourg, 2015.

Marshall, Barbara. "German Attitudes to British Military Government, 1945–47." *Journal of Contemporary History* 15, no. 4 (October 1980): 655–84.

―――. *The Origins of Post-War German Politics*. London: Croom Helm, 1988.

Masuda, Hiroshi. *MacArthur in Asia: The General and His Staff in the Philippines, Japan, and Korea*. Ithaca, NY: Cornell University Press, 2012.

Mayer-Rieckh, Alexander, and Pablo de Greiff. *Justice as Prevention: Vetting Public Employees in Transitional Societies*. New York: Social Science Research Council, 2007.

Mazower, Mark. *Dark Continent: Europe's Twentieth Century*. London: Allen Lane, 1998.

McAdams, Dan P., Ruthellen Josselson, and Amia Lieblich. *Identity and Story: Creating Self in Narrative*. Washington, DC: American Psychological Association, 2006.

McAdams, James. *Judging the Past in Unified Germany*. Cambridge: Cambridge University Press, 2001.

McIntosh, Elizabeth P. *Sisterhood of Spies: The Women of the OSS*. Annapolis, MD: Naval Institute Press, 1998.

Meehan, Patricia. *A Strange Enemy People: Germans under the British, 1945–1950*. London: Peter Owen, 2001.

Mesner, Maria, and Matthew Paul Berg. *Entnazifizierung zwischen politischem Anspruch, Parteienkonkurrenz und Kaltem Krieg: das Beispiel der SPÖ*. Vienna: Oldenbourg, 2005.

Meyer, Kathrin. *Entnazifizierung von Frauen: die Internierungslager der US-Zone Deutschlands 1945–1952*. Berlin: Metropol, 2004.

Miklaucic, Michael, and Michelle Hughes, ed. *Impunity: Confronting Illicit Power Structures in War and Transition.* Washington, DC: National Defense University, 2016.

Moeller, Robert G. *War Stories: The Search for a Usable Past in the Federal Republic of Germany.* Berkeley: University of California Press, 2001.

Möhler, Rainer. *Entnazifizierung in Rheinland-Pfalz und im Saarland unter Französischer Besatzung von 1945 bis 1952.* Mainz: Hase & Koehler, 1992.

Montgomery, John. *Forced to Be Free: The Artificial Revolution in Germany and Japan.* Chicago: University of Chicago Press, 1957.

Mouton, Michelle. "Missing, Lost, and Displaced Children in Postwar Germany: The Great Struggle to Provide for the War's Youngest Victims." *Central European History* 48 (2015): 53–78.

Mühlberger, Detlef. *Hitler's Followers: Studies in the Sociology of the Nazi Movement.* London: Routledge, 1991.

Mühlenberg, Jutta. *Das SS-Helferinnenkorps: Ausbildung, Einsatz und Entnazifizierung der Weiblichen Angehörigen der Waffen-SS, 1942–1949.* Hamburg: Hamburger Edition, 2010.

Müller, Tim B. *Krieger und Gelehrte: Herbert Marcuse und die Denksysteme im Kalten Krieg.* Hamburg: Hamburger Edition, 2012.

Murray, Gregg R. et al. "Convenient Yet Not a Convenience Sample: Jury Pools as Experimental Subject Pools." *Social Science Research* 42 (2013): 246–53.

Naimark, Norman. *The Russians in Germany: A History of the Soviet Zone of Occupation, 1945–1949.* Cambridge, MA: Belknap Press, 1995.

Nettl, J. P. *The Eastern Zone and Soviet Policy in Germany, 1945–1950.* London: Oxford University Press, 1951.

Neumann, Franz L. *Behemoth: The Structure and Practice of National Socialism, 1933–1944.* New York: Octagon Books, 1963.

The Cultural Migration: The European Scholar in America. Philadelphia: University of Pennsylvania Press, 1953.

Niethammer, Lutz. *Die Mitläuferfabrik: Die Entnazifizierung Am Beispiel Bayerns.* Berlin: Dietz, 1982.

Entnazifizierung in Bayern: Säuberung und Rehabilitierung unter amerikanischer Besatzung. Frankfurt: Fischer, 1972.

Niven, Bill. *Germans as Victims: Remembering the Past in Contemporary Germany.* Basingstoke, Hampshire: Palgrave Macmillan, 2006.

Novick, Peter, Helene Ternois, and Jean Pierre Rioux. *L'epuration francaise, 1944–1949.* Paris: Balland, 1991.

O'Brien, Andrea. "American-German Encounters and U.S. Foreign Policy in Occupied Germany, 1945–1949." PhD diss., University of California, Berkeley, 2012.

Oba, Kentaro et al. "Memory and Reward Systems Coproduce 'Nostalgic' Experiences in the Brain." *Social Cognitive and Affective Neuroscience* 11, no. 7 (July 2016): 1069–77.

Orlow, Dietrich. *A History of Modern Germany: 1871 to Present*, 7th ed. Boston: Pearson, 2011.

Overmans, Rüdiger. *Deutsche militärische Verluste im Zeiten Weltkrieg.* Munich: R. Oldenbourg, 1999.
Parkinson, Anna M. *An Emotional State: The Politics of Emotion in Postwar West German Culture.* Ann Arbor: University of Michigan Press, 2015.
Phillips, David. "War-Time Planning for the 'Re-education' of Germany: Professor E.R. Dodds and the German Universities." *Oxford Review of Education* 12, no. 2 (1986): 195–208.
Port, Andrew I. *Conflict and Stability in the German Democratic Republic.* Cambridge: Cambridge University Press, 2007.
Potter, Pamela M. *Art of Suppression: Confronting the Nazi Past in Histories of the Visual and Preforming Arts.* Berkeley: University of California Press, 2016.
Price, David H. *Anthropological Intelligence: The Deployment and Neglect of American Anthropology in the Second World War.* Durham, NC: Duke University Press, 2008.
Quinney, Kimber Marie. "The United States, Great Britain, and Dismantling Italian Fascism, 1943–1948." PhD diss., University of California, Santa Barbara, 2002.
Quint, Peter. *The Imperfect Union.* Princeton, NJ: Princeton University Press, 1997.
Rausch, Stefanie. "Good Bets, Bad Bets and Dark Horses: Allied Intelligence Officers' Encounters with German Civilians, 1944–1945." *Central European History* 53 (2020): 120–45.
Rees, Jonas H., Michael Papendick, and Andreas Zick. "This Ain't No Place for No Hero: Prevalence and Correlates of Representations of Victims, Helpers, and Perpetrators during the Time of National Socialism in German Families." *Journal of Pacific Rim Psychology* 15 (2021): 1–12.
Reinisch, Jessica. *The Perils of Peace: The Public Health Crisis in Occupied Germany.* Oxford: Oxford University Press, 2013.
Remy, Steven P. *The Heidelberg Myth: The Nazification and Denazification of a German University.* Cambridge, MA: Harvard University Press, 2002.
"The Heidelberg Myth: The Nazification and Denazification of a German University, 1933–1957." PhD diss., Ohio University, 2000.
Reusch, Ulrich. *Deutsches Berufsbeamtentum und britische Besatzung: Planung und Politik 1943–1947.* Stuttgart: Klett-Cotta, 1985.
Roberts, Geoffrey K. "Political Education in Germany." *Parliamentary Affairs* 55, no. 3 (July 2002): 556–68.
Roche, Helen. "Surviving Stunde Null: Narrating the fate of Nazi elite-school pupils during the collapse of the Third Reich." *German History* 33, no. 4 (2015): 570–87.
The Third Reich's Elite Schools: A History of the Napolas. Oxford: Oxford University Press, 2021.
Rösch, Felix. *Émigré Scholars and the Genesis of International Relations: A European Discipline in America?* Basingstoke, Hampshire: Palgrave Macmillan, 2014.
Rosenfeld, Frances. "The Anglo-German Encounter in Occupied Hamburg, 1945–1950." PhD diss., Columbia University, 2006.
Rosenwein, Barbara H. *Emotional Communities in the Early Middle Ages.* Ithaca, NY: Cornell University Press, 2006.

Ross, Dorothy. *The Origins of American Social Science*. Cambridge: Cambridge University Press, 1991.
Ross, Dorothy, and Theodore M. Porter. *The Modern Social Sciences*. Cambridge: Cambridge University Press, 2003.
Rühmkorf, Peter. *Wolfgang Borchert in Selbstzeugnissen und Bilddokumenten*. Reinbek bei Hamburg: Rowohlt, 1962.
Sa'adah, Anne. *Germany's Second Chance: Trust, Justice, and Democratization*. Cambridge, MA: Harvard University Press, 1998.
Sarbin, Theodore R. *Narrative Psychology: The Storied Nature of Human Conduct*. New York: Praeger, 1986.
Scharf, Claus, and Hans-Jürgen Schröder, eds. *Die Deutschlandpolitik Frankreichs und die Französische Zone, 1945–1949*. Wiesbaden: Franz Steiner, 1983.
Scheu, Just. "Der Fragebogen." In *Wir sind so frei: Kabarett in Restdeutschland 1945–1970*, edited by Volker Kühn, 61–62. Weinheim: Quadriga, 1993.
Schildt, Axel. *Medien-Intellektuelle in der Bundesrepublik*. Göttingen: Wallstein, 2020.
Schlemmer, Thomas, and Susanna Schrafstetter, eds. "After Nazism: Relaunching Careers in Germany and Austria." Special issue of *German Yearbook of Contemporary History* 5 (2021).
Schmädeke, Jürgen, and Peter Steinbach, eds. *Der Widerstand gegen den Nationalsozialismus: die deutsche Gesellschaft und der Widerstand gegen Hitler*. Munich: Piper, 1985.
Schmitz, Helmut. *A Nation of Victims? Representations of German Wartime Suffering from 1945 to the Present*. Amsterdam: Rodopi, 2007.
Schöck-Quinteros, Eva, and Jan-Hauke Ahrens. "'Was verstehen wir Frauen auch von Politik?': Entnazifizierung ganz normaler Frauen in Bremen (1945–1952)." Bremen: Universität Bremen, Institut für Geschichtswissenschaft, 2011.
Schramm, Percy E. *Kriegstagebuch des Oberkommandos der Wehrmacht: 1940–1945*. Frankfurt: Bernard & Graefe, 1961.
Schrenck-Notzing, Caspar von. *Charakterwäsche: Die Re-education der Deutschen und ihre bleibenden Auswirkungen*. Graz: Ares, 2015.
Schroeder, Steven M. *To Forget It All and Begin Anew: Reconciliation in Occupied Germany, 1944–1954*. Toronto: University of Toronto Press, 2013.
Schulte, Jan Erik, and Michael Wildt, eds. *Die SS nach 1945: Entschuldungsnarrative, populäre Mythen, europäische Erinnerungsdiskurse*. Göttingen: V&R Unipress, 2018.
Schuster, Armin. *Die Entnazifizierung in Hessen, 1945–1954: Vergangenheitspolitik in Der Nachkriegszeit*. Wiesbaden: Historische Kommission für Nassau, 1999.
Schwarze, Gisela. *Eine Region in demokratischen Aufbau. Der Regierungsbezirk Münster 1945/46*. Schwann: Düsseldorf, 1984.
Sebald, W. G. *The Emigrants*. New York: New Directions, 1996.
Luftkrieg und Literatur. Frankfurt: Fischer, 2002.
Sérant, Paul. *Die politischen Säuberungen in Westeuropa am Ende des Zweiten Weltkrieges in Deutschland, Österreich, Belgien, Dänemark, Frankreich, Großbritannien, Italien, Luxemburg, Norwegen, den Niederlanden und der Schweiz*. Oldenburg: G. Stalling, 1966.

Seruya, Teresa. "Gedanken und Fragen beim Übersetzen von Ernst von Salomons Der Fragebogen." In *Konflikt – Grenze – Dialog: Kulturkontrastive und Interdisziplinäre Textzugänge*, edited by Jürgen Lehmann et al., 227–37. Frankfurt: Peter Lang, 1997.

Sharp, Tony. *The Wartime Alliance and the Zonal Division of Germany*. Oxford: Clarendon Press, 1975.

Shibata, Masako. *Japan and Germany under the U.S. Occupation: A Comparative Analysis of Post-War Education Reform*. Lanham, MD: Lexington Books, 2005.

Sica, Emanuele, and Richard Carrier, eds. *Italy and the Second World War: Alternative Perspectives*. Leiden: Brill, 2018.

Sissons, Miranda, and Abdulrazzaq Al-Saiedi. "A Bitter Legacy: Lessons of De-Baathification in Iraq." *International Center for Transitional Justice* (March 2013): 1–46.

Smith, Bradley F. *Reaching Judgment at Nuremberg*. New York: Basic Books, 1977.

The Shadow Warriors: O.S.S. and the Origins of the C.I.A. New York: Basic Books, 1983.

Smith, Richard Harris. *OSS: The Secret History of America's First Central Intelligence Agency*. Berkeley: University of California Press, 1972.

Snowman, Daniel. *The Hitler Émigrés Revisited*. London: Research Centre for German and Austrian Exile Studies, 2013.

Sollors, Werner. "'Everyone Gets Fragebogened Sooner or Later': The Denazification Questionnaire as Cultural Text." *German Life and Letters* 71, no. 2 (April 2018): 139–53.

Standifer, Leon C. *Binding up the Wounds: An American Soldier in Occupied Germany, 1945–1946*. Baton Rouge: Louisiana State University Press, 1997.

Stein, Harold. *American Civil-Military Decisions: A Book of Case Studies*. Birmingham: University of Alabama Press, 1963.

Stephan, Alexander, and Jan van Heurck. *"Communazis": FBI Surveillance of German Émigré Writers*. New Haven, CT: Yale University Press, 2000.

Stiefel, Dieter. *Entnazifizierung in Österreich*. Vienna: Europaverlag, 1981.

Strunk, Peter. *Zensur und Zensoren: Medienkontrolle und Propagandapolitik unter sowjetischer Besatzungsherrschaft in Deutschland*. Berlin: Akademie, 1996.

Szanajda, Andrew. "The Prosecution of Informers in Eastern Germany, 1945–1951." *The International History Review* 34, no. 1 (March 2012): 139–60.

Taberner, Stuart, and Karina Berger, ed. *Germans as Victims in the Literary Fiction of the Berlin Republic*. Rochester, NY: Camden House, 2009.

Taylor, Frederick. *Exorcising Hitler: The Occupation and Denazification of Germany*. New York: Bloomsbury Press, 2011.

Zwischen Krieg und Frieden: Die Besetzung und Entnazifizierung Deutschlands 1944–1946. Berlin: Berlin Verlag, 2011.

Taylor, Nick. *American-Made: The Enduring Legacy of the WPA: When FDR Put the Nation to Work*. New York: Bantam, 2008.

Tent, James. *Mission on the Rhine: Reeducation and Denazification in American-Occupied Germany*. Chicago: University of Chicago Press, 1982.

Thacker, Toby. *The End of the Third Reich: Defeat, Denazification & Nuremburg January 1944–November 1946*. Stroud, Gloucestershire: Tempus, 2006.

Thompson, Steven K. *Sampling*, 3rd ed. Hoboken, NJ: John Wiley & Sons, 2012.

Thorne, Christopher. "Chatham House, Whitehall, and Far Eastern Issues: 1941–1945." *International Affairs* 54, no. 1 (January 1978): 1–29.

Trogdon, Gary A. "A Decade of Catching Spies: The United States Army's Counter Intelligence Corps, 1943–1953." PhD diss., University of Nebraska, 2001.

Tscharntke, Denise. *Re-educating German Women: The Work of the Women's Affairs Section of the British Military Government 1946–1951*. Frankfurt: Peter Lang, 2003.

Tsuchiya, Yuka Moriguchi. "Military Occupation as Pedagogy: The U.S. Re-education and Reorientation Policy for Occupied Japan, 1945–1952." PhD diss., University of Minnesota, 2004.

Tsvetkova, Natalia. *Failure of American and Soviet Cultural Imperialism in German Universities, 1945–1990*. Leiden: Brill, 2013.

Turner, Ian D., ed. *Reconstruction in Post-War Germany: British Occupation Policy and the Western Zones, 1945–1955*. Oxford: Berg, 1989.

van Melis, Damian. "Denazification in Mecklenburg-Vorpommern." *German History* 13, no. 3 (1995): 355–70.

Entnazifizierung in Mecklenburg-Vorpommern: Herrschaft und Verwaltung 1945–1948. Munich: R. Oldenbourg, 1999.

Vincent, Marie-Bénédicte. "La prise en compte de plusieurs générations dans la méthode prosopographique: L'exemple des hauts fonctionnaires prussiens sous l'Empire et la République de Weimar," *Genèses* 56 (September 2004): 117–30

"La sanction des falsificateurs de la dénazification ou comment s'élabore une éthique de la fonction publique ouestallemande après 1945, entre héritage weimarien et renouvellement," *Allemagne d'aujourd'hui* 208 (2014): 43–55

Vogt, Timothy. *Denazification in the Soviet-Occupation Zone of Germany: Brandenburg, 1945–1948*. Cambridge, MA: Harvard University Press, 1997.

Vollnhals, Clemens. "Die evangelische Kirche zwischen Traditionswahrung und Neuorientierung." In *Von Stalingrad zur Währungsreform: zur Sozialgeschichte des Umbruchs in Deutschland*, 3rd ed., edited by Martin Broszat, Klaus-Dietmar Henke, and Hans Woller, 113–67. Munich: R. Oldenbourg, 1990.

Weckel, Ulrike. *Beschämende Bilder: Deutsche Reaktionen auf alliierte Dokumentarfilme über befreite Konzentrationslager*. Stuttgart: Franz Steiner, 2012.

Weine, Steven M. et al. "Guidelines for International Training in Mental Health and Psychosocial Interventions for Trauma Exposed Populations in Clinical and Community Settings." *Psychiatry* 65, no. 2 (2002): 156–64.

Welsh, Helga A. *Revolutionärer Wandel auf Befehl? Entnazifizierungs- und Personalpolitik in Thüringen und Sachsen, 1945–1948*. Munich: Oldenbourg, 1989.

Welzer, Harald, Sabine Moller, and Karoline Tschuggnall. *"Opa war kein Nazi": Nationalsozialismus und Holocaust im Familiengedächtnis*. Frankfurt: Fischer, 2002.

Werner, Hans-Georg. *Deutsche Literatur im Überblick*. Leipzig: Reclam, 1965.
Whitby, Andrew. *The Sum of the People: How the Census Has Shaped Nations, from the Ancient World to the Modern Age*. New York: Basic Books, 2020.
Wiecki, Stefan. "Professors in Purgatory: Denazification of Munich University, 1945–1955." PhD diss., Brandeis University, 2009.
Wiesen, S. Jonathan. "Overcoming Nazism: Big Business, Public Relations, and the Politics of Memory." *Central European History* 29, no. 2 (1996): 201–26.
Williams, Isobel. *Allies and Italians under Occupation Sicily and Southern Italy 1943–45*. New York: Palgrave Macmillan, 2013.
Williams, Kieran, Brigid Fowler, and Aleks Szczebiak. "Explaining Lustration in Central Europe: A 'Post-communist Politics' Approach." *Democratization* 12, no. 1 (2005): 22–54.
Willis, Frank Roy. *The French in Germany, 1945–1949*. Stanford: Stanford University Press, 1962.
Winks, Robin W. *Cloak and Gown: Scholars in the Secret War, 1939–1961*. New York: Morrow, 1987.
Wolfe, Robert, ed. *Americans as Proconsuls: United States Military Government in Germany and Japan, 1944–1952*. Carbondale: Southern Illinois University Press, 1984.
Woller, Hans. *Die Abrechnung mit dem Faschismus in Italien 1943 bis 1948*. Munich: Oldenbourg, 1996.
Gesellschaft und Politik in der amerikanischen Besatzungszone: die Region Ansbach und Fürth. Munich: Oldenbourg, 1986.
Wyneken, JonDavid. "Driving Out the Demons: German Churches, the Western Allies, and the Internationalization of the Nazi Past, 1945–1952." PhD diss., Ohio University, 2007.
Zeren, Aysegul Keskin. "From De-Nazification of Germany to De-Baathification of Iraq." *Political Science Quarterly* 132, no. 2 (2017): 259–91.
Ziemke, Earl. *The U.S. Army in the Occupation of Germany 1944–1946*. Washington, DC: Army Historical Series, 1975.
Zülsdorf-Kersting, Meik. *Sechzig Jahre danach: Jugendliche und Holocaust: Eine Studie zur geschichtskulturellen Sozialisation*. Münster: Lit, 2007.

Index

Page numbers for illustrations and tables are in **bold**; page numbers for notes are in *italics*.

Aachen, 91, 120
academics, 6
  denazification, implemented by, 22
  dismissal of, 187
  Fragebogen, lead authors of, 75–76
  in GCU, 59
  in OSS Research and Analysis (R&A), 46–49
  post-war occupation, planning for, 35–37
  screening of, 136, 244
  subject areas of, 33–34, 46
ACC *see* Allied Control Council.
Ackermann, Anton, 27
Adcock, Clarence, 132
Adenauer, Konrad, 9, 149, 178, 206, 253, 262
Administration militaire française en allemagne (AMFA), 102–4, 150–51
  Cinquième Bureau, 100–1, 121
  denazification policy
    delegation to Germany, 144–46
    Fragebogen, use of, 137–39
    implementation of, 126, 138
    dismissals and exclusions by, 185, **186**
    establishment of, 125
Adorno, Theodor, 48
affiliation, Nazi *see* categorization, of Nazi affiliation.
agency, 191, 257
agricultural sector, 132, 140, 173
Allied Control Council (ACC), 9, 25, 126
  Directive 24, 88–108, 136, 139, 145, 147
  Directive 38, 145
  Nazi Arrest and Denazification Subcommittee, 107
  quadripartite questionnaire, 161, 217
Allied Military Government (AMG), 66, 72–73
Allied Military Government of Occupied Territories (AMGOT), 66–69, 75
  Political Intelligence Section, 70, 74

Allied Powers
  co-operation between, 160–61
  denazification, planning for, 22–28, 55–63
American Institute for Public Opinion, 77
AMFA *see Administration militaire Française en Allemagne.*
AMG *see* Allied Military Government.
AMGOT *see* Allied Military Government of Occupied Territories.
amnesties, 9, 157–58, 204
  legislation for, 206, 252–54
anti-Nazi people and groups, 35, 203
  denazification, contribution to, 116, 139, 147
  denunciation by, 216
  employment of, 116, 183, 194
  family stories of, 231
  Fragebogen questions on, 84, 108
  "white" list of, 37
anti-Nazism
  definitions of, 235, 238
  evidence of, 80, 124, **134**, 172, 183, 205, 233–34
  limited, 237–38
  false claims of, 234
  memories of, 238–50
  through passive resistance, 234–37
anxiety, 174, 229
appeals procedures, 88, 132, 135, 203
  Berufungskammern (Appellate Tribunals), 146
  in *Spruchkammern*, 154, 187
  unsuccessful, 206
Armstrong, Sinclair, 76, 79
arrests, 30, 117, 167–68
  automatic, 8, 89, 116–17
  numbers of, 163, 199–200
  policies on, 50, 117
  Soviet aversion to, 104

295

Index

artists, 136
Assmann, Aleida, *240*
Associated Press, 142
Atlantic Charter (1941), *24*, 28
atrocities, 162, 193
Austria, 7, 83, 85
autobiography, 210–11, 256
   Allied administrators' influence on, 231–33
   anti-Nazi resistance narratives, 233–38
   assistance/rescue narratives, 249–50
   denazification case files, 231–32, **231–32**, 241–43
   ego documents, 227–28, 251
   inauthentic, 228–30
   Selbstzeugnisse (self testimonies), 227–28, 231–33
   trauma narratives, 248
   truth and dishonesty in, 232–33

Babcock, William T., 65, 92
Bach, Julian, Jr., 131, 133, 158, 219
Bad Hersfeld *see* Kreis Hersfeld (Hesse).
Bad Oeynhausen, 125
Baden Baden, 122, 125
Baden-Württemberg, 24, 97, 122, 179
Badoglio, Pietro, 68
Balfour, Michael, *14*
banking/finance, 182–83, 195, 198
Bärensprung, Horst W., *48*
Bavaria, 24, 98, 160, 164, 219
   Fragebögen outcomes in, **134**
   Fragebögen, processed in, 121, 131, **148**, 156
Beattie, Andrew H., *5*, *17*
Bechler, Bernhard, 213
Beisel, Wilhelm, 183, 258
Berlin, 102, 121, 125, 143, 147, **170**
   cross-sector administration in, 25, 108
   denazification commission, 108
   denunciation in, 214
Berlin Bureau of Denazified and Ownerless Businesses (*Amtsstelle für die entnazifizierten und herrenlosen Betriebe*), 183
Berlin Document Center (BDC), 127, **128**, 215
Berlin Kommandatura, 161, 215
Berufungskammern (Appellate Tribunals), 146
Biddiscombe, Perry, *5*
Bienert, Richard, 193
Biess, Frank, *15*, 189, 215
Binder, Paul, 216
Birnbaum, Walter, 188

black market, 186, 205
   for *Persilscheine* (exoneration statements), 249
Bloxham, Donald, 232
Boehling, Rebecca L., *17*, 54
Boetticher, Friedrich von, 174, 250
Bonn, 120
Borchert, Wolfgang, *3*
Borgstedt, Angela, *3*
Bosnia and Herzegovina, 260
Boveri, Margret, 177
Bracci, Mario, 73
Brandenburg, 24, 108, 116, 152
BRD *see* Federal Republic of Germany.
Brecht, Bertolt, 48
Bremen, 24, 98, 147
Brentano, Heinrich von, 253
British Control Commission for Germany, 92
British Institute of Public Opinion, 77
Broszat, Martin, 225, 243
Brown, Norman O., 46
Brückweh, Kerstin, 33, 78
Brüning, Heinrich, 48
Buchanan, Andrew, *68*
Bund Deutscher Mädel (League of German Girls), 198
Byrnes, James F., 157

CAD *see* Civil Affairs Division.
Carruthers, Susan, *240*
Caruth, Cathy, 248
Casablanca Conference (1943), 35
case studies *see* Kreis Hersfeld (Hesse).
categorization
   of employment eligibility, 124, 135
   of Fascists in Italy, 68–69, 72
   of guilt, 145–46
   of Nazi victims, 247
categorization, of Nazi affiliation, 8, 37, 53–54, 79–80, 106, 154, 245–46
   active, 89, 115, 128
   vs. nominal, 80, 103, 126, 135
   ambiguities in, 61–62
   Belastete (Offenders), 146
   "black-grey-white" lists, 37, 50, 79, 117, 123, 167
   Entlastete (Exonerated), 146, 181, 246
   evaluation of, 123
   in GCU policies, 61–62
   Hauptschuldige (Major Offenders), 146
   ineffectiveness of, 141
   Minderbelastete (Lesser Offenders), 146, 203
   Mitläufer (Followers), 146, 176–78, 181, 203, 246
   numbers of, 157, 188, 204

Index

Müssnazi ("Nazi by necessity"), 104, 106
  nominal, 106, 115, 117, 129, 176
   and post-war employment, 117–18
   vs. active, 80, 103, 126, 135
  nominal, criticism of Fragebogen by, 177–78
  sympathizers, 31, 37, 83, 85, 115, 156, 194, 222
Cation, J. C., 59
CCG(BE)92 *see* Control Commission for Germany (British Element),
CCS *see* Combined Chiefs of Staff.
CDU *see* Christlich Demokratische Union.
Central European Section (CES, OSS), 22, 45–55
  "The Abrogation of Nazi Laws in the Early Period of MG [Military Government]", 49
  "Dissolution and the Nazi Party and its Affiliated Organizations", 50
  "General Principles of Administration and Civil Service in Germany", 50
character references (*Leumundszeugnisse*), 219, 244
character, German, 28, 30
Chatham House (Royal Institute of International Affairs), 36
Chauffour, Sébastien, 99
Chief of Staff to Supreme Allied Commander (COSSAC), Civil Affairs Division (CAD), 35, 55–56, 60
children, 139, 166, 184
  Fragebogen questions on, 103, 214
Christlich Demokratische Union (Christian Democratic Union, CDU), 9, 147, 176, 178, 201
Christlich Sozialistische Union (Christian Socialist Union, CSU), 176
church leaders, 116, 179
churches, 179, 197
  Evangelical Church in Germany (EKD), 130, 170, 176, 179, 217, 225
Churchill, Winston, 22, 24, 91
CIC *see* Counter Intelligence Corps.
civil affairs, 40–42
  Anglo-American development of, 35–36
  doctrine, 21
  intelligence gathering for, 45–46
  inter-Allied planning for, 55–63
  strategies for, 32
  training, 34, 38–43, **41**, 45, 56–57
Civil Affairs Center (CAC), Shrivenham, UK, 56–57, 87

Civil Affairs Division (CAD), COSSAC, 35, 55–56, 60
Civil Affairs Division (CAD), US War Department, 38, 50
Civil Affairs Handbook on Germany (OSS), 50
civil affairs officers, 8, 36, 114–15, 125, **128**
  in Italy, 68
civil servants, 137, 195–96, 199, 203
  Fragebogen, completion of, 128, 196
  lower-paid, 165
  Reichsbund der Deutschen Beamten (Reich Federation of German Civil Servants), 182, 199
civil service, 196, 235
  dismissal/exclusion from, 31, 36, 62, 123
  extent of Nazism in, 50
  specific Fragebogen for, 105
civilians, expert
  American, 39–42, **41**, 58
  British, 35–38
  employment of, 8, 22, 32–43
  French, 34
  in GCU, 58–59
  German, 34–35
  maturity of, 58
  military status of, 56
  professional backgrounds of, 58–60
  from Soviet Union, 34–35
Clare, George, 172
class, social, 53, 164–65
  Junker identity, 96, 129
  loss of standing, 187–88
  and victimhood, 242
classification *see* categorization.
Clay, Lucius D., 10, *28*, 130, 132–33, 141
clemency, 135, 158
clergy, 59, 116, 122, 179
coal industry, 135, 151
Cold War, 157, 260
Combined Chiefs of Staff (CCS)
  CCS 551 directive, 74
  "Removal of Nazis and Militarists" directive, 115, 128
communism, fears of expansion of, 26
community, 17
  denazification impact on, 17, 188, 252
  denunciation, damaged by, 225
concentration camps, 174
  German civilians, toured by, 114
  survivors of, 241–42
confessions, 232, 251
  absence of, 197, 250

Control Commission for Germany (British Element), (CCG[BE]), 94, 115
denazification, delegation to Germany, 144–45
denazification, implementation of, 121, 126
denunciation, use of, 213, 224
"Directive on Arrest and Removal", 134
dismissals and exclusions by, 185, **186**
establishment of, 125
Fragebogen, use of, 134–37
German Advisory Councils, 145
resource requests by, 122
Counter Intelligence Corps (CIC), 84, 117, 119, 212, 216
courts *see* tribunals and courts.
Craig, Gordon, 46
criminality, 28
Critical Theory, 50–54, 79
Crosslet, Archibald, 77
CSU *see* Christlich Sozialistische Union.
curfews, 114, 193

Dack, Mikkel, *12*
DAF *see* Deutsche Arbeitsfront.
Dagerman, Stig, 23, 142
Daniell, Raymond, 90
Dastrup, Boyd L., *13*
de Gaulle, Charles, 27, 91, 100
de-cartelization, 25
de-industrialization, 25–26
demilitarization, 25–26
democratization, 25, 52
denazification, 5–6
criticism of
as authoritarian, 171–79
German, 175–80
as immoral, 179
as undemocratic, 179
in US, 131–32
definitions of, 17–18, 163
of economic structures, 52–53
through encouragement of anti-fascism, 104
ending of, 149, 157–58, 253–54
Entnazifizierungsschlussgesetz (Law to End Denazification, Article 131), 253
evaluation of, 119
everyday, 16, 164–80, 254
experimental nature of, 32
German administration of, 9, 133–34, 144–58
"Denazification Panels", 145
denunciation, 215–17
"German Review Boards", 145
ministries and tribunals for, 146
Säuberungskommissionen (Chambres d'Épuration), 145, 151
Spruchkammer (special tribunal), 152–57
Untersuchungsausschüsse (Delegation d'Instruction), 145, 150, 182
workload, 156
German attitudes to, 162–64, 167, 175
German civilians employed in, 112
German experience of, 4–5, 166–80, 255–56
arrests, 167–68
beneficial, 183
community, 17
decisions, delayed, 174
Fragebogen completion, 169–74
humor and, 180, 191
impoverishment, 184–86, 205
individual, 17, 52, 79, 163
psychological, 187–91
for senior Nazi officials, 167–68
unemployment, 185–88
historiography of, 11–16, 190–91, 207
inconsistency of, 98, 124, 126
institutions of, 13
limitations of, 165–66, 251–52
opposition to, 1–3
perceived failure of, 10–11
planning for, 22–28, 31, 55–63
positive legacies of, 16
in post-invasion period, 114–25
reach of, 52
records of, 191–92
regular army attitudes to, 118
resources for, 112, 118–19, 126
rigor, levels of, 145
uniformity in, 107–8, 160–61
see also Fragebogen.
denazification policies, 28–31, 49–54
American, 13, 28–30, 88–91
British, 30, 92–94
French, 101–4, 115, 121, 126, 137–39, 144–46
pragmatic nature of, 30, 99–100
GCU, developed by, 60–63
implementation of, 115–16
intensification of, 89–91
OSS, 79, 117
perceived leniency of, 61, 244
Soviet, 14–15, 30–31, 99, 104–8, 115
denunciation, 84, 97, 106, 211–26, 251, 256
accusers, characteristics of, 220–21

Index

administration of, 213
American use of, 213–14
of anti/non-Nazis, 214
as authoritarian, 216
benefits of, 225–26
criticism of, 216–17
by denazification commission members, 216
denounced, characteristics of, 221
discouragement of, 224
as duty, 213
extent of, 217–19
false, 224
fear of, 224
Fragebogen, appended to, 172, 201
Fragebogen, invited by, 214–15, 251
in GDR, 224
German tradition of, 211–12, 224–25
under German-administered denazification, 215–17
influence of, 215
investigation of, 215, 221
motivation for, 218–19, 221–24
Nazi use of, 218, 221, 224
ordered, 122
of profiteers, 222
punishments for refusal of, 214
records of, 218–20
reliance on, 119, 212–14
as revenge, 216, 222–24
statements, 219–24
of sympathizers, 222
trustworthiness of, 213
voluntary, 84, 167, 194
deportations, 167, 184
Desch, Michael, 54
de-Stasification, 14, 261
detention *see* internment.
Deutsch, Harold C., 47
Deutsche Arbeitsfront (German Labor Front, DAF), 83, 199
Deutsche Studentenschaft (German Students' Union), 83
Deutsches Frauenwerk (German Women's Welfare Organization), 83, 182, 202
dismissal, 30, 185–88
of academics, 188
categories for, 53, 61, 79, 121, 124, 128, 145
in civil service, 62, 123
decision-making on, 61
discretionary, 79, 83, 91, 124, 129
exemptions from, 194
of Italian Fascists, 71
mandatory, 8, 79, 81, 83, 89, 107, 124

extension of scope for, 61, 91, 145
numbers of, 134
of mayors, 194
under Nazi regime, 242, 244–45
numbers of, 185, **186**
permitted delays in, 115
planned limitation of, 40
of police officers, 140
in private sector, 53
rank/office, dependent on, 83
displaced persons (DPs), 165–66
doctors, 136, 140, 174, 186, 196, 204
NS-Ärztebund ((National Socialist Physicians' League), 83
Dodds, E. R., 36–37
Domenico, Roy, 70
Donnison, Frank, 135
Donovan, William "Wild Bill", 43, 46–47
Dorn, Walter L., 46
Dorner, Rudolf, 139, 167–68, 216
Dos Passos, John, 134
DuBois, Cora, *46*
Dulles, Allen, 46
Dunham, Vera Sandomirsky, *46*

education, 183
history, screening of, 94, 103, 197
reeducation, 30, 100, 104, 168
see also teachers.
education sector, 129, 136
Eisenhower, Dwight D., 56
employment
anti-Nazis, opportunities for, 183
demotion, 186, 204–5
eligibility for, 124, **134**, 135, 153
exclusion from, 8, 124, 204–6
civil service, 31, 36, 62, 123
numbers of, 185, **186**
"ordinary labor", 186, 189, 203
permission for, 181–83
recommendation for, 79, 124
reinstatement, 9, 204–5, 252–53, 258
delays in, 174, 178, 202–3
retention, 203
suspension, 80, 202–3
variation in decisions on, 118
of women, 188–89
see also dismissal.
engineers
in GCU, 59
screening of, 196, 244
Entnazifizierungsgeschädigte (damaged by denazification), 263
Entnazifizierungskommissionen (denazification commissions), 108

Index

Entnazifizierungsschlussgesetz (Law to End Denazification, Article 131), 253
epuration (purification), 67, 73
Estel, Magdalena, 162
Ettle, Elmar, *13*
Euler, August Martin, 194–95, 200
European Advisory Council (EAC), 24, 50, 58
Evangelical Church in Germany (EKD), 130, 170, 176, 179, 217, 225
executions, 167
exoneration, 9, 252
 Entlastete status, 146, 181, 246
 Persilscheine (exoneration statements), 157, 202–3, 219, 249
Eyck, Frank, 111

Fahrenhorst, Eberhard, 201–2
falsification, 80, 130–31, 170–73, 187
 of anti-Nazi activities, 234
 clemency for, 158
 investigation of, 124, **148**, 148
 NSDAP membership and, 199
 prevention of, 94
 punishments for, 8, 136, 173
families
 impact of denazification on, 184–85
 memory narratives of, 230–31, 238, 251
 postwar reconstruction of, 189
farmers and farming, 132, 140, 173, 182
Fascism, Italian, 68, 72
fear, 191, 244
 of denunciation, 224–25
 of Fragebogen outcomes, 174
 of occupying forces, 162
Federal Bureau of Investigation (FBI), 47, 79
Federal Republic of Germany (Bundesrepublik Deutschland, FRG), 253–54
 questionnaires, use of, 149
 Wirtschaftswunder (economic miracle), 260
Ferdinand Johann of Schönaich-Carolath, Prince, 131
fingerprinting, 79
First World War *see* World War I.
Fitzgibbon, Constantine, 5
"Five D's", 25
food
 rationing, 112, 146, 153
 shortages, 162
Ford, Franklin L., 47
foresters and forestry, 165, 182, 202

Fragebogen (denazification screening questionnaire), 2
 achievements of, 5, 158–59, 258–59
 archives of, 11–12
  British, 14
  in former GDR, 14
  French, 14
 black market in, 180
 completion, **170–71**
  German experience of, 169–74
  in groups/public, 170–72
  incorrect, 142
  iterative, 151, 203
  mandatory, 128, 137
  manuals for, 170
  requirements, 135
 completion rates, 10, 121–22, 132–33, 159–60, **159–60**
  in American zone, 18, **148**
  in British zone, 135–36, 148
  in French zone, 138–39
  under German administration, 149–50
 criticism of, 3, 140–44
  American, 88, 91–92
  as authoritarian, 171–79
  British, 92–93
  as bureaucratic, 140, 180
  complexity, 141–42
  by denazification officers, 111
  French, 100–1
  German, 176–77
  as immoral, 179
  iterative completion of, 141, 150
  leniency, 142–43
  as undemocratic, 179
  as unfair, 141, 177–78
 cross-checking of, 8, 84, 123, 129, 135, **148**
  against "black" lists, 37
  Berlin Document Center (BDC), supported by, 127
 denunciation and, 84, 97, 106, 214–15
 development of, 6–8
 drafts, 7, 74–88
  approval of, 81
  Nazi affiliation categories, 79–80
  reviews of, 81
  scheda personale (personal questionnaire), influence of, 75–76
 drivers for use of, 52–54
 effectiveness of, 257–60
 emancipatory possibilities of, 251
 end of use of, 9–10
 evaluation, 123–24, 135
  anti-Nazism claims, 237–38
  by German civilians, 122, 133, 136

inadequate skills for, 142
instructions for, 83–84
process for, 129
training for, 120
experimental nature of, 64, 66, 109, 254
extent of use of, 4, 79–80, 132–34, 207, 258–59
flexibility of, 209–10
"Fragebogen Action Sheet", 124, 129
German administration of, 144–58
historiography of, 3–4, 11–12
implementation of, 8–9, 80–81, 84–85, 112–13
  distribution methods, 121–23, 169
  under German administraiton, 149–50
  inconsistent, 97–98, 152
  institutionalization, 120–21, 126–29
  instructions for, 86–87, 96, 103
  in post-invasion period, 119–25
  training for, 87, 101
  under German administration, 151
inclusivity, 5
limitations of, 5, 110, 158, 254–55, 257–58
mockery of, 180
ongoing use of, 149, 160
outcomes, 180–91
  for anti-Nazis, 183
  employment, **204**
  impoverishment, 184–86
  internment, 183–85
  permission to work, 181–83
  psychological, 187–91
  unemployment, 185–88
professions, screening of, 135–36, 195–96
questions of, 7, 81–84, 94–97, 102–3, 106–7, 217
reliance on, 77, 88, 98, 136–37, 159
resources for, 85, 87, 122, 143–44
revisions of, proposed, 93, 119
scheda personale (Italy), influence of, 72–74
strategic choice of, 76–79
submission receipt (*Quittung*), 153
supplementary evidence, 10, 84, 88, 107, 169, 200–1, 204
  autobiography in, 210–11
  Lebenslauf (resumé), 8, 18, 84, 105, 172, 200
suffering, accounts of, 246–48
therapeutic possibilities of, 248, 251
victimhood, questions about, 245
witnesses for, 173
workload, 131, 133, 136, **148**, 150
see also falsification; references.

Fragebogen versions, 7–8, 123
  American, **95**, 128, 237, 246–47
  historiography of, 14
  revision of, 91–92, 94–98, 214
  for Austria, 85
  British, 14, 94, 214
  French, 14, 102–4, 137, 214, 236
  industry-specific, 138
  SHAEF original, 81–84, **82**, 91–94, 97, 105, 214
  Soviet, 106–8, 214–15, 236–37
"Fragebogenkrank" (song), 2, 180
France
  denazification policy, 30, 99–104, 115, 121
  Directives pour notre action en Allemagne, 102
  Fragebogen, implementation of, 122
  French First Army, 100, 115
  Germany, animosity towards, 30
  government-in-exile, 100
  Mission Militaire pour les Affaires Allemandes (Military Mission for Germany), 101
  post-war occupation, planning for, 26–27, 34
  School of Military Government, 101
  Sûreté, 119, 137
  see also Administration militaire française en Allemagne; occupation zones/sectors, French.
Frankfurt am Main, 121, 125, **171**
Frankfurt School (Institut für Sozialforschung), 47–48, 50–54
Frankfurter Presse (newspaper), 177
Frankfurter Zeitung (newspaper), 177
Frei, Norbert, *15*, 253
Freisler, Roland, 193
Frevert, Ute, 252
FRG *see* Federal Republic of Germany.
Friedman, Wolfgang, 141
Friedrich, Carl J., 42
Fulbrook, Mary, *15*, *207*, 248–49
Fürstenau, Justus, 5

Gallup, George, 77
Gantner, Gösta, *16*
Gaskill, Gordon, 111
GCU *see* German Country Unit.
Gellately, Robert, 218
gender, 164–65, 188–90
  and denunciation, 220–21
Gerhardt, Uta, *16*, *207*

German Country Unit (GCU), 22, 55, 57–63, 74–88
  denazification policy, 60
  dissolution of, 90
  Fragebogen, implementation of, 120
  Handbook for Military Government in Germany, 60–61, 76, 86–98, 100, 115
  lack of French involvement in, 100
  Public Safety Branch (PSB), 76
  Public Safety Manual of Procedures, 60–62, 76, 86, 100, 123
  revision of, 89–90
German Democratic Republic (Deutsche Demokratische Republik, GDR), 11, 14–15
  amnesties in, 254
  denazification archives, 14
  denunciation in, 224
  Personalbogen (employment questionnaire), 149
  questionnaire use, following dissolution, 261
  Stasi (*Ministerium für Staatssicherheit*), 211, 224, 261
German people
  Allied troops, relationship with, 113–14
  attitudes to denazification, 162–64, 167, 175
  denazification work of, 112
  experience of denazification, 4–5, 166–80, 255–56
    arrests, 167–68
    beneficial, 183
    community, 17
    decisions, delayed, 174
    Fragebogen completion, 169–74
    humor and, 180, 191
    impoverishment, 184–86, 205
    individual, 17, 52, 79, 163
    psychological, 187–91
    for senior Nazi officials, 167–68
    unemployment, 185–88
  "refugee intellectuals", in OSS Research and Analysis (R&A), 47–49
  trusted, lists of, 50
Germany
  Allied invasion of, 113–14
  destruction in, 113
  economy of, 26
  governmental structures of, 61, 125
  invasion of, 193
  occupation, Allied Powers planning for, 22–28
  questionnaires in former GDR, 261
  Wehrmacht, 99, 113, 150, 172, 193–94, 235
  see also Federal Republic of Germany; occupation zones/sectors.
Gestapo (*Geheime Staatspolizei*), 193, 211, 216, 218, 221, 224
Gilbert, Felix, 48, 60, 79
Gimbel, John, 190
Goffman, Erving, 229
Gollancz, Victor, 144, 179
Goltermann, Svenja, 174
Great War *see* World War I.
Griffith, William E., 12, 62
Gritschneder, Otto, 216
Grohnert, Reinhard, *14*
Gropius, Walter, 48
Grossman, Atina, *15*
Guardian, The (newspaper), 150
guilt
  categorization of, 145–46
  collective, 28, 30
  presumptive, 146
Gurland, Arkadij, 48

Hagen, Wilhelm, 243
Halland, Gerald, 78
Hamburg, 24, 111, 116, 135, 185, 217
Harris, Joseph P., 39
Hayse, Michael, *210*
health and medical sector, 136, 140, 174, 182–83, 186, 196, 204
Heidegger, Martin, 146
Heineman, Elizabeth, 185
Heitmeyer, Paul R., 59
helplessness, 191
Henke, Klaus-Dietmar, *14*
Herf, Jeffery, *9*
Hersfeld *see* Kreis Hersfeld (Hesse).
Hersfelder Bekanntmachungen (periodical), 195
Hersfelder Zeitung (newspaper), 193
Herz, John H., 48, 153, 217
Hesse, 24, 98, **134**
Hessisches Hauptstaatsarchiv, 192
Heuss, Theodor, 177
Heyman, C. D., 93
Hilldring, John H., 38, 45
historiography
  Alltagsgeschichte (history of the everyday), 13–14
  of denazification, 11–16, 190–91, 207
  of Fragebogen, 3–4, 11–12
  of occupation zones/sectors, 15

Index

Hitler, Adolf, 162, 191, 228
  accusations of support for, 218
  Chancellor, appointment as, 192, 198
  claims of victimization by, 188, 238–39
  denunciations of, 226, 238, 259
Hitlerjugend (Hitler Youth, HJ), 83, 123, 198
Hoffmann, August Heinrich, 211
Hofmann, Walter ("Waldl"), "The Bridge to Freedom", **239**
Holborn, Hajo, 45, 48, 63
Hollins, Frank, 92
Holmes, Julius C., 81
Horkheimer, Max, 50
Hughes, H. Stuart, 46
humor, 96, 180, 191
Hunt, Irwin L., "Hunt Report", 21, 32, 44, 63

identity
  anti-Nazi, 236–38
  narrative (re)construction of, 227–31, 238, 250–51, 256, 259
  occupying nations, connections with, 250
  as rescuer of victims of Nazism, 249–50
  victimhood, 239–49
impoverishment, 184–86, 205, 244
imprisonment *see* internment.
informants *see* denunciation.
Institut für Sozialforschung (Frankfurt School), 47–48, 50–54
Institut für Zeitgeschichte, 235
institutions, internal purges by, 129, 136
intelligence reports, 52, 68
  limitations of, 119
Interkommunales Kreisarchiv Nordhessen, 192
International Military Tribunal (Nuremberg Trials), 5, 7, 127, 167, 176, 254
internment, 117, 163, 167–68, 183–85, 199
  camps, conditions in, 184
interrogation, 171, 194
  and denunciation, 213
introspection, 52, 171, 209, 251
  dissociation from, 248
  Fragebogen, initiated by, 230
  memory, impact on, 248
  necessity for, 52, 263
  as trauma, 262
Iraq, de-Baathification campaign, 261–62
Iredell, George S., 194–95
Italy, 66–74

Allied Military Government, 60
defascistization, 6, 55, 67–73
  criticism of, 69–70
  evaluation of, 76–77
  scheda personale (personal questionnaire), 70–76
Partito Nazionale Fascista (National Fascist Party, PNF), 68

Jähner, Harald, *16*
Japan, 7, 86
Jarausch, Konrad, *16*
Jaspers, Karl, *52*
Jewish people
  Fragebogen completion by, 241
  marriage to, Fragebogen questions on, 103
  narratives of assistance to, 249–50
  persecution of, 96–97
Jones, Jill, *14*
journalists, 136, 138, 183, 242
Junker identity, 96, 129

Kardorff, Ursula von, 179
Karlsruhe, 122
Kästner, Erich, *216*
Katz, Barry, 49
Kaysen, Carl, 46
Keegan, Charles E., 121
Kellerman, Henry, 48
Kent, Sherman, 46
Kettenacker, Lothar, *240*
Kiel, University of, 136
Kindleberger, Charles, 46
Kirchheimer, Otto, 48, 50–51, 209
Kissinger, Heinz (Henry), 112
Knappstein, Karl Heinrich, 177
Koeltz, Louis-Marie, 34, 101
Koenig, Pierre, 145
Kommunistische Partei Deutschland (Communist Party of Germany, KPD), 27, 105, 116, 176, 192, 201, 208
Kormann, John, 131
KPD *see* Kommunistische Partei Deutschland.
Krautheimer, Richard, 48
Kreis Hersfeld (Hesse), 191–206, 242
  arrests in, 199–200
  denazification in, 194–206
  demographics of screening, 196–97
  employment outcomes, 202–5, **204**
  Fragebogen implementation, 195, 200–1
  Meldebogen implementation, 195, 201

Kreis Hersfeld (Hesse) (cont.)
  Spruchkammer in, 195, 201–3
  women, screened by, 202
  denunciation in, 213
  dismissals, 189, 194
  education levels, 197
  income, 196
  internment/detention, 199
  military government, 193–94
  Nazi affiliation in, 198–99
  Nazi Party in, 192–93
  refugees in, 194
  religious beliefs, 191, 197
  voting history, 197
  World War II in, 193
Kuckhoff, Greta, 183, 233

laborers
  questionnaires completed by, 165
  screening, exempt from, 165
Laffon, Émile, 137, 145
land ownership, 96
Lange, Irmgard, *13*
Langer, William L., 44, 47
language skills
  Fragebogen questions on, 183
  lack of, 40, 142
  study of, 41
language, and identity, 229
lawyers
  in civil affairs work, 39, 59, 69, 75
  NS-Rechtswahrerbund, 200, 206
  screening of, 199–200, 206
LDP *see* Liberal-Demokratische Partei.
Leipzig, University of, 129
leniency
  criticism of, 142–43, 175
  perceived, 61, 88
Leßau, Hanne, *11*, 232
Leumundszeugnisse (character references), 219, 244
Lewis, Edgar, 57, 59
Liberal-Demokratische Partei (LDP), 147, 177, 201–2
Liberation Law *see* Office of Military Government, United States.
local government
  election to, 202
  Fragebogen use in, 135
  in Nazi period, 192–93
  reconstruction of, 116, 188 *see also* mayors.
Lochner, Louis P., 142
Louis-Demme-Stadtarchiv, 192
Lower Saxony, 24

Macpherson, Nelson, 54
Mainz, 116
Mair, John, *14*
Manual *see* Public Safety Manual of Procedures.
Marburg, 116, 122, 190
Marcuse, Herbert, 48, 50–51, 53, 76, *79*, 212
Marquardt-Bigman, Petra, *52*
Marshall, Barbara, *14*, 25
Marshall, Thomas H., 36
Martin, R. M. J., 101
Marxism, in denazification policy, 30–31
masculinity, crisis of, 188–90
Mason, John B., 42
Mass Observation, 77
Matthews, Noel, 117
mayors, 116, 182
  appointment of, 116
  denunciation of, 216, 220
  dismissal of, 194
  Fragebogen distribution by, 122
McDonald, John W., 127, 142
Mecklenburg, 24, 108
Meinecke, Friedrich, 48
Meldebogen (registration form), 9, 146, 152–56, **155**
  completion of, 172, 182
  completion rates, 156, **160**
  exemptions from, 165
  French use of, 103
Melis, Damian van, *15*
memory, 10, 17, 256
  of anti-Nazi resistance, 233–38
  of assistance/rescue, 249–50
  distorted, 229–31, 238
  Fragebogen influence on, 238
  narrative construction of, 228, 250–51
  narrative influence on, 227
  occupying nations, connections with, 250
  performativity of, 227–28
  private/public discrepancies in, 230
  recollection, 228
  of suffering, 239–49
men
  denazification, principal subjects of, 7, 164–65, 196
  denunciations by, 220–21
  impact of denazification on, 188–90
mental health
  denunciation and, 224–25
  Fragebogen outcomes and, 174, 187–91
  memory narratives and, 229
  national, 42
  trauma and, 248

Index

methodology, 16–18
　social science, influence of, 6, 33–34
midwives, 136, 175, 182, 189
militarism, 28, 100, 103, 115, 129, 222
military government
　civilianizing of, 32–43
　Germans, employed by, 123, 148
　Handbook for Military Government in Germany, 60–61, 76, 86–98, 100, 115
　in Italy, 66–74
　in Nazi-occupied territory, 83
　in occupation zones/sectors, 125–26
　ongoing screening by, 147–49
　planning for, 98
military personnel
　in civilian agencies, 44
　denazification processes for, 150
　in GCU, 59–60
military service history, 103, 196, 235
miners and mining, 151, 165, 204
Moeller, Robert G., 240, 241
Möhler, Rainer, *14*
Montgomery, Field Marshal Bernard, 36
Montgomery, John D., 13
Montreal Gazette (newspaper), 142
Moore, Stella, 137
Morgenthau, Henry, 25–26, 61, 88–90, 98
Morton, Frederic, 2
Moscow Tripartite Conference of Foreign Ministers (1943), 24, 28
Muelder, Milton E. G., 59
Murphy, Robert D., 91
Mussolini, Benito, 68

Naimark, Norman, 114
Napoli, Joseph F., 141
narrative, identity construction through, 227–31, 238, 250–51, 256, 259
nationalism, 28, 100, 178, 222
Nationalsozialistische Volkswohlfahrt (NSV), 199
Nazi Party (Nationalsozialistische Deutsche Arbeiterpartei, NSDAP), 6
　business dealings with, 96, 138, 156
　formal abolition of, 55, 61, 114
　in Kreis Hersfeld, 192–93
　members, 7, 106, 182, 198
　　"black" lists of, 37, 50, 117, 123, 167
　　denazification work by, 133
　　denunciations by, 221
　　identification of, 116–17
　　ongoing employment of, 118
　　removal from positions of influence, 6, 14, 128

　　senior, 174
　　victimhood, asserted by, 243–45
　　non-membership, consequences of, 244
　　questionnaires, use of, 168–69
　　ranked officials, 123
　　records, 8, 84–85, 120, 127, **128**, 148
　　　lack of, 119, 212
　　reported victimization by, 242–44
　　restricted membership of, 85
Nazi-affiliated organizations, 96, 102, 108, 123, 138, 182
　application to, 166
　Bund Deutscher Mädel (League of German Girls), 198
　Deutsche Arbeitsfront (German Labor Front, DAF), 83, 199
　Deutsche Studentenschaft (German Students' Union), 83
　Deutsches Frauenwerk (German Women's Welfare Organization), 83, 182, 202
　Fragebogen, listed on, 83
　Gestapo (*Geheime Staatspolizei*), 193, 211, 216, 218, 221, 224
　Meldebogen, listed on, 154
　NS-Altherrenbund (National Socialist League of Alumni of German Students), 199
　NS-Ärztebund (National Socialist Physicians' League), 83
　NS-Frauenschaft (National Socialist Women's League), 199, 221
　NS-Kriegsopferversorgung (National Socialist War Victims Care), 182
　NS-Lehrerbund (National Socialist Teachers' League), 83
　NS-Rechtswahrerbund (National Socialist Association of Legal Professionals), 200, 206
　NS-Reichskriegerbund (National Socialist Veterans' Association), 182, 198
　NS-Studentenbund (National Socialist German Students' League), 198
　Reichsarbeitsdienst (Reich Labor Service), 123
　Reichsbund der Deutschen Beamten (Reich Federation of German Civil Servants), 182, 199
　Reichskolonialbund (Reich Colonial League), 198
　Reichsluftschutzbund (Air Raid Protection League), 199
　Sturmabteilung (SA), 7, 83, 123, 193, 198, 204 *see* Schutzstaffel.

Nazism
  affiliation to
    allegedly coerced, 226, 238–39, 243–45, 247
    categories of, 62, 104
    definitions of, 115
    determination of, 62
    identification of, 157
  allegiance model of, 37
  as criminal belief system, 51
  as criminal organization, 28
  definitions of, 23, 31, 51, 104
  discrediting of, 251–52, 259–60
  disillusionment with, 162
  economic program, dismantling of, 53
  narrative distancing from, 182, 226–27, 251–52, 256
  as "sickness", 23, 28, 30
Neuer Westfälischer Kurier (newspaper), 176
Neumann, Franz L., 47–49, 51, 76, 79–80
Neustadt, 121
New York Herald Tribune (newspaper), 113
New York Times (newspaper), 89–90, 108, 132, 142, 154
Niethammer, Lutz, 13–14, 164
Niven, Bill, 240
NS-*Altherrenbund* (National Socialist League of Alumni of German Students), 199
NS-*Ärztebund* (National Socialist Physicians' League), 83
NSDAP *see* Nazi Party.
NS-*Frauenschaft* (National Socialist Women's League), 199, 221
NS-*Kriegsopferversorgung* (National Socialist War Victims Care), 182
NS-*Lehrerbund* (National Socialist Teachers' League), 83
NS-*Rechtswahrerbund* (National Socialist Association of Legal Professionals), 200, 206
NS-*Reichskriegerbund* (National Socialist Veterans' Association), 182, 198
NS-*Studentenbund* (National Socialist German Students' League), 198
Nuremberg Trials (International Military Tribunal), 5, 7, 127, 167, 176, 254

Oba, Kentaro, 229
occupation zones/sectors, **15**, 90, 255
  American, 18, 24, 152–57, 165
    criticism of denazification in, 176
    denunciation in, 213–14
    dismissals and exclusions in, 185, **186**
    employment policy in, 181
    extension of employment screening in, 132–34
    Fragebogen, implementation of, 122
    Kreis Hersfeld (Hesse), 191–206
  British, 18, 24, 134–37, 150, 165
    criticism of denazification in, 176
    denunciation in, 213
    dismissals and exclusions in, 185
    records of, 14
  denazification, variability between, 126, 166
  differences between, 4, 8
  employment policy, variability of, 181
  establishment of, 24–25, 125–26
  French, 18, 24, 99, 102–4, 150–51
    criticism of denazification in, 176
    dismissals and exclusions in, 185, **186**
    records of, 14, 99
  historiography of, 12, 15
  questionnaires processed in, **160**
  Soviet, 18, 151–52
    denunciation in, 213, 215
    dismissals and exclusions in, 185, **186**
    records of, 12, 14–15, 99
Office of Military Government, United States (OMGUS), 9, 18, 88, 98, 103
  Denazification Policy Board, 133
  denazification, delegation to Germany, 144, 146
  denazification, implementation of, 126, 174
  denunciation, use of, 213–14
  dismissals and exclusions by, 185, **186**
  establishment of, 125
  Fragebogen, use of, 127–29, 131, 160
  Kreis Hersfeld (Hesse), 191–206
  Law No. 8, 1945 ("Prohibition of Employment of Members of the Nazi Party"), 132–34
  Liberation Law, 1946 ("Law for Liberation from National Socialism and Militarism"), 146, 152, 182
Office of Strategic Services (OSS), 43–56, 60
  Central European Section (CES), 22, 45–55
    "The Abrogation of Nazi Laws in the Early Period of MG [Military Government]", 49
    "Dissolution and the Nazi Party and its Affiliated Organizations", 50
    "General Principles of Administration and Civil Service in Germany", 50
  Civil Affairs Handbook on Germany, 50

Index

denazification program, 49–54, 79, 117, 119
European field offices, 45
GCU, work with, 60
influence of, 46–55, 58
intelligence reports, 119
Research and Analysis (R&A), 43–55
 academic personnel of, 46–49
 Critical Theory, use of, 50–54
 Europe-Africa Division (EAD), 45–49
 German "refugee intellectuals" in, 47–49
 neo-Marxists in, 47–48, 52
 reports of, 44–45, 49–50
OMGUS *see* Office of Military Government, United States.
OSS *see* Office of Strategic Services.

Padover, Saul K., 118, 169, 234, 238, 243
paper shortages, 111, 143, 150, 180
pardons, 204
Parkinson, Anna M., 2
Partito Nazionale Fascista (National Fascist Party, PNF), 68
patriarchy, 189
Patton, George S., 118, 131, 133
Paul, Rudolf, 105
Persilscheine (exoneration statements), 157, 202–3, 219
 by Nazi victims, 249
Personalbogen (employment questionnaire, GDR), 149
Personalfragebogen (questionnaire for refugees), 105
Plischke, Elmer, 6
Poletti, Charles, 69–71, 73
police, 123, 174, 182, 192
 dismissals of, 140
 and Fragebogen
  completion of, 140
  distribution by, 122
 in GCU, 59, 78
 internment of, 173
 questionnaires, use of, 78–79
Political Adviser (US), Office of, for Germany (POLAD), 91
political parties
 Christlich Demokratische Union (Christian Democratic Union, CDU), 9, 147, 176, 178, 201
 Christlich Sozialistische Union (Christian Socialist Union, CSU), 176
 denazification, criticism of, 176–77
 electoral base, enlarging of, 253
 Fragebogen questions on, 237
 Freie Demokratische Partei (Free Democratic Party, FDP), 176–77
 Kommunistische Partei Deutschland (Communist Party of Germany, KPD), 27, 105, 116, 176, 192, 201, 208
 Kreis Hersfeld, support for, 192
 Liberal-Demokratische Partei (LDP), 147, 177, 201–2
 Partito Nazionale Fascista (National Fascist Party, PNF), 68
 Sozialdemokratische Partei Deutschlands (Social Democratic Party Germany, SPD), 170, 176, 192, 201
 Sozialisitische Einheitspartei Deutschland (Socialist Unity Party of Germany, SED), 147
 Spruchkammer committees, representation on, 201
 voting history, 97, 179, 197, 237
Pollack, Friedrich, 48
Pollock, James K., 42
Posener, Julius, 180
postal workers, 136, 151, 182
Potsdam Conference (1945), 25, 125–26, 168
Potter, Pamela M., 53
poverty, 184–86, 205, 244
Powell, Henry, 39
press, 138
 denazification, criticism of, 142–43, 176
 journalists, 136, 183, 242
prison *see* internment.
prisoners-of-war (POWs), 35, 138–39, 160, 212
private sector
 dismissal and exclusion from, **186**
 employees in GCU, 59
 Fragebogen
  distribution by, 122
  use in, 133, 135, 137
 Nazi membership in, 198
 owners and senior staff, 116, 196, 198, 204
 questionnaire use, 78
 small businesses, 185
propaganda, 45, 138
property
 land ownership, 96
 seized, 97
psychology
 and denunciation, 224–25
 and Fragebogen outcomes, 174, 187–91
 and memory narratives, 229
 national, 42
 trauma and, 248

public office
  appointments to, 115
  dismissal and exclusion from, 121, 185, **186**
  Fragebogen, mandatory for, 71, 80, 128, 135
  in Italy, 72
  Japan, purge of, 86 *see also* mayors.
Public Safety Manual of Procedures (the *Manual*, GCU), 60–62, 76, 86, 100, 123
  revision of, 89–90
Public Safety officers, 61, 76, 128, 170
  decisions by, 129, 141
  falsification, concerns about, 80
  in Italy, 69
  versions, use of, 97
  workload of, 133
punishment, 24, 26
  categorization of, 53, 73, 146
  civilian experts' unfamiliarity with, 42
  for falsification, 8, 130, 136
  French aversion to, 100
  vs. rehabilitation, 42, 64, 115, 126
  see also dismissal; internment.
purges, 17, 29
  administrative, 30, 50
  CES policy recommendations on, 50
  in civil service, 50
  diluted, 9
  extended, 50, 79, 91, 107–8
  in France, of collaborators, 100
  informal, 216
  institutions, conducted by, 129, 136
  in Italy, 67
  in Japan, 86
  moderate, 36, 100
  political, 6, 60, 67, 147
  reconstruction, impact on, 89

questionnaires
  for concentration camp survivors, 241–42
  evaluation, 72, 262
  inconsistent implementation of, 73
  non-use of, 261–62
  opinion polling, 77
  Personalbogen (employment questionnaire), 149
  Personalfragebogen (questionnaire for refugees), 105
  prevalence of, 77–79
  processing, failures of, 72
  for railway (*Reichsbahn*) workers, 105
  for refugees/displaced persons, 105
  resource demands of, 70, 72

scheda personale (personal questionnaire), 70–74
standardized, 33, 52
usage
  in Axis nations, 86
  in FRG, 149
  in GDR, 149
  police, 78–79
  post-conflict, 260–61
  in post-Soviet Eastern Europe, 261
  in pre-WWII Germany, 168–69

radio, 138
Raffa, Aldo, 75, 108
  Fragebogen, work on, 74–76, 79, 84, 87, 92, 140
  Italian defascistization, work on, 70–71, 73
railway (*Reichsbahn*) workers, 105, 136, 140, 151, 165
Ranke, Leopold von, 48
Reber, Samuel, 73
reconciliation, 100
Red Cross, 139, 196, 202
reeducation, 30, 100, 104, 168
references, corroborative, 93–94, 103, 241
  Leumundszeugnisse (character references), 219, 244
refugees
  displaced persons (DPs), 165–66
  in occupied Germany, 113
  repatriated German, 138–39
rehabilitation, 30–31, 157
  vs. punishment, 42, 64, 115, 126
Reichsarbeitsdienst (Reich Labor Service), 123
Reichsbahn (railway) workers, 136, 140, 151, 165, 235
Reichsbund der Deutschen Beamten (Reich Federation of German Civil Servants), 182, 199
Reichskolonialbund (Reich Colonial League), 198
Reichsluftschutzbund (Air Raid Protection League), 199
relief work, 117
religious beliefs, 103, 191, 237
removal *see* dismissal.
reparations, 27
Research and Analysis (R&A, OSS), 43–55
  academic personnel of, 46–49
  Critical Theory, use of, 50–54
  Europe-Africa Division (EAD), 45–49
  German "refugee intellectuals" in, 47–49
  neo-Marxists in, 47–48, 52
  reports of, 44–45, 49–50

Index

resistance *see* anti-Nazism; anti-Nazi people and groups.
restoration
  criticism of, 61
  economic, 26
retribution, 31, 216
Rhineland, Allied occupation of, 21, 60
  see also United States of America.
Rhineland-Palatinate, 24
Riefenstahl, Leni, 146
Roche, Helen, *210*, 232
Roetgen, 116
Roosevelt, Franklin D., 22–26, 43
  Germanophobia of, 28
  Handbook for Military Government in Germany, campaign against, 89
Roper, Elmo, 77
Rosenwein, Barbara H., 225, 252
Rowohlt, Ernst, *8*
Royal Institute of International Affairs (Chatham House), 36

SA *see* Sturmabteilung.
Saarland/Saar Protectorate, 24, 102, 139, 145
Salinger, J. D., 112
Salm, Johannes, 201
Salomon, Ernst von, 169, 180, 208
  CIC, criticism of, 216
  on confession, 232
  Der Fragebogen, 1–3, *8*, 11
  on Persilscheine, 249
Sarbin, Theodore R., 228
Säuberungsausschüsse (cleansing committees), 108
Saxony, 24, 108, 140, 152
Saxony-Anhalt, 24, 108
Scheu, Just, 2, 162, 180
Schleswig-Holstein, 24
Schmitz, Helmut, *240*
scholars *see* academics.
Schorske, Carl E., 46
Schumacher, Kurt, 183, 234
Schutzstaffel (SS), 83, 123, 184, 193, 198, 235
  membership, 7, *198*
  SS-Totenkopfverbände, 174
Schwäbisches Tagblatt (newspaper), 175
Scotsman, The (newspaper), 142
Sebald, W.G., *240*
Second World War *see* World War II.
SED *see* Sozialistische Einheitspartei Deutschland.
self-reflection, 171, 209, 251
  dissociation from, 248

Fragebogen, initiated by, 230
  memory, impact on, 248
  necessity for, *52*, 263
  as trauma, 262
sexual violence, 162, 193
SHAEF *see* Supreme Headquarters, Allied Expeditionary Force.
Shirer, William L., 113
Siegfried, André, 34
Smith, Richard Harris, 43, 54
Sobottka, Gustav, 27
social sciences
  development of, 33–34
  methodologies of, 6
Sollors, Werner, 2, *8*, 54
Sonderweg (special path), 51
Soviet Military Administration (SMA), 34–35, 105, 107
  Allied denazification campaign, alignment with, 107
  denazification, delegation to Germany, 144, 146–47, 151–52
  denazification, implementation of, 126
  denunciation, use of, 213, 215
  dismissals and exclusions in, 185, **186**
  establishment of, 125
  Fragebogen, use of, 124, 139–40, 174
  Nazi victims, categories of, 247
  Order 201, 147
Soviet Union *see* Union of Soviet Socialist Republics.
Sozialdemokratische Partei Deutschlands (Social Democratic Party Germany, SPD), 170, 176, 192, 201
Sozialisitische Einheitspartei Deutschland (Socialist Unity Party of Germany, SED), 147
SPD *see* Sozialdemokratische Partei Deutschlands.
Special Branch (denazification units), 81, 84, 135, 153
  and denunciation, 213
  establishment of, 61, 78
  expansion of, 129
  Fragebogen, continued use of, 149
  Fragebogen, evaluation of, 123
  on Liberation Law, 147
  resources of, 87, 93, 122
  training of, 87, 238
  workload, **134**, 148, 150, 185
Special Investigation Sections, 213
Spofford, Charles M., 69, 71
Spruchkammer (special denazification tribunal), 13, 146, 152–54, 164
  numbers of cases, 164, **204**, 207

Index

SS *see* Schutzstaffel.
Stalin, Joseph, 22, 27
Standifer, Leon C., 113–14
Standing Committee on Denazification, 136
Stasi (*Ministerium für Staatssicherheit*), 211, 224, 261
   de-Stasification, 14, 261
Stephens, Robert, 176
Stiefel, Dieter, *85*
Stimson, Henry L., *26*, 89
Stokes, Richard, 141
storytelling, identity construction through, 227–29, 238, 250–51, 256, 259
students, 165
Sturmabteilung (SA), 7, 83, 123, 193, 198, 204
Stury (cartoonist), **29**
Stuttgart, 122, 179
Sudetenland, 83
Supreme Headquarters, Allied Expeditionary Force (SHAEF), 7, 35, 56, 90
   disbanding of, 124
   FACS 93 directive, 91–92
   French relationship with, 100
   G-5 (Civil Affairs) Division, 56–57
   OSS R&A, work with, 45, 55
   Proclamation No. 1, 115
   Public Safety Division, 115, 117
   questionnaire use, 78
   "Removal from Office of Nazis and German Militarists" (directive), 91–92
   see also German Country Unit.

Taylor, Frederick (historian), *16*, 190
teachers, 136, 138, 140, 183, 196, 244
   exclusion of, 206
   NS-Lehrerbund (NS-Teachers' League), 83
Tehran Conference (1943), 22–23, 28
Thuringia, 24, 105, 108
Toynbee, Arnold, 36
trade unions, 203
trials *see* tribunals and courts.
tribunals and courts, 146
   archives of, 13
   Berufungskammern (Appellate Tribunals), 146
   for false/incomplete Fragebogen returns, 8
   Germans called before, 146
   Nuremberg Trials (International Military Tribunal), 5, 7, 127, 167, 176, 254
   presumptive guilt in, 146
   Spruchkammer (special denazification tribunal), 13, 146, 152–54, 164
   numbers of cases, 164, **204**, 207
   Volksgerichtshof (People's Court), 193
   war crimes, 7 *see also* appeals procedures.
Troubridge, Sir Vincent W., 60
truth
   autobiographical, 232–33
   perceptions of, 229
   tailoring of, 250 *see also* falsification.

UK Control Council, 78
Ulbricht, Walter, 27, 206
UN *see* United Nations.
unemployment, 205–6
Union of Soviet Socialist Republics (USSR)
   denazification policy, 14–15, 30–31, 99, 104–8, 115, 117–18
   deportations to labor camps in, 167, 184
   intelligence sharing with, 50
   NKVD (People's Commissariat for Internal Affairs), 119
   occupation by, 104
   post-war occupation, planning for, 27, 34–35
   Red Army, 27, 34, 104–5, 117–18
United Kingdom (UK)
   Cambridge University, 38
   Civil Affairs Staff Centre (CASC), Wimbledon, 38, 45, 57
   civil affairs training center, Eastbourne, 57
   denazification policy, 30, 92–94
   Foreign Office, 26
   Foreign Office Research Department (FORD), 36–37, 60
   Intelligence Training Centre (ITC), Cambridge, 38
   London School of Economics, 36
   Oxford University, 36
   post-war occupation, planning for, 26, 35–37
   questionnaire use in, 77
   Royal Institute of International Affairs (Chatham House), 36
   USA, joint working with, 35, 39, 42
   intelligence sharing, 50, 54
   limitations of, 58
   War Office, 38, 58, 60, 92, 122
   Germany and Austria in the Post-Surrender Period, 37
United Nations (UN), 25, 260
United Nations Relief and Rehabilitation Administration (UNRRA), 139, 165

Index

United States Forces European Theater (USFET), 97, 127–29, 195
United States of America (USA)
  Army of Occupation in the Rhineland, 21, 60
  Cabinet Committee on Germany, 28–30, 38
  Civil Affairs Center (CAC), Shrivenham, UK, 56–57
  Civil Affairs Training Schools (CATS), 40–42, 45
  Combined Chiefs of Staff (CCS), 58
  denazification policy, 13, 21–30, 88–91
  intelligence gathering, 45–46
  occupation forces, 14
  occupation policy, 92
  Political Adviser, Office of, for Germany (POLAD), 91
  post-war occupation, planning for, 25–26, 37–38
  questionnaire use in, 77
  School of Military Government, University of Virginia, Charlottesville, 39–42, *41*, 45
  UK, joint working with, 35, 39, 42
  intelligence sharing, 50, 54
  limitations of, 58
  War Department, 38, 49
  Civil Affairs Division (CAD), 38, 50
United States, Group Control Council (USGCC), 90–92, 98, 115, 120–21
  "Basic Preliminary Plan: Allied Control and Occupation of Germany", 120
  directive JCS 1067, 121
  "Public Safety Plan for Occupation for Allied Control and Occupation of Germany" (Annex XXIII), 98
US Army, 40
  Field Manual 27-5, 39
US National Archives and Records Administration, 18, 191
USFET *see* United States Forces European Theater.
USGCC *see* United States, Group Control Council.
Usingen, 165

Vermeil, Edmond, 34
Versailles, Treaty of, 32
vetting *see* employment.
victimhood, 239–49, 251, 262–63
  as commodity, 248–49
  Mitläufer status and, 188
  through victim association, 249–50
Victor Emmanuel III of Italy, 68
Vogt, Timothy, 15, 31, *99*, *151*, 215

Volksgerichtshof (People's Court), 193
Volkssturm (militia), 193
Vorwärts (newspaper), 178
voting history, 97, 179, 197, 237

Wagner, Robert, 167
Walters, Arnold, 39
war criminals, 117
Wehrmacht (German Armed Forces), 99, 113, 150, 172, 193–94, 235
Welter, Erich, 172
Wespennest, Das (magazine), **29**
Westphalia, 24
Wiesen, Jonathan, 187
Willis, Roy, *14*
Wilson, M. Keith, 75, *76*
  Chief of Denazification Section, OMGUS, 88, 120, 152
  Fragebogen, development of, *61*, 76, 87
Wilson, Orlando W., *76*, 79, 88
  Fragebogen, work on, 76, 84, 92, 119, 140
Winnacker, Rudolph, 47
women, 182
  denunciations by, 220–21
  employment of, 188–89
  in GCU, 59
  impact of denazification on, 173, 184, 188–89
  Meldebogen, required to complete, 154
  in OSS Research and Analysis (R&A), 46
  questionnaires completed by, 165, 196, 199, 202
World War I, 21, 33
World War II
  Allied invasion, 113–14
  Armistice of Cassibile 1943, 68
  Casablanca Conference (1943), 35
  German suffering in, 239–41
  German surrender, 113
  Kreis Hersfeld (Hesse), 193
  Moscow Tripartite Conference of Foreign Ministers (1943), 28
  Potsdam Conference (1945), 25, 125, 168
  Tehran Conference (1943), 22–23, 28
  Yalta Conference (1945), 24, 90
Wurm, Theophil, Bishop, 179
Württemberg-Baden, **134**

Yalta Conference (1945), 24, 74

Zemple, Arnold L., 59
Ziemke, Earl, 58
Zink, Harold, 21, 38, *57*, 98, 143
Zone française d'occupation (ZFO) *see* occupation zones/sectors, French.